ALSO BY MARC ELIOT ·

CARY GRANT
A Biography

DEATH OF A REBEL
Starring Phil Ochs and a Small Circle of Friends

ROCKONOMICS
The Money Behind the Music

DOWN THUNDER ROAD
The Making of Bruce Springsteen

WALT DISNEY
Hollywood's Dark Prince

THE WHOLE TRUTH

TO THE LIMIT
The Untold Story of the Eagles

DOWN 42ND STREET
*Sex, Money, Culture, and Politics at the
Crossroads of the World*

JAMES STEWART

A BIOGRAPHY

—•—

Marc Eliot

Aurum

First published in Great Britain
2006 by Aurum Press Limited
25 Bedford Avenue
London WC1B 3AT
www.aurumpress.co.uk

A catalogue record for this book is available from the British Library.

ISBN-10 1 84513 181 9
ISBN-13 978 1 84513 181 4

10 9 8 7 6 5 4 3 2 1
2010 2009 2008 2007 2006

Title page image courtesy of Lester Glassner Collection/Neal Peters.

Text design by Barbara Sturman
Printed and bound in Great Britain by MPG Books, Bodmin

This biography is dedicated with respect, admiration, and gratitude to the following:

ALFRED BESTER, WILLIAM GOLDMAN, HENRY MILLER, PHIL OCHS, HAROLD ROBBINS, AND ANDREW SARRIS.

In my youth, their work ignited the fires of my own creative passions, passions that burn within me still. . . .
And to the memory of SHEN ZHONGQIANG, *my eternal Shanghai brother-in-peace. Wherever your spirit rests today, it is also here.*

Contents

"He was the most naturally gifted actor I ever worked with. It was all instinct, all emotion; I don't think it came from training or technique . . . it came from forces deep within him."

THOMAS MITCHELL

"The story goes that when the news first hit Hollywood of Ronald Reagan's ambitions to be president, Jack Warner, the legendarily blunt mogul, responded, 'No, Jimmy Stewart for president, Ronald Reagan for best friend.'"

RELATED BY DAVID ANSEN IN *NEWSWEEK*

"That's the great thing about the movies . . . after you learn— and if you're good enough and God helps you and you're lucky to have a personality that comes across—then what you're doing is—you're giving people little, little, tiny pieces of time, that they never forget."

JIMMY STEWART, QUOTED BY PETER BOGDANOVICH

"I would prefer to place James Stewart in a triptych of equal acting greatness with Cary Grant and James Cagney . . . and say that Stewart is the most complete actor-personality in the American cinema, particularly gifted in expressing the emotional ambivalence of the action hero."

ANDREW SARRIS, FILM HISTORIAN AND CRITIC

"All the women want to mother Jimmy Stewart, that's his great quality."

FRANK CAPRA

"Stewart was closer to a representation of Hitchcock himself than any presence . . . his image was reshaped by Hitchcock to conform to much in his own psyche. He is, in important ways, what Hitchcock considered himself . . . with an alter ego attractive enough to engage the sympathies of his audience. Cary Grant, on the other hand, represents what Hitchcock would like to have been."

DONALD SPOTO, HITCHCOCK BIOGRAPHER

"When something is happening to a star, a Cary Grant or a James Stewart, the public feels it more."

ALFRED HITCHCOCK

"A show business optimist? That's an accordion player with a beeper. . . ."

JOHNNY CARSON

Introduction

James as in Jimmy, Art as in Life

A figure races in the darkness along a series of rooftops, like the flash of an idea across the mind. Just behind, an older, uniformed officer is in hot pursuit, and still farther behind him a third, tall and thin plainclothesman, bent like a fox at the hunt, struggles to keep up. Shots ring out, revealing the first is a criminal, running from the others. He makes desperate rooftop-to-rooftop leaps, the last across a dark, sheer-drop alley. The older and slower uniform makes it as well. The plainclothesman tries next, but, although thinner and apparently younger than the uniform (but not as lean or youthful as the thief), he doesn't quite get over. Instead, his body slams onto the side of the steep A-frame. He slips downward toward the edge. He dangles by his fingertips from a dangerously unhinged gutter drain. The uniform turns back to rescue the plainclothesman. He inches closer down that slippery slope, reaches out to grab the plainclothesman's wrist, loses his footing, and, with a final scream that rips apart the night, falls to his death. Horrified, the plainclothesman hangs, suspended and helpless, looking over his shoulder into the hungry, deadly abyss that eagerly awaits him.

These are the spectacular and spectacularly disturbing opening moments of Alfred Hitchcock's 1958 classic *Vertigo,* in which James Stewart, at the absolute peak of his acting form, plays the tragically flawed, insanely obsessed, and deeply existential John "Scottie" Ferguson. In *Vertigo,* Stewart's style of acting perfectly reflected not only his familiar cinematic persona—the ordinary man adrift, perhaps trapped in an abnormal world, longing to find his rightful physical, emotional, and spiritual place in it—but also to a greater degree than in any other movie he made, his real-life personality.

Stewart, like Ferguson, was withdrawn and a wanderer, a Presbyterian soul who fought against the perils of losing control of his own closely held emotions. He grew up in the shadow of an imperious, distant, at times completely absent Godlike father to become a man continually hanging by his fingertips above the canyons of disillusionment that beckoned throughout his otherwise high-flying and glorious life.

The crucial difference between the character Scottie and the actor Stewart lay in their relative sanity. Scottie's ultimate undoing is brought about by his belief in the power of possessive, obsessive sex as a curative, a liberating, redemptive act even after it has caused the death of his (so-called) loved one, a fatal trap disguised as a letting go that leads him eventually to the brink of suicide. The foundation of Jimmy's sanity, meanwhile, lay in his abject refusal to ever let go of his unwavering faith in the curative, redemptive liberation of love as the reflection of the moral righteousness of Western Christian ideology. These beliefs, in turn, helped him realize the power of his continual on-screen persona, that of a spiritually based, romantic all-American beacon of enlightenment to millions of Americans for more than half a century of turmoil and upheaval, from the depths of the Great Depression, through World War Two, the Cold War, Korea, Vietnam, and up to and including America's early involvement in the ongoing conflicts of the Middle East.

The idiosyncratic stylistics of Stewart's screen acting, the tools with which he used to project the inside of his characters onto the dreamlike surface of the silver screen, included a repertoire of physical tics, exaggerated gestures, and slowed-down jaw-boning that generation after generation (and multitudes of impersonators, both professional and party-level) came to recognize as "Stewartisms." Some were as simple as appearing to shake hands with himself during a scene while having a conversation with someone else (or, as in the case in Henry Koster's *Harvey* [1950], with some unseen "other"), the country-boy crackle of honesty and confusion in a high-pitched, drawn-out drawl, the slow, silent, frustrated shake of his head. Others were more subtle and complex, like the depth of his soul that shone so clearly through those piercing Pennsylvania steel blue eyes. Anthony Mann, a director who guided the actor through eight films in an intense five-year period during the first half of Stewart's greatest sustained period of filmmaking, the fifties, once observed, "All the great stars that the public love have clear eyes. . . . The eyes do everything: they're the permanent reflection of the internal flame that animates the hero. Without those eyes, you can only aspire to second-string roles."[1]

Indeed, Stewart's otherwise ordinary face—with its delicate, translucent skin so thin that the tiny blue veins on his cheeks were always visible, even under makeup, its square jaw rounded to just this side of soft, and its nose a bit too thick to make him leading-man handsome—was artistically lit by those startling blues that illuminated the passionate longing that lurked within. Whenever his brows arched upward, it was his eyes that gave in to helpless supplication, while the top of one wrist pushed back and forth against the bottom of his dropped jaw, making it seem as if he were rubbing away some recurring pain, physical or otherwise.

In Stewart's best work, the amazingly expressive eyes and face helped define his characters' quests to maintain their moral purity, their innocence threatened by an attractive if corrupting temptation that was almost always sexual in nature. In Hitchcock's *Vertigo* (1958) and *Rear Window* (1954) it takes the human form of the director's familiar, fetishistic ice-goddesses (Kim Novak and Grace Kelly, respectively), in other films it manifests itself in alluring objects that substitute for the "love interest"—the eponymous experimental plane in Billy Wilder's *The Spirit of St. Louis* (1957), the phallic rifle in Mann's *Winchester '73*, a seat in Congress in Frank Capra's *Mr. Smith Goes to Washington* (1939). These external manifestations triggered moral conflicts that repeatedly brought Stewart's characters to the brink of self-inflicted, near-crucifixionlike tragedy, until they were in the end rescued, redeemed really by the sheer force of their own will, the visible power of their inner spirituality (except for *Vertigo,* which makes the point by the sheer absence of redemption). As morality was conceived in the studio era, about the only thing that separated the continuum of Stewart's physical

---

1. The eight films were *Winchester '73* (1950), *Bend of the River* (1952), *The Naked Spur* (1952), *Thunder Bay* (1953), *The Glenn Miller Story* (1953), *The Far Country* (1955), *Strategic Air Command* (1955), and *The Man from Laramie* (1955).

persona from the standard Hollywood female heroine, whose purity was almost always reverent but whose corruption was almost always sexual, was that her redemption was almost always made possible by some supposed heroic male knight in shining armor. In that sense, James Stewart's cycle of hyper-sensitive self-surviving existentialists made him the best self-redemptive heroine Hollywood ever produced.

Jimmy's complex and unique film persona took a long time to perfect. It certainly did not come together during his disastrous early years at MGM, when the studio continually miscast him, up to and including his role as the killer in W. S. Van Dyke II's *After the Thin Man,* made in 1936, Stewart's eleventh movie in just over two years. Although he was never again cast as "evil," at times throughout his career, his characters' complex nobilities showed serious moral flaws: the professor in *Rope* (Hitchcock, 1948), the clown in Cecil B. DeMille's *The Greatest Show on Earth* (1952), one of two rival siblings in *Winchester '73,* the intimacy-fearing voyeur in *Rear Window,* the twisted obsessive in *Vertigo.* By the end of each of these films, the ability to convince audiences that his character has remained loyal—to someone else or, as was more often the case, to his own soul, whether riding off into the sunset or standing on the edge and resisting falling into the abyss—made him a star of legendary moral and heroic magnitude.

MGM's inability to properly cast young Stewart was a clear reflection of its inability to understand the essence of the talent of the new actor it had "discovered." Nowhere is this more evident than in his 1938 "official biography" released by the studio three years after Louis B. Mayer had signed him, which describes "James Stewart" this way: "His type is as normally average as the hot dog and pop at Coney Island. He is good looking without being handsome, quiet without being a bore, ambitious without taking either himself or his job too seriously and unassuming without being dull. Stewart's growing appeal has sometimes been difficult to peg. He's no Gable and certainly has none of the qualities of a Valentino. A sixteen-year-old fan seems to have hit it when she wrote to him, 'I like you because you're like the boy next door.' "[2]

---

2. He was always billed as "James Stewart" on-screen, preferred "Jimmy" in real life, was "Jimbo" to his father, "Jimsy" to his mother, and "Jim" only to his best friend, Henry Fonda.

— • —

Although Stewart was from a small town in western Pennsylvania, and his movie persona was most often a projection of a rural, working-class innocent whose unshakable morality and all-American common sense enabled him to outwit the big-city slickers, his lineage was, in fact, quite urban and sophisticated. Both sides of his family tree are rife with educated, self-made multimillionaires, beautiful women, perceptive land developers, adept businessmen, and, most consistently, military heroes who fought in virtually every American war, starting with the Revolution.

He was the only son of three children of Alexander M. and Elizabeth Stewart. Alex, as his charismatic father was known, owned and operated a popular hometown hardware store, but was, at heart, an adventurer who loved to periodically run off to play soldier as much as, if not more than, staying close to home and protecting the nest. When he was around, he proved a tough taskmaster who ruled his brood with an iron heart. When he was gone, his absences caused young Jimmy to assume the filial duties as "the man" to his mother and two sisters, a task that left indelible marks on his malleable personality, instilling at once a sense of manly responsibility and a resistance to the overly protective instincts of the women of the house. The result was the development of a Presbyterian courtliness and sexual aloofness in the boy that would, one day, form the basis for Jimmy's on-screen persona.

And it is within the complexities and contradictions of that persona that the depth of his talent is revealed. As a child he was in respectful awe of his father, even as he was forced to compete with him for the attention and affection of his sisters and mother, something he only really got when Alex was gone. He was also expected to follow in Alexander's footsteps, eventually to take over the family business, but when he got the chance, he rebelled, choosing instead a career in show business, a profession for which his father had no respect. And, quite as much as he loved being the head of his own house when his father was away, to Alex's dismay Jimmy avoided marriage and fatherhood until well past his fortieth birthday.

Instead, he remained a child at heart, making movies until he went to war. Not long after he won the Academy Award for Best Actor for his performance in George Cukor's *The Philadelphia Story* (1940), he was drafted into the armed forces and saw action as a fighter pilot. Five years and dozens of combat missions later, including one final bombing sortie into the heart of Berlin, Stewart returned to America a highly decorated, if extremely war-weary, hero.

Indeed, despite all the smiles and the post-mission medals, it was apparent to even the most casual of observers that the ravages of combat had profoundly changed him, both physically and psychologically. The boyishness of his face was finally gone, replaced with a tougher, more grimly etched visage. His body seemed stiffer and more defensive. His demeanor was no longer that of a callow youth but a hardened man. For the rest of his life he would refuse to discuss in any meaningful detail his wartime experiences, but the effects of what he had seen and done were always visible, living within him like a parasite on his psyche and his soul. Although he actively maintained his military commission until advancing age forced his mandatory retirement, he never agreed to play war heroes on-screen or would appear in any films that glorified combat.

After making Capra's 1946 sardonic postwar black comedy *It's a Wonderful Life,* whose rich, if dark, humor proved too intricately entwined with the haunting nightmare of a man obsessed with suicide to find success at the box office, Jimmy began to question whether or not he would ever return to the past glory of his career, and of his youth—until he commenced the decade that would finally lead him to lasting greatness. In 1950, at the relatively late age of forty-two, Jimmy made the first of his eight movies with Anthony Mann, four years later the second of four (three in the 1950s) with Alfred Hitchcock. These comprised eleven of the twenty-four features he would make before the decade ended, nearly a third of the eighty films he would appear in (plus numerous TV appearances and theatrical runs) over an astonishing fifty-five-year career, an even more impressive number when one factors in the five years of military service in which he made no features.[3]

---

3. In addition to Mann and Hitchcock, during his long career Stewart made multiple films for the following directors: Frank Capra (three), Clarence Brown (four), Andrew McLaglen (four), Henry Koster (five), John Ford (three) (Stewart did not appear in Ford's episode of *How the West Was Won*), W. S. Van Dyke II (three), George Marshall (two), William Wellman (two), H. C. Potter (two), and Richard Thorpe (two).

That same year, Jimmy-come-lately married divorcée Gloria Maitland—adopting her two sons from a former marriage and going on to have twin daughters of his own. During the Vietnam era, when one of his stepsons rebelled against his conservative pro-war values (which Jimmy took at least in part as a rejection of his own generation's military valor during World War Two, an interesting twist on his own early rejection of his father's choice of careers), Jimmy, in turn, stubbornly denounced that rebellion as severely as his father had his. Something essential is revealed when we discover that none of his four children ever expressed the least interest or desire to follow in their father's footsteps and try for a career in show business. One, however, did march off enthusiastically to Vietnam only to die by enemy fire in the line of duty. Following that tragic turn of events, Jimmy Stewart never made another meaningful movie.

After a run of increasingly mediocre pictures, he turned to television, a medium he hoped would launch one last mainstream connection for him to the outside world. He tried, without success, to launch two TV series, neither of which captured the imagination of the public. After that, he finally came home, took his shoes off, and called it a career as he sank softly into the living room sofa of his legend. He took to writing tongue-in-cheek "verse," called it poetry, and occasionally performed some of it on the *Tonight Show Starring Johnny Carson.*

He lost his wife to cancer in 1994. At home one night three years later, at the age of eighty-nine, he died quickly and quietly while watching television. To his personal friends and family, he bequeathed his private belongings. To the rest of the world, he left an eternal legacy of cinematic greatness.

In John Ford's magnificent *The Man Who Shot Liberty Valance* (1962)—a film that explores the relationship between legend and fact—Jimmy plays Senator Ranse Stoddard, who, during the course of the film, relates the true story of his lifelong friend Tom Doniphon (John Wayne). After confessing that it was really Doniphon who killed Liberty Valance and deserved all the glory, one reporter says, "When the legend becomes fact, print the legend!"

Fortunately, today, because of modern technology, we have the legend of James Stewart at our fingertips, easily accessible via DVD, videocassette, and cable TV's movie channels, where the artistic iconography of his eighty movies lives on. What follows, then, are the facts of Jimmy Stewart's life, reflected and refracted through an unforgettable body of work that, for the greater part of the twentieth century, thrilled number-less fans, even as it led him on a lifelong cinematic journey as the only character he ever really fully understood and always wanted to play.

Himself.

PART ONE

— . —

Jimsy and Genesis

The Stewart family at home in Indiana, Pennsylvania, 1918.
Ten-year-old Jimmy is seated to his father's left.

1

"My earliest memories are of hardware smells. The dry aroma of coiled rope. The sweet smell of linseed oil and baseball gloves. The acid tang of open nail kegs. When I open my nose, they all come back to me."

—JIMMY STEWART

*H*is mother, Elizabeth Ruth Jackson Stewart, whom everyone knew as Bessie, called her only son Jimsy. It was a rare sign of warmth and affection to the boy in the otherwise rigid, turn-of-the-century middle-class American Presbyterian household in which James Maitland Stewart grew up, a household with a proud lineage tinted with vivid reds, whites, and blues. Elizabeth was descended from a long line of Jacksons, the first having arrived in the Colonies in 1773. From their homes in Pennsylvania, every male first-generation Jackson eagerly signed on to fight in the Revolution. This call to arms soon became a family tradition as generation after generation of Jacksons unhesitatingly fought whenever freedom demanded it, including the War of 1812 and then the American Civil War.

In June 1863, Bessie's father, Colonel Samuel Jackson, heroically led the charge of his troops onto the infamous battlefield at Gettysburg, survived the bloody carnage, and was duly rewarded for his valor. His proud family in attendance, Jackson was promoted personally by General Grant to the northern army's elite rank of brigadier general.

After the war, Jackson moved his family farther west, to the burgeoning industrial town of Apollo, just outside of Indiana, Pennsylvania, and about fifty-five miles east of Pittsburgh, in the foothills of the Appalachian plateau. Once settled, Jackson agreed to allow investors to capitalize on his military fame as a way to help raise money to form the Apollo Trust Company. In return, he was made president of the Trust and given a permanent seat on its corporate board. Using Apollo money, Jackson supervised the financial reorganization and massive physical reconstruction of P.H. Kaufman Steel, which helped rejuvenate Pittsburgh's then war-weary industry and gave the entire state a much-needed economic boost. Not long after, the appreciative citizens of Pennsylvania elected him to several state and federal offices.

Along with social prominence and political power, Jackson accumulated a significant personal fortune, and at the ripe old age of thirty-four, decided it was time to start a family of his own. He met and married Mary E. Wilson, eleven years his junior, who, everyone agreed, was the most attractive unmarried woman in town.

Their union produced five children, the third of which was Elizabeth Ruth—Bessie—a popular child despite the fact that her looks were far from what the rakish Jackson had imagined a daughter of his and Mary's would be like. In truth, Bessie was rather plain, with a circular face accented by drooping eyebrows and a down-curved mouth, nothing at all like the long line of tall, lean aristocratic Jacksons. What she lacked in traditional beauty, however, she made up for in social skills.

For one thing, Bessie was an expert musician with a special affinity for the piano, good enough as a teenager to be asked to play the organ every Sunday at the Apollo Presbyterian Church services, which she did for nearly fifteen years. Her playing charmed everyone, but no one more than the thirty-four-year-old war veteran and prominent Apollo businessman Alexander M. Stewart.

His father was James Maitland Stewart the first, or J.M. as he was universally referred to, the tenth child of John Kerr Stewart, who had come to America from County Antrim, Ireland, in 1784, eager to make his mark in the New World.

J.M. Stewart was born in 1839, attended Dayton Academy and Westminster College, after which, in 1864, just shy of his twenty-fifth birthday, he enlisted in the Signal Corps to fight for the North in the Civil War. He saw action at Winchester, Cedar Creek, Fisher's Hill, and in several other battles near and about Richmond, Virginia. When the war ended, J.M. returned to Indiana County and became a partner in the retail hardware business Sutton, Marshall and Stewart, which had been started in 1848 by John and Peter Sutton and W. B. Marshall, and was later joined by J.M.'s older brother, Archibald. That same year, the Suttons and Marshall left the business, with Marshall forming his own retail outlet to sell dry goods and notions, while Archibald, with the help of J.M, continued on, merchandising hardware, groceries, grain, and lumber.

Three years later, J.M. married the town beauty, Virginia (Jennie)

Kelly, once she finally accepted the last of his many proposals, having already turned him down several times because of his excessive drinking. Although he promised he would stop, he didn't, and she then broke off their engagement a month before the scheduled wedding was to take place, until he swore "under God" that he would be a worthy husband and father.

Jennie eventually married J.M. and gave birth to four sons, two of whom died in childhood. One of the survivors was Alexander Maitland (A.M.), a tall, tough youngster who grew to manhood known affectionately as the "wild" Maitland, because of his love of fun and good times. His father, J.M., saw his own youthful reflection in the boy, and sent him off to Princeton in the hopes that the demands of higher education and religious formality would straighten him out.

Alexander dutifully majored in chemistry until his senior year, when the six-foot-three, good-looking, fun-loving, and hard-drinking young man became obsessed with the daily events that were leading up to the outbreak of the Spanish-American War. Only months before graduating, he left Princeton to enlist, leaving so quickly that it was said he didn't even have time to turn off his Bunsen burner. He was sent to Cuba, but was disappointed not to see any real action. When the war ended, he returned to Apollo, determined to settle down and make a decent life for himself. He made a deal to buy out his aging father and uncle, and became the hardware store's sole proprietor. Then he decided it was time to find a wife.

In 1906, Alexander proposed marriage to thirty-one-year-old Bessie Jackson, saving her from the unfortunate but seemingly inevitable old-maid life predicted for her by the growing whispers about town. The church wedding was held on December 19, 1906, after which the squarely built, muscular Alexander carried her across the threshold of their new home on Philadelphia Street that he sanctimoniously christened "The Garden of Eden." On Wednesday morning, May 20, 1908, the Stewarts became the proud parents of James Maitland Stewart, named after his paternal grandfather.

Whatever fun-loving, youthful adventurism Alexander had left quickly evaporated, replaced by an increasing Fundamentalist-driven devotion to the store. His face became an endless map of brow-wrinkling concern, as the weight of responsibility for the family's now-struggling business fell heavily upon his broad shoulders. He worked diligently, believing, as both the church and Princeton had taught him, that hard work and productivity were the pathways to earthly success, and that, in turn, was the only true avenue to heavenly immortality. Likewise, anything unproductive was the devil's doing, even his Bessie's nightly parlor-room playing of the family Steinway grand piano—unless it was church music she was practicing, which, all too often, Alexander knew, it was not.

Nor did he appreciate her "social singing," fine for the church choir, but not the local music club's amateur shows. When she agreed to take a role in *Madame Butterfly*, Alexander's spirited, preachy protestations only made her laugh. Marriage, she was reminded of once more, had indeed changed her "wild" Alexander more than she thought it ever possibly could. His singular focus had shifted from seeing how much whiskey he could drink to how late he could keep open the doors of the J.M. Stewart and Company Hardware Store, or the Big Warehouse, as it was known to everyone in the neighborhood. To that end he now expected Bessie to play the dutiful, supportive wife, and her appearance in *Madame Butterfly* was not exactly what he had in mind.

Although Bessie called her little boy, whom she adored and showered with affection, Jimsy, he was Jimbo to his father because of his chubbiness, which annoyed the ramrod-tight, tough, and trim Alexander. It also didn't help matters any that Jimbo was utterly enchanted by his mother's music. He loved to sit in the parlor after the family had finished dinner and listen to Bessie's sweet and simple ¾ melodies. One day he asked his mother to teach him how to play, a suggestion that Alexander immediately discouraged and that set off a battle between him and Bessie as to the need for music in the home at all. The standoff ended only when Alexander received a most unexpected form of remuneration for a bill one of his customers could not afford to pay.

It was Alexander's policy, influenced no doubt by his Fundamentalist tilt, to encourage hospitality to those less fortunate, including, interestingly, any and all local traveling entertainment companies that happened to pass through Indiana. Alexander believed that those who earned an honest living, even if in (the wholesome side of) show business, were doing some form of God's work. When young Jim, who loved horses, convinced his father to take him to watch a carnival set up their tents and attractions, Alexander, as a gesture of goodwill, invited several of the carnies home to dinner, and even extended some of the performers credit to purchase supplies at the store. As it happened, one of them was unable to pay his bill, and offered instead an accordion he claimed had been in his family "for generations." Alexander reluctantly accepted the instrument. Fine for them and their tents, unacceptable for him and his home. But as a good Christian he took it, put it away, and forgot about it. That is, until Bessie found it one day and decided to teach Jimsy how to play some melodies on it. Although Bessie's knowledge of the instrument was limited to the right, or keyboard, hand, the friendly local barber, who had learned to play the music box as a child on the streets of his native Italy, volunteered to teach the boy the rest of what he would ever need to know about music.

— • —

Bessie gave birth to Mary Wilson, or "Doddie," in January 1912. Two years later, in October 1914, Virginia Kelly, or "Ginny," arrived. As soon as she was old enough, Ginny was given the seat next to Bessie on the piano bench and taught to play harmony on the higher keys while Doddie was trained on the fiddle. After dinner Bessie and Ginny liked to play piano duets, with Jim on the accordion and Doddie creaking along on her little string box.

At times even the reluctant Alexander joined the makeshift family band. Although known for his booming bass at church, he purposely sang softly at home so as not to drown out the others. And he always made a point of balancing the mirth with a healthy dose of preaching: the meaning and value of the Ten Commandments, the Golden Rule, or one of the many stories he had memorized word for word from the New Testament.

Bessie did not really object all that much to Alexander's strict, if ritualistic, home rule. Rather, she found in it evidence of an intense level of care and affection from a faithful, hardworking husband. Even when Alexander raised his voice to rail against some local injustice, real or imagined, or something one of the children did that displeased him, she never challenged him directly, preferring to use her calming influence to quietly talk things over later, after the children were all soundly asleep.

She especially appreciated the close relationship Alexander had developed with their son. Once the two girls were born, it quickly became apparent to her that Jimsy, who for the first three and a half years of his life had flowered as the sole object of her maternal attention, had developed an intense shyness at home whenever his father was away at the store. Things were no better at school. He did not make many friends there or participate in any of the group after-class activities, preferring to come directly home and head for the basement, where he worked on hobbies he was able to pursue and be entertained from by himself until his father arrived at night.

Of these, his outright favorite was building model airplanes. After the 1903 miracle flight the Wright brothers had made off the shores of North Carolina, a decade of youth grew up dreaming of one day flying above the clouds and into the hitherto unknown of the clear blue skies. Benefiting from his father's endless supplies of nails, wood, glues, hammers, and saws, and the many 100-to-1-scale model parts Alexander bought for him, young Jimmy used kites, string, metal rings, and the works of a broken-down alarm clock for a motor to turn a push-mobile he had been given one Christmas into a model two-seater large enough for him to sit in and "fly" around the family backyard.

One day, after convincing himself his "plane" was aerodynamically sound, the precocious nine-and-a-half-year-old dragged the thing up the staircase to the attic, where he pushed it through the large windows onto the adjoining sloping roof of the wash house and "took off." Just then, his father, hearing the commotion, rushed from the house and dove beneath the falling contraption, softening the impact and allowing the boy to escape with only a few minor bruises and cuts.

After making sure his Jimbo was not seriously hurt, Alexander firmly admonished the boy for being so reckless, but carefully avoided discouraging his sense of daring and adventure, which, in truth, he wished he saw more of. He was concerned the boy was being "smothered" by his mother and two sisters, and was not getting enough exposure to "real men." Despite the near tragedy of the model airplane incident, it reassured the senior Stewart that his son was beginning to show signs of more "manly" pursuits than playing the accordion. Still, believing the boy needed a safer hobby, he bought one of the new crystal sets that had just come on the market and encouraged Jimbo to pursue another of the new century's phenomena, radio.

If Jimmy was upset at having his plane-hobbying time reduced, he dared not show it, at least not directly. He feared going up against the hard rule of his father. With no other male in the house, Jimmy's main companion became his loneliness. While throughout his life, in public at least, he chose to recall only the perfection of his happy childhood, privately he confessed to friends a somewhat different version. "I worshipped my parents and felt protective toward my sisters; I knew I had to please the folks . . . but in some ways I was lonely—*damned* lonely. There was some things I just couldn't talk about."

Jimmy turned ever more inward, taking up mechanical drawing, spending countless hours by himself designing aircraft, or, less enthusiastically, studying chemistry in preparation for eventually following in the family tradition and going to Princeton. Alexander happily supplied his son with a home chemistry set, which Jimmy used one day to attempt to concoct a combustible fuel, an experiment that resulted in his nearly setting the house on fire.

Alexander then decided to put an end to Jimmy's afternoons in the family basement. On the occasion of his tenth birthday, once daily classes ended at school, Jimmy was required to come directly to the hardware store, to "help out," as he later put it. Alexander constantly reminded his boy why: one day the hardware store was going to be his, and he needed to learn how to run such a big and complicated business. Fine, Jimmy would always say, and do as he was told, sorting nails, oiling tools, mixing paint, racking lumber, never once objecting or complaining about any of it. "I wouldn't say he was a loner," his sister Virginia recalled years later, "but he could spend a lot of time absolutely alone, his own best company, and never mind it."

Jimmy agreed, except when it came to his dad. "Doing things with my father was more fun than doing them alone, for his imagination outstripped my own and his participation added a dimension in the process. When, at the age of ten, I announced that I was going to Africa at the end of the school year, to bring back wild animals, my mother and sisters pointed out my age and the problems of transportation and all such mundane and inconsequential facts. But not Dad. He entered right into the project, brought home books about Africa, train and boat schedules for us to study, knapsacks and water canteens, and even some iron bars, which we used to build cages for the animals I was going to bring back. As the departure day approached, I was becoming a little apprehensive; but Dad brought home a newspaper that told of a wreck on the railroad that was to take me to Baltimore. This, of necessity, postponed my trip for a while, and by the time the train tracks were repaired, he and I were off on some other project that seemed more exciting even than wild animals.

"When President Harding died and his body was being returned to his home state, the funeral train was scheduled to pass through a town about twenty miles from ours. I wanted desperately to go and see this train; but Mother pointed out that it passed at 3:30 in the morning of a school day. And that ended the discussion. At 2:30 that morning, however, I was wakened by Dad's hand on my shoulder. He said, in a voice as neat as a whisper as his nature would allow, 'Jim, boy, get up. It's time to go see the funeral train.'

"We drove through the night without talking much, but bound together by the comradeship of disobedience. When we came to the railroad station, we found a half dozen people talking in hushed tones and from time to time stepping to the edge of the platform to look down the tracks, which had turned silver in the moonlight. Suddenly the tracks gave off a low hum—the funeral train was coming! Dad shoved two pennies into my hand and said, 'Run, put them on the rails. Quick!'

"I did as he directed and jumped back to hold his hand as the monstrous engine thundered past us, pulling a glass-windowed observation car, in which we saw the flag-draped casket, guarded by two Marines, their glistening bayonets at attention. I could hardly breathe, so overwhelming were the sight and sound. After the train had roared off into the night, I retrieved the two flattened pennies from the track. Dad put one in his pocket, and I kept the other. As we drove home, I examined mine and found the Indian's features had been spread and the few feathers of his headdress had become a great plume. On the other side, the two slender stalks of wheat had grown and burst, as if the seed had ripened and scattered. For years, Dad and I carried those coins flattened by the weight of history. And the knowledge that what was in my pocket was also in his made me feel very close to him."

— • —

By the time Jim had started helping out after school, the family business had become more than the county's hardware supply outlet. Through the years the store had gradually turned into the town's official, if informal, meeting place, a version of other burgs' local saloon, only without the whiskey and the beer. Here, the male citizenry of Indiana, the county seat, could get together and discuss business and local issues, often the same thing, over coffee, even play some no-stakes cards in the back.

Alexander often led these politically oriented meetings, and proved so good at it that every so often one of the other townsmen in attendance would urge him to run for office, an idea he always rejected with a smile, a headshake, and his hands held up in the air, palms toward the heavens. It was one thing, he knew, to help out neighbors, for instance to let them pay on credit when they had no money, or to allow them to trade services for goods, even meet at the store to discuss the problems of the day. Politics, however, was a different game altogether. The way he remembered it from stories Bessie's father had told him, holding office meant being strangled in bureaucratic red tape, or having to collect taxes from good friends, even relatives, whether they had the money or not. Alexander wanted none of it. He preferred other, more useful forms of public service, actions not only practical and worthy, but that he could enjoy openly as well, such as being a member of the Indiana mounted volunteer fire brigade, for which he declared a reluctant Jimbo, amidst bellows of laughs from the other volunteers, its mascot.

The hardware business continued to prosper, and in 1918 Alexander moved the family into a grand new Dutch Colonial home in Indiana on Vinegar Hill, just two blocks north of Philadelphia Street. This was both good news and bad for ten-year-old Jimmy. On the one hand, he hated leaving the only home he had ever had. He knew every crack, every corner, every little hideaway in the house, the special places he liked to go to whenever he needed to get away from the others. On the other hand, the big new dwelling offered the opportunity for the kind of privacy the smaller one lacked.

The move also necessitated a change of schools. Jimmy was now eligible for and promptly enrolled in the Model School, an adjunct of the Indiana State Teachers College, reserved for the brightest or most privileged children in this new and upscale neighborhood. It was at Model that he met a trio of boys with whom he would remain friends for the rest of his life: Joe Davis, Hall Blair, and the one he would become closest to, a budding amateur magician by the name of Bill Neff.

And Jim discovered something else he liked at Model, the pretty, flame-haired little girl who sat three rows over from him. During his first year he was invited by his teacher to play one of the spear-carriers in the school's Spring Festival pageant. Afterward, at the cast party, the red-haired girl stood next to Jimmy and politely offered him half her cake. The two quickly became inseparable, and while there was never anything between them that could be described as intimate as even dating, the girl with the red hair was, nevertheless, the trigger that fired the opening round of what would prove to be the awkward and difficult years of adolescence for young Jimmy Stewart.

Things became infinitely more complex for him when, without warning, everything in his life was suddenly turned upside down. It happened one day in 1918 when Alexander came from the hardware store to announce to the family that he had enlisted to fight in World War One. The news, coming after the fact, left no room for discussion or debate about a decision that would deeply affect all of their lives.

The family gathered to see him off to Camp Dodge, Iowa, where he was to undergo military training before being shipped off to France. Just before he boarded the train, he knelt and told young Jimmy, "You are the man of the house for now, so act accordingly."

This was a great honor and Jimmy took his assignment quite seriously, but it was also one that filled him with a certain dread. Alexander, despite (or because of) his strong, manly camaraderie and endless protection and encouragement, always seemed more deity than daddy. Now, present in spirit but missing in body, Alexander became to Jimmy a Presbyterian spirit of majesty and mystery, an even more powerful presence *because* he was not there. There was no way, he believed, that he could adequately fill his father's formidable shoes. A lifetime of being "the mascot" had assured him of that, as did his father's stentorian manner and formidable physical prowess. Besides, he had no idea how he could possibly "protect" a houseful of women his father had so easily and willingly left behind. From what?

As any boy who has grown up with sisters knows, there is a certain mystery that is missing from an adolescent's blossoming imagination about the excitement of the opposite sex, a mystery solved by knowing how they look in the morning without makeup, how they smell without perfume, what they talk about when other, i.e., "real" boys aren't around, what their rooms are like, their moods, their fights, their pouts, their frowns. For ten-year-old Jimmy the onset of puberty brought about an acute sense of hormonal self-consciousness, sexual urges he was beginning to feel but had no idea what to do with. Surrounded by women in a house where he was now both "husband" and "father" as well as brother infused these urges with a particularly thick overlay of guilt and shame. Even before Alexander had left, Jimmy tried, without success, to talk to him about the new feelings he was having. Years later, he told fellow actor, friend, and roommate Myron McCormick about the difficulties that the onset of adolescence had brought. "There were . . . things I couldn't talk to Dad about—like playing with yourself [sic] and what to do about girls or about other people who would approach me in a funny way in the woods or at the toilet in the town hall."[1]

Also later on, close friend Henry Fonda would remember Jim's describing to him his adolescence as impossibly inhibiting and his boyhood one of family-imposed chasteness: "Jim claimed that he never attended a circle-jerk [sic], though I'm sure that, alone, he did what all of us did. If he didn't, he was either an adolescent saint or a eunuch."

The only actual response young Jimmy had gotten from Alexander before he left was a stiff admonition to just let things work themselves out.

But what things? *And how?* Although he was not at all satisfied (or relieved) by these answers, Jimmy had dared not press his father any further, and then he was gone. Like most boys of that age and that time, he found the answers he needed at school from boys his own age, even if they were likely as ignorant as he was in the ways of sex. Nevertheless, they spoke with school-yard authority when they warned him to be careful not to "catch" anything from girls, who were all dirty and carried horrible diseases, and who liked to "do things" to boys. They also told him to steer clear of the town toilet, that it was a bad place where bad men took bad girls and bad boys when they wanted to have sex with them.

More confused than ever, an acutely embarrassed Jimmy finally went to his mother for answers. Bessie, always aware of her children's behavior, knew by now that her son was having a difficult struggle with adolescence (she was also the household laundress). One thing that no one could miss was the sudden spurt of physical growth that stretched him to well over the six-foot mark (on his way to a full six-foot-three, one inch shorter than Alexander), accompanied by an equally dramatic sudden loss of his baby fat. Finally, in the most general and gentle of

---

1. Stewart never explained to anyone who these "other people" might have been.

ways, Bessie sat Jimsy down and calmly told him to always remember to keep pure and clean, to "save" himself for the girl he would one day marry, that his body was a temple that should always be properly cared for and worshipped.

At the same time, she began to stuff him with as much food as he could eat, which was a lot, always insisting Jimsy finish double portions of oatmeal in an attempt to regain some of his lost weight (a ritual that left him with a lifelong aversion to the hot cereal). Nothing helped, and for the rest of his days, the tall Stewart remained scrawny, nonmuscular, and underweight, with narrow shoulders, no hips, and a chest that seemed at times to be so hollow it bordered on the concave.

— • —

Bessie's motherly advice helped lead Jimmy to find other safer and cleaner outlets for his newfound energy and desires. Not long after his father left, he decided to put on a series of live solo "shows" in the family basement. He both wrote and starred in these, occasionally strapping on the accordion and enthusiastically pumping himself into and out of his original specialty numbers. These shows always had the same topic, World War One, with props supplied from the many souvenirs Alexander continually sent home from France—German gas masks, helmets, and blades.

The first full-scale, fully cast production by the founder and star of the Stewart Basement Players was "To Hell with the Kaiser," in which Jimmy played a heroic American soldier, assigning his friend Bill Neff and his sisters all the other parts. The show proved a hit, even with the penny admission Jimmy charged the other boys and girls in the neighborhood, many of whose fathers had, like Jimmy's, gone off to fight the war. When "To Hell with the Kaiser" had its run, he went directly to work on another production. He called this one "Slacker," about a reluctant war hero who gets decorated by General Pershing himself, the supreme commander of the American Expeditionary Forces.

In both of these shows, Jimmy was, perhaps without even realizing it, blossoming as something of a local "star" while idealizing the image of his absent father. Years later he would talk about the fear he had during those times that his father might never come back (a fear that in psychological terms might also have been a suppressed wish).

— • —

Alexander Stewart returned to Indiana from the war on May 1, 1919, a year after his enlistment. At first he seemed unchanged, as strong and sure of himself as ever, but it soon became evident, at least to Bessie, that he was not exactly the same as he had been before. He spoke a bit more quietly now, and less often, especially about the business and the town's local issues.

Jimmy noticed it, too. Whenever he tried to talk to his father about what being in battle had been like, Alexander would look away and answer in the most indirect of ways, leaving out any of the specifics of what he had experienced. Instead, he told his son that whenever things seemed most dire or hopeless, he put his faith in God. It was God, not the surrender of the Germans, that had brought him home.

— • —

At the age of thirteen, Jimmy discovered a new thrill, going to the movies, when he took a summer job at the Strand, the local Indiana nickelodeon, as the theater's weekend projectionist. This allowed him to watch the same films over and over again, and he marveled at the way the actors performed for audiences through the eye of the all-seeing but invisible camera. In these early days of theater cinema, projectors were still hand-cranked, used dangerously hot carbon-arc lamps, and required the changing of colorizing "tinting plates" as instructed by the studio in a set of printed instructions, all of which Jimmy quickly mastered. It was his hardest job to date, but the one he loved the most. If it were up to him, his summer at the Strand would last until he was old enough to run the family business, then find himself a wife, have children of his own, and live happily ever after. His ultimate dream, unlike most of his ancestors, was to stay firmly rooted to the family. As far as he was concerned, he never had to see Paree.

However, Alexander had other plans for his only son. He wanted him to follow in his footsteps and attend Princeton. About this there could be no discussion. The one time young Jimmy suggested to his dad, ever so politely, that he might want to go to Annapolis instead, to pursue a career in the navy and possibly become a pilot, Alexander slammed the door shut. His boy was Princeton bound, end of story.

There was, however, one small problem that might still upend the grand family plan. Jimmy was, at best, an average student. With his popularity having grown among the other students due to his one-man shows at the same time his father had gone off to war, he had slacked off on his studies, to the point where it appeared he would not likely be accepted at the famed Ivy institution. To solve that problem, upon his graduation from Model, Alexander enrolled Jimmy in Mercersburg Academy prep school, a hundred miles southeast of Indiana.

And so it was that in the fall of 1923, fifteen-year-old Jimmy Stewart left home for the first time, leaving behind his sisters, his mother, and his father for what would be a five-year residence at Mercersburg Academy. The occasional holiday visit and one extended convalescence were the closest he would ever get to returning to the life he dreamed of living in Indiana, Pennsylvania, filled with "hard work, community spirit, God, church and family."

In the years to come, he would unfailingly recall his youth with affection and melancholia, particularly when he spoke of his father and how he had left once to go off to war, only to return to say good-bye again, this time when he sent his only boy, Jimmy, away by himself to a far-off place called Mercersburg, a hundred miles east of Eden.

2

"There wasn't a role for me in the first play, so I was assigned to play my accordion in the Old Silver Beach Theater Tearoom next to the theater. The patrons talked right through my playing, in fact, some just told me to shut up. So I bowed out . . . deeply humiliated, and took to building sets, painting scenery and was sweeping out until they had some bit roles for me. . . . Anyway, I'm grateful to [those] patrons, because they were really responsible for my career as an actor."

—JIMMY STEWART

Mercersburg Academy is located in the small town of Mercersburg, Pennsylvania, not far from the Maryland border. In 1923 it was considered one of the most prestigious prep schools in the Northeast, known for its ability to place a large number of its all-male graduates in Princeton and other Ivy League universities. The majority of its students were from well-to-do families, the sons of the wealthy who perhaps needed and could certainly afford a little extra attention and assistance to qualify for entrance into their family's preferred university.

Nevertheless, Mercersburg had not been Alexander's first choice for Jim. He'd preferred Kiski Prep because of its strong athletic program, believing football training would build up Jimmy's tall but still slight physique. However, Kiski wouldn't accept the boy because of his poor academic record, and at first neither would Mercersburg, until Alexander called in a favor from the Indiana Presbyterian Church, whose influence extended from the steps of the prep school straight to the ivied halls of Princeton.[1]

Mercersburg had begun as a German Reform seminary, and Presbyterianism remained a heavy presence on the school's campus.

---

1. Fifty-four out of the 104 students in Stewart's class went on to Princeton.

"Offenses" such as student drinking, gambling, or, as stated in the cat-alog, "other signs of immorality" were not tolerated. First offenders were subject to weekend-long sessions in detention; repeaters faced irreversible expulsion. None of this posed any threat to Jimmy in the five years he spent at Mercersburg, from the age of fifteen until he graduated a young man of twenty. Despite his raging hormones, he not only never had a steady girlfriend, but also, to the best that anyone who was there has ever been able to recall, never went on a single date. It wasn't that he didn't have time for socializing. Rather, he feared going out with the "wrong" type of girls, the ones his high school friends had warned him about—as had his parents, if more dis-creetly, no less effectively. Moreover, his father had jokingly told him shortly before he left for Mercersburg that if he didn't do well there, he would shoot him.

The regimen at Mercersburg was tough. By the end of the first year, a full quarter of the freshman class had been given their walking papers. Even the highly supervised social program was no walk in the sun. Carefully prescreened females, the young daughters of the most prominent families in Chambersburg, were bused in on Saturday nights, invited to attend unremittingly formal "mixers." All the Mer-cersburg boys were required to be present and wear full tuxedoes, the women ball gowns, and the only physical contact allowed between them was when their fingertips touched during fast-dancing to such in-person big-band stars as a very young Jimmy Dorsey.

The following Mondays always saw a rise in "private consultations" between the boys having the most difficulty dealing with their fully charged batteries and the school's religious advisors. Prayer was the an-swer, they were told, along with a healthy dose of active patriotism to burn off their "extra energy." Allegiance to God and the spirit of Teddy Roosevelt, in that order, were Mercersburg's prescribed cure-alls for any and all nonspiritual thoughts, feelings, or urges.

When Jimmy wasn't holed up in his room studying, he thought about joining one of the school's mandatory extracurricular teams or organizations. Developing teamwork skills was considered an essential part of the Mercersburg program, especially for students like him who, unless forced to, would prefer to never leave their rooms except to go to class. He half-heartedly tried out for the football team, knowing his slight, nonmuscular 140 pounds did not work to his advantage. He made third string, but only because the school did not allow for the absolute rejection of any student who tried out for anything. However, everyone knew that third string meant no string, and he soon voluntarily quit.

He then joined the debating team, the John Marshall Literary Society, where his drawling delivery was deemed too slow to be effective, and once again he was relegated to the third-string (tier) team. He also applied to and was accepted into the choir and the glee club, but found no excitement or stimulation in either one.

His only true enjoyment the first year at Mercersburg was the same as it had been his last year in high school, going to the movies. He went to the town's local theater every weekend, Saturday or Sunday afternoons, sometimes both. In the dark, he could reconnect with happier days when he was a projectionist in Indiana, alone with the images of his projected, idealized heroes starring in his most private dreams.

— • —

As the spring of 1924 finally came to a close, Jimmy eagerly looked forward to returning home and spending the summer working in the hardware store alongside his father. Alexander, however, had other ideas. Concerned about his son's still-gaunt look, he insisted Jimbo get a job doing physical labor in the hopes it would bulk him up a bit, as well as balance the mental exertion he had been through that first year at school. Although disappointed, Jimmy did not protest. From May through August he labored as a brickloader for a local Indiana construction company. At night he hung with his pal Bill Neff, three years older and a freshman at Penn State. Neff had by now developed a nice touch as an amateur magician and loved showing Jimmy his latest tricks. He also happily showed them to young Emma Stewart, an ever-present girlfriend (no relation) who Jimmy seemed to have acquired for the summer.

All was well until an incident with near-fatal consequences. Apparently after having gone hunting, Jimmy was cleaning his .22 caliber rifle at the table while alone with Emma in her kitchen when the gun suddenly went off, the bullet missing Emma's head by less than two inches.

According to Stewart, he dropped the gun and ran out of the house and never saw Emma again.[2]

— • —

That September 1924, safely back at school, he was unable to work up any real enthusiasm for a second round of dry studies and restricted social activities. Another uneventful academic year passed slowly and in the spring of '26 he returned once more to Indiana, this time consigned by his father to spend the summer painting traffic lines on the sticky streets of the hot city.

The social highlight of Jimmy's first senior semester was the October 26 ceremonial dedication of the school's new campus chapel, attended by President Coolidge's wife; both of Jim's parents and his sisters attended.

Not long after, Jimmy came down with a sudden and severe case of scarlet fever. His condition was considered serious enough for him to be sent home to Indiana. During his bedridden convalescence his sisters cared for his every need, while his mother tutored him daily to make sure he kept up with his studies. In March, just as it appeared he was well enough to return to Mercersburg for the final months before graduation, he developed a serious kidney infection and accompanying high fever. His condition worsened and for several weeks he lay uncomfortably close to death. More than once a priest was called to the Stewart home to administer last rites (although they were not Catholic).

The fever finally did break, and after a few more weeks of recuperation, the family doctor said a still frail and ever-skinnier Jimmy was well enough to return to school. By now it was too late to finish Mercersburg on time, which seemed to bother his father far more than it did Jimmy. Acceptance to Princeton would be at least another year off now, if it ever came at all.

While still recovering, Jimmy turned his attention, along with the rest of the world, to the highly anticipated May 20–21, 1927, solo flight

---

2. Stewart's first and only public mention of Emma Stewart, whose father was a prominent Indiana lawyer, came nearly sixty years later, upon his return to Indiana to celebrate his seventy-fifth birthday. According to others in attendance that day, a laughing Stewart vividly recalled the incident.

of Charles Lindbergh in the *Spirit of St. Louis* from Long Island, New York, to Paris, France. In the weeks leading up to the big day, Jimmy began working on a hand-carved wooden model of the *Spirit of St. Louis*. As he painstakingly worked on the body, he asked his father for a large piece of beaverboard, on which he drew a map of the North Atlantic. Using crayon, he then added the skyline of New York City on the left and the Eiffel Tower on the right. With some basic heating techniques, he warped the board, so as to approximate the curvature of the earth. Into this diorama he attached his model plane. So impressed was Alexander, he decided to display the "work of art" in the hardware store's front window.

Jimmy and his father followed every moment of the grand media buildup, via radio, to the day of Lindbergh's planned 3,600-mile flight. If Jimmy and his father appeared more heavily invested in the heroics of "Lucky" Lindbergh than most, it likely had to do with the fact that the person who had built the real plane that carried the aviator across the Atlantic and into history was one appropriately named Benjamin Franklin Mahoney, Mercersburg class of '18.

As it happened, the flight began on Jimmy's nineteenth birthday, which he took to be a sign of some special, cosmic connection to Lindbergh. The night of the flight, Jimmy followed as much of it as he could by radio. "I don't think I got any more sleep than Lindbergh did," Stewart said, later on. "Lindbergh's problem was staying awake; mine was staying asleep that Friday night while he was unreported over the Atlantic between Newfoundland and Ireland." Early the next morning, when Lindbergh's plane was cited off the coast of Ireland, young Jimmy rushed to his father's store to move the plane farther along the diorama, closer to the Eiffel Tower.

Lindbergh, upon completion of his daring feat, became the twentieth century's first true-life media-created American hero. So great was his popularity that for a while his face was more familiar throughout the world than Charlie Chaplin's, the international superstar of the movies, even though Lindbergh's only exposure to the public was through newspaper photos, radio interviews, and brief newsreels. Jimmy was always struck by the shy, reticent manner of the tall, lean, handsome, diffident if a bit distant adventurer, and he couldn't help but notice the resemblance of Lindbergh, in manner as well as appearance, to Alexander. As far as Jimmy was concerned, Lindbergh was the perfect reflection of his father.

Jimmy, in turn, fixated on the physical characteristics of his hero. He consciously tried to incorporate Lindbergh's mannerisms into a personality and style all his own—the slight downward, one-sided tilt of his head when he talked while keeping his eyes riveted on his subject, his jaw traveling to one side of his face during long, unsure pauses.

Reluctant to take another municipal job, and grateful that his mother forbade any physical work so soon after his illness, Jimmy hooked up with and spent most of his spare time and summers with Bill Neff, who was determined to put together a summer tour for himself. His skills were developed enough to get him a job with a traveling carnival as a resident magician, Houdini style, and he was looking for an assistant who could help perform the tricks and possibly serve as his opening act. When Neff offered the job to Jim, he jumped at it, and soon the two were busy planning a publicity campaign to bolster attendance at the carnival. Neff came up with the idea. The afternoon before opening day in each town they played, Neff would tie a piece of thick rope around his ankle, attach it to the roof of the tallest building, then dangle from the side while strapped into a straitjacket and bearing a sign hand-painted by Jimmy that displayed the name of the act and where it was going to appear. Meanwhile, Jimmy played the accordion. Once a crowd gathered, Neff would wow them by wriggling out of his constrictions and, still dangling from one leg, urge everyone at the top of his voice to come and see the rest of the "even more spectacular" live show.

During actual performances, Neff, with Jimmy's assistance, performed all types of complicated tricks, many of which utilized the special equipment they had built in Jimmy's garage, including a breakaway box for sawing a woman in half, a "volunteer" from the audience who was actually an accomplice planted by Neff, none other than Jimmy's sister Ginny. As Neff later recalled, "We had a real magic show, complete with floating women, disappearing acts, guinea pigs and rabbits and all that stuff."

These days out on the road with Neff and Ginny were happy ones for young Jimmy, who enjoyed playing his accordion in front of crowds and helping with the tricks. Neff, who upon graduation would go on to have a successful career as a professional magician, appreciated

Jimmy's assistance and never failed to tell him how good he was, a nat-ural crowd-pleaser, that even his painted signs were terrific. This much-needed boost to Jimmy's ego inflated it like a helium balloon until it finally burst at summer's end when he had to leave show business be-hind to prepare for his fifth, and what he hoped would be his final, year at Mercersburg.

— • —

Back at school, Jimmy's postsummer boredom intensified dur-ing the long free hours he had between the few remaining classes he had left to make up. One day he called Neff for advice on how best to use his time. His friend suggested he try out for a part in the school's winter play put on by the Stony Batter Club (like everything else in this Colonial-rooted part of the country, the club was named after the birth-place of a president, in this instance James Buchanan). Nah, Jimmy said. Theater was about the last activity he felt qualified for.

That spring the Stony Batters were putting on Romain Rolland's *The Wolves,* loosely based on the celebrated Dreyfus case. Although rel-atively obscure, Rolland's play was a natural for student productions, with its single courtroom set and, most important for Mercersburg, all-male cast.

After auditioning, done at Neff's insistence, to his surprise and delight Jimmy was given one of the leads, that of Buquet, a civilian revolutionary hero who rises to power after the fall of the monarchy during the French Revolution. Although the Stony Batter production was, not surprisingly, amateurish high-school-level stuff, the Monday night it "opened," February 20, 1928, marks nineteen-year-old Jimmy Stewart's first official stage performance in a full-length play before a live audience.

There was, apparently, little in evidence of what would one day come to be regarded as the familiar Stewart style of acting. The direc-tor, Carl Cass, later described Jimmy's performance as "clumsy," the actor a "funny-looking long-legged kid" who had to be carefully coached lest he trip over himself and fall flat on his face. The school paper, the *Mercersburg News,* was less judgmental than Cass when it described Jimmy's performance as "excellent," "swaggering," with "the confident manner of a polished star."

Regardless of what anyone thought of his acting, Jim was definitely on a social upswing because of the play. Two nights after it closed, he made his debating debut at the inter-society play-offs, and was a member of the winning team with its spirited defense of the Volstead Act.

The only thing left now was graduation, a day that seemed to Jimmy to be forever in coming. After finally receiving his diploma in front of his entire family, Jimmy was loaded into the family car and returned to Indiana, his academic future still uncertain.

Although it was not yet too late, Princeton had so far remained noticeably silent about whether or not they were going to accept Jimmy Stewart. To pass the days while he waited for their answer, Jimmy returned to bricklaying, until one hot August afternoon, while on the construction site of Indiana's new First National Bank building, he looked up to see Alexander rushing toward him, waving a letter back and forth above his head. Jimmy stood and ran to his father, who handed him the already opened notice. He stopped, carefully held up the single page, and read out loud. *Good news!* "Admissions Committee . . . pleased to inform you . . . accepted for the fall 1928 . . ."

The long months of speculation were over. He would, after all, be able to fulfill his father's dream, even if it was not exactly his own. At this moment, pleasing felt almost as good as being pleased. As for Alexander, he was indeed elated. He heartily shook his son's hand and patted him on the back as he congratulated him.

As the time for his departure to Princeton grew near, Jimmy began his familiar pattern of separation anxiety, but Alexander would have none of it. His son was going to Princeton or he was going nowhere. And, he told his son in no uncertain terms, to forget about staying home. If he intended to be a bricklayer all his life, he could find himself another town to live in.

A day or two later, Alexander personally drove his son to Princeton's New Jersey campus for an overnight tour of the grounds. As Stewart would recall the visit years later, in a statement he gave to a press gathering at Princeton in 1990, "We got there in the evening, and the next morning [my dad] took me out and introduced me to Princeton in the best way anybody can ever be introduced: through the front gate, with Nassau Hall rising up ahead, and the sun set perfectly in the morning sky. I'll never forget it. And I suppose that was the whole idea to begin with." Whether or not he was truly impressed with the Ivy institution's splendor, Jimmy made no further protestations.

According to a 1938 MGM publicity release, "Princeton and Jim Stewart were made for each other. . . . He knew it from the first day he walked up the main drag, known as University Avenue. He took pride in the rich traditions of the school, in the stories handed down to him by his father. He made friends easily. He enjoyed every moment of that first year." This description of Stewart's early days at Princeton has since been taken as the last word, a kind of sacrament of remembrance reinforced, perhaps, by the selective sentiments of Stewart himself, who was as eager as his first studio to forget some of the less pleasant, more complicated events between his entrance and his ultimate graduation from the storied institution.

To begin with, as even Stewart later admitted, Princeton had remained a reluctant choice, a product of the defeat of his will that had come up against his father's, whose insistence that his son attend the university had everything to do with family pride, if little to do with family. In truth, Jimmy was less in awe of the immediate campus than in fear of what lay ahead. It was already part of Jim's character to take the way of least confrontation, to comply rather than to confront. But, as he was soon to discover at Princeton, passivity could sometimes be a nascent form of rebellion all its own, yielding the most remarkable, if unexpected, results.

— • —

Like Mercersburg, Princeton was steeped in ritual and tradition. It wasn't until early into the twentieth century that its longstanding policy of restrictions began to weaken. Until then, any young man not brought up Presbyterian was not seriously considered for admission (Catholics got in before Jews, Jews before African-Americans). Women were kept out until 1944. Such were the ways of American higher education in those days, nowhere more glaringly than in the Ivy League.

As Jimmy quickly discovered, hallowed convention was at the foundation of everything at Princeton. It was the best way to ensure the continuation of a family's educational lifeline, and as such, freshman were required to identify themselves to upperclassmen, their surrogate older brothers and fathers, by wearing a dink, a little black cap worn everywhere except the shower and in bed that marked the newbie for what and who he was. Although it has always been reported that Jimmy's major was architecture, Princeton did not offer an undergraduate degree in that field. He actually majored in electrical engineering at the university's School of Engineering, with mechanical drawing his unofficial minor, to help him qualify for eventual acceptance into the university's graduate program of architecture.

Jim's first roommate at Princeton was Stephens Porter Brown, a geology major and fellow native Pennsylvanian whose father, an insurance salesman, had also managed to get his son into Mercersburg. As freshmen, they were assigned to the worst housing on campus, a single room they shared in Reunion Hall, itself a ritual of we'll-make-a-man-out-of-you endurance. That first winter they were so cold, they took to burning furniture to keep their unheated quarters warm (or so Jim claimed in an interview he gave to the *Princetonian* in 1947 without giving any insight or specifics as to how this feat could safely be accomplished indoors). In any event, the two were friends, but their separate interests prevented them from becoming truly close.

Although Jimmy's academic preparation for becoming an architect was meant to return him home with a knowledge of construction that would serve him well in the family business, a career in aviation was the private dream he still harbored. However, this inner conflict quickly devolved from one of battling tradition and familial conformity to one of simple incompetence. Although he might have subconsciously understood that failing mathematics would not only automatically disqualify him from his intended major but also liberate him from his father's predetermined vision of the continuation of the family business, it is possible Jimmy was just no good with numbers, and lacked the motivation and therefore the discipline to master them.

Instead of getting down to the daunting matter of learning calculus, Jimmy concentrated on another and to him far more pleasant diversion— running track. Because all freshmen were required to take at least one physical education course, Jimmy went out for the track team, and, to his surprise, made it, although the coach ordered him to drink two glasses of milk a day to keep his weight up. But as hard as he tried, Jimmy couldn't keep on the extra pounds. Knowing he would never make first string, he dropped off the team (they went undefeated that year) and spent a lot more time alone in the dark at the movies, though he later claimed he used it to concentrate on his mathematics studies.

Midway through his first year at Princeton, Jimmy had discovered the town's two local movie theaters. Every campus has them, broken-down neighborhood palaces that screen idiosyncratic films intended to specifically appeal to the student body that supports them. In this instance, they were the Garden and the Arcade. Jimmy took to going on a regular basis, every Friday and Saturday night, and eagerly joined in the tradition of the mostly undergraduate Princetonians who talked loudly and sometimes mockingly at whatever was taking place on the screen. "Look out, there's someone behind you," or "Kiss her, you sap, can't you see she's in love with you?"

Jimmy quickly developed a list of his favorite stars. At the top were silent-film-star-turned-talkie-sensation Norma Shearer—especially in Ernst Lubitsch's *The Student Prince in Old Heidelberg* (1927), Sam Wood's *The Latest from Paris* (1928), and Robert Z. Leonard's *A Lady of Chance* (1928)—and all-sound-all-the-time Ginger Rogers in James Leo Meehan's *Campus Sweethearts* (1929), a film that made him wish Princeton was coeducational.

If films were his only relief, they also proved a costly distraction. In the summer of 1929, Jimmy had to attend remedial classes on campus due to his dangerously low grade-point average caused by his poor performance in math. Among other things, this prevented him from returning to his beloved Indiana, which turned out not to be a disappointment. He had, after nearly a year at university, finally begun to enjoy his newfound sense of freedom.

By the start of fall classes, he had managed to avoid academic catastrophe and, at least for the time being, happily looked forward to his second year at Princeton.

— • —

Jimmy and Brown benefited from their sophomore status by being granted far better living accommodations at Brown Hall. Once they settled in, Jimmy went about putting together his schedule of extracurricular activities. Having failed at sports, he decided to join the Glee Club as a second tenor. Within weeks, he felt confident enough to audition for *The Golden Dog,* an original musical production being put on by Princeton's esteemed musical dramatic society, the Triangle Club.

Part of his motivation for auditioning was obvious. Although the all-male Triangle Club rarely had the opportunity to use women in its productions, there seemed to be no shortage of them around when the group took their shows out on the road to nearby towns, which they always did.[3] By now, twenty-one-year-old Jimmy was desperate to meet just one.

He worked up an audition piece he thought would show off his talents. For weeks he practiced a single tune, "So Beats My Heart for You," accompanying himself on the accordion. Traditionally, every production featured a live, specialty accordion number—why, no one really knew except that it was "tradition." Jimmy was all too well aware that his singing voice was only adequate and that he could barely carry a tune. If he had any hope of making it as a Triangle player, it would be through the one talent they could really use—his ability on the accordion.

The Golden Dog was an original show written by Al Wade, a senior, and his musical production partner, a talented if moody junior by the name of Josh Logan, who was also president of the Triangle Club. They first noticed Jimmy when he auditioned for the show's faculty director and supervisor, Dr. Donald Clive Stuart. Years later, Dr. Stuart would remember Jimmy's audition this way: "It wasn't Jim, it was his accordion. I had made a solemn resolve to ban accordion specialties forever. Every Triangle Club show for years had had one. The 1929–30 production of *The Golden Dog* was, as far as I was concerned, going to struggle along without one."

At the audition, Robert Perry, another accordion player and a friend of Jimmy's from Mercersburg, went out for the same part. Jimmy's audition, however, completely charmed Logan, whose attention had been caught by the boy's thin, pretty face and small-town demeanor. He thought him perfect for one of the roles, and convinced Wade to take on both Stewart and Perry, who Dr. Stuart strongly preferred, although his impression of the latter was neutral, at best. Logan's desire not to butt heads with Dr. Stuart was the real reason he kept Perry in the show.[4]

Over Dr. Stuart's objections, Logan cast both boys in the play to

---

3. From the club's formation thirty-seven years earlier by Booth Tarkington, it was the club's tradition to take their productions "on the road."

4. Perry, like Jimmy, was from Indiana. They had known each other from childhood but were never particularly close. After graduation Perry returned to Indiana and married Jimmy's sister Doddie.

perform the obligatory accordion number, "Blue Hell." Throughout re-hearsals, Dr. Stuart was at a loss as to why Logan had insisted on keep-ing Jimmy and the number in the show, with the way he bent over the accordion, the serious look on his face, and the protruding lower lip that, according to Dr. Stuart, "stuck out like a balcony." Not only that, Stuart insisted that when the boy spoke, it was difficult to hear him, as he had no idea how to project his naturally soft voice. Logan worked with Jimmy to teach him how to play without bending over so low, and to try to keep his lip in check so as not to distract the audience from the rest of what was happening on stage. And when he did so, Logan no-ticed he wasn't half bad.

During rehearsals one day, Logan approached Jimmy and asked if he had any ideas about becoming a professional actor. According to Logan, Jimmy's response was to pull back, as if in surprise, before au-tomatically saying, in a low, deliberate drawl, "Good Gawd, no. I'm going to be an architect."

"He walked away as if I had slandered him," Logan recalled.

To be sure, Logan's awareness of what he later described as Jimmy's "attractive personality" was a loaded one. Born in Texas in 1908 four and a half months before Jimmy (he was a year ahead at Princeton be-cause of Jimmy's makeup year at Mercersburg), Josh Logan was raised in Mansfield, Louisiana. From the day his lumberjack father had com-mitted suicide when little Josh was only three, tragedy seemed to follow Logan everywhere he went. Not long after, his mother remarried, and the boy was brought up by an abusive stepfather who nicknamed him "Sissy" because of his feminine manner. By the age of twenty, Logan had swanned into an extremely good-looking young man interested in two things—the theater and other men (with the former the perfect venue for finding the latter). He found a comfortable niche for his sex-ual proclivities in Princeton's theatrical activities, the one place on campus where nobody seemed to care if anyone was gay. In fact, to the other clubs and especially the teams, it was a good place to park them. The director Logan was more than likely attracted to Jimmy for reasons other than just his ordinary-at-best acting or musical abilities displayed in *The Golden Dog*. As for Jimmy, just getting through the ordeal with-out major embarrassment was an accomplishment he ranked high on his list of achievements at Princeton. He considered it at once a tri-umphant debut and a fitting farewell to his career in the theater.

— • —

The following fall, Jimmy, now a junior, moved into his own room at Foulke Hall, the just-built, highly sought-after housing unit strictly reserved for upperclassmen. In an attempt to boost his grade point average for acceptance into graduate school, he added more drawing classes and declared architecture his pre-major, which was allowed at the junior level under the auspices of the Department of Art and Archaeology. Each candidate was then personally supervised by students in the Graduate School of Architecture. The curriculum was, according to the Princeton catalog, mostly liberal arts courses augmented with Ancient Architecture, Elements of Drafting, Introduction to Design, Principles of Drawing and Painting, Ancient Art, Renaissance Sculpture, Oriental Art, and Modern Architecture. These classes proved easy for Jimmy, whose natural ability to draw helped him make the honor roll that year.

He also joined one of Princeton's eighteen "eating" clubs. The Charter Club, founded in 1909, was a place where upperclassmen could gather for evening meals in jackets and ties and discuss their individual progress as well as their plans for the future. Accepting the Charter Club's invitation was a big deal for Jimmy, especially since his father had belonged to the Cottage Club, one of the oldest "eaters" at the school and, traditionally, where any member's son was automatically accepted. For some reason, the Cottage had ignored Jimmy, possibly because his theatrical activities and association with the flamboyant Logan had led some members to believe he might himself be gay, and gay members were not welcome at the Cottage.

A friendly competition arose among the eating clubs as to who could throw the best weekend parties. With his accordion, Jimmy quickly became one of the most popular of the Charters. He soon discovered what most young musicians do—playing an instrument is a great way to attract girls. Many young women attended the parties, some hopeful to snag a Princeton boy for a future well-to-do husband, some just looking for a good time. Jimmy, always wary of anyone who wanted to get too close, nevertheless was unable to get any of the party girls who swarmed around him when he played to go out with him after. For some reason, by the end of the evening he'd find himself home alone, frustrated and confused, his squeeze-box dangling lifelessly from one of his long arms.

— • —

That December, Logan asked Jimmy to try out for the Triangle Club's 1930 presentation, one that Logan had written with several other students called *The Tiger Smiles*. Although Logan was committed to what was his senior and therefore final production for the Triangle Club, he already had much loftier goals in his sights.

Two years earlier, in the winter of 1928, Logan had been invited, as president of the club, to attend a Manhattan cocktail party honoring Vladimir Nemirovich-Danchenko, cofounder of the Moscow Art Theatre. Nemirovich-Danchenko was in America to spread the word of the new phenomenon that was sweeping the stages and classrooms of Russia, the Method acting of the great Konstantin Stanislavsky.

In truth, Nemirovich-Danchenko, like the rest of the theatrical Muscovites in America that year, was less interested in spreading the word to the working people than in the moneyed benefactors of their free society. They successfully courted those who were financially able to support them, inviting the wealthiest as well as the most promising college students to a tony bash hosted by wannabe New York directors Bretaigne Windust, the president of Princeton's other theatrical group, the nonmusical Intime, and Charles Crane Leatherbee, the president of the Harvard Dramatic Society.

The party had had an electrifying effect on Logan. After drinks at a nearby hotel bar with Windust and Norris Houghton, a set designer from Cape Cod who had worked with Leatherbee at Harvard, Logan vowed to start an acting company of his own, dedicated to maintaining the highest standards of classical theater.

That night, with raised glasses and solemn voices, they toasted their own future as the University Players.

— • —

The main character of *The Tiger Smiles*, a satire about Princeton sports teams (the Tigers), is Bruce Pelham, an athlete who suffers a blow to the head and imagines what life will be like a hundred years in the future. Logan insisted that Jimmy play Pelham, the leading role (not telling him that he, Logan, had written the part with Jimmy in mind), and Jimmy accepted the offer. He had a total of six musical numbers in the show, both with and without the accordion, among them "On a

Sunday Evening," a performance Logan later described lovingly as "gangling and hilarious."[5]

The play opened on December 17 and ran two nights at Princeton. Then Logan took it out on a regional tour that was reviewed by *Time* magazine, which in its brief notice praised Logan for his originality and the show's "excellence [that] easily equals anything the [Triangle] Club has done since it was founded." The article was accompanied by a photo of Jimmy in full costume regalia. The tour traveled during the Christmas school break and played in Philadelphia; Columbus, Ohio; Chicago; Milwaukee; Cleveland; and Baltimore. As Logan later remembered, "As president of the Triangle Club I was charged about seeing writers, lyricists, musicians, scenic artists, choreographers. But [after *The Tiger Smiles*] closed, I suddenly stopped and seemed misty-eyed and vague. My head was not up in the clouds. It was in Moscow . . . the juvenile lead for *The Tiger Smiles* was written for James Stewart, with his droll Pennsylvania drawl in mind. He spoke in a stately pavane even then. He *still* felt he was going to be an architect. This stage 'monkey business' was just fun. But he was so good I knew deep down he loved acting but was too embarrassed to admit it."

When the tour ended, there were only a few days left before spring classes began. Logan and Leatherbee, who had since become lovers, decided to use the time to make a pilgrimmage to Moscow. They arrived the first week of 1931 and were warmly received by the Moscow Art Theatre in a somewhat exaggerated fashion as the toasts of New York's burgeoning show business intelligentsia. While there, they took in as much theater as they could and happily caroused with the actors in the various companies. On their way back to America, they stopped to pay their respects to the great Max Reinhardt in Vienna. By the time they returned home, Logan's heart was already miles away from Princeton. It was in Cape Cod, to be exact, where Leatherbee's mother had generously donated part of her expansive home to serve as the new living quarters for the University Players.[6]

---

5. The Logan-penned song was later recorded by Guy Lombardo, who had a minor hit with it.

6. The fledgling company had already gone broke once, struggling to keep up with the lease it had signed with the Elizabeth, the local motion picture theater that was

That spring of 1931, upon graduation, Logan, Leatherbee, and Houghton moved their company to the Cape and began in earnest to pursue their grand theatrical dream of running an annual summer theater of national prominence that they absolutely believed would change the course and direction of modern American theater.

— • —

Back at Princeton, meanwhile, Jimmy, finishing up his junior year, found that he missed the excitement of belonging to and performing with the Triangle Club. It wasn't so much the plays themselves he missed as the camaraderie that he had developed with Logan.

In his senior year, Jimmy appeared in the Logan-less Triangle production of *Spanish Blades,* in which, accordion strapped as ever around his narrow shoulders, he played a small role that offered two solos on the squeeze-box. He was disappointed by the experience, finding nothing of the excitement or professionalism that he experienced when Logan had been in charge of things.

The show, nevertheless, would mark a key turning point in Jimmy's life. In the audience for its single campus performance was Billy Grady, a rosy-cheeked, bulb-nosed former talent agent who bore an uncanny resemblance to W. C. Fields, and who had been hired by Metro-Goldwyn-Mayer as an East Coast talent scout for the Culver City–based studio. That afternoon, while driving down to Atlantic City to see a pre-Broadway tryout of his friend George M. Cohan's latest show, Grady had stopped for lunch at a roadside diner and checked in with his office. When he found out that that evening's performance had been postponed due to technical reasons, "in order not to waste the rest of the day I decided to attend the annual Princeton University Triangle show opening that evening. Princeton shows were always interesting; this one was no exception. It got off to a good start with a line of thirty-two male undergraduates in female chorus garb, trying to emulate Broadway showgirl ensemble routines. They were a motley group, and like all amateurs, accentuated their ridiculous appearance with excessive mugging and gestures. All but the skinny guy on the end. He was six-foot-four [*sic*], towered over all the others, and looked uncomfortable as hell. While the others hammed it up, the thin one played it straight and was a

---

otherwise dark Monday and Tuesday nights, for which they had agreed to pay a crippling 50 percent of their gross receipts.

standout. Later in the show the thin one did a specialty, singing a song to his own accompaniment on an accordion. He could not seem to coordinate the lyrics and the instrument . . . the audience thought it was a comedy routine and rewarded him with loud applause."

Grady had enjoyed Jimmy's performance so much that he went backstage to introduce himself. In his notebook, Grady wrote that Jimmy had "an ingratiating personality" but, unfortunately, was a type that would be "of no particular interest" to the studio.

As it turned out, Grady was not the only talent scout in the audience that night. Max Arnow, of Warner Bros., also caught the show and also went backstage to see Jimmy. He gave him his card and asked him to call his Manhattan office sometime. Jimmy thanked him, put the card down somewhere in his dressing room, and quickly forgot about it.

— • —

Two weeks before Jimmy's spring 1932 graduation, Josh Logan paid him a visit at school. Over a cup of coffee in the student lounge, he pointed his finger at Jimmy and said, "You're my new leading man!"

Logan ignored Jimmy's dropped jaw as he made him an extraordinary invitation, to come to Cape Cod and be the leading man for the 1932 summer season of the University Players. Jimmy, stunned by the offer, profusely thanked him but reluctantly said no, because he was planning to return home to Indiana to spend the summer with his folks before beginning classes at Princeton's graduate School of Architecture.

But Logan wouldn't take no for an answer. For the next three hours he tried to convince Jimmy to change his mind, which he finally did by using his ace-in-the-hole. Having exhausted all other arguments, Logan played his Sullavan hand. He told Jimmy he had hired Margaret Sullavan to be the company's leading lady.

Logan had first used her in his sophomore year, after Leatherbee had cast her in a Harvard Dramatic Society show and had recommended her to Logan for the Triangle production of *The Devil in the Cheese,* in which Jimmy had served as stage manager. As Logan later recalled, "Returning to Princeton for my sophomore year I made a token appearance in enough classes to avoid expulsion and the loss of the Triangle Club. . . . When Charlie recommended Sullavan for *The Devil in the Cheese* she was nineteen, from Virginia. . . . I learned one thing at rehearsals. This new girl Margaret Sullavan was all Charlie had promised. She had a pulsing and husky voice that could suddenly switch, in emotional moments, to a high choir boy soprano. Her beauty was not obvious or even standard. It showed as she tilted her head, as she walked, as she laughed, and she was breathtakingly beautiful as she ran. One of my girlfriends complained that I talked too much about Sullavan and she was right. We were all in love with her."

But not like Charles Leatherbee. He was not only crazy about Sullavan but also sleeping with her every night. And not like Jimmy, who, knowing nothing about her relationship with Leatherbee, had formed an intense crush on the actress, and had tortured himself all during the production over whether or not to ask Sullavan to be his escort at one of the Charter Club functions. He finally did, she happily accepted, and they went together, but before Jimmy could even think about taking things any further, she was picked up almost immediately by the Shubert Organization and whisked to New York City to make her Broadway debut. The last he had heard of her was that she was performing in a play called, ironically enough, *A Modern Virgin*.

As Logan was well aware, Jimmy had not been able to get her out of his mind. Not even when the news had come down that she had married a young actor by the name of Henry Fonda. The headline Logan delivered that day, that they had divorced after only two months, and that Fonda had quit the company as well, caused Jimmy's eyes to widen. It was the promise from Logan that he might actually get to act with Sullavan that prompted Jimmy to agree to join the University Players.

There was, however, one condition; Logan had to help him get Alexander to agree to let him do it. Even though he was by now nearly twenty-four years of age, Jimmy was still too afraid to ask Alexander himself, fearing his father would actually explode at the mere suggestion his son waste his summer acting in a stock company for the unprincely sum of $10 a week, plus room and board, which meant a built-in bed on the Leatherbee yacht (the women were given a small house complete with chaperone in nearby Quisset). Logan laughed and told him not to worry, that he would talk to Alexander himself. Fine, Jimmy said, and if you can get him to let me come, I'll be there. Logan patted him on the shoulder and told him to relax and leave everything to him.

True to his word, the next day the director spent several hours on the phone with Alexander persuading him to let Jimmy join his company for the summer. He went so far as to remind Alexander that in these hard Depression times, studying architecture, even on the scholarship that Stewart had been offered, might not be the most practical direction the boy should take. Who was going to be able to afford to build houses in this economy? Don't worry, Alexander had said, he's going to join me in running the hardware store. Sure, Logan replied, that's fine, so why not let him have a few weeks of harmless fun before facing a life selling nails?

Oh all right, Alexander finally said, but he had his terms as well. He insisted the boy had to act like a man and tell him to his face.

Years later, Jimmy recalled what happened next. "I went home to Indiana, and one night I told my father what was on my mind—that I was thinking of trying my luck as an actor. There was a moment of stunned Presbyterian silence. Presbyterians don't actually feel that theater-going, card playing and dancing are instruments of the devil; still my father couldn't help thinking that the practice of Architecture was more respectable than becoming an 'actor fellow.' 'If that's the way you want it, Jim,' he said, 'then okay.'

"Dad was upset. My father didn't like it at all—till the day he died he didn't like it . . . he kept shaking his head, saying, 'No Stewart has ever gone into show business!' Then he lowered his voice and whispered, 'Except one who ran off with a circus. And you know what happened to him? He wound up in jail!' "[7]

The same day he received his degree, Jimmy caught a train for West Falmouth Harbor at Dennis on Cape Cod, Massachusetts. Logan had told him to look for a reception committee that would be at the station waiting to greet the newest member of the 1932 University Players.

He wondered if Miss Sullavan would be among them.

---

7. There is no reliable primary or secondary source that confirms this part of the story.

3

"If I hadn't become an actor, I think I'd been mixed up in flying. . . . Acting was like getting bit by a malaria mosquito."

—JIMMY STEWART

*E*ven before Jimmy's arrival, the University Players had already run through most of its operating budget for the entire season and lost a lot of the company's resident talent. Starting a new theater is always difficult, but in those economic hard times it was impossible. The stock market crash of October 1929 had come less than a year after Logan, Windust, and Leatherbee had first decided to work together. Moreover, the competition was tougher than they expected. Another regional organization had been formed. The extremely popular Group Theater had also taken its inspiration from the techniques of the Russians, but, unlike the University Players, pledged allegiance to the Communist flag. Created by Harold Clurman and Lee Strasberg, the group saw itself as the conscience of the American left.

The University Players, on the other hand, was strictly theater-for-theater's sake, commercialism rather than politics its primary driving force. Because of this, an internal struggle over the company's direction and leadership had begun almost as soon as it was formed, dividing the three founding members and its highly talented original cast of actors into various political factions. Many of the University Players' core performers would go on to distinguished careers, including resident character man and Princeton alumnus Myron McCormick, perhaps best remembered today by filmgoers as Paul Newman's manager in Robert Rossen's *The Hustler* (1961); leading man Kent Smith, a Harvard alumnus, who would have a successful film career starring in a number of memorable, if off-beat, movies, most notably Jacques Tourneur's *Cat People* (1942); Barbara O'Neil, who would go on to portray Scarlett O'Hara's mother in Victor Fleming's *Gone With the Wind* (1939) and whom Logan would marry (for companionship) during her residency at the University Players; utility actor Johnny Swope, who would become a successful photographer before marrying actress Dorothy McGuire; and Bart Quigley, out of Harvard premed, who worked in the theater for several years (and whose daughter, Jane Alexander, would become an acclaimed Broadway and film actress, best remembered for her award-winning portrayals both on stage and screen as the ill-fated wife in the Jack Johnson story, *The Great White Hope*,1969 on Broadway, 1970 on film).

Even before Jimmy's arrival, several other new performers had also joined the company, including Mildred Natwick, Arlene Francis, and Martin Gabel, the latter two aspiring young actors who would shortly marry, after which Francis would go on to a successful television game- and talk-show career, while Gabel would become an enduring classical stage actor, with occasional forays into live television drama.

Despite the new influx of talent, deep political divisions among the surviving members of the original company remained. Some felt that theater didn't operate in a vacuum and should reflect at least some of what was happening in the country. Others expressed their disappointment that this was a group established by college professors who weren't serious about anything in the real world, least of all politics. As one of these original and now departed players, one of the first to be signed and one of the first to leave, later recalled, "The [founders of] the University Players were in it strictly for the fun, only a step above a college lark. How could it not have been, when they were mostly to-gether for summers, like some kind of extended, organized vacation, hardly the atmosphere for considering serious political and social goals, like the Group was doing." His name was Henry Fonda.

— • —

Born in 1905 in Nebraska, where he spent his childhood, Fonda had completed two years at the University of Minnesota major-ing in journalism before flunking out, returning home, and joining a local theater group, the Omaha Community Playhouse run by Dorothy "Doe" Brando, perhaps better remembered for her other contribution to the American theater and film world, her son Marlon.

Fonda studied at the playhouse for three years, then took off across America to live the imagined romantic life of an itinerant actor. In the summer of 1931, he found himself working at the Cape Cod Playhouse when he heard that the nearby University Players had just signed a new actress to the company. He had known Margaret Sullavan from a brief walk-on appearance he had done with the Harvard Dramatic Society earlier that year, in April, in which he had had the dubious pleasure of being slapped across the face by her. He'd been angered by both the ferocity and enthusiasm of her slap. When Fonda complained to Leatherbee, who was directing the show, he said, in weary response, Don't worry, you'll soon come under her spell; which the actor did. So much so that Sullavan broke up with Leatherbee and set herself loose on Fonda.

When he picked up from the regional actors' grapevine that the struggling University Players were still assembling their cast for that summer's season, and that Sullavan had agreed to join the company, he called Leatherbee and told him he wanted in. The director wasn't particularly happy to hear from Fonda, hoping that somehow he, Leatherbee, might be able to salvage his relationship with Sullavan, but Fonda was an actor, a good actor, and the company was bleeding good actors. The pay wasn't much, Leatherbee told him, five dollars a week, which was fine with Fonda. And he would have to help out with the sets. No problem there. Why would it be? He was making nothing at the Cape Cod theater and building their sets as well.

Sullavan had, indeed, agreed to join the company. She had gone from the Triangle Players to rip her way through Harvard's stage and Leatherbee's heart before she quickly and effortlessly landed on Broadway, and found herself in a national tour on the Shubert circuit with then stage director and writer Preston Sturges's 1931 hit comedy, *Strictly Dishonorable*. Logan had wanted Sullavan to join the company from the very beginning, and it was this decision that began what would be a long-simmering dispute, due partly to company direction and partly to jealousy, between him and Leatherbee, so loaded that it would eventually end their personal and professional associations.

The situation came to a head shortly after Fonda arrived that summer of '31, exacerbating an all-out three-way war between Windust, Leatherbee, and Logan, each of whom differed as to the necessary academic qualifications of their company members. Their name was, after all, the University Players. Logan, never big on the academic angle, insisted Fonda was eligible because of his two years at the University of Minnesota. Windust agreed. Leatherbee, however, was vehemently opposed, for reasons having less to do with academics than with Fonda's affair with Sullavan.

Logan accepted Fonda's credentials, but was, like Leatherbee, bothered by the actor's heavy-handed, heated courtship of the equally eager, "highly sexed Sullavan," as Logan would later describe her in his memoirs. However, for the sake of the company, he tried to overlook it. This was, after all, a professional acting company made up of free-willed professionals, not a college campus. Shortly after an erotically charged University Players production of *Lysistrata* saved the company from going out of business, with a run that was extended through the late fall of 1931 and again over the Christmas holidays, Fonda and Sullavan surprised everyone and no one when they tied the knot. As Logan recalled, "It was through a newspaper item that we first learned that Fonda and Sullavan had applied for a marriage license. And Sullavan even denied it at first. But on Christmas Day, 1931, at eleven in the morning, the company gathered in the dining room and witnessed the marriage, performed by Horace Donegan."

Nobody was angrier than Charlie Leatherbee, or happier when, even before the last of the wedding day rice had been swept out of their hair, bliss turned to nightmare. When the long University Players season finally ended that December, Fonda and Sullavan moved to a small garden apartment behind a big house in New York's Greenwich Village. As Fonda later told his biographer, "Living with Sullavan was like living with lightning. Her tantrums struck at any hour and on any subject. Scenes are what actors play best and Sullavan created them over everything. The weather, the food we ate, the clothes she wore, the plays we tried out for, anything. I began to match her, argument for argument." Fonda would later insist, "I never knew I had a temper until I got married. It got to the point where we didn't live on love. We were at each other constantly, screaming, arguing, fighting. It's all a blur now. I don't know whether I stamped out in a rage or whether Sullavan threw me out."

According to University player Kent Smith, "She was too fiery to handle."

And Logan: "She delighted in kicking over the traces. Henry Fonda, husband number one, later recalled his abject humiliation."

In February, when Fonda found out that Sullavan was having a hot and heavy affair with Broadway producer Jed Harris, he went out of his mind. Overnight he followed them—back to his and Sullavan's place—watched them go up, and waited for Harris to come down so he could pummel him. Only Harris never came down. An infuriated Fonda barged in while they were having passionate sex. It was enough of an emotional blow to make him think about quitting acting altogether. Before the month was over, Sullavan filed for and was officially granted a divorce from Fonda. Their marriage had lasted less than sixty days.

The formal end of the Fonda-Sullavan marriage threw the University Players into even further disarray, as the plays for the upcoming 1932 season had been picked to match the talents of its two "stars." In the weeks that followed word of Fonda and Sullavan's split-up, both Kent Smith and Johnny Swope, believing it was too late to rethink the new season, quit the troupe and most of the remaining original members soon followed. Logan was devastated, although less surprised than Windust and Leatherbee. He had warned them about being too closely aligned with educational theater. Aspiring actors would always see the University Players as a stepping-stone to a real professional career, he had told them, rather than part of the career itself.

With their roster decimated, the company faced still more problems. The owners of their Cape Cod performance space, the Elizabeth, decided renting to the University Players wasn't profitable enough and canceled its lease. Desperate to find a new home, Logan and the others tried to rent an abandoned power plant, but even after promising to fix it up, they were turned down. With no money left and no new projects scheduled, it appeared the group was finished until, at the last minute, Leatherbee came up with a $20,000 loan from his grandfather, enough to take over an old 395-seat movie theater adjacent to Old Silver Beach, one of the loveliest sections of the Cape, complete with a tearoom for refreshments before curtain, during intermission, and after the last act. Logan immediately made arrangements to move whatever was left of the company to its new site for the upcoming summer season.

Logan now needed to find a new young leading man for the company, and fast. After rifling through the hundreds of eight-by-tens he had on file, he came upon one of young Jimmy Stewart, the accordion player from Princeton.

Logan then set up the meeting with Jimmy where he pointed his finger at him and declared, "You're my new leading man!"

— • —

And so it was that summer of 1932, upon his arrival into the wake of chaos and confusion, that Jimmy Stewart arrived, suitcase in one hand, his mother's accordion in the other, to begin what he believed was to be his last summer of fun and frolic before the show closed and real life took over.

A month later he made his debut in the University Players' production of Booth Tarkington's *Magnolia*, an old-style southern costume comedy that had been one of the big hits of the 1923 Broadway season and was now a staple of summer stock. He followed that in quick succession with a brief appearance in an original University Players production of a comedy by Allan Scott and George Haight called *Goodbye Again*.

In the third act of the play, a novelist is asked by a wealthy woman to sign a copy of his book. She sends one up to his hotel room with her chauffeur, played by Jimmy in his only appearance of the night, and is refused. In response, the chauffeur says, "Mrs. Belle Irving is going to be sore as hell." He managed to wring a laugh out of it with his slow delivery and raised hands, a laugh that impressed Logan, Leatherbee, and Windust. One of the few things the three ever agreed about was Jimmy's sense of comic timing.

"The rest of the time," Jimmy later recalled, "I just watched [actor Osgood] Perkins and learned a lot that way." Despite the third-act laugh, Jimmy's part was by no means memorable. "When I joined the curtain call at the end, I'd see people in the audience pointing at me wondering what I was doing there."

He had taken a liking to Osgood Perkins and was fascinated by Perkins's understated but effective style of acting. A veteran of the Broadway stage, Perkins had acquired the reputation of a "fixer," as in if the play's broken in tryouts, get Osgood and he'll fix it for you. He studied the physical detail in the way Perkins lit a cigarette, poured a cup of coffee, took a drink. He began to break down the mechanics of acting, observing how a simple physical act, if it was the right one, could move an audience to laughter or to tears. Surprise, he realized, could be expressed as easily as taking a half-step back. Emotional pain could be illustrated by grabbing his stomach and bending over. Fear was cupping one hand under his chin (as Perkins often did) and half-covering his mouth with the other. Pathos was the outstretch of those same hands, and love, perhaps for Jimmy the hardest of all to emote, could be shown by a simple tilt of his head and a bodily lurch, a reach for love.

Playwright George Haight, who was in residence that summer, later reflected upon Jimmy's fascination with Perkins: "He'd watch his every move, his every mannerism. It got to be a joke the way Jimmy idolized that man. If Osgood nodded his head in one direction, you could be sure that Jimmy would soon do the same. If Osgood waved his hands, Jimmy would adopt the gesture. I remember once during rehearsal this caused a bit of a stir. Osgood raised his hand the way kids do at school. He merely wanted to take a brief recess to relieve himself. Sure enough, Jimmy's hand shot up, too. He hid his face when Osgood headed for the bathroom." (Osgood Perkins was the father of future actor Anthony Perkins, the tall, lanky, quiet, thoughtful actor best remembered for his role in Alfred Hitchcock's *Psycho,* a role whose vocal and physical mannerisms in the first third of the film easily bring a young Jimmy Stewart to mind.)

Despite Logan's remembrance of Jimmy's performance in *Goodbye Again* as "howlingly funny as a lanky Southern slob," it had become painfully clear to everyone that Jimmy was not going to be able to bring the kind of presence and impact that Fonda had to the company, the dark, burning intensity, the leonine body movements, the soft, deep, handsome face of a poet. Or the inner rage. Where Fonda had electrified, Jimmy tickled. Soon enough he was reduced to playing his accordion in the tearoom to entertain audiences between the shows in which the real actors appeared, while Logan and the others brought in various actors to play the remaining leading-man roles.

There was something else missing as well, and it could be summed up in two words: Margaret Sullavan. She had decided at the last minute not to come back, or at least that was the version Logan told his actor when he asked when she was scheduled to appear. Jimmy was crushed but kept it all inside. Logan, of course, knew the truth, but kept it from Jimmy: that she had never signed on at all. It had all been nothing more than a lure to get him to come to Cape Cod.

By August, while Jimmy began to prepare for his inevitable, if reluctant, return to Indiana, a series of events was unfolding that would change everything for him.

If Logan's trickery had worked in getting Jimmy to join the company for the summer, it had backfired in the way Jimmy had failed to spark much interest or excitement as a leading man. As the summer slogged on, the University Players were once more hovering on the brink of bankruptcy. Desperate for an influx of fresh operating capital, Logan, Windust, and Leatherbee took a meeting in New York City with producer Arthur Beckhard, whose *Another Language* by Rose Franken had unexpectedly turned into a Broadway smash. Beckhard, a decade older than Logan and the others, overweight, overwrought, mustachioed, and a chronic sweater, had been around the Great White block too many times, producing failure after failure, following a losing streak of concert promotions and summer-theater ventures in Woodstock, New York, and Greenwich, Connecticut. He was the classic example of the producer who lived for one hit in the hopes that it would not only redeem his professional career but also bail him out of an ever-deepening hole of theatrical debt, which is precisely what *Another Language* had done.

Despite Beckhard's reputation as a money-loser, because of his hit, the University Players were eager to forge an economic alliance with him, even if it meant removing the last vestige of the company's original goal of "pure," Russian-influenced, college-bred theatrics. The deal that turned the company, or what was left of it, into the strictly commercial, profit-oriented business none of its founders had ever wanted it to become was a simple one. Beckhard would invest in the University Players, produce shows on the Cape in the summers, and if anything seemed promising, he would take it to Broadway in partnership with Logan, Windust, and Leatherbee.

The first Beckhard/University Players production was Frank McGrath's *Carry Nation,* an epic biography of the primal feminist/Prohibitionist that required a cast of fifty, typical of the ever-impractical nature of Beckhard's usually failed visions. Beckhard had happened to see Jimmy in the University Players' production of *Goodbye Again* doing his chauffeur bit, and insisted he be offered a role in *Carry Nation.* Logan and the others were a bit miffed with what they considered to be Beckhard's rather arrogant demand. They had understood their deal to mean that Beckhard was the money man, but that all artistic decisions would be left to them. However, to keep a harmonious relationship, they agreed, and Jimmy found himself back among the company's regular roster of leading actors.

But before *Carry Nation* could open, Beckhard pulled another power play, telling Logan, Windust, and Leatherbee that he wanted a new, outside director, Broadway veteran Blanche Yurka, to be brought in to handle the production. Logan was outraged. It had always been understood between him and the others that he would have first choice to direct anything the University Players put on, that he reserved that right, and he had just assumed he would be at the helm of *Carry Nation*. Even more unacceptable to Logan was Beckhard's insistence that his wife, Esther Dale, play Carry. Logan had envisioned his new bride, actress Barbara O'Neil, in the title role. The standoff threatened to turn ugly, which sent Windust and Leatherbee into a panic. While neither thought much of Dale as an actress, they feared that if they didn't use her, there likely would not be a show at all.

Esther Dale got the role.

The big surprise to Logan was not how well Dale did, but how funny Jimmy turned out to be playing one of the hordes of police who seemed to be forever crawling all over the stage throughout the show. For the first time, he thought that Jimmy might actually have the kind of acting chops necessary to carry the University Players. As Logan later recalled, "Perhaps [Jimmy] could carry us all on his shoulders, as Fonda and Sullavan could have done . . . for a short time we thought our Broadway connection would help our beloved company. We even began to dream of moving [the University Players] to New York and having a permanent repertoire. But then came the ax blow."

Beckhard decided to move *Carry Nation* to Broadway, and take the University Players along with it.

— • —

Carry Nation opened at the West Forty-seventh Street Biltmore Theater on October 29, 1932, to high expectations, a packed house, and, the following day, loathsome notices by the critics. It closed after seventeen performances. "The reviews were lugubrious," Logan remembered. "I read them in the flickering light of a subway car, crumbling them into the corner before getting off." It was at that moment that Logan knew the University Players were finished.

Jimmy and the other actors and actresses knew it, too.

Jimmy had been paid thirty-five dollars a week for his role in *Carry Nation,* but had gotten something far more valuable from the University

Players than the cash; he had found the beginning of a genuine approach to acting, with all the hand, voice, and facial gesture–and–tic stylistics that would one day be familiar to movie-goers around the world.

Bitten by the bug, he decided to stay in the city for a little while longer, and moved into an apartment that Logan and Myron McCormick had rented, keeping his bags always half-packed, ready to move out and back home on a day's notice. The place was a small cold-water flat on West Sixty-third Street just off Central Park West, two floors below a thriving local whorehouse, and consisting of what Logan would later describe as a soot-colored bedroom with twin beds, a living room with two sprung studio couches, a bathroom with a mildewed shower, and a huge kitchen stove out in the hall. The apartment was affectionately referred to as "Casa Gangrene" by Fonda when he moved in with them. He, too, had decided to remain in New York after the divorce; he was out of work and starving, and embittered over Sullavan's success—she had recently signed on as the lead in the Broadway production of Frederick Lewis Allen's *Only Yesterday* (based on Allen's own novel). The others, including Jimmy, welcomed him and his contribution to the rent.

Despite Jimmy's lack of steady work, he enjoyed the freewheeling boho atmosphere of Depression-era life in New York City. It fueled his appetite for living (as well as for food, including Fonda's specialty, a dish he'd learned as a boy from his mother: Mexican rice and Swedish meatballs, made from ground veal, beef, and milk-soaked bread crusts. Jimmy was known to down eighteen in one sitting, killing the house budget as well as the lining of his stomach).

"I'll never forget our Thursday Night Beer Club," Jimmy told one interviewer years later. "The charter members included Hank Fonda, Buzz [actor Burgess] Meredith, Josh Logan, Myron McCormick and me." A membership fee of $1 each covered the cost of beers and "hobo" steak sandwiches. Fonda and Johnny Morris, another ex–University Player and weekly regular, would take thick slabs of raw meat dipped heavily in kosher salt and put them under a broiler. Once cooked, Morris would lift the salt off the pieces of meat like plaster from a wet wall. Fonda would then slice the steaks, cover them with butter, and put chunks on bread. "We met in an old basement spot on West Fortieth Street. It was a heady atmosphere, with Broadway players dropping by constantly to take advantage of the all-you-can-eat-for-a-buck deal the proprietor allowed us to offer anyone in show business." The deal attracted a lot of the current Broadway crowd, including Meredith, Katharine Cornell, Helen Hayes, Ruth Gordon, players from the nearby NBC radio studios, and established musical stars such as Benny Goodman, who at the time was a member of the network's house orchestra that accompanied all the live national broadcasts. Mildred Natwick, another of the regulars, took pity on Fonda and Jimmy and covered their bill because they seemed so broke she feared they might actually starve to death.

One night Jimmy decided to go out and explore his new neighborhood. He passed one of the expensive high-rises and struck up a conversation with the doorman, who told him, quite casually, that the notorious gangster Jack "Legs" Diamond had lived two doors down the street until the day he was murdered in December 1931. Jimmy rushed back to tell Fonda, who seemed unaffected by the news. "Oh yeah, this whole street's full of gangsters, whores and pimps," Fonda said. "But there's a nice clean YMCA across the street with a free gym. We could get in shape and fight 'em off."

More imminent was the ongoing battle with their landlord whenever they couldn't come up with the $35 rent. Every month they'd come home to find the apartment door padlocked and have to go scrounging for money to get back in. Fonda got the bright idea that he and Jimmy could pick up some change if he sang and Jimmy played his accordion on a busy street corner in Times Square. Jimmy went along with the idea, and their first night, after four hours of "Ragtime Cowboy Joe," "Dinah," "Wait 'Til the Sun Shines Nellie," and something vaguely resembling Gershwin's *Rhapsody in Blue* (transposed from piano to accordion, with a highly original vocal added), they had earned a total of 37¢. Fonda blamed it on Jimmy's singing; Jimmy insisted the problem was Fonda's flattened Midwestern twang. The patrol cop who passed by at four in the morning blamed both of them. A low slap with his nightstick behind Jimmy's knee put an end to their musical experiment.

Gradually, the two became closer to each other than the rest of the fellows in the apartment. They were, after all, younger than McCormick, and felt a professional distance from Logan, who had been their director at the University Players and, due to his accomplishments and confident manner, seemed at least ten years older, although they were approximately the same age. Jimmy and Fonda also looked a little alike; both had the tall, lean builds that attracted girls, a fact that the much more experienced Fonda encouraged his still virginal friend to take advantage of. This was a big deal to Jimmy, who never forgot for a moment that Fonda had actually been married to Sullavan, his own secret love. If he had harbored a kind of mother/sister fondness for Sullavan (a good way to disguise his darker and more lustful feelings for her), then Fonda surely had to represent in some fashion the brother Jimmy never had, or, more likely, a friendlier version of his own father. Because of it, he could never truly resent Fonda for having "taken" Sullavan, or ever be put off by his "icy" manners and sullen, intense moodiness, what Jane Fonda would later describe as his "cold, shut-you-down, hard-to-come-back-from Protestant rages." They became so close, in fact, that he and Fonda shared a single mattress, simply because there was no room for another bed in the already crowded apartment, and the heat from their two bodies helped keep each of them warm during the long winter months.

If Jimmy could last that long. Since the November closing of *Carry Nation,* despite the occasional part and all the "good times" he was having with Fonda, the hard truth was that having come from a big warm house with lots of homemade food and the privileged life of Depression-protected Princeton, roughing it was not something he was particularly good at. In truth, he missed his three squares a day, the old house in Indiana, and the familiar comfort of being around his mother and father, his sisters, even his grandfather. As his options dwindled, he began once more to prepare himself to make the march of the defeated back to Indiana, and then on to Princeton grad.

He was saved from having to do that, by, of all people, Arthur Beckhard, who had somehow managed, after legally separating himself from any remaining ties with Logan and the rest of the University Players, to raise enough money to open what he considered his best, if last, shot at making it as a producer on Broadway—a revival of the summer production he had first seen in Cape Cod that past summer, *Goodbye Again.* With everything in place for a "go," he called Jimmy and invited him to repeat his third-act, one-line chauffeur laugh-getter.

On December 28, 1932, *Goodbye Again* opened at the Theatre Masque on West Forty-fifth Street to out-and-out raves. Every major publication applauded the farce as a welcome addition to an already bustling Broadway season packed with the newest offerings of Philip

Barry, Clifford Odets (by the Group Theater), Noel Coward, Kaufman and Hart, George Gershwin, Cole Porter, and Rodgers and Hart. When *The New Yorker* singled out Jimmy's performance, noting how "Mr. James Stewart's chauffeur . . . comes on for three minutes and walks off to a round of spontaneous applause," it created a loud buzz along Broadway about the hot new comic actor in town.

The play settled in for a long run that would take it through the winter. In the spring it moved to a still-larger theater, the Plymouth, where it stayed for another two months before going on a national summer tour. During the show's run, Jimmy went from being a hanger-on at the Thursday Night Beer Club to one of its resident celebrities, easily (and finally) able to mix with some of the most attractive women on Broadway. Gradually he began to warm to them, and they to him, including Katharine Cornell and Helen Hayes, as well as the endless line of pretty and easy chorus girls Fonda could somehow always manage to round up to bring to the party.

Until he was stopped dead one night after his performance in *Goodbye Again* when a sparkling, giggling, altogether radiant Margaret Sullavan came through the front door of the saloon. Jimmy was stunned when she ignored Fonda, who was glowering in the far corner of the room, and came right over and kissed him on the cheek, as if they had gone to the college dance the night before.

She was there, she said, because she had "big news" for everyone. Universal Pictures had signed her to a film contract and she was leaving Broadway immediately for Hollywood to star in John Stahl's production of *Only Yesterday*, a melodrama about a young, pretty girl who has a one-night fling with a soldier during World War One, becomes pregnant, has the baby, and raises it herself. As she looked around the room, still avoiding Fonda's hard gaze, her eyes came back to Jimmy, who had not been able to take his off her. She giggled, turned to Buzz Meredith, pointed to Jimmy, and said, "That boy is going to be a major Hollywood star!"

Jimmy swallowed hard and tried not to look like what and how he felt inside, a gurgling combination of desperation, fear, and irresistible longing for this fabulous, if forbidden fruit.

4

"It was a very exciting time. It was at the very bottom of the Depression . . . people wanted to go out and go into a theater and be lifted up a little. There were parts, big parts, small parts, but you had to go out and hustle for them. Actually, it was a great time to get into the business."

—JIMMY STEWART

*D*espite his great reviews and the talk on the street that followed *Goodbye Again,* once it closed, Stewart had trouble finding another acting job. The Depression was in full throttle and the theater was one of the industries hardest hit. Much cheaper talking pictures had taken away a lot of paying customers. By 1934, most of Broadway's live venues had been refitted with projectors and converted to movie houses.

"I was having a rough year," Jimmy recalled later on. "From 1932 through 1934 I'd only worked three months. Every play I got into folded, so I took a job with the Shuberts in a play called *Journey at Night,* in which I played an Austrian hussar with an accent I hoped sounded Austrian. We got such bad notices out of town, and the play had such constant re-writing and re-rehearsals, we thought it would never get to Broadway. We finally did open in New York, and during the opening night's performance, I had a scene in which I opened a door. The door wouldn't open. I tugged at it so hard, I lifted the whole scenery wall and it crashed down on my head. Having heard of 'the show must go on' adage, and not knowing what else to do, I lifted the scenery back into place. When the wall came down on me, the audience howled, and I lifted it back in place. They had hysterics. As for me, I got so flustered I forgot my accent. Next night, the door opened on cue, but the play folded."

During this period, to keep himself in food and lodging, Jimmy took a job as a stage manager for a Boston-based production of *Camille,* a position he didn't really want and found hard to focus on. The star of the production was Jane Cowl, known in those years for her ability to chew scenes into emotional sawdust, who worked *Camille* audiences into a pin-drop, tissued frenzy with her final-act death scene.

In the years before cueing a show was largely a computerized push of a button, a stage manager's job was complicated and busy; one mistake all that was necessary to ruin an evening's performance. One particularly warm night, while running down the cue-book, Stewart heard what he later described as "unusual noises" coming from the side alley. He went out to take a quick look and discovered a drunk throwing stones against the side of the theater. Jimmy shooed him away and returned to his backstage perch, only to discover that he had missed cueing the final curtain to drop just as Camille expires. Afterward, Cowl was so furious she pointed a finger at Jimmy, screamed that he had ruined her entire performance, and had him fired before many of the patrons had even left the house. The next morning, suitcase in hand, he found himself back in New York City.

A few days later, Fonda returned from Mount Kisco, having completed a season of summer stock at the behest of the company's star performer, none other than Margaret Sullavan, who had agreed to do a few weeks of promotional live theater between pictures. Whether or not she felt pity for her ex-husband, wanted him around for recreational activities, or simply just to torture him, Fonda had reluctantly taken the job.

Back in New York City, Fonda filled Jimmy in on the sorry details, how he had to watch his ex-wife play to cheering, packed houses while he was relegated to the status of lowly servant, both on and off stage. Stewart told Fonda how awful life had been at the hands of Jane Cowl. They spent the first night crying in each other's beers, until, with neither of them having a decent place to stay (the West Sixties apartment long gone), they decided to chip in and share a room. The few dollars they had bought a drab and dusty, ruby-and-gray flat at the rundown Twenty-third Street Madison Square Hotel.

They also resumed the weekly steak-and-beer parties. "I'm afraid Jim and I overdid it a bit at one of those," Fonda remembered. "The slogan might have been 'Eat as much as you want and drink as much as you can,' but that particular night, we did a helluva lot more drinking than eating. We drank beer by the pitcher instead of the mug. We finally decided to go home, and we went outside. There had been a snowstorm during the evening, and it already had been shoveled into high banks along the curbs and against the buildings. We caught a subway train and we were sitting there and I said to Stewart, 'I can't straighten up. My bladder's so tight from beer.' And he said, 'That's how I feel.' When we left the subway, we had about four blocks to reach the Madison Square Hotel. Stewart said, 'Hank, I don't think I can make it to the hotel. There's no place open, and there's no people on the street. Let's do it here.' I said, 'It's a good idea. Let's have a contest. We'll see who can piss the longest continual line in the snowdrift. If a car passes, it'll just look like we're walking along, admiring the snow.' 'It's a deal,' Stewart replied. Then I had a better plan. 'Say, let's write our names in the snow.' We must have been pretty pie-eyed because he agreed. Now, I walked two blocks going real slow, and Stewart walked about three blocks. He complained later that my name was shorter than his, but I had broken the rules anyhow, I only printed my initials. He wrote his whole name in those drifts. Come to think of it, Stewart must have had a helluva lot more to drink that night than I did."

— • —

As the first cool winds of late autumn hinted at the coldness to follow, Fonda struck stage gold, a hundred and four performances worth of pure glitter in the Broadway production of *The Farmer Takes a Wife*. It wasn't that the show was so great—it wasn't—but it did result in Fonda's being screen-tested by 20th Century Fox. The studio had bought the film rights and wanted him for the lead opposite Janet Gaynor in the movie to be directed by Victor Fleming when the play's Broadway run ended. Jimmy, meanwhile, once more began to think about packing it in. In response, Fonda, free during the days (except for Wednesday and Saturday matinees), suggested that instead of moping around, Jimmy should occupy his time by working with him on something useful, like assembling model airplanes.

The kid in both of them responded instantly to the notion. They began to buy parts and plans and quickly became so obsessed with their newest hobby, they locked themselves inside their hotel room and wouldn't allow anyone in, not even the chambermaids, while they buried themselves up to their ankles in balsa wood shavings. They worked especially hard on a replica of a United States Army Air Corps

Martin bomber. "We finished the framework and covered it in silk," Fonda later recalled, "and the instructions called for us to paint it. The paint came with the kit, but when *Farmer* folded and Hollywood wanted me, I left the decorating job to Stewart."

— • —

Fonda's departure left Jimmy feeling more alone than ever, genuinely happy for his friend but sad that he was gone. He was about to start packing for home, when, once again, as if on cue, Arthur Beckhard reappeared, and again offered him a role, this time in his new production of Nene Belmonte's English adaptation of Gregoria Martínez Sierra's Spanish play *Spring in Autumn,* about a temperamental opera singer who takes charge of the arrangements for her daughter's upcoming wedding with the aid of the girl's father from whom she has been long estranged. (Whatever humor there may have been in the Spanish original is entirely lost in the translation.) Beckhard's offer had some strings: Jimmy had to agree to help out with some of the stage-managing, and, in the climactic wedding scene, play the accordion. After a not particularly successful out-of-town tryout, the play opened on October 24, 1933, at the Henry Miller Theater, and closed twenty-six performances later.

Three weeks after *Spring in Autumn* folded, Jimmy found himself back on the boards, this time as Johnny Chadwick, one of the so-called lost-generation Depression-era young men living in Paris in *All Good Americans,* a satire by S. J. Perelman and his wife, Laura. In this one, he not only played the accordion, but at one point had to throw it out the window. Early on, during rehearsals, to save his accordion—he had to supply his own to get the part—Jimmy convinced the director to let him substitute a cheap banjo instead.

The play opened at the Henry Miller Theater and closed after thirty-nine performances.

"I played the accordion at the party following the play's last performance," Jimmy recalled later on.

— • —

Not very long after, still another play came Jimmy's way, Sidney Howard's *Yellow Jack.* Based on the book *The Microbe Hunters* by Paul de Kruif, it chronicled Walter Reed's involvement in the aftermath of the outbreak of yellow fever in Cuba at the turn of the century. This time, Jimmy was cast as the lead, Private O'Hara, a character based on Reed. The original director of the production was the notorious (to Fonda) Jed Harris, Sullavan's former lover. When he was replaced mid-rehearsals by Guthrie McClintic, married at the time to the already legendary Katharine Cornell, Jimmy managed to hold on to his own part. The show's single, elegant set was designed by the great Jo Mielziner.

Yellow Jack opened on March 6, 1934, at the Martin Beck Theater, and for the first time, the critics were unanimous in their praise for all its component parts: the production, the writing, the direction, and its principal player, James Stewart. Brooks Atkinson, the dean of Broadway critics at the time, writing for the all-powerful *New York Times,* called Stewart's performance "excellent." Robert Garland of the *New York World Telegram* singled him out for special praise, noting, "Especially [how] I admire the Private O'Hara of James Stewart . . . here is a performance that is simple, sensitive and true. And replete with poetic underbeat."

"Appearing in 'Yellow Jack' convinced me that I really wanted to follow acting as a career," he said later on. "Before, I had been only playing at it. But the role of Sergeant [sic] O'Hara was so powerful, the experience such a tremendous one, that my mind was made up, for the first time the thought of eventually turning to an architect's desk was totally erased from my mind."

Jimmy invited his parents to the opening, but only his mother came; Alexander refused to make the trip to see his son all dandied up as a fake soldier on a New York stage. However, after Bessie returned to Indiana and wouldn't stop raving about how great Jimmy was in the show, Alexander decided he would, after all, see it for himself. He attended a Friday-night performance, and when the show concluded, sent word he was coming backstage to see his son. Not knowing what to expect, but hoping for the best, Jimmy stood in the dressing room as Alexander entered. Jimmy stuck out his hand and tried to read his father's eyes as they greeted each other. After an awkward silence, Alexander finally spoke. "Your soldiers are wearing their hats wrong." Jimmy nodded his head slowly up and down. "Here's the way they should be worn." With that, he picked up one of Jimmy's costume hats and put it on his own head. That was as much as an encouraging word as he would get from his father that night.[1]

Jimmy's reviews were so good that even when the show closed that June after only seventy-nine performances—it proved ultimately too downbeat to attract the kind of upscale audiences needed to keep a play afloat during those hard times—the director, McClintic, immediately signed Jimmy for a leading part in his highly anticipated fall production of the new Judith Anderson vehicle *Divided by Three.*

— • —

Before he left the city for the summer to do a few weeks of summer stock at Long Island's prestigious Red Barn Theater, Jimmy was offered a small part in a movie being shot by Vitaphone. The New York–based film company had flourished during the silent era before being bought by Warner Bros., after which it had relocated most of its production facilities to Hollywood, maintaining only a small "Vitaphone" shooting operation in the city.

The film was called *Art Trouble,* a comic twenty-minute two-reeler intended to fill out the rest of a double bill. This one starred comics Harry Gribbon and Shemp Howard (the latter one of the future Three Stooges) as a couple of house painters who somehow get mixed up with two rich boys, one of whom was to be played by Jimmy. He had no real interest in the role, and the existing film demonstrates how awkward and stiff he felt making it. Considerations for sound recording had severely limited his movements and forced him to throw his voice toward the microphone. He always claimed it was just another job, and that he took it only because he needed the extra fifty dollars per day it paid.[2]

While at the Red Barn, he appeared in two plays, John Stuart Twist and Catherine Henry's *We Die Exquisitely,* a drama set aboard a commercial airline and the communal suicide plot that has been made among several of the passengers, and Alfred Savoir's *All Paris Knows*

---

1. In 1938, MGM made *Yellow Jack* into a movie directed by George Seitz with Robert Montgomery playing the role Stewart had created on Broadway.

2. Forgotten by the public, *Art Trouble* almost never appears in any James Stewart filmographies, but it nevertheless remains notable as his first official appearance in motion pictures.

(which, according to the reviews, wasn't very much). Then it was back to New York for the 1934–35 season, where, that fall, he was set to star in *Divided by Three*.

— • —

Opening night was October 2, 1934, a glittering social affair with a packed house that included Joseph P. Kennedy, Irving Berlin, Moss Hart, and Bernard Baruch, among dozens of other luminaries from New York's social, cultural, theatrical, and literary circles. Also in the audience, seated in the same row as Henry Fonda (who had flown in for the occasion), was MGM scout Bill Grady, the recipient of a coveted opening-night ticket, compliments of a young actress in a small role in the show by the name of Hedda Hopper. (Before she was to become one of Hollywood's most powerful gossip columnists, Hopper had aspired to a career as a performer, having already made numerous appearances in New York–produced "B" movies that had earned her the unwanted sobriquet of "Queen of the Quickies." Unfortunately for Miss Hopper, the nickname lent itself all too easily to numerous variations of the same obvious joke from everyone on the Great White Way. Everyone, that is, except Jimmy, who saw nothing funny in the joke, which immediately endeared him to Hopper.) Grady appreciated the invitation from the hopeful actress, but was more interested in seeing the performance of James Stewart, the actor he had first noticed that night, three years earlier, when Cohan's New Jersey performance had been canceled and Grady had gone to see the Triangle Club 1931 production of *Spanish Blades* instead.

Although the play received mostly negative reviews, Jimmy not only escaped the critics' razor blades, but actually received excellent notices. When Bosley Crowther of the *New York Times* called his performance "a masterpiece of characterization," it became clear to everyone on The Street that Jimmy had stolen the thunder from the magisterial Judith Anderson. Grady was impressed, enough to put a call in to his boss, Louis B. Mayer, the head of MGM, urging him to sign the young actor before another studio got its hands on him. Mayer then instructed Al Altman, the studio's top East Coast talent scout, to go see the play and check this Jimmy out. He did, and as Grady knew he would, he liked what he saw.

Everyone from Arthur Beckhard to Guthrie McClintic to Hedda Hopper was excited by Stewart's big break (and for the rest of their lives would all try to take the credit for it).[3] Stewart, however, despite Grady's and Altman's enthusiasm, told anyone who bothered to ask him how he felt about it that he had no interest in making any more movies.

It was Fonda who stayed up all night with Jimmy and finally talked him into at least taking MGM's screen test. Fonda was scheduled to leave the next day to return to Hollywood and promised Jimmy he would personally be there to pick him up if and when he decided to come out. But when nobody called from MGM, Jimmy thought the whole thing had been a bad joke.

Then, a few weeks later, Grady telephoned to say that MGM was prepared to fly him out and test him, and, if all went well, which he was sure it would, to offer him $350 per week to sign on as a contract player for up to seven years, at their option.

Which is why, on a dark, cloudy, humid night in June of 1935, twenty-seven-year-old Jimmy Stewart, with one suitcase, a wooden case, and his accordion, and a hat on his head tilted forward and to the side, took a taxi to Grand Central Station and boarded a train for Chicago. There, the luxe Twentieth Century would take him all the way to the West Coast, to Hollywood, to the gorgeous, high-heeled, beautifully made-up, fabulously fake but hopelessly irresistible promised land.

And Margaret Sullavan.

---

3. Once Hopper changed her career and became a syndicated columnist, she continually took credit for "discovering" Stewart. As late as July 14, 1964, Hopper said in the Los Angeles Times that "I appeared in a play with [Stewart] in New York . . . when I returned to Hollywood, I told Metro about him."

PART TWO

—·—

Learning to Carioca

An early MGM publicity shot of James Stewart.

5

[Stewart] has a different kind of appeal than that of Valentino or Garbo or Robert Taylor. He has an alert, kiddish, eagle-beaked appearance and everybody likes him. He is the kid from Elm Street who rents his tux to go to the junior prom. . . . The audiences seem to like him and the movie lasses draw straws to see who will be the next lady of the evening. One noted Hollywood person could see no mystery in his appeal. It's simple enough. A big, good-natured kid like that, they like to mother him.

—*COLLIER'S* MAGAZINE

On Saturday, June 8, 1935, a typically warm Southern California spring night, Henry Fonda stood waiting at the platform for the Chief to come to a stop. When Jimmy emerged, Fonda threw his arms around him and welcomed him to Los Angeles. As they got into the waiting taxi, Fonda told Stewart he should take off his stylish (and socially obligatory East Coast) hat because sunny California was the kind of place where nobody cared about any of that. Jimmy smiled as he threw his bag, the wooden case, and squeeze-box, then his hat, into the back seat. He laughed out loud when Fonda asked if he'd also brought "the bomber," meaning the model plane they'd worked on so feverishly.

Fonda took him to his faux Mexican farmhouse on Evanston Street that 20th Century Fox had rented for him (everything in Hollywood was faux; it was part of the charm and style of the community built by an industry whose only viable product was the selling of make-believe). Most impressive to Jimmy was the fact that Fonda's next-door neighbor was screen legend Greta Garbo. To Jimmy's amazement, Fonda was living like a crowned king compared to everybody he knew in New York City, where actors, even successful ones, lived like drain rats. Good living seemed to agree with Fonda; his usually pale skin looked healthy, his teeth were whiter than Stewart remembered them, and, if possible, he was even more trim and tightly wound.

One thing that hadn't changed was the communal nature of actors helping other actors. Also living at Fonda's house were, at various times, former Trianglers Josh Logan, whose stage career had stalled and who had since come west to work as a dialogue director for David Selznick; and Johnny Swope, who had taken Fonda's strong advice and relocated to L.A. to find work, eventually landing a job as an assistant director). As far as Fonda was concerned, what was his was theirs. (Logan, as it turned out, was both envious and jealous of Fonda and Jimmy. He had been the big enchilada at the Triangle, and now he was living off the good graces of Fonda, who was already making movies, and Jimmy, who was about to.)

The interior of the place was decorated with what looked like props from the studio's ample supply house, which in fact they were—chairs; sofas; patio furniture *for a patio;* thick, multicolored, and artificially aromatic foliage everywhere. And cats, lots of cats, wild ones from the hills that regularly came down to be fed, which Fonda did on a regular basis.

After Jimmy unpacked, he and Fonda had a drink in the living room, and Stewart handed his friend the box that contained the wooden replica of the bomber, the unfinished totem to their as-yet-still-unshaped careers.

"Well, [on my way to California] I went home first to Indiana, Pennsylvania, and I held it in my hands the whole way," Jimmy later recalled. "And then I got a helper at the hardware store to build a case for it. The only trouble was the case looked like a machine gun carrier. I painted it black. It looked exactly like a machine gun. It was quite a trick, sleeping with it in the upper berth of a Pullman. The conductors kept saying, 'What do you have in that thing?' Everyone was trying to figure it out. 'It's a model airplane with the wings folded back,' I told them and they'd say, 'That's too good an answer for us, so we'll let it go.' "

When Fonda first left for Hollywood, Jimmy had spent a lot of his free time thinking about how one day he might actually get into one of those things and let it fly him directly to his dreams. The trains had taken a little longer, but here he was, finally, strapped into the cockpit and ready to take off.

— • —

Fonda had already finished shooting *The Farmer Takes a Wife,* and signed a contract with Fox to be their third-tier leading man, behind Tyrone Power and Don Ameche, both of whom were hot on the studio's hierarchy of movie stars. That same year Will Rogers had died in a plane crash, creating an opening for a rural wisdom-in-his-manner, charm-in-his-bite type of leading man, and Joseph M. Schenck, the head of the studio, thought Fonda could perfectly fill that hole. Unfortunately, *The Farmer Takes a Wife* proved to be Schenck's swan song as head of the studio. While his movies did well enough after the stock market crash and subsequent Depression, the studio, founded by William Fox in 1915, was tottering on the brink of bankruptcy. That it survived as long as it had was primarily due to the series of Shirley Temple movies it cranked out until Temple got a little too old to be called baby-cute. Her entry into adolescence marked the beginning of the end of her superstardom. The studio was saved from bankruptcy when Darryl F. Zanuck agreed to merge his 20th Century studio with Schenck's, to create 20th Century Fox. Zanuck set about to recast the image of his studio with younger, more broadly appealing stars. He particularly liked what he saw in Fonda and determined to make him the studio's newest savior.

Stewart, on the other hand, was not so fortunate. MGM, the studio he had signed with, was making lots of money and riding high. It was the Rolls-Royce of studios, swathed in a mystique promoted by its own glittery self-congratulatory slogan: *More stars than there are in heaven!* With sky diamonds like Greta Garbo, Clark Gable, Norma Shearer, Wallace Beery, Robert Montgomery, Joan Crawford, the Barrymore clan, William Powell, Myrna Loy, Jean Harlow, and Mickey Rooney, Louis B. Mayer and his young executive protégé, the dynamic Irving G. Thalberg, were not looking for a skinny Broadway unknown whose legs were too long, whose pants were too short, whose jaw was too soft, and whose speech was too slow.

Within days after his arrival, Jimmy was put to work—not on a film, but as male wallpaper opposite the numberless starlets who had managed to get past the obligatory casting couch and onto the next stage of their hoped-for careers, the screen test. So as not to be distracted by anything but the faces and figures of the young and pretty dreamers as they searched for the next Garbo, Dietrich, or Harlow, the producers used the neutral Stewart opposite the young women they tested.

The very much hands-on, paternalistic Louis B. Mayer—a common joke in Hollywood at the time was that actors would rather come down with T.B. than have to work for L.B.—had just scored a major coup, having "stolen" Spencer Tracy from Fox. Tracy's contract had loopholed during that studio's merger/takeover by Zanuck. Zanuck didn't care, believing Tracy had neither the looks nor the talent to fit into the studio's new focus. Mayer snapped up Tracy and immediately cast him in Tim Whelan's sixty-nine-minute B job, *The Murder Man* (1935). Other than marking the actor's debut at MGM, it is an ordinary and forgettable murder melodrama in which the actor plays Steve Grey, a reporter who kills one of the two men he believes responsible for driving his wife (Virginia Bruce) to suicide after a bad business deal, then frames the other for the murder. In the Code-enforced climax of the film, Grey confesses to both the murder and frame-up.

When Bill Grady heard about the production, he immediately pushed for Stewart to be given the small role of Shorty, one of Tracy's fellow newspapermen, a fourteen-line bit of no consequence. Grady also had his eye on a role for Jimmy in the upcoming sequel to the surprisingly successful movie *The Thin Man*. The William Powell and Myrna Loy vehicle, in which they played the alcohol-loving, high-living, sexed-up husband-and-wife team who happen to solve murders between martinis, had proven an enormous hit. At the height of the Depression, W. S. Van Dyke's II's *The Thin Man* provided perfect pop escapism, and Mayer wanted to crank out as many versions of it as he could.

The start of production on Van Dyke's *After the Thin Man* was still months away, but Grady knew that if he didn't get Stewart into something before then, he had little chance of landing him a decent role in one of the studio's hottest properties. Grady, aware that *Murder Man*'s producer, Harry Rapf, was having trouble casting his film, buttonholed him outside the commissary and recommended Stewart for the part, even though he already knew Rapf had envisioned Shorty the size of a jockey.

Rapf told Grady to get lost. The two argued loudly until Grady finally left in disgust. He wasted no time in getting hold of Tim Whelan, an old friend, scheduled to direct *Murder Man*, and called in a favor. Whelan, who hadn't yet cast the role, agreed to use Jimmy, sight unseen. When Rapf saw the dailies, he blew a gasket and went directly to Mayer, insisting that both Grady and Stewart be fired. Mayer summoned Grady to his office, chewed him out, and threatened to hand him his walking papers, until Grady reminded the studio head that he had just signed a new five-year contract, and that according to its provisions, should he be fired, he would still have to be paid. Mayer then decided to wait until the movie was finished and see how it did before taking any further action.

Jimmy, who had no idea of the behind-the-scenes battle that had taken place over his being cast in *The Murder Man*, focused all his attention on Tracy during the filming, following the actor around like a star-struck kid. As the production continued, Jimmy began to learn how making a film worked—the long process of waiting around, the time often spent kibitzing with the other bit actors while the stars retreated to their dressing rooms until someone called "Places" and a few seconds of footage was shot. One time during a particularly long break, Tracy turned to Jimmy, who happened to be standing nearby, and said, wistfully, "Gosh, I never get to go anyplace. I sit around all day and do nothing but wait." Jimmy, astonished that the star had actually shared such a private thought with him and unaware that Tracy was the kind of drinker who never remembered anything he said, particularly on-set and *especially* to another actor, remarked, without thinking, "That's ridiculous, Mr. Tracy. When this picture's through, let's you and me fly around the world." To his amazement, Tracy seemed to go for the idea enthusiastically. "So we got maps," Jimmy later recalled, "started planning the trip, and everything was soon arranged. A few days later I asked him what luggage he was going to take on the trip. 'What luggage? What trip?' and [he] walked away from me."

— • —

Once *The Murder Man* opened, in July 1935, and proved a hit, all the off-screen skirmish over using Jimmy was quickly forgotten, and he was now being cast in one film after another, watched over carefully by Grady, who was waiting patiently for production to begin on *After the Thin Man*.

Meanwhile, back at the farmhouse, Stewart and Fonda had begun to live it up, Hollywood style. Fonda had hooked them up with a couple of actresses, one a long-legged, dyed-redhead, gum-chewing starlet with a flair for comedy who could also dance, the other a bleach-blond, tall-stepping dancer who had become a star sharing screen time with Fred Astaire. At Fox, Fonda had first struck up a relationship with Lucille

Ball, who then fixed up her girlfriend, twice-divorced Ginger Rogers, with Fonda's roommate, Stewart. Rogers had recently dissolved her marriage to actor Lew Ayres, who had gained fame as the antihero of Lewis Milestone's 1930 film version of Erich Maria Remarque's novel *All Quiet on the Western Front*. High on his own fame, Ayres had become a self-righteous, real-life peace advocate (and a future conscientious objector). His politics made him too quiet and scholarly and intellectual for her, Rogers told friends, and his philandering and drinking didn't help, either. She was free and single and ready to rumba.[1] And the ladies were both more than willing to spend time with these two tall, good-looking, *working* young actors.

For Jimmy, dating a hot beauty like Rogers was an especially unbelievable rush, for it was not so very long ago, while still a student at Princeton, that he had sat alone in the Arcade Theater, mind-lusting after the young blond beauty. Now here he was, getting personal lessons from her at some of Hollywood's most famous nightclubs on how to do the carioca. Not surprisingly, he was totally smitten with Rogers, the first woman to bring his long-suffering manhood to the altar of love.

In other words, she slept with him.

Having Rogers take Jimmy's cherry was an accomplishment for which Fonda somehow insisted on taking all the credit. He commemorated the milestone the following night with a bottle of champagne, reassuring his friend as he popped the cork that he was not about to turn to salt for what he had done. With the quiet, assured logic that Fonda would become known for on-screen, he tried to alleviate the massive dose of postcoital guilt Stewart was reeling from by reminding him over and over again that he wasn't Rogers's first and that she wouldn't be his last, and the world hadn't come to an end because of what happened.

— • —

Soon Jimmy and Ginger were a regular Hollywood gossip column item. One afternoon, after spending a day sleeping off the night before, Jimmy woke Josh Logan, who was staying at the house, and told

---

1. Rogers's first marriage was to vaudevillian entertainer Jack (Cul) Pepper.

him they (Jimmy, Fonda, and Logan) were all going over to Ginger's for dinner. Logan, who had never met the actress, became animated at the thought of actually getting to hang out with some genuine Hollywood royalty. On the drive over, Logan, still clinging to his academic mindset, insisted on discussing the financial merits of the newly released Max Reinhardt version of Shakespeare's *A Midsummer Night's Dream,* and, to his horror, discovered that Jimmy was no longer the artistic purist he once believed him to be.

" 'I saw it and it stinks,' said Jimmy.

" 'How can you say that? It's a work of art!'

" 'It won't make a nickel.'

"In my fuzzy condition I decided it was time to save my friend from this insidious Hollywood commercialism," Logan later recalled. " 'How could you change so quickly from a man of ideals? You sound like a crass distributor who can only think in picture grosses.'

" 'That's the way they judge films out here—and anyway, it still stinks.' "

A little later Logan, having had too much to drink during dinner, tried to find a bathroom. As he later recalled, "Down the hallway I wobbled to a likely door, opened it and plunged down a ladder twelve feet into the basement. Heaven must protect drunks, for I got up unharmed, climbed back to find Fonda and Stewart waiting for me.

" 'Come on outside, Josh,' Fonda said.

"I followed them, thinking they were going to drive me home. Fonda said, 'We don't like the way you're behaving.'

" 'Well, I don't like the way Mr. J. Hollywood Stewart talked to me. I think you've all sold out for the money. I'm gonna move out of your money-tainted house. You go your way and I'll go mine.'

" 'Okay with me,' Fonda shrugged.

" 'And with me,' said Jimmy."

But in his heart Jimmy knew that what Logan had said contained a kernel of truth. Everything about him was changing. He had left Logan and the rest of his Princeton/Triangle/University Players days behind him. Even Broadway was beginning to fade into the sunset. He was a new man now, flying in a new world.

And he liked it.

— • —

Between their shooting schedules, Fonda and Stewart fantasized about what their next-door neighbor Garbo was really like. Her house was surrounded by high fences and neither had ever seen her. One day they decided to dig a tunnel under their house to get into hers. The story, endlessly retold by Jimmy and surely apocryphal (and always denied by Fonda), served as their much-needed excuse for what drove Garbo to move as far away from the two of them as she could. The real reason she upped and left was far less romantic than the silly "digging" Stewart dreamed up. It was, in fact, literally odorous; the thirty-five stray cats Fonda had more or less adopted had stunk up not only his living room but the entire neighborhood, including Garbo's house. She simply couldn't stand the smell, or Fonda because of it, and left.

— • —

Margaret Sullavan had been in Hollywood for three years working steadily at Universal. After starring in John Stahl's *Only Yesterday* (1933), the screen adaptation of the play she had appeared in on Broadway, she made William Wyler's *The Good Fairy* (1935), a weeper about a girl from an orphanage who becomes the "good fairy" to others, notable for the real-life romance it produced between the director and his leading lady. Sullavan and Wyler were married during the making of *The Good Fairy.*

Sullavan's next film, made on loan to Paramount, was King Vidor's *So Red the Rose* (1935), a standard Civil War romance based on the Stark Young novel that made the best-seller list in the rash of *Gone With the Wind* copycats. It received decent enough reviews—Richard Watts Jr., writing in the *New York Herald Tribune,* praised Sullavan's "proper lyricism"—but did nothing to advance Sullavan's steady but as yet unspectacular film career. Back at Universal, the disgruntled actress turned down script after script, until she came across a Melville Baker screenplay based on an Ursula Parrott novel, *Say Goodbye Again,* which chronicled the disintegration of a young couple's love when the husband, a journalist, is assigned overseas, during which time she becomes a major Broadway star. Complicating matters is the unexpected arrival of a baby. The film takes a melodramatic, soapy turn when the husband contracts a rare, fatal disease while stationed in China, and, during a tearful reunion with his wife, insists they get divorced so she can marry the new man in her life, but (to satisfy the Production Code) he dies before that can happen. She tearfully vows never to forget him, even as her new fiancé realizes he cannot marry her after all. The studio eagerly green-lighted what it saw as a surefire vehicle that could very well take Sullavan to the top of the top, changed the working title to *Next Time We Live,* then changed it again, at Sullavan's insistence, to the more provocative *Next Time We Love.*[2]

The script didn't particularly impress Sullavan, who told Wyler she considered it weak. When Wyler, who was directing the film, insisted she make it, she in turn insisted to the powers at Universal that the role of her husband be played by James Stewart, "that great new actor from the Broadway stage who has already done some pictures at MGM."

Fine, the studio said, except, they insisted, they'd never heard of James Stewart. No one in Universal's casting department could remember him in anything he'd been in, including *The Murder Man* or his second movie, W. S. Van Dyke II's *Rose-Marie,* a Jeanette MacDonald/Nelson Eddy vehicle in which Jimmy was cast rather unconvincingly as a killer. Neverthess, Sullavan cited them as proof of just how good a film actor he was. She remained adamant, and insisted she would make the film only if Universal made a deal with MGM to borrow him, an offer Mayer jumped at, having no idea what else to do with the young, gangly actor he was paying $350 a week whether he was working or not.

No one at Universal could understand why Sullavan was willing to risk her big-break movie on an unknown co-star. In fact, the catalyst for Sullavan's lobbying for Jimmy had been a chance encounter between the two one afternoon on Hollywood Boulevard, where Sullavan, being driven to the studio from her Beverly Hills home, happened to spot him walking along by himself, hands in his pockets, head down. She had the driver pull over, rolled down her window, and called him over. Soon he was sitting alongside her, reminiscing about New York City and Broadway.

Jimmy, whose relationship with Rogers had by now begun to cool—she found him just too inexperienced, too callow for her heat, she told friends—was ripe-ready for the return of Sullavan in his life, in any

---

2. The film was released in England as *Next Time We Live.*

form, while for her, Jimmy was not exactly the one who had gotten away, but one of the many she liked and for one reason or another had let get away. With him, though, she was careful about breaking a heart so tender, one that he wore so plaintively on his sleeve. It was that very nonvoracious quality about him that she had always been attracted to. "She was protective, loving, maternal toward him," Myron McCormick told Sullavan's biographer. "She wasn't usually like this with most men. If she wasn't getting sexually predatory with them she was indifferent, or contemptuous."

Now she determined to flex her muscles and turn him into the star she had always felt he would become. However, when she brought his name up to Carl Laemmle, the hard head of Universal, he told her that Francis Lederer had already been cast in the role. Lederer was one of Hollywood's vaguely exotic European leading men (he was actually Czech), whom the studio, in all its infinite wisdom, had earmarked for the part in the film of the "young, all-American Princeton type." Unable to shake Sullavan's resolve, Laemmle passed off what he started calling "the *final* casting" to the film's assigned director, Edward Griffith, an able if ordinary silent screen veteran who had a dim flair for breezy contemporary comedy and who would go on to become the favored director of icy screen goddess Madeleine Carroll. Griffith, not wanting to rock this temperamental star's boat, chose the path of least resistance for himself, okayed Jimmy for the role, and the loan-out deal with MGM was made.

Filming for *Next Time We Love* began on October 21, 1935, with a noticeably anxious Jimmy Stewart, and before long, Griffith was feeling the pressure from Laemmle, who was unhappy with the dailies and wanted Jimmy replaced before any more film was shot. In her memoirs, Brooke Hayward, Sullavan's daughter, wrote, "They were both particularly fond of the scene [in *Next Time We Love*] in which Jimmy had to go away on assignment, leaving his young wife and baby behind. Jimmy felt that the situation called for a tear or two on his part, and had no difficulty filling his eyes for the first take, but the baby threw something at him and they had to cut. The second take was likewise ruined by the baby and the third and the fourth. By the fifth take, Jimmy was unable to summon up any more tears. He didn't know about glycerin, which is often used in movies to stimulate tears and, in any case, would probably have been too embarrassed to ask for it, so he went behind the scenery, lit a cigarette, and held it to his eyes in the hope that the smoke would make them tear up. This experiment transformed his eyes into two raw blobs, and he almost threatened to shoot the child. Mother was delighted, particularly by the cigarette."

Sullavan calmly guaranteed both Griffith and Laemmle that Stewart would come through for them. To make it happen, after the cigarette scene, she worked privately with him, every night after shooting, coaching him for the next day's scenes, showing him exactly how he should move (and *not* move), encouraging him to tone down the more mannered aspects of his stage-trained persona—the hand movements, the projected voice, the neck turns, the awkward bent-forward posture—and instructed him to look directly into her eyes when he spoke to her, and to keep on looking at her, and only her, when she spoke to him.

All of this extracurricular coaching did not help Sullavan's already shaky marriage to the insecure Wyler, who was off making *These Three* for Samuel Goldwyn, the third movie version of Lillian Hellman's controversial lesbian drama originally written for the stage as *The Children's Hour.* In addition to directing his cast, Wyler had to play referee to the verbal fisticuffs between jealous-of-each-other co-stars Miriam Hopkins and Merle Oberon.

Stewart remained oblivious to the whispers floating around that the nights he was spending with Sullavan had less to do with rehearsals than romance. And in a sense, they were correct. Sullavan was, in her fashion, seducing Stewart with her talent, treating him like a doting mother dressing up her favorite little boy and teaching him how to behave in public. *How to act.*

These were not just the only formal "lessons" Jimmy ever had; they were also the best he could have ever hoped for. Sullavan taught him the secret to channeling his most private desires into characters whom audiences could understand and relate to, and, most important, be moved by. It was this understanding of how to bring his emotions to the surface that would lead him for the first time to experience the true art of film acting—to make the connection between what was inside of him and what an audience saw, the bridge to what they would both feel. These sessions with Sullavan, in their way, were as "real" as any romance would have been. Being close enough that he could smell the perfume of her shampoo while she carefully tutored him was intoxicating and, for Jimmy, an act more intimate to his way of thinking and feeling than any he had ever done with Ginger Rogers. And, as a result, he would never be quite the same way as he was before, not as an actor and not as a man.

The difference in his acting was noticeable. He'd gained a new confidence in his approach, and stopped hiding behind the mechanics of his automatic mannerisms; he'd become naturally charming on camera, instead of trying to mimic the gestures of a charmer.

Next Time We Love opened early in 1936, and the high quality of Jimmy's performance was noticed by everyone. Many thought it was his first film, and for years after, Griffith, who enjoyed an unusual (for him) success with the film as well, always credited Sullavan for having made James Stewart a star.

Jimmy agreed with that assessment, and, not surprisingly, had difficulty separating his professional gratitude from his personal feelings. "I'll never marry until I find a girl like Margaret Sullavan," Jimmy told a reporter from a Hollywood fanzine.

— • —

Despite Universal's success with the film and Jimmy's new-found popularity, Mayer remained without a clue as to what to do with him next. Mayer no longer doubted he could act, but still had no idea how to cast him. Some at the studio thought with his unusually long legs he had the makings of a good screen comedian. Others saw a spark of romantic leading man in his boyish good looks, but were put off by his awkward mannerisms. Still others thought, with a little building up, he might make a good action hero. In 1936, his first full year at MGM, Jimmy appeared in seven features, all made at the studio, small roles in unimportant pictures in which Stewart played a variety of characters while MGM tried to figure out how best to use him (and Grady waited to get him into *After the Thin Man*). In W. S. Van Dyke II's *Rose-Marie*, he played a killer. In Clarence Brown's *Wife vs. Secretary*, a Clark Gable/Jean Harlow vehicle, he played a typical all-American young man. In William Wellman's *Small Town Girl*, a Janet Gaynor/Robert Taylor vehicle, he played essentially the same role. In Edwin Marin's *Speed*, co-starring Una Merkel, he played a young race-car driver. In Clarence Brown's *The Gorgeous Hussy*, an MGM all-star showcase, with Joan Crawford, Robert Taylor, Lionel Barrymore, Franchot Tone, Melvyn Douglas, Louis Calhern, Beulah Bondi,

Sidney Toler, Gene Lockhart, and at least a dozen other familiar names, he played a young, romantic aristocrat. And in Roy Del Ruth's *Born to Dance,* an Eleanor Powell vehicle, playing a young naval officer, Jimmy danced for the first and only time in his entire career in the manner of Fred Astaire or Gene Kelly (as opposed to ballroom, or cheek-to-cheek, which he did in several films).

In the midst of all this speculation, Mayer personally had Jimmy test for the part of Ching, a supporting role in the studio's upcoming big-budget production of Pearl S. Buck's sprawling novel of the life of Chinese peasants, *The Good Earth,* to be directed by Sidney Franklin, with Paul Muni and Luise Rainer in the first leads. Jimmy was sent to makeup, where he was fitted with a tight hair cap, his eyes were glued up on either side, and his eyebrows and eyelashes were cut off. The screen test proved a disaster, and Mayer gave the part to Ching Wah Lee, one of the studio's standard-issue "Orientals." After that, Mayer ordered Jimmy to gain weight to make him more castable, and assigned one of the studio's personal trainers to see to it he stuck to his regimen. Finally, he was cast in the role of the apparent nice guy who is really the killer in W. S. Van Dyke II's *After the Thin Man.*

— • —

Throughout that rush of films, during his off-time, Stewart continued to hang out mostly with Fonda, with whom he had moved to a larger (and catless) house in Brentwood, with Josh Logan and Johnny Swope more or less permanent houseguests. Almost from the day they took over the place, there were parties practically every night, where the most beautiful starlets in Hollywood, which meant in the country, which meant in the world, came to play and in most instances, to stay, at least until the next day.

Fonda and Jimmy's off-days usually began with an eggnog and brandy. As Jimmy recalled later on, "We were both too skinny, and one time we decided to gain a little weight . . . a little . . . so a fella told us for breakfast every morning we should drink an eggnog with brandy. But the thing was, we noticed that the eggnog kept getting darker and darker, and by eleven A.M. we were both *pissed!*"

And stayed that way until it was officially party time. Sometimes they would continue the festivities into the night on the Sunset Strip, an unzoned mile or so of anything-goes situated between Beverly Hills and Hollywood, with the clubs owned by the stars themselves and where whiskey, drugs, and sex flowed as freely as the popcorn and soda pop at most movies' concession stands. They usually got things rolling at the Trocadero, before moving on to the Cocoanut Grove, hangouts that catered to the industry, stayed open all night, and always looked the other way, no matter what or who was going down.

It was at the Cocoanut Grove that Stewart first met many of the stars who were to become his lifelong friends and some his eventual neighbors, including Jack Benny and his wife, Mary; George Burns and Gracie Allen; Harold Lloyd; William Powell; Norma Shearer; Dolores Del Rio; Red Skelton; and a teenage Judy Garland always escorted by her mother. Occasionally he would run into his ex, Ginger Rogers, but if he held any lingering heartbreak over her, he didn't show it. For one thing, he was too busy fighting off the actresses and starlets eager to get a chance with him. He may not yet have been a top-ranking star to the rest of the world, but to the young ladies of Hollywood, he was a working actor who had actually made some movies, had a few dollars in his pocket, didn't smoke those smelly cigars, and was under sixty, the age of the men they usually wound up dating when they were on the career make.

Fonda later recalled how stars and starlets were always the aggressors, sending them flowers with little notes attached the way a man would ordinarily treat a woman. And they loved it, even when the women were as aggressive as their screen image. Barbara Stanwyck, just divorced after seven years of marriage to actor Frank Fay, chased Stewart all over town, but had trouble convincing him to take her home to his bed. He was always opting instead for parties, and hanging out. Stanwyck nicknamed him "the problem child," called him crazy to his face, and walked out on him: the end of yet another romance that never was.[3] Meanwhile *Collier's* magazine, a popular rag of its time with literary pretensions and loads of Hollywood gossip, dubbed Jimmy the newest "Blade of Beverly Hills."

All the duo's skirt-chasing, or perhaps more accurately in Jimmy's case, all the being chased by skirts, ended when Fonda returned from

---

3. A few years later, in 1939, Stanwyck got married for a second time, to movie heman Robert Taylor, who had a reputation as an intense, real-life ladies man. Their marriage lasted twelve years.

London, where he had gone to make a movie, and announced that he had gotten married. Again. On September 6, 1936, while overseas, Fonda had tied the knot with Manhattan socialite Frances Seymour, the young widow of George Brokaw (who had been married once before, to Clare Boothe). Frances and Fonda had been introduced by her wealthy uncle, the former head of Standard Oil, while Fonda was shooting *Wings of the Morning*. He proposed to her in Budapest, she accepted in Paris, they were married in New York City, and they spent their honeymoon at the Beverly Hills Hotel.

This meant, among other things, that the house he had shared with the others passed on to Jimmy, or, as his friends referred to him now, "Bachelor Number One." As a wedding present, however, Jimmy, Logan, and Swope let Fonda and his new wife, Frances, stay on in the house, while they all found another one that just happened to be located a block away from where Margaret Sullavan was now living.

— • —

After the Thin Man opened on Christmas Day, 1936, and went on to become a big hit, the sixth highest grosser of the year. The *New York Herald Tribune* called Jimmy's performance "a characterization as surprising as it is effective," and *Variety* singled him out for special praise: "James Stewart is calm until the blow-off when he does his best work." "The blow-off" was the final scene in which Stewart, to this point in the movie little-noticed, suddenly turns into the villain, with a strong ten-minute breathtaker in the slick, Dashiell Hammett–Van Dyke–*Thin Man* fashion of rapid-fire revelation to resolution.

Everyone, it seemed, except Mayer was suddenly aware now of the hot new young actor in town. Mayer promptly agreed to loan out the actor to 20th Century Fox in order to star in Henry King's *Seventh Heaven* to the tune of $1,000 a week, complete with a $3,000 signing bonus (all of which went to MGM). As far as Mayer was concerned, if someone else wanted to pay that kind of money for the contract player's time, that was just fine. Because he was now operating without the youthful visionary Irving Thalberg by his side (whose unexpected early death in 1936 left no one to help guide the studio), Mayer still did not have a clue as to what, or who, Jimmy Stewart was.

But others did. Both on-screen and off.

6

"I loved being in pictures. Right away—didn't miss the stage at all. Loved it. All that stuff ya hear 'bout how the big studio was nothing but an enormous factory—this just isn't true . . . it was wonderful."

—JIMMY STEWART

When Darryl F. Zanuck, the head of the newly merged 20th Century Fox, signed twenty-five-year-old French film sensation Simone Simon, she had only made two pictures in America. Zanuck decided to use her in the Janet Gaynor role for his planned remake of the 1927 silent classic, Frank Borzage's *Seventh Heaven*. In need of product, he had decided to raid his own catalog of premerger and rarely seen silent Fox Films. The story of *Seventh Heaven* concerns the adventures of Chico, a Parisian sewer worker who falls in love with Diane (Simon), a young and beautiful prostitute thrown into the streets for not making enough money for the brothel. A priest advises them to get married and start over. They set a date, but before they can officially become man and wife, World War One breaks out and Chico enlists. Word soon reaches Diane that he has been killed. She renounces her life as a prostitute and remains faithful to his memory, until, miraculously, he returns, after the war, blinded but still alive. She tells him it doesn't matter about his eyesight, that she will be his eyes from now on. They move into a small garret they name Seventh Heaven, where they live happily half blind ever after.

Zanuck had wanted to pair Simon with Tyrone Power, one of the top stars on 20th Century Fox's A-list roster, but Power flatly turned down the role. He hated the script and feared that "playing French" opposite one of France's most popular leading ladies could hurt him. When Zanuck failed to come up with anybody at his own studio who was either willing to play the part or whom Simon approved of, he finally asked her for her personal wish list of leading men. At the top of it was James Stewart.

She had seen him in a couple of movies and liked what he did on-screen, especially his nonthreatening manner. If he co-starred, she believed she wouldn't have to worry about the film being stolen from her. Zanuck then approached Mayer, who turned to Bill Grady for advice about what to do. Grady told him to agree to the loan-out, and Mayer made the deal.

Production on *Seventh Heaven* began at the Fox studios on December 2, 1936, under the direction of Henry King, a former silent-screen actor and director who Zanuck liked to use for what he called house projects, films that came down the pike and were made by chosen directors on assignment via the head of production or, as in this case, Zanuck himself.

As one might have predicted, the chemistry between the hot, sultry actress and her chosen screen co-star was nonexistent. Simon was one of those European imports, like Garbo and Dietrich, who had the look, sound, and shape that set isolationist-era American men on fire, the kind of woman who the studios loved to use to satisfy the public's exotic, i.e., sexual fantasies, and the kind who had no problem taking care of their own while they were at it. It was, for instance, well known around Hollywood that those in the business who gained Ms. Simon's favor were rewarded with a gold key that opened the door to her private boudoir.

Stewart was not one of those who received that particular prize. So turned off was he by Simon's upfront sexuality that he virtually ignored her during the entire making of the movie and spent whatever off-camera time he could talking with Henry King about flying private planes, a subject they both had a far deeper interest in than either the picture or its female lead.

The film opened in March 1937 to mixed reviews, the movie criticized for its obvious back-lot imitation Paris, Stewart's unbelievable French accent, and what seemed Simon's near-total lack of acting ability, especially when compared to the silent film version's original star, Janet Gaynor.

— • —

Back at MGM, Jimmy gained little forward momentum from the loan-out and found himself back playing in another slew of supporting roles behind some of the biggest stars of the day. His next film,

Edward Ludwig's *The Last Gangster* (1937), was a vehicle for Edward G. Robinson, one of Warner's custom-cut "gangsters," who'd first made it big with his portrayal of Enrico Bandello in Mervyn LeRoy's *Little Caesar* (1930). That film's closing line—"Is this the end of Rico?"—had made Robinson an instant star. Although he had tired of playing heavies, Robinson nevertheless agreed to make *The Last Gangster* because of the huge amount of money he was offered.

Stewart doesn't make his entrance until midway through the film and then has to age ten years in the last half hour. To make the transition more believable, he was given a pencil mustache. The picture, an anachronistic look at late-twenties gangsterism, a genre about to be made obsolete by the larger forces of evil threatening the world, was an out-and-out flop, and as such did nothing for either Robinson or Stewart's careers.

Running on the contract hamster wheel, Stewart made two more movies in 1937. In Sam Wood's *Navy Blue and Gold* (1937) and Clarence Brown's *Of Human Hearts* (1938), he reverted to type and played all-American college boys.

In *Hearts,* he benefited from playing a supporting role to the great Walter Huston in a scenario set on the Ohio frontier in the middle of the nineteenth century. Stewart plays Jason Wilkins, a young man who grows up under the strictures of a stern cleric of nonspecific denomination (Hollywood's favorite religion), played by Huston, and who rebels by running away and going to medical school—science being the symbol of his lack of faith. After struggling through medical school, with the tireless help and sacrifice made by his widowed mother (Beulah Bondi), he becomes a battlefield surgeon during the Civil War following the death of his father.[1] Having heard nothing from him in two years, his mother is convinced her son is dead (as was Simon regarding her husband in *Seventh Heaven*). In her grief, she writes a letter to Abraham Lincoln (John Carradine), asking for information as to where she might find the remains of her son. Wilkins is then summoned to the

---

1. Bondi would go on to play Stewart's mother in several more movies, including George Stevens's *Vivacious Lady* (1938), Frank Capra's *Mr. Smith Goes to Washington* (1939), and again in Capra's *It's a Wonderful Life* (1946). She and Stewart also appeared in Joseph Mankiewicz's *The Gorgeous Hussy* (1936), but not as mother/son, and had no scenes together.

White House by Lincoln himself who, in the middle of the war, has somehow found the time to chastise him for neglecting his mother. Sufficiently upbraided, Stewart returns home and tearfully reunites with long-suffering Mom.

Of Human Hearts premiered in February 1938 in Greenville, South Carolina, the title the result of a publicity contest sponsored by MGM to replace the awkward original title, *Benefits Forgot*. The film received fairly good notices. The *New York Times* lauded the cast, singling out Stewart for special praise, in a role he likely understood better than most—that of a boy trying to rebel against an overly stern father and in doing so, gains the motherly love and support he so desperately wants and needs: "James Stewart's and Master Reynolds' farm boy [Reynolds played the Wilkins character before he grows up to become Stewart] and all the others are flawlessly typical." *Movie Mirror* magazine agreed: "There is no fault to find with production, direction or acting. The individual performance of each cast member—especially of Mr. Stewart, Miss Bondi, Huston and young Reynolds—are flawlessly typical."

However, the film's downbeat vision of war at a time when the country was being drawn into international conflict did not find an audience. After thirteen films, Jimmy, approaching thirty years old, had not as yet been able to break out as a major star and remained, for now, just another of Hollywood's familiar nameless faces in the crowd.

— • —

In the studio era, once an actor was cast as a "type," that was what he or she usually played. Character-juveniles, a strange hybrid of which to this point Stewart was considered to be, rarely evolved into leading men. More often a "char-juv" evolved into a "char-man," as was the case with Mickey Rooney. Jimmy was not considered by MGM as able to keep up with the Gables, Flynns, Grants, Nivens, Colmans, Coopers, Powers, even the Fondas, when it came to what they believed a romantic, heroic lead had to be. American film critic Howard Barnes summed up MGM's feeling in 1936 when he described Jimmy this way: "[H]e has been denied Robert Taylor's beauty and endowed with none of the strong, silent intensity of Gary Cooper."

Jimmy believed he had no choice but to go along with whatever MGM wanted him to do, whether he liked it or not: As he said in 1979, "I was a contract player. It was a full-time job. You worked a six-day week, fifty-two weeks a year. If you weren't making tests with new people the studios were thinking of signing, you were in the gym working out to keep in shape. Taking voice lessons. Going out and exploiting pictures you weren't even in. Beating the drum for motion pictures. You didn't pick your movies. You did what you were told. Your studio could trade you around like ball players. . . . Each morning I had to check which one [of five movies] I was working on that day and see what part I was playing. You did small parts in big pictures and big parts in small pictures."

The problem went even deeper than he was willing to acknowledge. His nonsexual on-screen persona had by now led Mayer to wonder if, in fact, there was something "wrong" with him. Whereas other MGM names had to be literally pried loose from the bevy of starlets they were bedding, despite the fact that the men were all married—such as Gable, whom, it was said, often took to bed the chambermaids of whatever hotel he happened to be staying in; Franchot Tone, whose suavity had led him into the arms of some of Hollywood's most fabulous beauties; and Spencer Tracy, a known womanizer from the moment he first stepped on a sound stage—Jimmy kept himself away from all of that, preferring the company of one steady woman, and if he didn't have one, he was content to have none, rather than five.

Single MGM actors over the age of twenty-five, like Jimmy, often came under the suspicion of Mayer, especially when they failed to project heterosexual heat on-screen. To alleviate the situation, and to quite literally separate the men from the boys (meaning in this instance the straights from the gays) as well as to protect his star females from unwanted and unprofitable pregnancies and his own selfish desires for them, Mayer had a private brothel built within walking distance of the studio's front gate. Attendance there was as mandatory as it was for the studio gym, and Mayer, it was said, kept a close inventory on the comings and goings of his male stars. According to Grady, "The whores were hand-picked; starlets who had given up on their careers; cast-off girlfriends of well-placed men who wanted to make a buck; some were imported from Mexico for the guys who liked them Spanish. Mayer's boys got them thoroughly tested for venereal disease . . . every effort was made to suit the girl to the actor—if we could find Gable's or Tone's type, so much the better. They were a horny bunch and most of them thought of it as a convenience."

The word went out that any other MGM male who wasn't married and who didn't "perform" at the bordello would be released. Known homosexuals, such as Ramon Navarro and William Haines, who steered clear of the bordello, were eventually linked in separate gay sex scandals and were fired by Mayer in 1935.

It fell to Grady to read the riot act to Stewart, even though he had been "linked" to almost every female star he had made movies with, including Virginia Bruce (*The Murder Man* and *Born to Dance*), Rose Stradner (*The Last Gangster*), and, of course, Ginger Rogers. According to Grady, "I had to lay down the law to him. I had to tell him, Jim, if you don't go and give a manly account of yourself at least a few times, Mayer and the others will start lumping you in with Navarro and Haines . . . and it will undermine all the casting efforts I'm making for you. So get your ass over there and get those rocks off with at least two of those broads."

If there was any comfort for Jimmy in the mandatory visits to the brothel, it was in how they resonated with the echoes of his father's high moral tone. At home, as a boy, Stewart had been admonished for even *thinking* about girls by his father. Here, at the studio, where he *played* boyish *types,* he had put himself in jeopardy by resisting the paternal guidance of Louis B. Mayer into the studio's whorehouse. Somewhere between the layers of guilt and the promise of liberation lay a measure of physical pleasure, something he realized following his first visits to "prove" his manhood to Mayer. After that, he made fairly regular visits, and whenever Grady asked him how he liked the way these most talented and highly trained girls made him feel, he would only shrug his shoulders and say he'd rather be in love when he "did it."

Try acting, Grady told him.

— • —

Ironically, it was the film he made before *Of Human Hearts, Navy Blue and Gold* (1937), that would change everything, although no one at the studio seeing the film before its delayed release predicted that. In it, Stewart was paired with another contract player, Robert Young, who the studio was also trying to make into a star and who also seemed to be going nowhere. The film traces the careers of three candidates at the naval academy, Annapolis, linked by their desire to play football. In his second year, Ash (Young) is relegated to a substitute while his two pals, Truck (Stewart) and Richard (Tom Brown Jr.), become the stars of the team. At one point Truck hears a lecture about an officer who disgraced the army. The officer turns out to have been his father. He angrily defends him and is suspended for it, while the rest of the team goes to the "big game." He is benched until the fourth quarter, sent in, given the ball by Ash, and in turn unselfishly passes it to Richard, who makes the big final play and wins the game. While he gets all the glory, Truck is recognized as a true team player, an all-American in the highest sense, not just physically recalled but spiritually redeemed.

The film opened at New York's Capitol Theatre the day before Christmas 1937, and proved a hit with audiences and critics. Stewart received the best reviews of his career, in a far different and more profound performance than the usual romantic play-acting he kept being assigned by the studio.

Six days before *Navy Blue and Gold* opened, Stewart began work on George Stevens's *Vivacious Lady,* which was to be his last role of 1937. It was another loan-out, this time to RKO where he co-starred with his ex-lover Ginger Rogers. Although he was, at first, hesitant to take the part, he did so on the advice of his new agent, Leland Hayward, who also just happened to have recently become Margaret Sullavan's third husband.

Sullavan had in the last year divorced Wyler and married Hayward, whose hot roster of talent included, among others, Garbo, Fred Astaire, Ginger Rogers, Ernest Hemingway, Lillian Hellman, and Dashiell Hammett. The handsome, well-groomed, and always elegant Hayward wore impeccably tailored custom suits and highly polished black shoes, and had his hair cut every five days. He was, like Jimmy, a Princeton man, having attended in 1920 but lasting only a year before flunking out, prompting his wealthy father to cut off his allowance. He then became a newspaper reporter for the *New York Sun,* but was unable to get along on his meager (for him) $25-a-week salary. He applied for and was reinstated at Princeton, only to leave again, this time at his own choosing, to marry wealthy Texas socialite divorcée Lola Gibbs. They divorced after two years, then remarried seven years later (then divorced again after four years).

The first divorce left his pockets lined sufficiently, and he took off for Hollywood with ambitions to become a producer. Instead he wound up eking out a living as a bottom-feeding press agent. In 1932, he returned to New York City and opened the Leland Hayward Talent Agency as an East Coast branch of Myron Selznick's Hollywood Talent Agency (Myron was the brother of David O. Selznick). This time the plan worked; during the next five years Hayward signed several New York–based actors and writers and promptly sent them west, to Myron, who then secured lucrative studio deals for them. Their partnership lasted until 1937, after which Hayward moved back to Los Angeles, this time into posh Beverly Hills, and married Sullavan. He was, by then, riding high from his cut of the agency's profits, especially the success he'd made of Hammett's original *The Thin Man*, which he sold in 1933 to MGM by explaining Nick Charles as a kind of idealized extension of himself. The original film eventually became an eleven-year, six-film studio franchise that returned handsome residuals to Selznick and Hayward.

In 1936, Hayward expanded his agency and partnered with Jimmy's relatively small-time agent, Leah Salisbury, who later that same year decided to sell out her remaining interest to Hayward, a move that gave him sole control over a roster of actors that included Jimmy and Fonda. The incestuous nature of all this was pure Hollywood. Jimmy was in chaste love with Sullavan. Sullavan enjoyed playing Jimmy's muse. Fonda was her first husband and Jimmy's best friend. Jimmy had played the villain in the sequel to the first *Thin Man* film, and Hammett was represented by Hayward, Sullavan's third husband. And now they were all not only friends and associates but, except for Fonda, happy neighbors.

Hayward believed the only way Stewart would ever rise in the hierarchy of MGM's talent was through loan-outs, where he could have the opportunity to play the kind of parts he was never going to be offered at his home studio. When Rogers, who was now one of the biggest female stars in Hollywood, specifically requested Stewart as her co-star, it was Hayward who urged Jimmy to take the part.

Rogers knew what she was doing. Having made her career as Fred Astaire's dancing partner, which she had been for most of the decade, she now sought to establish herself as a serious nonmusical actress and was looking for a leading man who would not overwhelm her on-screen. Jimmy, she believed, was the perfect choice, precisely because she didn't think he was strong or aggressive enough to do it. In their romance, that had been the man problem. For her career, it was the perfect solution.

If there were any bad feelings on Stewart's part for Rogers, he never showed it, at least not on screen. The picture is a light, breezy romantic comedy involving a shy botany professor, Peter Morgan (Stewart), who falls in love with a dazzling New York nightclub singer, Francey Brent (Rogers), marries her, and then frets over how to tell his gruff father and his sickly mother. Yet again, the parallels to Jimmy's own family life helped him imbue his acting with an impressive emotional depth.

His performance was so good in *Vivacious Lady* that Stevens gave him equal co-billing with Rogers, which ticked her off, as her gamble had resulted in having the exact opposite effect she had hoped for when lobbying for Jimmy to be her co-star. Still, the film accomplished what she had wanted it to. Their unexpected on-screen chemistry was so powerful, it delighted audiences; the film did remarkably well, and Rogers once more shimmered in the starlight she craved.

However, as successful as it was, it didn't provide Stewart with the platform from which he could make the leap onto the A-list roster. One element remained missing from all sixteen movies he had made thus far—a great director who could focus in on and precisely exploit Stewart's unique talents.

7

When Frank Capra hired James Stewart he was a minor MGM contract player, thirty years old, with Princeton, Broadway, and only three years of Hollywood experience behind him. The director had spotted Stewart in *Navy Blue and Gold,* directed by Sam Wood, in which Stewart played a midshipman at the U.S. Naval Academy. [Capra]: "He had a minor part, he wasn't the star. He did a little something defending a fellow naval student. When I saw him I thought, 'Oh, my lord, *there's* a guy.' "

—FROM JOSEPH MCBRIDE'S *FRANK CAPRA*

The unexpected death in 1936 of thirty-seven-year-old Irving G. Thalberg, legendary head of production at MGM, threw the studio into turmoil. This turned out to be fortuitous for Jimmy when, in 1938, he was given the opportunity to work again with Margaret Sullavan, a deal cannily put together by Hayward. The film was *The Shopworn Angel* (1938), to be directed by H. C. Potter. Thalberg, his reputation as one of the great studio heads notwithstanding, was known to meddle in projects often to the point of overbearance, leaving his stamp, rather than his stars' or directors', on their films. This would not be the case with *The Shopworn Angel.*

When Jimmy read the script, he knew immediately he was perfectly suited to play the role of Private Bill Pettigrew. In the film, Pettigrew is stationed at Camp Merritt, just outside of New York City. One evening a limousine driving the "New York Entertainer" Daisy Heath (Sullavan) accidentally runs him down and nearly kills him. Pettigrew happens to have idolized Heath for as long as he can remember. Once healed, Pettigrew starts to see her on a regular basis, until he is shipped overseas to fight in World War One. She then tells her somewhat jealous lover, Broadway producer and "mentor" Sam Bailey (Walter Pidgeon), that she's going to marry the boy, to give him a reason to stay alive and return safely, after which, she says rather glibly, she can always divorce him. Bailey reluctantly agrees. Then, one night while performing, she receives word that Pettigrew has been killed in the line of duty. The film ends with Heath and Bailey in the throes of grief and guilt.[1]

By now, Sullavan had developed a formidable reputation as a man-eating manipulator and a woman who married to advance her own ambitions. Many critics saw her character in *The Shopworn Angel* as an extension of Sullavan's public persona, a further cashing-in on the reputation she had built. She more or less plays with the Stewart character, and marries him partly out of the need to want to see him stay alive, but also partly as a joke to be shared with Sam Bailey. However, a deeper look at Sullavan's Daisy reveals a more complex character. Full of life, talented, famous, and funloving, she is in a relationship with a man she doesn't love (in many ways a Wyler substitute) and is attracted to and reinvigorated by a younger, innocent boy, one who ignites her latent maternal needs and desires (Stewart). The guilt that both she and Bailey feel at the end of the movie is due at least partly to her having married on a lark, so to speak, but also to their not realizing the precious commodity that life really is. For all her continuing flamboyance on stage, the real fire in her life burns out with Pettigrew's death.

And, of course, there is Jimmy's portrayal of the soldier. His unrequited love for Sullavan is mirrored by Pettigrew's for Daisy. Key to the film, Sullavan's life, and Stewart's, is the vague sexual relationship that drives the story. Here is what Pidgeon later told interviewer Lawrence Quirk: "I really felt like the odd-man-out in that film. It was really all Jimmy and Maggie, and that was the way it should have been. It was so obvious he was in love with her. He came absolutely alive in his scenes with her, playing with a conviction and a deep sincerity I never knew him to summon away from her. . . . Of course, they both kept up the

---

1. This was the kind of film that Thalberg would never have green-lighted. The story was too precious, the relationships too undefined, and the ending too downbeat to qualify as a so-called typical MGM picture. It was, in fact, more suited to Columbia or Paramount. The script was based on "Private Pettigrew's Girl," a short story that originally appeared in the *Saturday Evening Post* in 1918, at the height of World War One, and had been filmed twice before, once in 1919 as a silent, George Melford's *Pettigrew's Girl,* then again in 1929 as a part-silent, part-talkie directed by Richard Wallace and starring Gary Cooper and Nancy Carroll, this time called *The Shopworn Angel.* It would also be done again in 1959 by Sidney Lumet, as *That Kind of Woman,* starring Sophia Loren, Tab Hunter, and George Sanders.

front that they were friends, and that their mutual affection was purely platonic. For her it may have been, though sometimes I felt she was more emotionally involved, off-screen, with Jimmy than she consciously was aware she was. Or maybe, being the flirtatious Southern belle she was, in most situations, she got some ego-kick out of his adoration of her. . . . Sullavan was in love with love, and she loved Jimmy being in love with her; it enhanced her feelings about herself."

None of this was lost on Hayward, whose natural jealous tendencies were painfully exposed by the romantic scenes Sullavan and Stewart had together. Although he was well aware of how much Stewart loved Sullavan, his notions of the emotional, nonphysical complexities of that love were not very sophisticated. For instance, he often suggested to Sullavan that both Fonda, her ex, and Stewart were really gay; after all, they were always living together and neither one appeared "man enough" to keep a woman, especially her, sexually satisfied. Hayward remained noticeably ill at ease throughout the making of the film, however, and overly possessive of Sullavan, behavior that only led to more speculation in the gossip columns that Stewart and Sullavan were "once more" an item.

The chemistry that Jimmy and Sullavan had on-screen in this film was pure dynamite. Women cried openly in theaters at the film's ending, while men sat uncomfortably grim and silent. Critics raved, rightly giving their performances far better reviews than the overall picture itself. The *New York Herald Tribune* called the pairing of Stewart and Sullavan evidence of "two of the finest actors appearing on the screen today." *The New Republic* said that "the human quality here is owing partly to the schooled restraint of writing and direction, but even more to the unaffected appeal and warmth of Margaret Sullavan, James Stewart (and Walter Pidgeon). . . . Stewart is the deep slow yokel because he has created the illusion of a personal hurt and belief."

The film had a legion of female followers, one in particular who happened to be in a position to get closer to Jimmy than the others. Even before the July 1938 release of *The Shopworn Angel*, Norma Shearer, Irving Thalberg's widow, had fallen madly in love with him.

— • —

Marrying the boss, or as film critic and historian Andrew Sarris once called it, "boudoir careerism," has always been one of the surest and shortest routes to the top of the Hollywood heap. Indeed, when Norma Shearer wed Irving G. Thalberg, after making ten years of mostly forgettable silent films, she soon found herself the recipient of the 1930 Oscar for Best Actress (for Robert Z. Leonard's *The Divorcee*), over some of the fiercest and most talented competitors of the day.[2] Cynics took great delight in pointing to the former beauty queen with the slightly crossed eyes and insisting she would never have stood a chance without the industry muscle of the formidable Mr. Thalberg.

Shearer had originally come to Hollywood via the pageant route, where she was discovered by and subsequently married MGM's head of production. By the time she became a widow at the age of thirty-four, she had been nominated for four Academy Awards, had won one, and was young, rich, and suddenly very much on the loose in LaLaLand.[3]

After Thalberg's unexpected passing, Shearer's career began to lurch unevenly. Her appearance in the 1938 production of *Marie Antoinette* (directed by the usually reliable MGM helmer W. S. Van Dyke II), the first film she made after her husband's death, co-starred Tyrone Power, whom she insisted be borrowed from 20th Century Fox so they could work together while they carried on a so-called torrid love affair. Because Power's bisexuality resulted in an early end to the romance, such as it may have been, Shearer came unescorted to the annual William Randolph Hearst–Marion Davies December costume ball, in those days the most coveted invitation in Hollywood.

That she was asked to attend at all came as a surprise to her. Hearst was Thalberg's only true Hollywood rival in terms of power, and he had a mistress, Marion Davies, whose career he navigated as surely as Thalberg had Shearer's. So sensitive was the rivalry that when, in 1934, Shearer was cast by Thalberg for the lead role in Sidney Franklin's *The Barretts*

---

2. Double-nominee Greta Garbo (Clarence Brown's *Anna Christie* and his *Romance*), Nancy Carroll (Edmund Goulding's *The Devil's Holiday*), Ruth Chatterton (Dorothy Arzner's *Sarah and Son*), and Gloria Swanson (Goulding's *The Trespasser*) all lost out that year to Shearer.

3. Shearer was nominated for Best Actress in 1929/30 for E. Mason Hopper's *Their Own Desire,* won an Oscar for Robert Z. Leonard's *The Divorcee,* was nominated again in 1931 for Clarence Brown's *A Free Soul,* again in 1934 for Sidney Franklin's *The Barretts of Wimpole Street,* and again in 1936, the year Thalberg died, for George Cukor's *Romeo and Juliet.* All of these films were made under the auspices of Thalberg. Her career never fully recovered its momentum after his death, and she retired in 1942.

of Wimpole Street—after Hearst had lobbied heavily to get Davies the part—Thalberg and Shearer were not only immediately excluded from all social activities that took place at Hearst's legendary Castle at San Simeon, but the movie magnate saw to it that Davies's contract was transferred from MGM to Warners (something Thalberg, for a number of reasons, was more than willing to make happen).

When the invitation came for the costume party, Shearer chose to wear the same provocative costume she had in the ballroom scene from *Marie Antoinette*. By several accounts, including George Cukor's, Shearer was on the hunt that night and had her radar turned up for the first eligible bachelor she could find.

That blip turned out to be Jimmy Stewart.

Josh Logan accompanied Jimmy to the party. Stewart came dressed as a cowboy, outfitted head to toe courtesy of the MGM wardrobe department, and almost immediately upon his arrival he locked eyes with Shearer.

As Logan later recalled, "In a moment of alcoholic gallantry, Jim told Norma, one of the early idols of his Princeton movie-going days, that the five foot one actress was the most gorgeous creature he had ever seen. That was enough for Shearer. Despite the age difference between them—Shearer was eight years older than the just-turned-thirty actor—'The Merry Widow,' as the always aloof Shearer was referred to behind her back [after Thalberg's death] by those on the lot, was determined to sleep with every available man at MGM (and a few not so available) to convince herself, among other things, that she was still young enough to be alluring."

She wasted no time latching on to Jimmy, who, by all accounts, didn't quite know what hit him. She wanted him, and badly. He had the same boyish qualities as her late husband, even if Jimmy was tall, Presbyterian, slow, and drawling. Thalberg had been short, articulate, intellectual, and Jewish. Both men, however, were young, and different from most of the eligible men in town by their lack of skirt-chasing addiction, and Shearer sensed something familiar in Jimmy's innocence. If for no other reason than to deny the reality of her husband's passing, "The First Lady of MGM," as she was known among the gossips, promptly dumped Mickey Rooney, whom she had just started seeing after Power, and went after Jimmy.

They were suddenly seen everywhere, including in the papers.

"Jimmy gave Norma what she wanted: proof that she was still young, beautiful and desirable," was the way Mickey Rooney summed up the whole thing. Indeed, she lavished him with gifts, took him places he never would have gone by himself, and imbued his image with something it had never had before, a sexually sophisticated incandescence that put a new sheen to the youthful innocent he had perfected in *The Shopworn Angel*.

According to Logan, "Jimmy was being skittish about the lavish attentions of the studio queen, as she took royal possession of him. She transported him around town openly in her yellow limousine, even though he slumped down on the back seat hoping that his friends would not recognize him. As proof of her 'ownership' she gave him a gold cigarette case sprinkled with diamonds. That meant that whenever she asked for a cigarette in front of others, the gift would advertise the giver. Jimmy didn't want any sly looks. He would fumble in every pocket until he came up with a crumpled pack of Lucky Strikes, his badge as a free man."

If Stewart had been obsessed by what he perceived as the chaste lure of Margaret Sullavan, he was desperate to escape the heated web that Shearer had spun around him. While he remained polite and cooperative for a while, knowing full well that even with her husband gone, she still wielded a great deal of power at the studio, his resistance to her seductive ways eventually turned her off and she gave up, staying on friendly terms with him, even letting him have the lighter as a keepsake. She hoped it would be a permanent reminder to him of his refusal to allow her to light him up.

Although the gossip columns assured everyone the break was "mutual and amicable," in truth it wasn't, for all the obvious reasons why it couldn't work—the age difference, the career conflicts (his star rising, hers falling), the financial inequity (she paid for everything), and the fact that Jimmy simply couldn't take the heat of her pursuit.[4]

---

4. So powerful was the intensity of this affair that in 1939, a year after his return to New York, Josh Logan directed a Schwartz/ Fields/McEvoy musical called *Stars in Your Eyes* that played upon the highly publicized Shearer-Stewart romance. The show starred Ethel Merman and Richard Carlson in the "Shearer-Stewart" roles. Jimmy Durante was also featured, as was Logan's old friend and former University Player Mildred Natwick. The plot of *Stars in Your Eyes* revolves around an aging movie queen who once owned a movie studio and falls in love with a young, upcoming director. See the chapter notes for more.

— • —

During this hectic period of melodramatic romance in Jimmy's life, someone else had taken notice of him as well, although in a far-different and creative context. As the decade lurched toward its end, with the Depression at its peak and the world about to explode into another world war, one director with a camera and a Crucifixion complex was intensely searching for the perfect all-American innocent upon whom he could attach the cross of decency and democracy, not necessarily in that order. The director's name was Frank Capra, and the actor he wanted most for his own personal Jesus was Jimmy Stewart.

Frank Capra was a product of an immigrant upbringing during which he worked his way not just through college, but, as he often liked to tell people, "through grammar and high school" as well. A child of the ways of the old world, he always sent money home to his mother, even when he was making as little as $90 a month. He attended the Throop College of Technology (which would become Cal Tech) on a scholarship, after which he enlisted in World War One. He spent his entire tour of duty in San Francisco, and upon being discharged tried a variety of jobs, including door-to-door child photography, which eventually led him to Nevada and that state's many gambling venues. It was there among the state's many legal tables and the wheels that Frank Capra first developed his skills as a hustler.

While living in Nevada he met a vaudevillian by the name of Montague who made his living performing Kipling's epic poem "The Ballad of Fisher's Boarding House." At the height of the silent film's first wave of popularity, Montague hit upon the idea of filming his performance, using lines burned into the negative that flashed above his head as he acted out the poem's action. Capra was intrigued with the idea and convinced Montague to let him direct it.

Capra had stumbled onto his calling, and soon made his way to Hollywood, where he landed a job as a gag writer at Mack Sennett's silent film studio. He did numerous scripts for the *Our Gang* comedy series and helped develop the personality of and physical bits for screen clown Harry Langdon. Feeling held back by the Sennett laugh-a-minute machine, Langdon left the studio for First National and took Capra with him, where the comedian's feature films made him nearly as popular as the other silent comedy gods of the era, Chaplin, Keaton, and

Chase. Langdon made his reputation via the original comic persona that Capra helped him develop, the see-no-evil, hear-no-evil, do-no-evil, blessed innocent eternally redeemed by his goodness, i.e., God (i.e., Capra).

Capra wrote and directed three Langdon features, *The Strong Man* (1926); *Tramp, Tramp, Tramp* (1926); and *Long Pants* (1927)—all of which rank among the finest of the silent era comedies.[5] Langdon then decided he didn't need Capra, or anyone, anymore, that like Chaplin and the other comic screen kings did, he could write and direct as well as star in his own movies. He also modified his character into what Capra later described as a "Jack the Giant-Killer"—the little man as heroic and romantic savior. That was more or less the end of Langdon.

At first, the split between the two marked both of them as industry losers, and for a while Capra could not find work in Hollywood. He moved to New York City, where in 1927 he was hired to direct an independent feature, *Love o' Mike,*[6] starring an as-yet-unknown stage actress by the name of Claudette Colbert. The film was a financial disaster and Capra, with nowhere else to go, returned once more to Hollywood, broke and apparently without any future, when he happened to bump into Max Sennett one day while both were strolling along Hollywood Boulevard. They talked awhile and Sennett offered to rehire him as a silent-screen gag writer at $75 a week, considerably less than he had been paying him when Capra left. The grateful director took the job.

Also in 1927, Harry Cohn of Columbia Pictures, the so-called poverty row of the major studios, hired Capra away from Sennett, on the strong advice of Cohn's second-in-command, Sam Briskin, to direct *That Certain Thing,* starring Viola Dana and Ralph Graves, a former actor and fellow gag writer of Capra's at Sennett. Graves had convinced Briskin that Capra was perfectly suited to direct *That Certain Thing,* because of the way the script romanticized the working class, something that resonated with Capra, and Briskin in turned convinced Cohn. The film opened on New Year's Day 1928, received rave reviews, and revived Capra's career, turning him into one of Columbia Pictures' hottest "new" directors.

---

5. Although Capra, in his memoir, claimed to have directed all three and most film authorities agree, based on stylistic evidence, several other sources state that Harry Edwards directed *Tramp, Tramp, Tramp.*

6. Aka *For the Love of Mike.*

Thus began a long and sometimes contentious association between Capra, Cohn, and screenwriter Robert Riskin.[7] Riskin was a former Broadway playwright whose sense of story, character, and class-conscious comedy melded perfectly with Capra's. The Capra/Riskin creative partnership turned out some of the most socially aware Hollywood comedies in the history of film, among them *American Madness* (1932), *Lady for a Day* (1933), *Broadway Bill* (1934), *Mr. Deeds Goes to Town* (1936), *Lost Horizon* (1937), and *You Can't Take It With You* (1938). The most successful Capra/Riskin collaboration was 1934's *It Happened One Night*, starring Clark Gable and Claudette Colbert, the first Hollywood film ever to win all five major Academy Awards—Gable for Best Actor, Colbert for Best Actress, Capra for Best Director, Riskin for Best Screenplay, and Capra (as producer) for Best Film of the Year.[8] By the time *It Happened One Night* went into production, Capra had become the most popular and successful studio director of his time.

If there was any single element missing from *It Happened One Night*, it was Capra's notion of the ideal leading man. While Gable was great in the movie, he was, to the director's way of thinking, a bit too insensitive for the kind of hero he'd envisioned, someone who was more reminiscent of the Langdon-like innocent he could both protect and elevate to the level of blessed, if tortured, sainthood.

Two films later, Capra first thought he had found his man in Gary Cooper, who starred in the director's masochistic self-denying *Mr. Deeds Goes to Town* (1936), and then in Ronald Colman, in 1937's utopian-tinged socioreligious resurrection fantasy *Lost Horizon*. Neither film nor actor proved to be exactly what Capra was looking for. Cooper, like Gable, was simply too inherently sexual to be Capra's pop-culture Jesus, Colman too exotically Continental.

---

7. From 1931's *Platinum Blonde* through 1950's *Riding High* (Paramount), a total of nine screenplays and four additional films were made from Riskin material, including two remakes.

8. This five-award sweep of all the major categories holds a unique spot in Hollywood lore, an achievement made all that more remarkable by the fact that Columbia, at the time, had no voting members in the Academy (Capra was, however, heavily involved in the politics of the industry and an ardent supporter of the Academy. He became its president in 1937 and served in that capacity for five years). In the seventy-two years since the *One Night* coup, only two other films have ever pulled off the top-five sweep: Milos Forman's *One Flew Over the Cuckoo's Nest* (1975) and Jonathan Demme's *Silence of the Lambs* (1991).

It wasn't until Capra saw Jimmy Stewart in MGM's delayed release of *Navy Blue and Gold* that he knew he'd finally found the right actor. Where everyone else saw a light, all-American type, Capra picked up on Stewart's darker, more anguished turn in the film. "I had seen Jimmy Stewart play this sensitive, heart-grabbing role and sensed the character and rock-ribbed honesty of a Gary Cooper, plus the breeding and intelligence of an ivy-league idealist. One might believe that young Stewart *could* reject his father's patrimony [in *You Can't Take It With You*], a kingdom in Wall Street." It was Jimmy's strong performance that convinced Capra he could turn the gawky, shuffling, stuttery, underused, and overlooked contract player into the most popular movie star in the world.

PART THREE

—·—

Mr. Christ Goes to Calvary

Katharine Hepburn and Jimmy, in his only
Best Actor Oscar–winning performance, as Macauley Conner,
in George Cukor's *The Philadelphia Story* (1940).

8

"He's the easiest man to direct I've ever seen. A man who gets what you're talking about in just a few words. You wonder if you've told him enough about the scene, and yet when he does it, there it is. He knew by looking at me, and I can look at him and know him. It's not because I've worked with him so much; I think he's probably the best actor who's ever hit the screen."

—FRANK CAPRA

Jimmy Stewart began filming Frank Capra's *You Can't Take It With You* on April 25, 1938, under strict orders from Capra to gain weight; he was far too thin to carry a movie, as far as the squat Italian director was concerned. To Capra, coming from a world where food was as sacred as it was scarce, Stewart's slight frame bordered on the sacrilegious. Throughout production Stewart continually stuffed his face with Butterfinger candy bars, but it made no difference; his weight remained a constant 140 during the entire shoot.

For all the apparent consternation that caused Capra, it was still a far cry from the problems he'd had with Gable during the filming of 1934's *It Happened One Night,* when the dashing star, feeling that MGM was punishing him for his outlandish womanizing by sending him down to the minors—loaning him to Columbia Pictures to be in Capra's under-budget on-the-run comedy—displayed his anger and frustration by showing up the first day drunk and did his best to stay that way for the rest of the shoot. Compared to Gable, Stewart was Capra's chaste and sober prince.

This was no casual coronation. Capra was an old-world family man. In an industry where paternalism was a way of life, where producers acted as industrial-strength father figures treating grown actors and actresses as their unruly children, the most visceral connection a director like Capra could make to an actor was a surrogate one. It was, in fact, the scene in *Navy Blue and Gold* where Stewart rises up from his seat in class to defend his father that had convinced Capra that Stewart could do the job in *You Can't Take It With You*. Of Stewart's acting in that scene, Capra said, "He grabbed you as a human being. You were looking at the man, not an actor. You could see this man's soul . . . when you're dealing in the world of ideas and you want your character to be on a higher intellectual plane than just a simple man, you turn to persons like Jimmy Stewart because he has a look of the intellectual about him. And he can be an idealist . . . a pretty fine combination. . . ."

What adds a deeper understanding to Capra's sentiments was the real-life drama he was going through at the time with his infant son, John, born stone-deaf and diagnosed at the age of three as mentally defective. It was something Capra was ashamed of and wanted to cover up.[1] His fairly far-reaching descriptions of his discovery of Stewart, on the other hand, were filled with a bursting fatherly pride and idealism.

For Jimmy, the emotional pull was equally strong. As far as Jimmy was concerned when he was chosen by Capra to star in his new film, Hollywood had become one big happy extension of his family. In response he expressed unqualified, almost worshipful appreciation. As he told Joseph McBride, the director's biographer, "I just had complete confidence in Frank Capra. I always had, from the very first day I worked with him. . . . I just hung on every word Frank Capra said."

You Can't Take It With You was Capra's most complex film to date, a risky venture that would not only, upon its release, solidify his position as the most popular director in Hollywood, but make Jimmy Stewart the quintessential Capra hero. Based on the Pulitzer prize–winning smash Broadway play by George S. Kaufman and Moss Hart *You Can't Take It With You*, and freely adapted by Capra and Robert Riskin (about 25 percent of the original concept and dialogue remained), it seemed on the surface another of the zany thirties comedies that loosely fit the definition of screwball but violated one of that genre's sacred rules by inserting a layer of serious social commentary beneath the uneven weave of the humor's crazy-quilt pattern. Riskin described the theme as "the accumulation of gold beyond a man's need [being] idiotic." It was a tough message for a so-called funny film, especially one made at the height of the Depression when most screen comedies were based on the notion of escapism.

---

1. Most likely the boy was autistic.

Capra had nearly left Columbia Pictures when his previous film, *Lost Horizon* (1937), proved an unqualified disaster, so much so that Capra threatened to sue Harry S. Cohn, the head of the studio, to get out of his remaining contract. Cohn, however, refused to let him go, even though the film's huge budget and subsequent box-office failure had nearly bankrupted Columbia. To keep his disgruntled director in place, Cohn uncharacteristically doubled Capra's salary and bought the rights to *You Can't Take It With You* for him, after the director had caught a performance of the show on Broadway and expressed an interest in turning it into a movie.[2]

The story concerns the goings-on inside the mansion of the Vanderhof-Sycamore family, "a house where everybody does exactly what he wants to do," the screenplay says, because the family has so much money they don't work anymore and, as the head of the household keeps reminding them, they might as well have fun now because they can't take any of it with them when they die. The patriarchal grandfather, Martin Vanderhof (Lionel Barrymore as a Vanderbilt-type patriarch), collects stamps and buys friends. His daughter, Penny Sycamore (Spring Byington), writes plays that remain unproduced. Her husband, Paul (Samuel S. Hinds), makes fireworks in the basement. Penny's daughter, Essie (Ann Miller), ballet-dances barefoot all day under the direction of her personal Russian tutor (Mischa Auer). The only so-called normal member of the clan, Alice (Jean Arthur), actually has a job working as a stenographer for Tony Kirby, played by Jimmy Stewart. The part of Kirby was greatly expanded from the original play so that the focus of the film became the love story between Alice and Tony, rather than the antics of her family.

Tony's father, as it turns out, has designs on the mansion, and there is a strong suggestion that the romance may, in fact, be a ruse for a land grab. Eventually the two families meet, zaniness dominates, everyone is hauled off to jail (as so often happens in screwball comedies), Tony denounces any claim on the land, Vanderhof gives it away

---

2. L. B. Mayer had also wanted it for MGM, one of the reasons Cohn was so quick to grab the rights to the play, for a then-unheard-of $200,000. Capra had no love for Mayer, who had fired him during Capra's days making silent movies. He maintained a lifelong grudge against the studio head, and vowed he'd bury him with the Oscars that *You Can't Take It With You,* made at Columbia, would win.

anyway, everyone learns a good Christian lesson of one kind or another, and they all live unburdened with their material trappings, happily ever after, after all.

If this was a typical screwball comedy, it was decidedly "Capra-corny" in style (as some pundits had already begun referring to the director's from-bleakest-to-brightest comedies). Clearly, the more conflicted, darker elements of the director's point of view had begun to emerge in this movie. In retrospect, the film's plot seems uncomfortably close to the failed *Lost Horizon,* where the rest of the troubled world is left behind by a group of travelers when they discover a seemingly perfect, if isolated, Shangri-La, the Vanderhof mansion (the hub of the Family of Man) being a more Americanized version of the isolated utopia the characters in the film *Lost Horizon* believe they have stumbled upon. As allegories of pre–World War Two isolationist freedom from an oppressive system, the physical locale of both films—the exotic Shangri-La and the world-in-the-Vanderhof-mansion—appear too separate and elitist to qualify as landmarks of perfection for the working-class movie-goer. In addition, the original Kaufman-Hart play had an element of paranoid anti-Communist humor that the film completely eliminated; on-stage the fireworks in the basement were meant to ward off the coming Red Menace, the great threat to the upper-class privileged surrounded by poverty in the American proletarian thirties. In the film the two families have no political inclinations whatsoever. (Interestingly, 1938, the year the film was released, also marked the formal start of the House Committee on Un-American Activities, an outgrowth of the ultra–right wing Motion Picture Alliance, and no one, least of all Capra, wanted to come off in his work wearing the slightest shade of pink. Any reference to Communism, pro *or* con, was considered too dangerous, and therefore treated in American motion pictures to a great extent as if it didn't exist at all.)

Ironically, while Capra was making "populist" films that championed the little guy, by the time of *You Can't Take It With You,* he was a millionaire and a registered Republican. A year earlier, he'd voted for Alf Landon for president because Capra feared Roosevelt's Depression-era politics would result in all the money being taken from the rich, including himself, and given to the poor, his target movie-going audience.

Capra's complex balance of the conflict between his personal politics and his public idealism manifested itself in his off-screen, at times seemingly contradictory, activities, most vividly in the duality of his being at the same time president of the Academy of Motion Picture Arts and Sciences—the conservative power wing of the industry—and a founding leader of the upstart Directors Guild, the lib-rad faction of Hollywood's workers. Capra's cunning fence straddle partially protected him from career-threatening attacks from both sides of the industry's widening political divide, but in the end satisfied neither.

By the mid-thirties, the Academy was floundering in the wake of the industry-wide pro-union movement, and to its many mogul members, the lovable eccentrics in the Vanderhof mansion looked a bit too uncomfortably like themselves—with the decision by them at the end of the movie to "give everything away" seemingly a little too closely to some on the management side like Capra's hoped-for capitulation by the Academy to the unions. And the fact that the whole family was Looney Tunes did nothing to assuage their feelings.

In that sense, the character of Stewart's young Kirby, who begins as a schemer to marry Alice as a way of acquiring her family's property for his own father, then realizes he truly loves her, was a projected self-idealization (and justification) of Capra himself, as was Kirby's political duality. He is the only "sane" one in an otherwise crazy, if privileged, populace (industry) who manages to happily reconcile the two opposing sides (similar to the role that Cary Grant would play later in *Arsenic and Old Lace,* yet another of Capra's adaptations of Broadway plays that focused on an isolated, lunatic family—in this instance the perception of evil being relative, and the hero being the great bridge between the two opposing worlds, reality and unreality, the comic equivalents of moral and immoral).

What made Jimmy so perfect a choice for Capra was how well he projected the character's surface while missing, or ignoring, any of the intrinsic politics or deeper, perhaps darker morality of either Tony or the movie. To him, like most viewers, it was just another Depression movie, the soothing message being that wealth makes you a prisoner of the craziness it produces, while poverty keeps you sane and happy. Apparently, none of the movie's darker undertones resonated with Jimmy.

A month after the film's release on September 1, 1938, awash in rave reviews and surging box-office receipts, Capra was devastated when his son suddenly and unexpectedly died following a simple surgical procedure to remove his tonsils. In the wake of that tragedy, the emotional and artistic bonds between the director and his leading man grew noticeably tighter and substantially more entwined. Like an about-to-be lit fuse, they were now set to explode into the stratosphere of cinematic super-starlight.

9

"My father first thought of Gary Cooper for *Mr. Smith,*
but decided that Jimmy had everything Cooper did, with one thing more—
he projected an Ivy League intelligence that was crucial to the character
of Jefferson Smith, and it was something Cooper did not have. Stewart
was the perfect garden variety of citizen with just the right touch of Phi
Beta Kappa."

—FRANK CAPRA JR.

Although *You Can't Take It With You* made James
Stewart a top-of-the-line star, he was not considered
for an Oscar for his performance (except for Spring
Byington in the Supporting Actress category, no one else in the cast was
even nominated). Robert Riskin was nominated for Best Screenplay,
but did not win; nor did Joseph Walker, also nominated, for Cinematography. It is all the more surprising then that the movie itself managed to win Best Picture and brought Capra his third Academy Award
for directing.[1]

By the night of the Awards banquet, held at the Biltmore Hotel
on February 23, 1939, Capra was hoping to use the occasion to bring
together the unions and studio heads. Somehow, each side hoped to
benefit from having him as their leader.

---

1. Best Actor that year went to Spencer Tracy, in Norman Taurog's *Boys Town,* over
nominees Charles Boyer in John Cromwell's *Algiers,* James Cagney in Michael Curtiz's *Angels with Dirty Faces,* Robert Donat in King Vidor's *The Citadel,* and Leslie
Howard in *Pygmalion,* directed by himself and Anthony Asquith. Capra won out over
Michael Curtiz for *Angels with Dirty Faces,* Curtiz again for *Four Daughters,* Taurog
for *Boys Town,* and King Vidor for *The Citadel.* Spring Byington lost to Fay Bainter
in William Wyler's *Jezebel.* Riskin lost to Ian Dalrymple, Cecil Lewis, and W. P. Lips-
comb for their adaptation of George Bernard Shaw's *Pygmalion.* At the time, the
Academy made no distinction between original screenplay and adaptation; it did between screenplay and original story, the latter for which Riskin was not nominated,
as the film was based on the Broadway show. Walker lost to cinematographer Joseph
Ruttenberg for *The Great Waltz.* Capra had previously won Best Director for *It Happened One Night* (1934) and *Mr. Deeds Goes to Town* (1936).

In 1935, to reward Capra for all the success he'd had in keeping the fragile industrial peace between management and the still-unorganized workers, the Academy had elected him their president, even as he was secretly rallying the directors to declare their independence by forming their own guild, which they did in November 1938. As a result, the night of the awards, he found himself ever more entangled in the worsening situation, as both Academy peacemaker and union instigator, when a day before, the guild sent a behind-the-scenes threat to the Academy, notifying it that every guild director at the banquet was prepared to walk out *during the presentations* if their organization was not finally, fully, and formally acknowledged right then and there as a legal guild. As he had done so successfully before, most recently after *Mr. Deeds* had been nominated, Capra managed to broker a temporary peace by convincing each side to give in a little. The result was a begrudging industry acceptance of the guild, an uninterrupted ceremony, and, perhaps most astonishingly, feelings of gratitude on both sides for Capra's ongoing leadership (although some in the industry felt that Capra had used his influence to play one side off the other in order to make himself look like a hero when the situation was resolved). Whatever the truth, the result that night was yet another big industry win for him: an Oscar for Best Director. For now, at least, it appeared Capra could do no wrong. Somehow his canny machinations had made him the most popular operator in Hollywood, with the most popular rising actor at his beck and call.

— • —

After filming *You Can't Take It With You,* before its release and his subsequent rise to the top of the box office, Jimmy had been anxiously waiting for MGM to find a new project for him. When none materialized, he did some work in radio, broadcast versions of his own and other stars' movies. While many performers refused to lower themselves and appear on the crackling (and free) medium, Jimmy proved an immediate hit; his distinctive voice was instantly recognizable to audiences everywhere. He appeared regularly on the *Lux Radio Theater,* the *Silver Theater, Good News,* and the *Screen Guild Theater.* In the ultimate form of flattery, comedians and impersonators began exaggerating his drawl and the already slow pace of his talking.

Leland eventually received an offer for Jimmy from independent producer David Selznick, who had been in charge of production at MGM for a short time following Thalberg's death. He then left to form his own production company. With America's isolationist era about to come to an end and the world approaching a new international conflict, Selznick wanted to reflect the country's changing mood with a "serious" picture for Carole Lombard, who had made her name in thirties screwball comedies, such as Howard Hawks's *Twentieth Century* (1934), Gregory La Cava's *My Man Godfrey* (1936), and William Wellman's *Nothing Sacred* (1937). This type of grin-producing comedy had already started to fade in popularity as the humor could no longer keep away the frown of reality. To extend Lombard's career, in 1939 Selznick wanted her to "go dramatic" by showcasing the actress's hitherto little-seen dramatic side.

To ensure the focus would stay on Lombard, Selznick wanted to avoid any of the three hottest romantic leads of the day, Gable, Cooper, and Grant, even if any of them had been available, which, for various reasons, they weren't. Instead he chose Stewart, who he felt would be the perfect nonintrusive foil for a dramatic Lombard in *Made for Each Other.* His only worry was that she might so overwhelm the young actor on-screen that audiences would find it difficult to believe such a callow fellow (as Selznick believed he was) could actually win the affections of a lioness like Lombard (as he believed she was).

To direct, Selznick hired John Cromwell, a journeyman body-mover hired to work the soapy script built around the everyday lives of a young Manhattan lawyer (Stewart) who goes against his mother's wishes and, instead of pursuing the wealthy boss's daughter, marries for love (Lombard), and then struggles with her to make it in the big city. The first part of the film is fast-paced, light domestic comedy; the second, strictly soapsuds as the sudden illness of the couple's newborn moves Stewart to confront his stingy boss (Charles Coburn) to finance a desperate last-minute delivery of a life-saving serum. In the final scenes—the serum is delivered, the baby lives, and Stewart, for showing the courage to stand up to his boss, is promoted to the law firm's vice presidency.

The film opened in February 1939, the same month that the Academy Awards had crowned Capra as Hollywood royalty, but, unlike *You Can't Take It With You*, it was not a box-office hit. In a year crowded with costume classics—William Wyler's *Wuthering Heights,* John Ford's *Stagecoach,* and Victor Fleming's *Gone With the Wind*—towering performances by Laurence Olivier, John Wayne, and Clark Gable, respectively; the top-drawer comedy of Ernst Lubitsch (*Ninotchka*) with Greta Garbo and the intense melodrama by Edmund Goulding (*Dark Victory*) that showcased the red-hot Bette Davis, *Made for Each Other* quickly fell behind and faded.

Lombard was devastated by the film's failure. *Life* magazine put the final nails in its coffin when, later that year, it proclaimed that screwball comedy, the most popular form of screen humor in the thirties that had begun in 1934 with a slick, fearless, and screamingly funny Lombard in Howard Hawks's *Twentieth Century,* had ended the moment Lombard began sobbing seriously in the climactic hospital scene of *Made for Each Other.*

Jimmy was disappointed as well. He blamed its shortcomings on the absence of a strong director like Capra and a solid screenwriter like Riskin (Jo Swerling did the screenplay). In one scene, in which *he* had to cry, when Cromwell was unable to talk him through it, Stewart took a break, slipped outside the studio, lit a cigarette and, as he had with Margaret Sullavan, held it close to his face to allow the smoke to burn his eyes. Unfortunately, he feared there might be far more cigarettes available than great dramatic roles for him to use them in.

— • —

Offscreen, meanwhile, Jimmy continued to enjoy an ever-expanding roster of willing and available women. At least some of his "dates" during this period were created, arranged, and controlled by the studio, such as MGM's leaked "rumor" in 1939 that Jimmy was "seriously" dating Olivia de Havilland. Always eager to keep their bachelors bathed in women, especially the men thirty and over (Stewart had just turned thirty-one) and living with male roommates (Swope, McCormick, and Logan were all still revolving semiregulars at the house in Brentwood), the studio came up with the idea to have de Havilland accompany Jimmy to the December 1939 New York premiere of her new and highly anticipated movie, Victor Fleming's *Gone With the Wind,* independently produced by David O. Selznick and distributed by MGM, a lavish, publicity-soaked affair that helped intensify the planted rumors of a Stewart/de Havilland romance.

De Havilland, who played Melanie in *Wind,* just happened to be represented by Leland Hayward, who was also good friends with Irene

Selznick, David O.'s wife, and it was her idea, one with which Hayward enthusiastically agreed, to bring the couple together for the premiere. Although their "passion for each other" burned up the gossip columns, de Havilland later confessed, "At the New York premiere, Irene Selznick arranged for Jimmy to be my escort. At the time, I didn't even know him, just about him."

Next came a highly publicized "double-date" with Stewart, de Havilland, John Swope, and Elsie West Duval, a local southern girl from Newport News, Virginia. Duval happened to be best friends with actress and model Kay Aldridge, at the time one of the ten most photographed women in the world. When Duval sent a friendly letter to Aldridge via MGM and included an old high school photo she had come across, the letter and the photo somehow both wound up in *Life* magazine. Immediately after, MGM brought Duval to Hollywood. When a "double-date" between de Havilland and her "current beau," Jimmy Stewart, his part-time roommate Swope, and Aldridge fell though at the last minute because Aldridge "couldn't make it," the studio asked Duval to accompany Swope in her place. Forty years later, Duval still remembered quite vividly the show the studio put on for her, and the one they did together for the world. "It was a great picnic. Olivia brought a delicious catered lunch with matching paper plates and napkins. After, Jimmy played the piano at his home and sang silly ditties before we went to the MGM studio for a private movie showing. What I recall most of all is that Jimmy, whether playing piano or flying model airplanes on the desert, seemed just like he was in the movies!"

With de Havilland running hotter than ever because of *Gone With the Wind*, and Jimmy sizzling off the collective heat of *You Can't Take It With You*, they were a couple literally and figuratively made in studio heaven. MGM even insisted that de Havilland take flying lessons so she could indulge in Stewart's favorite hobby. Less than six months later, in May of 1940, *Motion Picture* magazine, the *People* of its day, wondered aloud on its front cover, "WHAT KIND OF HUSBAND WILL JIMMY STEWART BE?" and inside leaked the "scoop" that the couple had told their respective families they were seriously in love and planning to wed.

If MGM was working the PR mills overtime for Stewart, it was at least in part because they still didn't know exactly what to do with him next, and hoped that keeping him in the public eye would buy them some time. If they couldn't show him off in a movie, they could keep him around in the gossips. He remained, as far as MGM was concerned, despite his success in *You Can't Take It With You,* too tall, too thin, too gawky, and too lukewarm for long-term stardom. Mayer told cohorts that in his opinion James Stewart was no Gary Cooper, Paramount's extraordinarily hot young leading man (and another Capra star).[2] Mayer had a million ideas of what to do with Cooper if he could only get his hands on Hollywood's number one male star.

If Jimmy was concerned about Mayer's lack of enthusiasm, he didn't show it in public. Instead, he played the good soldier, keeping busy doing interviews regarding his impending "marriage," which he deftly managed to sidestep with his requisite politeness while he was secretly carrying on a real and top-secret affair with actress Loretta Young. Known in Hollywood's whisper circles as a charter member of the clique of leading ladies who sexually devoured their co-stars, Young was in the front rank of "manizers," beaten out for the top crown only by Marlene Dietrich, who, as one close to the scene recalls, "man or woman or both, fucked anything and everything that moved."

Young had been married for a short time in her teens to actor Grant Withers, before divorcing him in 1930 and subsequently going on a sexual tear through Hollywood's best men; whether they were married or single made no difference to her. At various times she had been linked romantically to Clark Gable (with whom she had an illegitimate child), Spencer Tracy (he was married at the time), George Brent, Gilbert Roland, Ricardo Cortez, Wayne Morris, Joe Mankiewicz, Robert Riskin, Jock Whitney, Tyrone Power, Cesar Romero, David Niven, and . . . Jimmy Stewart. Years later, Young told *Parade* magazine that when neither was married and they were "dating," she "prayed like mad that Jimmy Stewart would ask me to marry him. And he didn't! Jimmy took me out many times, but he just wasn't sending the same signals I was."

Indeed. Stewart, who was not at all in love with Young, was, rather, fearful of, a bit confused by, and more than a little tinged with guilt about her strong sexual advances, believing she would "pollute" him, his parents' favorite biblically tinged word for what unmarried sex did to the soul. At the same time, Alexander had been regularly writing Jimmy let-

2. Gary Cooper was in Capra's *Mr. Deeds Goes to Town* (1936) and, later on, *Meet John Doe* (1941).

ters, admonishing him for having not as yet found the right woman and settling down, never failing to add, in what seemed like the supreme contradiction, that he didn't see how it was possible in a place like Hollywood for any man to find a decent woman. Translation: Come home, find a Christian wife, and take over the family business. His mother, on the other hand, quietly encouraged him to stay in Hollywood, take his time and choose carefully, to play the field and wait until the right woman came along: "Save your clean manly body for the right woman—bring it to her as an undefiled, unpolluted temple." Well, that was a bit too little and a lot too late for anyone to ask of him. Besides, if he listened to his father, he was, in a way, disobeying his mother. And if he listened to Mother, he was disobeying his father.

Jimmy spent many evenings talking late into the night with Fonda about his problem. Although he was remarried, Fonda found time to help his friend through these difficult emotional times and went so far as to confess that he, too, continued to have problems with women and suggested to Jimmy that maybe he'd be better off getting out of the starlet sweepstakes altogether, at least for a while.

— • —

Jimmy's next movie, *The Ice Follies of 1939*, directed by Reinhold Schünzel, featured the real International Ice Follies, a spectacle act and the raison d'etre for the film. In it, Larry Hall (Stewart) is part of an ice-skating team, along with his wife, Mary McKay (Joan Crawford), and his "best friend," Eddie Burgess (Lew Ayres). When the act fails to catch fire, Mary decides to try her luck as a solo, and lands a contract with "Monarch Studios," with the understanding that she is single, both as a performer and in real life. She lies about her marriage and goes on to become a huge movie star. After a long separation, during which Stewart is struggling to put on an ice show in New York City, they meet up, reconcile, and Crawford decides to give up her career and return to being a full-time wife. To save the day (and, presumably, the movie), Monarch decides to hire Stewart to produce his wife's next movie and even hires Lew Ayres to be in it. The films ends with a "spectacular" ice ballet in glorious Technicolor (the rest was shot in black and white).

The film may best be summed up by Crawford's description of

it: "Everyone was out of their creative minds when we made *Ice Follies*. Me, Jimmy Stewart and Lew Ayres as skaters . . . preposterous! A dancer I am, a skater I'm not . . . It was a catastrophe."

The director was not one of the studio's brighter talents, and the producer, Harry Rapf, was usually consigned to B-movie projects. These were sure signs of how Mayer regarded not just the film, but the status of his three stars. Ayres, coasting for a decade on the crest of Lewis Milestone's *All Quiet on the Western Front* (1930), had begun to look passé on-screen, and Crawford hoped the film would reinvent her as a singer to broaden her filmmaking options. That five of the seven songs she recorded for the movie ended up on the cutting room floor—this despite the film's original (and unused) campaign slogan, "Crawford Sings!"—indicates how her vocals were received by the studio. Even the supposed "romance" between the newly divorced Crawford (from Franchot Tone) and her single, equally billed co-star barely received any play in the gossips, and the film quickly faded.

As for Stewart, the film's failure pushed him deeper into radio. He starred in a two-part production of *Up from Darkness* opposite Rosalind Russell for CBS's weekly *Silver Theater*, which played on two consecutive Sunday afternoons. Fearing his voice was becoming more popular than his face, he was relieved when he was offered a part in an MGM ripoff of its own highly successful *Thin Man* series, W. S. Van Dyke II's hastily shot *It's a Wonderful World*.

Even with its pedigreed screenplay by such studio heavyweights as Ben Hecht and Herman J. Mankiewicz (who conceived it as a screwballer at a time when this style of film had all but exhausted itself), nothing about the film worked. Guy Johnson (Stewart) is a detective assigned to safeguard millionaire playboy Willie Heyward (Ernest Truex), who has too much to drink one night and winds up on the wrong end of a murder frame-up, originally intended for Johnson. Heyward is convicted for murder and sentenced to death, while Johnson also faces a year behind bars as his accomplice. En route to prison via train, Johnson escapes, meets poet Edwina Corday (Claudette Colbert), and although she is initially kidnapped by him, eventually falls in love and assists him in finding the real killer, thereby exonerating both him and Heyward. This film, too, quickly disappeared without a trace.

— • —

Stewart's career remained stuck in the ranks of the unremark-able until Frank Capra, now the highest-priced and most-powerful di-rector in Hollywood as well as the undisputed king of Columbia's helmers, called him for another film. Dissatisfied with his deal and with Harry Cohn's stubborn, macho-mannered refusal to renegotiate it, Capra quietly began entertaining separate offers from both Zanuck and Samuel Goldwyn to make films for their respective independent stu-dios. Capra's struggle to become independent from what he perceived as the necessarily corrupted, or impure, Harry Cohn studio mentality toward talent, including directors, helped shape the thematic founda-tion of what was to be his next, and arguably greatest, film: *Mr. Smith Goes to Washington.* In it, Jimmy Stewart's incredible performance as Jefferson Smith would not merely redeem his faltering career, but place him alongside Capra at the very top of Hollywood's elite roster of bank-able A-list box-office giants.

The making of *Mr. Smith Goes to Washington* was fraught with con-troversy from the beginning, reaching all the way to the highest govern-mental authority in Hollywood, Joseph L. Breen, then the head of the industry's self-regulated Production Code Administration. It was one thing for a director like Capra to make a satire about Utopia, as long as it was set in some far-off Shangri-La, or a wacky comedy about a wealthy, out-of-touch family of millionaires living in a Shangri-La–like mansion exempt from the realities of the "real" world. But, as Capra was to discover, it was quite another to attempt a head-on, non-metaphoric feature about the pervasive, ongoing political corruption set within the great, vaunted walls of the United States Congress.

In 1937, Harry Cohn had optioned a short treatment written by Lewis R. Foster called *The Gentleman from Montana,* which concerned the gradual disillusion of an optimistic freshman senator. Foster was an "idea man" who, like Capra, started in silent comedy but had seen his career dissipate in the first decade of talkies until he was re-duced to freelancing original treatments he'd written for the studios. Cohn liked the premise of *The Gentleman from Montana* but initially thought about shelving it after Breen, whose office insisted it be shown all material that any studio considered filming, personally wrote back to Cohn in January 1938 rejecting the treatment because of its "general unflattering portrayal of our system [that is] a covert attack on the dem-ocratic form of government."

The project then languished from studio to studio. Everyone who read it liked it, but no one in a position to get it made was willing to challenge Breen's powerful office, until Harry Cohn decided to take a chance on it. He believed he could soften up its rougher, more controversial edges and optioned it as a project for Soviet Georgian émigré director Rouben Mamoulian. Cohn had been searching for something for Mamoulian, hoping he could sign the director to a contingent long-range contract at a bargain rate. Moreover, if a controversial project like *Mr. Smith* failed, he could always put the blame on what he would describe as Mamoulian's Soviet-bred anti-Americanism.

Meanwhile, Capra had gotten bogged down trying to make a movie based on the life of composer Frédéric Chopin. When he got the chance to read the Foster treatment for the first time, he insisted to Cohn he had to have it and suspended his work on the Chopin film. He traded in to Cohn an option he had taken on the Broadway play *Golden Boy* for the rights to *The Gentleman from Montana*. Cohn then assigned Mamoulian to direct *Golden Boy*, with new Columbia contract-player William Holden.

Capra needed someone to work with him on the script. This was no easy task as he had recently lost his longtime collaborator Robert Riskin to Samuel Goldwyn, who had signed Riskin and boosted his annual $100,000 salary at Columbia to a cool half-million.[3]

Capra was furious that Columbia had let Riskin get away, and his departure hastened Capra's decision to leave Columbia as well. He informed Cohn that this next film, the final one under his present contract, was to be his last for the studio. Capra then turned to contract screenwriter Jo Swerling, only to discover to his dismay that Swerling, too, was jumping ship and joining Goldwyn, so was therefore not eligible to work on the movie. With time running out, Capra next turned to Columbia screenwriter Sidney Buchman, whom he had worked with on the marginal *Broadway Bill* (1934) and the unsuccessful *Lost Horizon* (Buchman had worked with Riskin on the script), but who had since

---

3. Their relationship had always been competitive and at times contentious. There is still much debate today about which of the two is responsible for what in their collaborative efforts. After the failure of *Lost Horizon*, Riskin had begun looking for a new deal, and when the Goldwyn offer came along, he jumped at it.

written the elegant and successful *Holiday* (1938), directed by George Cukor and starring Cary Grant and Katharine Hepburn.[4]

Capra always insisted that the minute he read the original treatment of *The Gentleman from Montana* the only two people he could see playing the two leads, Jefferson Smith and Saunders, his "hard-boiled" assistant, were James Stewart and his co-star from *You Can't Take It With You,* Jean Arthur (who had also co-starred for Capra opposite Gary Cooper in *Mr. Deeds*).

In truth, Stewart was not Capra's first choice; Cooper was. So much so that the director saw the film as a sequel to his 1936 *Mr. Deeds Goes to Town* (for which Capra had won his first director Oscar) and for a while even thought of calling the new film *Mr. Deeds Goes to Washington. Deeds* did not become *Smith* until January 26, 1939, only a few weeks before Stewart was officially signed, and a few weeks *after* Goldwyn, who now also had Cooper under contract, refused to loan him to Capra. At that point, the director went to MGM for Stewart, where he knew he would have no trouble getting him from Mayer.

— • —

Principal photography on *Mr. Smith Goes to Washington* began in April 1939. The interiors were mostly shot on a giant sound stage that Columbia Pictures had converted into an impressively detailed reproduction of the actual Senate chamber. Early into filming, Capra decided to personally escort his principal players to Washington, D.C., to shoot some location scenes while hopefully instilling in his cast a deeper patriotic feel for the material they could use in their performances. Along with Stewart and Arthur, Capra took the always spectacular and profoundly underrated Claude Rains (Senator Joe Paine), the Capra regular and ever-dependable Edward Arnold (state machine boss and corrupt publisher Jim Taylor), Thomas Mitchell (perennially tipsy D.C. beat reporter Diz Moore), and Harry Carey (benevolent vice president and president protem of the Senate).

---

4. Buchman would go on to write several more Cary Grant movies, including Frank Lloyd's *The Howards of Virginia* (1940) and George Stevens's *The Talk of the Town* (1942). Buchman, with Seton I. Miller, won an Oscar for Best Screenplay in 1941 for *Here Comes Mr. Jordan*, directed by Alexander Hall.

It was the first time Jimmy had been to the nation's capital since he was a boy, when he'd once gone with his mother and sisters to visit Alexander while he was stationed there during World War One just prior to his being shipped out to the front lines of France. This time Stewart fell deeply in awe of the capital, particularly the monuments, and especially the Lincoln Memorial, which was to play such a crucial role in two of the movie's pivotal scenes. Later on, Jimmy remembered the shooting of those location scenes this way: "Director Frank Capra, who taught me a lot about acting while we were making *Mr. Smith,* refused to build synthetic Washington street scenes at the Columbia lot or use process shots; he took the cast to Washington and caught scenes at the exact moments when natural settings dovetailed with the story. In order to get a certain light, we made a shot at the Lincoln Memorial at four in the morning. To catch me getting off a streetcar, a camera was hidden in some bushes. I got on a regular car, paid my dime and, to the motorman's amazement, departed, two blocks later— in front of the bushes. For shots of me going up the Capitol steps, I sat in a car and, at a given secret signal, went trudging up through the swarming lunch-hour crowd. This search for absolute realism, plus the superlative work of the supporting actors, had a great deal to do with 'making' the picture. I think especially of the grand performances of Claude Rains, Thomas Mitchell and Jean Arthur, a fine comedienne who proved in *Mr. Smith* that she could handle dramatic moments with equal skill."

The final script had undergone extensive changes and development since the original Foster treatment, aided in part by several improvisational rehearsals that Capra encouraged as a way to develop the spoken language of his leading characters and in part by the rhythm of the gags.[5] By the time shooting began, the character of young Jefferson Smith (Stewart) had morphed into a small-town newspaper publisher and supervisor/guidance counselor of the Boy Rangers, a vaguely defined group of preteen clubs that most closely resembled the Boy

---

5. There may have been another reason as well. It was felt by some that besides being politically explosive, the original treatment too closely resembled a Pulitzer prize–winning play by Maxwell Anderson, *Both Your Houses.* The similarity was discovered by lawyers at Columbia near the completion of Capra's film, and to avoid any potential legal problems, the studio eventually bought the rights to the Anderson play as well.

Scouts (after the film's release and subsequent controversy, they were said by some who hated the film to have also borne an uncomfortable likeness to the Nazi Youth organizations of Hitler's Germany, something that particularly infuriated the extremely liberal Capra).

Jefferson Smith, like his three historical namesakes (Thomas Jefferson, Adam Smith, Jesus Christ) is a purist and literalist who believes in the clear skies of the great American dream, who never sees any clouds of conflict that might otherwise mar the endless horizon of democracy. As such, he becomes the unwitting, and therefore perfect, stooge for his state's corrupt political machine.[6] The film begins with the great Dimitri Tiomkin's rousing, patriotic score incorporating dribs and drabs of music from all corners of the Americana songbook, including "Columbia the Gem of the Ocean," "My Darlin' Clementine," "Yankee Doodle Dandy," "Glory Hallelujah," "Of Thee I Sing," and "Found a Peanut." This colorful cacophony is in direct contrast to the central theme of the opening montage: death (a subject still very much on Capra's mind with the passing of his son earlier that year). The film flies through its plot-establishing scenes with a series of clip-clop cuts that Capra uses like flash cards to inform the audience that a state senior senator has died and an immediate replacement is needed. This exposition climaxes with a terrific unifying gag as Governor Hubert Hopper (Guy Kibbee), convinced by his children that Smith would make the perfect replacement senator, goes to Smith's home, rings the front door, and is blown away by the responsive sound of a full brass band. Smith, it turns out, is rehearsing the Boy Rangers' band, and they've kicked in just as Hopper presses the buzzer. Capra's perfect sense of physical comedy puts a neat cap on the film's breathtaking opening.

The state's surviving and now senior senator, Joseph Paine (Rains), another character name laden with physical, political, and religious symbolism, was a close friend of Smith's late father, a behind-the-scenes politico never seen but nevertheless an influence in the film. It wasn't much of a stretch for Jimmy to play Smith as a man who revered the spirit of a powerful, absent father, a man whose shoes of greatness he now must attempt to fill (the actual dialogue between Rains and Jimmy involving the recollection of the senior Smith's death came out

---

6. Because of the widespread corruption suggested by the script, Capra decided it was best to leave the state unnamed.

of a series of improvisations between the two actors that served as the basis for the final scripted version).

The audience quickly learns that Paine and state boss and media giant Jim Taylor (Arnold) are in the midst of an illegal moneymaking land-grab involving the building of a federally funded dam in their home state, the legislation for which is carefully buried inside another, more important bill, and that they have conspired to appoint Smith to the Senate to assure themselves of his needed go-ahead vote on the project.

During the first of the naïve Smith's two visits to the Lincoln Memorial, he is inspired by the grand scale of democracy as represented via the Memorial, in which it appears that a giant-sized Lincoln is smiling down directly upon him (and, by extension all the other "little" people there including a former "Negro" slave—this Capraesque moment is somewhat tempered by an earlier scene in which African-Americans are depicted in their much more typical Hollywood studio–era roles as wide-eyed and dopey train porters). Afterward, Jefferson Smith returns to his office determined to contribute something worthwhile to the government in the name of the hometown people he represents. One of the first things Smith does is introduce a bill that would build a free summer camp for boys of all ages, not knowing that the land he wants designated is the very same parcel Paine and Taylor have earmarked for their dam site.

Meanwhile, to tighten his grasp on Smith, Paine, at Taylor's directive, instructs his gorgeous, sexy daughter, Susan (Astrid Allwyn), to seduce and therefore distract him. Paine's daughter is one of the women the film's male coterie of power euphemistically refers to as "high-heeled," suggesting she is not only a professional, but also at the social beck and call of her father and other powerful men.

Enjoying his new celebrity, Smith is stopped dead in his tracks at the prearranged introduction to the gorgeous Susan, swathed in mink, who lets him know she is "available" to him. Standing before her, Smith can't seem to keep his hat on or even hold it firmly in his hands, another expert Capra comedy bit, illustrating Smith's sexual intimidation (and possible impotence); at one point, Susan, enjoying his frustration, asks if she can hold it for him.

A little later, when it becomes clear to Paine and Taylor that Smith is trying to acquire the very same land they want, they decide to convince him to back down, and enlist Susan to help in the "persuasion." When all else fails, the assignment falls to Paine, whom Smith continues to idolize as a surrogate father, to explain to Smith how things actually work in Washington, D.C. It is a lesson in corruption and cynicism from within, and when Smith still refuses to play ball, he becomes the dupe in a plot to discredit him, instigated by Taylor and enforced by Paine.

Alone, defeated, and humiliated, Smith makes his second visit to the Lincoln Memorial, accompanied this time by his assistant, Saunders (Jean Arthur), who, when we first meet her, is cold, cynical, and well aware of the so-called politics of reality. Her inability to act against Paine and Taylor, to the point where she works as an informal spy assigned to keep tabs on Smith, further implicates her along with, apparently, everyone else in Washington. Now, though, in the ever-watchful shadow of Lincoln (to Smith a father figure cut in stone), impressed with his honesty, integrity, and, of course, this being Hollywood as much as it is D.C., his good looks, she convinces him to keep on fighting for what he believes in. She has obviously fallen in Capraesque-style love with him. No conventional beauty, and not particularly sexually becoming (like Susan), Saunders's love is decidedly not skin deep; it is, rather, interior, spiritual, maternal. She emerges because of it transformed, along with Smith, from the shadow of Lincoln, as Smith's strong, knowing ally. At this point Susan (Mary Magdalene?) is out and Saunders (Mother Mary?) is in.

Smith then takes his uphill battle directly to the Senate floor, where he expects to be mercilessly ripped to political shreds by Paine, or, as Susan has warned him earlier, "crucified." In a last desperate attempt to survive false but convincing charges of his own corruption, Smith, guided by Saunders from the public viewing box, attempts a filibuster. Holding the Senate captive and mute for twenty-three hours, he reads aloud the Declaration of Independence, the Constitution (which elicits a groan from the other Senators), and, in case the symbolic crucifixion has not been hammered home enough, passages from the Bible.

The film builds toward its inevitable climax in which everything miraculously resolves itself in happy democratic justice and contentment but not before what Andrew Sarris once described as the "obligatory Capra scene of the confession of folly in the most public manner possible." During this sequence, Capra shoots Stewart in ever tighter close-ups, full-face shots with no visible background, his wrists curved downward like swans' necks under his chin, his eyes darting from side to side, his face awash in sweat and agony.

As Jimmy later remembered, "It was the filibuster speech that Capra started way back in the gallery with the camera and ended up two feet from my face. Capra said, 'Jesus, do it right, 'cause this is what we're going to use. He kept getting closer and closer. By the time he got there I had the thing all worked out."

To induce the appropriate level of hoarseness for a twenty-three-hour filibuster, Capra had Stewart consult a doctor, who administered daily doses of deadly mercury dichloride directly onto the actor's vocal cords.

According to Jean Arthur, "When Jimmy was working in that picture, he used to get up at five o'clock in the morning and drive five miles an hour to get himself to the studio. He was so terrified that something was going to happen to him, he wouldn't go any faster." Eventually, his intensely reverential approach to the role of Jefferson Smith unnerved Arthur, who made no secret of her preference for playing opposite the likes of the sensual Gary Cooper than to the chaste Jimmy Stewart.

This was to be the first time American audiences would see Jimmy as an actor of dimension playing a character with both desperation and depth, and one capable of galvanizing a nation sorely in need of a cinematic patriot brave enough *and smart enough* to stand alone against the rising tide of economic swindle and worldwide Fascist threats to democracy. So popular was the character of Jefferson Smith that Jimmy Stewart himself became an immediate American symbol of intellectual purity, tall, dark, and *smart*—Clark Gable with a college degree, John Wayne with a driver's license (no Cary Grant to be sure, but no Claude Rains either).

To modern audiences *Mr. Smith Goes to Washington* may come off as too oversimplified a fairy tale of right triumphing over wrong, one more in the endless replays Hollywood has given the world of the David-and-Goliath tale, even if this one is staged in the arena of Washingtonian democracy. However, in its day, the film's defiant view of the reality of American politics was nothing less than populist dynamite. Nothing like it had been seen in an American mainstream movie. No filmmaker had ever before made such massive accusations about the pervasiveness of the corruption inherent in the hitherto untouchable hallowed halls of Congress. Because of it, *Mr. Smith* deeply resonated with a citizenry that had lived through a decade of the Depression and was now engaged in a battle over whether or not America should enter into the dangerous battlefield of World War Two.

To understand the film's widespread appeal, despite all the creeping and creepy darkness that pervades its bundle of overly simplified neos (Marxist, Weberian, New Deal, Jeffersonism, fascist, Christian) is to understand just how popular and important the director himself had become. At the time of the making of *Mr. Smith Goes to Washington,* Capra was the master of populist American entertainment. He was not only the biggest star director that Columbia Pictures had ever produced, he was the only "name" it had who could more or less "guarantee" a film. For all his Catholic guilt and resurrection complexes, what critic Andrew Sarris once described as a cinematic continuum of "near crucifixion and redemption," Capra had managed to become a personality of such identifiable force and familiarity to movie-goers that Columbia agreed to title the film in all advertising and in its opening credits as *Frank Capra's Mr. Smith Goes to Washington.*

With this film Capra had not only perfected his thematic, if ritualistic, screen style, he found the perfect expression of his own idealized personality in the acting style and physical manner of Jimmy Stewart. "He played [Jefferson Smith] with his whole heart and his whole mind, and that is what made it so real, so true," Capra later said of this most extraordinary of performances.

— • —

The film held a special premiere in October 17, 1939, in Washington's Constitutional Hall, preceded by a laudatory Press Club luncheon in Capra's honor. The four thousand invited guests, mostly Washington bigwigs and Hollywood heavy hitters, appeared to have a good time, despite the film's two stars not being present. Arthur begged off claiming she was shooting her next movie, but the rift that developed during filming between her and Stewart may have been the real reason for her absence. As for Jimmy, he, too, claimed a schedule conflict, but in truth he may have been frightened off by the growing criticism being hurled against Capra in the political as well as the cinematic press.

Indeed, the apparent (and by Capra unexpected) reception of the premiere's invited audience to the film's "radical" politics was the start of a mountain slide of criticism, much of it aimed directly at Capra. The very next day, senator after senator and political columnist after political columnist publicly questioned the film's depiction of the everyday machinations of American politics. Washington columnist Willard Edwards wrote that at the premiere "members of the Senate were writhing in their seats [over their] resentment . . . the Senate believes itself to have been maligned by the motion picture industry [and] is preparing to strike back at Hollywood." Frederic William Wile of the *Washington Star* wrote what was perhaps the most stinging attack on Capra when he insisted that the film "shows up the democratic system and our vaunted free press in exactly the colors Hitler, Mussolini, and Stalin are fond of painting them."

The controversy quickly took on a life of its own, with Capra taking virtually all of the heat, while the film's stars, especially Jimmy, managed to avoid the fray.[7] When things quickly got too hot for Capra, he rather unfortunately suggested that maybe the blame really belonged to the film's screenwriter, Buchman, who was, Capra reminded everyone, a member of the Communist party, someone who'd "betrayed" everyone (including Capra himself) by inserting certain party "codes" into the movie.[8]

Much to the relief of Capra and Cohn, the film's public premiere a week later, at New York's Radio City Music Hall, brought rave reviews from the general press, and it went on to become a box-office blockbuster. The *New York Times* approached the film's growing political controversy by saying, "Capra has gone after the greatest game of all, the Senate . . . operating, of course, under the protection of that unwritten clause in the Bill of Rights entitling every voting citizen to at least one free swing at the Senate . . . Mr. Capra is a believer in democracy as well as a stouthearted humorist . . . *Mr. Smith* is one of the best shows

---

7. Stewart never made any negative public statements about either Arthur or Capra, their professionalism or their politics. It should be noted, however, that he never again worked with Jean Arthur, and did not make another movie with Capra until both had returned from their respective duties serving in the armed forces during World War Two, when neither was able to find film work that easily. Stewart made eight movies before he and Capra reunited one last time to make *It's a Wonderful Life* (1946) for Capra's independent Liberty Pictures.

8. A persistent rumor of the day had Joseph P. Kennedy offering $2 million to Harry Cohn to buy the negative of the film before it officially opened, so he could destroy it.

of the year. More fun, even, than the Senate itself." The *New York Daily Mirror* called it "inspiring grand entertainment." The *New York Herald Tribune* praised it as "a moving and memorable motion picture." The *Daily News* flatly declared it "Capra's masterpiece." *The Nation* solemnly declared *Mr. Smith Goes to Washington* "by far the best film of the year," and said about its star, "Jimmy Stewart as Jefferson Smith takes first place among Hollywood actors. . . . Now he is mature and gives a difficult part, with many nuances, moments of tragic-comic impact. And he is able to do more than play isolated scenes effectively. He shows the growth of a character through experience. . . . In the end he is so forceful that his victory is thoroughly credible. One can only hope that after this success Mr. Stewart in Hollywood will remain as uncorrupted as Mr. Smith in Washington."

Andrew Sarris later described Jimmy's performance as "lean, gangling, idealistic to the point of being neurotic, thoughtful to the point of being tongue-tied," by a movie star who was "the most complete actor-personality in the American cinema, particularly gifted in expressing the emotional ambivalence of the action hero."

At the age of thirty-one, by virtue of his performance as Jefferson Smith in Frank Capra's *Mr. Smith Goes to Washington,* Jimmy Stewart had become a superstar and everyone wanted a piece of him now. Reporters tripped over themselves trying to get an interview, a comment about the film's controversy, or maybe even what his favorite color was. The only problem was, no one could find him.

10

"She'd slept with him from day one. It was a dream: It had been magical. For him, too. Suddenly, she was able to speak about it. It had all been poetic and romantic, hour by hour. That had held her bound to him, making her happy and unhappy. She never knew from one week to the next. He had never talked about love, but told her he was not in love, couldn't afford it. It hadn't bothered him not to be responsible for anybody. She had become pregnant by him the first time they'd slept together . . . she didn't want to abort the child, in order to continue sleeping with him. But she gave in to his wishes . . ." —FROM THE PUBLISHED DIARIES OF GERMAN NOVELIST ERICH MARIA REMARQUE REGARDING MARLENE DIETRICH'S AFFAIR WITH JIMMY STEWART DURING THE MAKING OF *DESTRY RIDES AGAIN*

Upon completing *Mr. Smith Goes to Washington,* a muted, increasingly introspective Jimmy Stewart found himself with two months free before having to report to work on his next film and booked passage for himself on the luxury liner *Normandie,* the preferred celebrity pond-crosser, despite the fact that by now war had been officially declared throughout Europe and Hitler was threatening to devour the entire continent. Shortly after the film opened, Stewart spoke directly to his father by telephone. During the conversation, Alex once again ran the litany, telling his son to forget about all this film nonsense, come home, share in the running of the family business, get married, and start a family. That was when Jimmy decided instead to go to Europe.

With a single suitcase and a home movie camera, he wanted to travel alone and incognito, shooting the sites like any tourist. After one day in England, he traveled to France, where he spent nine days roaming the countryside in a hired car. At one point he found himself in Bourges, the same town where Alexander had been assigned during

World War One to help rebuild some of the structures that had been blown up, "huge, empty steel buildings hidden away in the woods outside the city," as Jimmy would later describe them. He wound up in Cannes, along the way shooting dozens of rolls of amateur 16-mm footage.

Having just finished playing a character betrayed by a fictional father figure, Senator Paine, while being directed by a real-life one he truly admired, Frank Capra, and still unable to get the kind of recognition or encouragement from Alexander he so desired, Jimmy had fallen into the first of what would be a recurring series of isolating, dispiriting depressions. Now, as if to make the mixing of his emotions even finer, his amateur movie-making enabled him at once to act out the parts of the father, the son, and the directorial Holy Ghost.

He began his return trip to the States just as the Nazi army invaded Poland, bringing Britain and France into the war. The *Normandie* was forced to sail at night without lights, the passengers not allowed to illuminate their rooms as they crossed the increasingly treacherous waters of the Atlantic.

— • —

Upon his return in late summer of 1939, he remained out of sight in Los Angeles, reemerging just in time to begin work on his next film. While he was away, Leland Hayward had arranged yet another loan-out, this time to Universal, where Jimmy was cast as a cowboy in his first Western, opposite the sexually voracious Marlene Dietrich. Mayer's thinking was, If *Mr. Smith* proved too controversial and ultimately bombed, it was better to have the fall-out land at another studio. On the other hand, if the film proved a legitimate hit, MGM still had him under contract. The way Mayer saw it, it was a no-lose situation. For *him*.

Dietrich made no secret of the fact that she intended to make a full-course meal out of the handsome, if overly ripe, young actor who, everyone now agreed, had an absolute lock on winning Best Actor for his unforgettable portrayal of Jefferson Smith.

Miss Dietrich, of course, had a different role in mind for him.

The film, the fifth and final one he would make in 1939, was George Marshall's *Destry Rides Again,* more a spoof of than an actual Western, with the lead role tailored to fit him as perfectly as a thousand-dollar custom-cut cowboy suit.

— • —

Marlene Dietrich had made a spectacular entrance into the American filmgoing consciousness via her star turn in Josef von Sternberg's 1930 *The Blue Angel (Der Blaue Engel)*. Intended as a vehicle for German expatriate Emil Jannings (who had become a sensation for his performance in Sternberg's *The Last Command* [1929] and for which Jannings won the first Best Actor Academy Award, after *The Blue Angel* hit theaters in America), the film also made Dietrich a star.[1] Paramount eagerly signed her to a long-term contract and made Sternberg, who had fallen by now helplessly in love with her, Dietrich's "official," i.e., exclusive, director.

They would go on to make seven films together, during which time their tempestuous love affair, scandalized by the fact that both were married, rocked the gossip columns and helped sell tickets to their increasingly tempestuous, sexually provocative films.[2] Eventually, however, their pairing wore itself out, and by the time the last one they made together, *The Devil Is a Woman,* was released, their pairing had run its course. Dietrich, who had, for a while, become the highest-paid actress in Hollywood, was unceremoniously released by Paramount, and, unable to return to a war-torn Germany whose Nazi leadership she bitterly opposed (Hitler put a price on her head), turned freelance in the hopes of reviving her stalled career in American movies.

She was not the only star to descend from the heavens of Hollywood. By the end of the thirties, many of the biggest film actresses had lost their allure, as audiences seemed to tire of them en masse. What-

---

1. Jannings actually won the 1928 Oscar for two performances, *The Last Command* and Victor Fleming's *The Way of All Flesh*. Academy rules were eventually changed so that only one performance in any category could be considered for an award, thereby preventing an actor or actress from competing against him- or herself. The other nominees that year were Richard Barthelmess for both John Francis Dillon's *The Noose* and Alfred Santell's *The Patent Leather Kid*, and Charles Chaplin in his self-directed *The Kid. The Last Command* also shared Best Picture honors with William Wellman's *Wings*.

2. The seven films they made together as director and star include *The Blue Angel* (1930), *Morocco* (1930), *Dishonored* (1931), *Shanghai Express* (1932), *Blonde Venus* (1932), *The Scarlet Empress* (1934), and *The Devil Is a Woman* (1935). During this period, Dietrich made one non-Sternberg film, Rouben Mamoulian's *Song of Songs* (1933).

ever the reasons, in the wake of a coming war the handful of women who had once personified on-screen the decade of Art Deco, of unreal wealth for Depression audiences, of endless beauty, and suggestive costumes and glamorous sets, began to appear as aging, unsentimental throwbacks to the past. Along with Dietrich, such Hollywood mainstays as Katharine Hepburn, Joan Crawford, Greta Garbo, Kay Francis, and others were having a difficult time landing either the roles they sought or the salaries they demanded.

The one director who remained interested in Dietrich was Frank Capra, who wanted her to play Georg Sand in his stalled movie biography of Chopin that he still hoped to make. (Sternberg wanted to continue to work with her too, but on top of Paramount's reluctance, the entanglements he was facing with his troubled production of *I, Claudius* that kept him in England, and the studio's abject refusal to resurrect the once-golden team, made that wish all but impossible.) An opportunity for her to play Dallas in John Ford's 1939 *Stagecoach* also fell through.[3]

In June of that year, Dietrich's agent arranged a meeting for her with German-Jewish writer Erich Maria Remarque, who had gained international fame for his antiwar novel *All Quiet on the Western Front*, which had been made into a successful Hollywood movie in 1930 directed by Lewis Milestone and later forced Remarque into exile when the Nazis took over Germany. Although he was married (twice to the same woman, once in Germany, the second time in the States for American citizenship requirements), Remarque was immediately attracted to Lady Marlene, and an intense romance erupted. Dietrich had gained an off-screen reputation as a ruthless European temptress that far exceeded her on-screen one as a sinful goddess with a warm if devilish soul. She had earned it by her highly publicized affairs with a roster of willing-and-ables that included, besides von Sternberg, Gary Cooper, Robert Donat, Charles Boyer, William S. Paley, Douglas Fairbanks, Ernest Hemingway, Jean Gabin, and others, including several of Hollywood's most attractive American actresses ("Women are better [than men], but you can't live with them" became one of her most often-quoted comments).

---

3. The part went instead to Claire Trevor.

Late in 1939, while vacationing in France at the famous Hôtel du Cap, she received a phone call from Universal producer Joe Pasternak. Pasternak was interested in Dietrich for a saucy Western he wanted to make, in a part that the studio had once earmarked for Paulette Goddard. Pasternak offered Dietrich $75,000, a huge cut in her normal fee but money she now desperately needed. She accepted, Goddard was out, Dietrich was in.[4]

The film was to be a light-hearted, loosely based musical remake of a 1932 oater entitled *Destry Rides Again* (aka *Justice Rides Again*), directed by Benjamin Stoloff. In the original version (based on a Max Brand novel, the title character played by Hollywood cowboy hero Tom Mix), Destry was a gunslinger framed for a murder he didn't commit and sent to jail. Upon his release, he finds the real killers and shoots them dead. There is no character called Frenchy, a "saloon singer" (named that to justify Dietrich's thick accent).

The new movie perfectly reflected the mood of the country as it shifted reluctantly, if inevitably, into the role of the savior of freedom in a war-torn Europe. The major contextual difference between Jimmy's previous picture, *Mr. Smith,* and *Destry* is the acknowledgment in the latter of an evil from beyond the shores of America, a recognition of the gathering European and Asian storms, so to speak, while in *Mr. Smith* America seems to be the entire world, with all its troubles internal ones. In *Destry* the hero arrives in peace, unarmed, not wanting any trouble and certainly not looking for any. The town of Bottleneck has, like Europe had been by an earlier generation, "cleaned up" by Destry's unseen father, only to have once more fallen to the forces of evil. Dietrich's presence further cements the Germanic link, giving the saloon she works in a decidedly exotic, foreign flavor. America's struggle with isolationism versus entering World War Two on the side of the Allies hovers all over this movie.

Destry, the son of the original, is brought in by the townsfolk to

---

4. This situation had been resolved by Charles Chaplin, who was married to Goddard at the time and had her under an exclusive contract that gave him final say over what movies she could appear in. Never enthusiastic about *Destry,* he jumped at the chance to force Goddard out of the film. Chaplin then cast Goddard in his own new movie, *The Great Dictator.* One final curious note: Goddard and Chaplin divorced in 1942, and sixteen years later she married Remarque, Dietrich's lover at the time of the making of *Destry.*

clean up Bottleneck as his father had done before him. However, where the old man was rough and tough, Destry Jr. is a dedicated pacifist. He doesn't even carry a gun and quickly becomes a laughingstock when he arrives in town, until near the end of the picture when circumstances force him to take up arms and he becomes a legitimate six-gun–toting hero. He cleans up the town, but pays an enormous price. Frenchy, the favorite town whore (who sings), has gradually come to love and respect Destry, to the point that, during the film's climactic shoot-out, she throws herself in the path of a bullet meant to kill him, and dies nobly in his arms (and conveniently for the sake of the censors who could not allow a prostitute, no matter how great her singing voice, to live happily ever after). A few songs round out the screenplay, most notably one that would become a Dietrich signature, "The Boys in the Back Room."

There are nevertheless filmmaking echoes of *Mr. Smith* throughout *Destry*—although the lack of *Mr. Smith*'s script, stellar supporting cast, and the direction of Frank Capra, or the absence of it, make all the difference in the world. To begin with, the character's name—Thomas Jefferson Destry—suggests that *other* Jefferson, Jefferson Smith. Like Smith, Destry was the new boy in town, and the old West, particularly the corrupt local politics that take place within the saloon, easily recall the shenanigans that took place in Capra's halls of Congress. And, like Smith, Destry first tries reason to deal with the corruption he sees. In the end, the difference between the directorial visions of Frank Capra and George Marshall is the use of guns as the crutches of cowards, such as Senator Paine, versus being the instruments of the heroic, as in *Destry*. Finally, there is the fundamental difference between the two films' leading ladies. Although in both films Jimmy's characters appear oblivious to the allure of the women who befriend them, teach them the ways of the real world, and, ultimately, fall in love with them, the sexualization of Frenchy reduced this film's level of "spiritual" love, and by doing so doomed her for being the sinner that she truly was. In *Mr. Smith*, Saunders has her hard heart softened by the love she finds in the virginal purity of her Jefferson; in *Destry*, it is the hooker who already has a heart of gold that ultimately causes her demise. In the former, Jefferson and Saunders presumably live happily ever after. In the latter, Frenchy dies, also happily and forever, the after left ambiguous in the spiritless context of the film.

— • —

Further complicating matters on *Destry Rides Again* was Paster-nak's own infatuation with Dietrich. Well aware of her reputation for sexual voraciousness, he figured all he had to do was line up and take his turn. She rebuffed him in no uncertain terms by telling him she would sleep with him "over Hitler's dead body" (she would use that line often, and after 1945 continued to rebuff Pasternak and all the others who came on to her by telling them with a smirk she still couldn't sleep with them because Hitler was secretly alive in Argentina). Her rejection of Pasternak was revealing for several reasons. First, because at the time she was actively involved with Remarque, who, perhaps knowing his lover all too well, insisted on being present for the entire shoot, glued to Dietrich's side. Secondly, the director-as-mentor route she had taken with Sternberg had resulted, once their celebrated teaming lost its steam, in a precipitous cooling off of her career. And thirdly, because from the first time she laid eyes on the tall, slim American boy with the pretty face cast to play Destry, she went into serious heat. As Pasternak was to recall years later, she literally rubbed her hands in delight at the sight of the ripe, young prospect before her. Ultimately, it would do Re-marque no good to hang around once she set her sights on Jimmy.

It took less time than it would to remove a six-gun and garter belt before Dietrich had taken Jimmy to her bed and showed him the way European women treated their men. If other women had been turned off by Jimmy, disappointed by his shyness or mistaking it for a rural aloofness, Dietrich was driven crazy by it. She loved playing the temptress, the seducer, and the more passive he was, the more aggres-sive she delighted in becoming.

Like so many of her best film characters, such as Lola in *The Blue Angel* and Catherine the Great in *The Scarlet Empress* (1934), the throaty goddess luxuriated in the role of both teacher and participant, ecstatically feminine and always in charge. Seven years his senior at the time (Stewart was thirty-one, Dietrich thirty-eight), she played the Madonna-whore role offscreen as well as on to perfection. For Jimmy, this was the first woman he had found who, to say the least, did not re-mind him of his mother (at least not consciously). He reveled in his late-to-arrive-but-last-to-leave-the-party of Dietrich's current love life. Even as the gossip columnists continued to cluck about the possibility of his upcoming marriage to Olivia de Havilland, Jimmy was busy div-ing into the deep waters of Dietrich's ocean of sexual delights. The facts that she was married and carrying on with another man at the time (the ever-present Remarque) didn't seem to bother him at all. It may have, in fact, made it better, giving him a free ride, as it were, with the "trap" of marriage an impossibility.

Predictably, none of this sat well with Remarque. When his jealous, fuming presence became a problem on the set, Dietrich simply had Pasternak remove him, which the producer, already jealous himself of the heated open-secret romance going on between his two co-stars, was only too happy to do. However, if Pasternak had any ideas about making any moves himself, that ended when the clever and manipulative Die-trich, aware that Jimmy liked to spend much of his offscreen time in his dressing room reading Flash Gordon comic books, presented him with a custom-made life-size doll of his movie-serial hero in the likeness of actor Larry "Buster" Crabbe, who played Flash on the screen. She de-livered it to him personally like a young momma bringing her baby boy a new toy to play with, all shiny and gift wrapped, complete with big red bow. Then she locked the door behind her. It was not the last time the two would spend hours in love-lock on the set during the making of *Destry Rides Again*.

A few months later rumors of a Dietrich pregnancy, via Jimmy, swirled through Hollywood, beyond the reach of even the carefully con-trolled realm of the MGM PR machine.

Stewart remained characteristically silent about this relationship until years later, when he referred to it in the most oblique fashion, telling an interviewer, "I liked taking Marlene out to dinner and to dance back in the days of *Destry* . . . and so we dated quite a few times, which was fairly romantic . . . I was taken off guard by her adult con-cept of life."

According to Remarque, Dietrich, during the making of the film, went on to build in her apartment a virtual shrine to Stewart made of photos and surrounded by flowers, and even hired detectives to find out how real the relationship was between de Havilland and Jimmy. As naïve as he may have been in some areas, Jimmy was astute enough to suspect that these were the actions of an obsessive woman, a Holly-wood has-been with European pedigree who wanted to latch on to a new star. His eventual retreat from Dietrich's clutches was said to have infuriated her, to the point where decades later she barely mentioned his name in her 1987 memoirs, and then only to dismiss him and any notion of their one-time affair by describing him as nothing more than a dundering, humorless fool, in real life exactly the young, confused fellow he played to perfection on the screen; as the originator and perfector of the "whatever happened to my other shoe" style of acting.

Destry Rides Again was rushed into release on November 29, 1939 (only five weeks after *Mr. Smith Goes to Washington*), to qualify for Oscar consideration. By that time, the "romance," such as it was, between its two romantic stars had cooled. The film, however, opened hot and heavy and stayed that way through its entire initial domestic run. Dietrich's career fully recovered from its thirties slump, and she would go on to become one of the biggest Hollywood stars for the next quarter-century.

Jimmy, too, began the new year on a high note, as awards season brought its usual celebrity fever to both the industry and public alike. He was named Best Actor for his performance in *Mr. Smith Goes to Washington* by the New York Film Critics, no small accomplishment for what was considered the second most prestigious prize after the Oscar. It made him look like a sure thing to win an Academy Award.

To nobody's surprise, *Mr. Smith Goes to Washington* received a handful of Academy nominations besides Jimmy's, including one for Best Picture, Harry Carey for Best Supporting Actor (one of the nasty jokes going around at the time was that Carey shouldn't have been nominated for a role that had about eight lines of actual dialogue and that the honor should have gone instead to the Lincoln Memorial, whose heavily shaded reaction-shot performance in the film was far more moving), Capra for Best Director, Lewis Foster for Original Story, Sidney Buchman for Best Screenplay, Lionel Banks for Interior Decoration, John Livadary for Sound Recording, Dimitri Tiomkin for Best Score, and Gene Havlick and Al Clark for Best Editing.

The Oscar ceremony was held on February 29 at the Cocoanut Grove of the Ambassador Hotel in Los Angeles, hosted by Bob Hope. A stiffly tuxed Stewart showed up alone at the Awards and took his place at the MGM table near a beaming Frank Capra and his wife. He could not help but notice when Vivien Leigh, on the arm of David O. Selznick, arrived and sat at the head of the specially designated *Gone With the Wind* tables in the MGM section next to Olivia de Havilland (in black evening dress with lace inserts and a white ermine jacket), who was wrapped around Leigh's husband, Laurence Olivier. Dietrich, accompanied by Joe Pasternak, sat several sections away from Stewart, in the Universal Studios section, and avoided his eyes, as he did hers.

— • —

In those years, the Academy Awards ceremony was built around a rubber-chicken dinner served at large round tables, with each studio designated an appropriate number and arranged strategically near the aisles to reflect the likelihood of that night's winners and losers. After the meal was served, the actual presentation ceremonies began, at eleven o'clock.

Capra, in his last days of his final term as president of the Academy, had pulled off one final coup by selling the exclusive rights to the awards ceremony to Warner Bros., who paid $30,000 to make a short film of the evening. Thus the modern media black-tie affair and eventual annual televised broadcast of the event was born. On this night Capra was scheduled to officially hand over the presidency to his successor, Walter Wanger.

The end of Capra's run as the head of the Academy was the result of a tidal power shift in Hollywood that, ironically, he had helped bring about, namely the legalization of the trade and talent unions (that had been so bitterly opposed by the Academy, which was mostly comprised at the time by management and moguls). The burgeoning power of the unions had caught the attention of the federal government, which began a series of investigations into possible Communist infiltration; fear of reprisals began to pervade the industry. For his union activism, Capra had come under suspicion as a possible subversive even before *Mr. Smith* was released. His resignation as the head of the Academy, coinciding with the end of his directing contract at Columbia, which neither he nor Harry Cohn had been eager to renew, all combined to kill what would otherwise have been the picture's "can't-miss" status, despite an all-but-hysterical Hedda Hopper declaration in her pre–Oscar predictions column that "*Mr. Smith Goes to Washington* is as great as Lincoln's Gettysburg speech!"

Indeed, Capra, once seen as a hero for brokering a peace between the Directors Guild and the studios, was now largely regarded by those same studio heads (with reinforcement from Washington) as a troublemaker, sympathetic to unions and therefore to Communism, and his films were suspected of being filled with a disturbing level of anti-American propaganda. The industrial-strength resentment toward Capra became evident as the night wore on and the juggernaut that was *Gone With the Wind*, Selznick's independent colossus of a motion picture celebrating the glory of the past century's great civil war, went on to be the night's big winner. It won Best Picture over *Mr. Smith* and a host of other first-rate films that dominated that year's awards.[5] Victor Fleming won out over Capra as Best Director for *Gone With the Wind*.[6] And, in what was one of the biggest upsets of the night, a double upset really, Clark Gable, the acknowledged king of Hollywood, lost Best Actor, not to Jimmy, but to Robert Donat, the star of *Goodbye, Mr. Chips*; if Gable somehow didn't get it, the thinking had been going into the awards, Stewart surely would.[7] When he didn't and Donat did, he said nothing, smiled, and, if he was upset about losing, didn't show it. Instead, as always, he played the good soldier, congratulating Donat afterward for his great performance.

— • —

Despite his losing bid for an Oscar, Jimmy's performance in *Destry* proved, among other things, that he was not merely an extension of Frank Capra's dark/light vision of Depression-era America, that he could play period (Western) comedy, and that he now held a special niche in the middle-Americana mode of modern movies. Alongside Henry Fonda and his own Lincoln-laden movie (John Ford's *Young Mr. Lincoln,* in which the nineteenth-century president was at once humanized and lionized in yet another Depression reminder of purist democratic ideals), Stewart had become a part of Hollywood's new youth movement, the first generation of male movie stars who had not just

5. Edmund Goulding's *Dark Victory,* Sam Wood's *Goodbye, Mr. Chips,* Leo Mc-Carey's *Love Affair,* Ernst Lubitsch's *Ninotchka,* and Lewis Milestone's *Of Mice and Men.*

6. The other nominees were John Ford for *Stagecoach,* Sam Wood for *Goobye, Mr. Chips,* and William Wyler for *Wuthering Heights. Destry Rides Again* was shut out in this and every other category, having received no nominations.

7. The other nominees were Laurence Olivier in *Wuthering Heights* and Mickey Rooney in Busby Berkeley's *Babes in Arms.*

risen to stardom after the onset of the sound era, but had also helped render the silents obsolete even as they replaced the leading men who had appeared in them.

— • —

While the rest of the country hailed Jimmy as one of their own, MGM, increasingly unable to feel the cultural pulse of the nation, and without its one true visionary of the thirties, the late Irving Thalberg, failed again to capitalize on his surging popularity. It was Jimmy's good fortune to be the choice of another top director, Ernst Lubitsch, of the famous "Lubitsch Touch" (often described as being the imagined scene played off-screen in so many of his films, but also a definition of his so-phisticated, if offbeat comic pace set against the sugary romanticism of his movie imagination).

Lubitsch was, in every way, the polar opposite of Capra: light where Capra was heavy, heavy where Capra was light, romantic where Capra was pedantic, and timelessly sharp-witted where Capra was pointedly political. Having scored in Hollywood after emigrating from Germany at the behest of Mary Pickford, Lubitsch was quickly signed by Paramount. He racked up an impressive roster of fake European "kingdom" comedies and romantic costume musicals that both celebrated and mourned the continent that Germany, this time under Hitler's maniacal rule, was about to annihilate once more. As the filmmaker himself often liked to say, "I've been to Paris, France and Paris, Paramount. Paris, Paramount is better."

He had already successfully paired Jeanette MacDonald and Maurice Chevalier in *The Love Parade* (1929), the film that would not only make the two leads into stars but Lubitsch into one as well, proving that he, too, could make the transition from silent films to sound. After such classics as *One Hour with You* (1932), *Trouble in Paradise* (1932), the Code-bending *Design for Living* (1933), and *The Merry Widow* (1934), he wanted to film an adaptation of yet another European romantic comedy fantasy, this one based on Nikolaus Laszlo's Hungarian stage play *Parfumerie*, but ran into strong studio resistance. Paramount wanted more modern America and less antique Europe in its comedies.

Another, deeper problem for Lubitsch regarding the massive cultural shift in the Hollywood of the thirties was that many of the first wave of silent leading men and women had been left behind by the industry's aural modernization. In 1937, Lubitsch lost his best leading man when the heavily accented Maurice Chevalier left Hollywood and returned to France (where he would remain for the next twenty years). Not long after, Lubitsch, frustrated with Paramount's apparent lack of enthusiasm for his work, signed a two-picture deal at MGM. The first was 1939's *Ninotchka,* starring Greta Garbo in full legend mode. The other, made that same year, was his long-simmering adaptation of *Parfumerie,* retitled *The Shop Around the Corner.* It was to be Lubitsch's fondest remembrance of a rapidly disappearing Europe, of small shops with quality service operated by well-dressed capitalists for whom the whole world existed within their retail establishments (while their shops served as a cinematic microcosm of the whole world). They were run by a solicitous, formally attired staff and frequented by well-heeled clients who felt superior to the clerks, over all of whom the proprietor (rightly, in Lubitsch's old-world view) played God.

The plot concerns the sinister ambitions of one clerk, Ferencz Vadas (Joseph Schildkraut), who wants to be the manager of the shop, run by Mr. Hugo Matuschek (Frank Morgan). Two other young clerks, Klara Novak (Margaret Sullavan) and Alfred Kralik (Stewart), are conducting a romance via anonymous love letters, during which they fall in fantasy-love, while continuing to dislike each other in person. The climax of the film revolves around Kralik's unmasking of Vadas, Matuschek's promotion of him to manager, and the blossoming of real love between Novak and Kralik.[8]

If Jimmy had had any reservations about working on his fifth film in 1939, one that appeared, at least in script form, as an ensemble piece, a lateral career move at best, they paled beside the fact that he would have the opportunity to play the lead opposite Margaret Sullavan. Once again, it thrilled him to know he would be acting alongside the object of

---

8. The film was remade in 1949 by MGM as a turn-of-the-century American musical vehicle for Judy Garland and Van Johnson, Robert Z. Leonard's *In the Good Old Summertime,* adapted for an original Broadway musical in 1963 called *She Loves Me* with words and music by Jerry Bock and Sheldon Harnick, and remade again as a non-musical movie in 1998 by Nora Ephron, from her own script, updated and reset in New York City as the e-mail romantic comedy *You've Got Mail,* with Tom Hanks and Meg Ryan in the Stewart/Sullavan roles.

his romantic desires on the big screen, kissing and mooning in properly chaste but for him intensely erotic posturing, for all the world to see. For her part, Margaret Sullavan considered performing with Jimmy like walking through a beautifully green park in early spring, before the first mowing of the new grass.

The character of Kralik seems in retrospect a bit too passive and a bit too precious, especially in the field of romance, but all is forgiven for the scene in which Sullavan, bedridden, reads a letter from her thus far unidentified secret admirer, while Stewart, sitting beside her, must listen to his own words and pretend to know nothing about the person who has written them. Years later, reflecting upon the magic of the moment, Sarris said it best when he noted the high level of acting in the sequence, how it was "dangerously delicate. It would have been very tempting for a flickering triumphant expression to have passed over Stewart's face, but instead an intensely sweet and compassionate and appreciative look transfigures the entire scene into one of the most memorable occurrences in the history of the cinema [and] I could not think of any other actor who could have achieved an effect of such unobtrusive subtlety. . . . The stellar electricity generated by Sullavan and Stewart energizes even Lubitsch's elegant style to a new peak of emotion."

The great French critic André Bazin once identified a cinematic phenomenon he called doubling, wherein the characters in a film mirror the relationship between the characters in real life, with the resultant sparks supercharged—the reality of the actors' lives off-screen adding depth to the lives of the characters they portray, and vice versa. Nowhere is that more evident than in the courtly shyness of Kralik/ Jimmy toward his untouchable goddess Novak/Sullavan, whom he both fears and hopes will remain unattainable (or unpolluted). What the audiences sees when they watch *The Shop Around the Corner* is the real chemistry between the two, Jimmy's worshipful reticence to express his true emotions (while in love with a woman who stands before him but he cannot see) and Sullavan's always ambiguous feelings toward the one person in her real-life circle she not only didn't marry but also didn't sleep with. In an otherwise unexceptional movie, these moments deliver the finest form of docu-biography that exists and by doing so exhibit one of the great emotive powers of film.

The Shop Around the Corner was shot in sequence (its scenes filmed in the same order they appear on screen), a highly unusual happenstance in movie production, made possible because of its single primary setting, and was completed in a mere twenty-seven days (shooting began the day after Jimmy filmed his final scenes for *Destry*). While this might not make any apparent difference to general audiences, for both Jimmy and Sullavan, each of whom had begun in live theater, it was a rare opportunity to make a film in which they could build the emotions of their performances in unified chronological scenes rather than in individual shots taken from the end, beginning, or middle of the script for the economic consideration of locale setups. This is one of the reasons the film's dramatic build works so well, and the romantic chemistry between the two actors so compellingly latches on to the viewer's emotions.

The haste with which the film was made, on a relatively modest budget, was a strong indication of MGM's lack of confidence in the project, underscored by its release on January 12, 1940, traditionally one of the slowest box-office periods, immediately following the big holiday rush. This also made it ineligible for 1939's crop of Oscar nominees, which, as it turned out, didn't matter, as the film was not a crowd-pleaser and did not break any box-office records after it opened.[9] It was more or less dumped by the studio, with Mayer dismissing it as something of an anomaly, made at the wrong end of the decade, with artificial "old Europe" sets and overly mannered caricatures of clerks, customers, and courtliness; and its director somewhat over the hill, whose career had peaked with *Ninotchka* and was now trailing off and near its end. He wasn't entirely wrong, at least not about Lubitsch, who would make only six more films before dying in 1947 of a heart attack.[10]

---

9. The film has since been rediscovered by film enthusiasts and is generally considered to be one of the best movies of the thirties, often ranked by critics and polls in the top one hundred films of all time.

10. *That Uncertain Feeling* (1941), *To Be or Not to Be* (1942), *Heaven Can Wait* (1943), *A Royal Scandal* (1945), *Cluny Brown* (1946), and *That Lady in Ermine* (1948). The best of these was *To Be or Not to Be*, a political farce disguised as a screwball comedy that starred Jack Benny and, in her last movie, Carole Lombard (who died in a plane crash in Nevada shortly after completing a War Bond drive. At the time of her death, she was only thirty-four years old and had made an astonishing seventy-one movies). *Heaven Can Wait* was Lubitsch's most elegiac movie (not to be confused with the Warren Beatty/Buck Henry *Heaven Can Wait* [1978], which was actually a remake of Alexander Hall's *Here Comes Mr. Jordan* [1941]). Lubitsch died eight days into the filming of *That Lady in Ermine*. The film was completed and credited to Otto Preminger.

Shop received good, if not particularly enthusiastic reviews. The *New York Times* singled out the cast, noting how "James Stewart, Margaret Sullavan, Frank Morgan and Joseph Schildkraut make *The Shop Around the Corner* a pleasant place to browse in." *Time* magazine focused on Stewart, acknowledging his ascent to "screen personality" by saying that he "walks through the amiable business of being James Stewart." Only *The New Yorker* seemed to feel the film was an unqualified success: "*The Shop Around the Corner* is close to perfection—one of the most beautifully acted and paced romantic comedies ever made in this country."

Although Jimmy's performance did not hurt his soaring career, it didn't particularly help it, either, and in industrial Hollywood, then as now, stepping sideways meant stepping backward. *The Shop Around the Corner* was, ultimately, too small of a picture for him to follow the successes of *Mr. Smith* and *Destry,* and because of it, he and the film were more or less buried by the bigger pictures of the year, which included John Ford's outstanding adaptation of John Steinbeck's *The Grapes of Wrath,* starring Henry Fonda; Chaplin's *The Great Dictator* (a film whose political controversy put it on the front pages of every newspaper in the country); Ford's *The Long Voyage Home;* Alfred Hitchcock's *Rebecca;* Sam Wood's *Kitty Foyle;* and William Wyler's *The Letter*—all of which, in their own way, looked forward, acknowledging the darkening clouds of impending warfare. In the end, Jimmy's performance in *Shop* was too Americana to suggest anything like the wistfulness of old European sentimentality that the role demanded (and that the supporting cast, mostly European immigrants, superbly exuded). Whereas Capra had been able to use his spirituality as the basis for conflict in order to elevate Jimmy's character in *Mr. Smith Goes to Washington* to active heroic proportion, Lubitsch's use of the actor was hampered by an emphasis on lovelorn passivity that did nothing so much as shift *Shop*'s focus to Sullavan, who ultimately dominated both Jimmy and the picture.

— • —

He appeared in two more movies in 1940 as he tried to regain his career's upward momentum. But before starting work on Frank Borzage's *The Mortal Storm,* a somewhat worn-out Jimmy decided to go home for the holidays, something he had not done in two years. He took his time making the journey to Pennsylvania by rail, taking the Los Angeles–Chicago–New York route, spending a few days in Manhattan before actually heading back west to Indiana.

While in the city, he met up with his two sisters, Doddie and Ginny, who looked forward to passing time in the city with their now famous movie star brother. They accompanied him everywhere, and when he walked them down Fifth Avenue, they were delighted by how many strangers came up to shake his hand or ask for his autograph. "When people stared at him as we strode down the street," Ginny later recalled, "Doddie and I tried to appear blasé: but it was undeniably exciting . . . the little girl who jumped on the running-board of the taxi and begged for an autograph 'for Geraldine'; the aristocratic little lady who wished him a Merry Christmas on the Avenue . . . for three days we sailed around New York, doing exactly what we wanted to do and having a wonderful time. One evening as we were leaving a night club, photographers appeared in the lobby. 'Get him with a girl,' one of them whispered. I fled, but someone pushed poor Doddie and the two of them were snapped looking like frightened sheep.

"On Christmas Eve, we had dinner at Ralph's [a New York restaurant they had discovered years earlier on occasional trips to the city to visit their unemployed brother]. We ate there for sentimental reasons, for Ralph's had known us in other less cheerful days. As the evening passed and sounds of carols and holiday merriment floated in from the street, we grew reminiscent and nostalgic and very wistful. At midnight, we boarded the train, exhausted and grouchy, and before we knew it morning had come. It was Christmas and we were home."

The visit home proved a brief one for Jimmy. There was little said between Alexander and his successful, famous actor son besides the usual litany of lectures, this time with a strong choral backup supplied by Elizabeth. When was he going to get married? both his father and mother wanted to know. All decent young men past the age of thirty had wives and, if no children, certainly were in the planning stages, weren't they? And when was he going to come back home and take over the family business? *When was he going to act like a Stewart?*

One might have felt a touch of envy in the air, as Alexander tried to maintain his position of undisputed head of the Stewart-Maitland empire. In truth, his son had managed to overshadow him in every way except in the ever-shakier convictions of his own superiority. By the time

Jimmy boarded the train bound for Chicago and then on to Los Angeles, the emotionally taut wire between the two had become even more tightly stretched than ever and he could not wait to return to the comforting reality of Hollywood unreality.

— • —

Frank Borzage, the director of Stewart's next movie, *The Mortal Storm*, had already built a career in silent films before making the successful transition to sound. By 1931, he had two Oscars on his mantel and a solid, if unspectacular reputation among movie-goers.[11] Actresses especially liked to work with him because, as most of the silent directors had discovered in their (and the industry's) pioneering days, the simple but extraordinary power of the female close-up on the screen was unmatched by anything a script or a special effect could do to the viewer. That was why he was always one of Margaret Sullavan's favorite directors, and how he came to be chosen for her next project, following *The Shop Around the Corner*. For her co-star, despite *Shop*'s lackluster reception, she once again insisted on Jimmy, in what would turn out to be their last on-screen pairing.

Based on the popular prewar (1938) novel of the same name by Phyllis Bottome, *The Mortal Storm* is one of those films made in the years before Pearl Harbor when England and the rest of Europe were engaged in war with Germany and Asia was being shredded by the Japanese, while the United States maintained an official neutrality.

During the American prewar years, Hollywood was warned by Washington not to violate any of the three Neutrality Acts (1935, 1936, 1937) by making explicitly anti-Nazi or anti-Japanese movies. At the time, a raging domestic battle behind the scenes in the film industry was taking place over whether or not the United States should stay isolationist or expand its presence, and its power, in Europe and Asia. The government insisted that Hollywood name no specific enemy in its late-thirties, early-forties "prewar" films, to purposefully keep the enemy vague, a generic rather than geometric evil. For the most part, despite personal feelings, the heads of the studios did what they were told.

The story of *The Mortal Storm* concerns the plight of the Roth

---

11. *Seventh Heaven* (1927, silent), awarded in 1929, and *Bad Girl* (1931, sound).

family during the rise of a nearly generic European tide of Fascism (about as close as MGM could come to attacking Hitler without specifically naming him or Nazism). The father, Professor Roth (Frank Morgan), the head of a respected Jewish Bavarian family, is a favored teacher in his hometown university. His daughter, Freya (Sullavan), falls in love with both Martin Breitner (Stewart) and Fritz Marberg (Robert Young). She likes Fritz more, until she discovers his pro-Fascist sentiments. Things become darker and more threatening, and Professor Roth is expelled from his position because he is Jewish and sent to a concentration camp, where he dies. Breitner, meanwhile, continues to oppose the Fascists, and escapes to Austria, only to return to rescue Freya, even as Fritz plots to hunt her down and kill her. Just as Breitner is about to carry her over the threshold to Austria, Freya is shot and killed. With tears in his eyes and the body of his beloved in his arms, Breitner delivers her body, and with it her soul, to freedom.[12]

Although he had never been overtly political in any of the more than eighty films he previously made, Borzage dove into *The Mortal Storm* and its story of the increasingly savage pursuit of Jews trying to escape the widening, murderous grip of what was obviously Hitler's Nazism. The intensity of the film proved so powerful that a decade later it would still be remembered by some as too "pro-Communist," and bring its director before the unforgiving investigation of HUAC. As a result, Borzage was blacklisted for much of the fifties and he gained the incorrect reputation of being essentially a political filmmaker, and a left-leaning one at that. This not only fatally shortened Borzage's career, it left a taint on all his films, regardless of their content. That is why, despite what would become the best pairing of Jimmy and Sullavan, *The Mortal Storm* and Borzage are less fondly remembered (if at all) than *The Shop Around the Corner* and Lubitsch.

The Mortal Storm had its world premiere at New York's City's Capitol Theatre on June 20, 1940, and while the reviews were consistently good—the *New York Times* called it "magnificently directed and acted,"

---

12. Because of his thin, nonmuscular frame, Stewart could not lift Sullavan and carry her in his arms for any length of time. As a result, he acquired the on-set nickname of Stringbean. The situation was so bad that a special pulley system had to be concocted to make it appear that Jimmy was able to "heroically" carry Sullavan, a full foot shorter and thirty pounds lighter than him, across the border.

the *New Republic* declared that "Margaret Sullavan, James Stewart and Frank Morgan are fine," *Variety* said "the performances are excellent," and the *New York Herald Tribune* declared James Stewart "one of the finest actors alive today"—the film did not do particularly well at the box office. Perhaps it was a bit overly sentimental, if such a thing were possible in a film that dealt with the grim realities of Nazism, ending on a whimsical note that looked back on the past. Or, perhaps, despite Stewart's bravura performance, his character's heroic rescue, and Sullavan's character's impassioned flight for freedom, the film was no match for the real-life drama of the headlines in the daily papers.

Two days after the film opened, France fell to Hitler.

Jimmy Stewart knew now that it was only a matter of time before America entered the war, and when the time came, he would do what every Stewart and Maitland had done before him, *take up arms and fight to the end against any and all tyrants who sought to take away freedom and destroy the democratic way of life!*

But first he had to make another comedy.

11

"Stewart's most distinctive quality is his voice. If you listen to him, it's hard not to start imitating him, stammering out a 'Whal, gosh,' or two. The stars with staying power all had distinctive voices that were essential to the continuing thread in their characterizations. Stewart's voice isn't hesitant because he's unsure of himself, though there's some of that; it's more that he doesn't want to rush things, come on too fast or too strong. Voice is at the heart of the appeal of *The Philadelphia Story*. With Stewart, Katharine Hepburn, and Cary Grant, the picture is a veritable summit meeting of memorable voices." —DAVID FREEMAN

*I*n the spring of 1940, for his work in *The Shop Around the Corner* James Stewart was named one of the Best Actors of 1939 by the National Board of Review. This sent a signal to the powers at MGM that perhaps they should consider taking "Stringbean" out of action-adventures and back into romantic comedies. The only problem was, they didn't have a property for which they thought he was suited. Instead, Mayer decided to lend out Jimmy once more, for the last picture due on the option the studio had given David O. Selznick (Selznick International Pictures—SIP) for Jimmy's services that had begun with *Made for Each Other*, the completion of which set into motion a series of events that would, improbably, lead to Jimmy's winning his first and only Academy Award.

Less than two weeks after *The Mortal Storm* opened to rave reviews but indifferent box office, Stewart found himself at Warner Bros. preparing to star in William Keighley's *No Time for Comedy* (1940). Selznick, a degenerate gambler and uncontrollable womanizer forever in need of immediate cash and fresh-faced beauties, had developed a way of saving on payroll by trading with the studios for their most popular stars. While waiting for Jimmy to finish *The Shop Around the Cor-*

ner, Selznick had traded his option on him to Warner in return for the services of Olivia de Havilland, whom Selznick had desperately wanted to play Melanie Hamilton in *Gone With the Wind.*

Warner gladly gave de Havilland to Selznick because the studio thought Jimmy was perfect for its long-overdue screen adaptation of *Goodbye Again,* the play in which he had made his Broadway debut as Kenneth Bixby. However, when Jack Warner couldn't get MGM to postpone *Shop Around the Corner,* he renamed the project *Honeymoon for Three* and assigned Lloyd Bacon to direct. Warner put George Brent in the role of Bixby.

While waiting for his opportunity to use him, Jack Warner reluctantly gave to other actors several projects he had sequentially intended for Jimmy. The star, however, at least according to MGM, was never available. This led the increasingly impatient and at times paranoid Warner to believe that Selznick must have known of Jimmy's unavailability all along and had somehow pulled a fast one on him to get de Havilland.

Warner then green-lighted the purchase of the movie rights to S. N. Behrman's Broadway hit *No Time for Comedy* as a mollifying vehicle for Bette Davis for the then-enormous sum of $55,000. Davis, however, was at war with the studio head over the types of roles she wanted to play (as opposed to the ones they wanted her to play) and stubbornly refused to make the film. Warner gave that part instead to Rosalind Russell, hot after coming off her successful turn starring opposite Cary Grant in Howard Hawks's *His Girl Friday.* Just before the film was slated to go into production, Jimmy finished work on *The Mortal Storm* and was now available. At Jack Warner's personal directive, the studio's producer of the film, Hal Wallis, cast him as the male lead.

However, it quickly became clear that Jimmy was not the ideal choice to play a role the suave, sophisticated Brit Laurence Oliver had created on Broadway (opposite Katharine Cornell). Wallis ordered Julius and Philip Epstein, two brothers on the studio's writing payroll, to do a complete rewrite, to make *No Time for Comedy* more suitable for its star. In the original play, the quite urbane hero, Gaylord Esterbrook (Oliver on stage, Jimmy on film), having struggled for several years, suddenly finds success as a playwright on the New York stage. He is, at the time, married to actress Linda Paige (Cornell, Russell), but, after becoming famous, is "tempted" by another actress, Amanda Swift (Genevieve Tobin), toys with the idea of leaving his wife, but eventually reconciles with her.

In the film, Gaylord is a single newspaper reporter from the Midwest who, in his spare time, writes a comedy about New York City and sells his play to Broadway. When the production falters in rehearsal, he is suddenly called to New York City to do major rewrites. Once there, he falls for actress Linda Paige, now a "sophisticated New York woman" who shows the naïve youngster the ways of the world (a custom-tailoring of the role for Stewart that perhaps even the Epsteins, Wallis, and Jack Warner may not have realized at the time). Paige eventually convinces Esterbrook he must write only "serious drama," he realizes he is in love with her, proposes, and they get married. His new sense of his artistic self leads him to fall for the leading lady of his new, "serious" play, the married Amanda Swift. To "get even," Paige seduces Amanda's husband, Philo Swift (the always funny Charlie Ruggles). It is only when the play flops that everyone "comes to their senses," Amanda returns to Philo, Gaylord to Linda.

Echoing the infinitely superior *Mr. Smith Goes to Washington* in its depiction of an attempted corruption of purity (in *Smith* a purity of soul, in *No Time* a purity of craft), and anticipating the far greater *Sullivan's Travels* (Preston Sturges, 1942) in sorting out the dramatic differences between tragedy and comedy, grimness and greatness, pretense and passion, the film, released September 6, 1940, proved to be nothing more than a typically pragmatic Hollywood trampling of a once legitimately entertaining New York stage comedy. Audiences thought so, too, and stayed away.

By now it was impossible for Jimmy, who hadn't had a solid hit since *Mr. Smith Goes to Washington,* to avoid the reality that the upward momentum of his career had stalled, and his once red-hot name was in danger of lingering forever in the loan-out mediocrity of Hollywood's functionary middle roster, movieland's equivalent of what's-his-name.

To prevent that from happening, the always shrewd Leland Hayward hit upon the idea of putting Jimmy together with George Cukor, who had gained a reputation for being a "woman's director" primarily for his successful New York stage work with such Broadway divas as Dorothy Gish, Ethel Barrymore, Laurette Taylor, and Helen Hayes.

After Cukor moved to Hollywood, at the insistence of Katharine Hepburn (who was represented by none other than Leland Hayward and had just signed with RKO Radio Pictures, then under the leadership of David O. Selznick), his direction of 1932's *A Bill of Divorcement* made Hepburn the newest star of the silver screen. What followed for her was ten years of a career whose arc resembled a roller coaster. In 1936, co-starring opposite Cary Grant, she suffered a major blow, however, with the Cukor-helmed production of the commercially disastrous *Sylvia Scarlett*. Although the film flopped and Hepburn was blamed for her poor performance by the critics, it did wonders for Grant, who received great reviews and continued to work, as did Cukor, without interruption.

In 1939, Cukor was then hired by Katharine Hepburn to make a movie out of Philip Barry's *The Philadelphia Story*, a project she and Howard Hughes, her secret investor (and lover), had commissioned Barry to write for her and had taken to Broadway in an attempt to reestablish her popularity. Hayward, meanwhile, who had navigated Hepburn out of her free-fall and anticipated a major comeback with the film version of her smash-hit Broadway vehicle, looked to play the role of fixer for Jimmy as well by getting him a role in what was shaping up to be one of the most anticipated movies of 1940. If anything could save Jimmy's career, Hayward figured, it was *The Philadelphia Story*.[1]

Not that getting the film made was all that easy. Despite *The Philadelphia Story*'s soaring success on stage that made it the talk of the 1939 Broadway season, its New York–based cast of actors and actresses—Joseph Cotten as C. K. Dexter Haven, Tracy Lord's (Hepburn's) divorced first husband; Van Heflin as Macaulay Connor, the sardonic gossip columnist; and Shirley Booth as Macauley's wisecracking sidekick, Elizabeth Imbrie—failed to impress Hollywood when the studios came

---

1. Generally credited with resurrecting Hepburn's career, Cukor always claimed to have "discovered" Cary Grant, although Grant had made twenty movies before *Sylvia Scarlett,* and had developed something of a name for himself playing opposite Marlene Dietrich for Josef von Sternberg in *Blonde Venus* (1932) and opposite Mae West two times, in Lowell Sherman's *She Done Him Wrong* (1933) and Wesley Ruggles's *I'm No Angel* (1933). In 1954, Cukor, at producer Sid Luft's urging, performed another female career resurrection à la Hepburn, this time for Judy Garland, against Warner Bros.' wishes, after she had been released by her contract at MGM, by casting her as the female lead in *A Star Is Born.*

looking to buy the rights for a film version. Nobody wanted Cotten, Heflin, Booth, and especially Hepburn. When Selznick initially wanted to buy the property as a star vehicle for Bette Davis, Hepburn adamantly refused to sell to him. When MGM wanted it for Joan Crawford, Hepburn again said no. When Warner Bros. wanted it for Ann Sheridan, ditto. When independent film maker Samuel Goldwyn was willing to take Hepburn to get the rights to the play, but only if Gary Cooper were her co-star and William Wyler directed, Hepburn flatly turned him down. She then made it clear to one and all: either George Cukor directed her in the film version of *The Philadelphia Story* or there was not going to be a movie version.

Finally, Louis B. Mayer put an offer on the table that Hepburn liked—$175,000 for the rights, $75,000 for her to reprise her Broadway performance as Tracy Lord, and George Cukor at the helm. Mayer envisioned Clark Gable, Spencer Tracy (whom Hepburn had not yet met), or Robert Taylor in the role of C. K. Dexter Haven, and in the role of the gossip columnist Macaulay Connor (as a favor to Hayward, after the agent suggested to Mayer he could make the deal happen), James Stewart.

Gable, Tracy, and Taylor all turned down the film, presumably because they each felt it was still too risky a career move to star opposite box-office dud Hepburn. (Besides, Gable was already looking ahead to playing Rhett Butler in *Gone With the Wind* and didn't want to work with Cukor, anyway, who was gay, and who the homophobic Gable believed favored filming female stars over their male co-stars.)[2]

Jimmy's reaction to being offered the role of Macauley Connor was, on the other hand, one of pleasant surprise. "When I first read the script," he said later on, "I thought I was being considered for that fellow engaged to Hepburn. But as I read it, I thought to myself, ooh, that reporter part [Connor] is a good one, I'll be happy to play it."

Unfortunately for Jimmy, Grant wanted to play Connor rather than the part he had been offered, of Lord's ex-husband Dexter Haven, believing, although it was essentially a supporting role rather than the male lead, it was better written and funnier. However, as far as Cukor and Hepburn were concerned, Grant had to be her romantic co-star. In

2. Cukor was hired to direct *Gone With the Wind,* but was quickly fired at Gable's insistence, replaced by his friend, macho film veteran Victor Fleming.

the context of the film's reworked script, so as not to impede too much on the film's romantic track, the role of Connor was reduced to little more than a foil to Grant's star turn as Tracy's disgruntled but still-in-love, once-and-future husband.[3]

Stewart accepted the role of Connor without hesitation, even after he learned from Hayward how much more money Grant and Hepburn were being paid. Grant, four years older than Stewart and with a far more established screen presence, had become the first actor to successfully overcome the hitherto-ironclad studio salary system in 1936 by not renewing his original five-year deal with Paramount. Instead he signed two nonexclusive multiple-picture deals with Columbia and RKO, and reserved the right to negotiate his fees and percentages on a per-film basis. When Mayer offered him *The Philadelphia Story,* he agreed to sign on with two conditions. The first was that he be paid $137,500—twice what Hepburn was getting, figuring correctly that she would make her money on the back end if the film proved a hit. The second was that he receive top billing, to which Hepburn also agreed.

For Mayer, it was a sweet deal, especially considering that for all he was paying for Hepburn and Grant, he had Jimmy under a tight financial rein. He was paying him $3,000 dollars a week, which meant that for the five weeks the film was in production, from July 5 through August 14, Jimmy would earn a total of $15,000. Although he was not happy about the discrepancy in salaries, he also knew he was in no position to complain and said nothing. But he wouldn't forget either when, two years down the line, it would be time to renew his own contract with the studio.

Furthermore, unlike Gable, Jimmy was eager to work with Cukor, believing it was a real opportunity to perform for one of Hollywood's top directors who seemed to "get" him. Like Capra, Cukor was another European immigrant sentimentalist (although a far more sophisticated one), the child of Jewish-Hungarian immigrants who had settled in

---

3. When Grant went to Hepburn to enlist her help to get him the part of Connor, she assured him he could have the role if he really wanted it, but if he were smart, he would listen to Cukor and stick with Haven, a sure-thing Oscar for whatever actor played him. If there was one thing the Oscar-less Grant wanted more than the part of Connor, it was a gold statue from the Academy. Always unsure of himself when it came to casting, Grant went against his own doubting instincts and followed Hepburn's advice, leaving the role of Connor to Stewart. Cukor assured Grant he had made the right choice.

New York's Lower East Side. And finally, Jimmy didn't mind being the "new kid" for another reason; he had already begun to develop one of his chaste co-star crushes, this time on Hepburn. He expressed it early on during the production by doing little gags and bits he performed for her between setups, at times running around with a flowerpot on his head imitating Carmen Miranda. That always brought a frothy giggle from Hepburn, as did the long, drawling stories of his struggle to make it with Henry Fonda at his side back in New York City.

During filming, Stewart immediately offered to share with Hepburn his boyhood fascination with aviation, aware as he was of Hepburn's affair with the billionaire Howard Hughes and his obsession with flying. For her part, Hepburn was eager to learn as much as she could from Jimmy about flying, if only to impress Hughes the next time he took her aboard one of his planes.

After offering several times to take her flying, and always receiving a laughing no, Jimmy surprisingly got his chance when one time an obviously nervous Hepburn accepted an invitation: "I had learned to fly," Jimmy later recalled. "I had my pilot's license. It was a Friday, a break in shooting. She said, 'I'll meet you out at Santa Monica airfield. I want you to take me for an airplane ride.' I didn't have a plane of my own, so I rented one for the occasion—it was, after all, a very important occasion. It was a single-engine Fairchild, with a cabin; she could sit in the co-pilot's seat. She was there right on the dot that afternoon. We got in, and I started the engine. She sort of took over; she wanted to know what everything meant on all of the gauges. As I was taxiing, she told me I was taxiing too far; when I ran up the engine, she said it didn't sound right at all; she questioned a reading I had made on one of the gauges, saying it was quite wrong. I wasn't sure whether she was ready to take off, because she had so much to say that indicated she'd rather not fly with me at all.

"Finally, she said, 'All right, you can go up.' During the takeoff run, she kept talking and *talking*, saying what things were wrong about what I was doing. She'd snap, 'We don't seem to be gaining speed. The airplane will never get off the ground if we go like this.' Finally we did get in the air, and there was a little turbulence, which she blamed me for! As we made the first turn, she said, 'No, don't do that; let's just go straight.' Which meant going right out over the ocean! I told her that, and that we had to turn. She said, 'Wait until we get higher, and then we can go out.' I didn't know what she was talking about. She kept coming back to the instruments; she was concerned with the tachometer, which lots of times fluctuates a little—that's the rule rather than the exception. She didn't understand it at all. Its behavior was totally unacceptable to her. Her seat was very uncomfortable; she wasn't able to see enough; she kept saying, 'You can't see anything. You can't see up, you can't see back, it's impossible.' I told her, 'Kate, I think maybe we'd better go back.' She agreed. I was so nervous by this stage that I made a terrible landing; terrible, terrible! We bounced several times, and Kate absolutely had no kind words to say about that at all! Finally I taxied up, and she said, 'Thanks very much. I'll see you at work on Monday' and left! I was a wreck! I felt I'd been through a terrible thunderstorm and lost the engine. It was a nightmare! I never went flying with her again!"

— • —

At Cukor's insistence, Jimmy dropped most of his manneristic yawling and arm-lurching that had informed so much of the boyish innocence of his earlier portrayals, particularly those he'd done for Capra. Cukor was after something else from him, a cinematic rather than theatrical performance, one that would deliver a measure of emotional screen intimacy that he had failed to sustain with either Capra, Lubitsch, Borzage, or any of the other directors he had thus far worked with. Most of them, including Capra in *Mr. Smith Goes to Washington*, were content to capture Stewart's innocence and charm, emphasize it with the cinematic italics of cutting and close-ups, put him in front of the entire Senate or have him skiing across the Alps and montage-mutilate his most intimate, climactic moments.

The only rough patch Jimmy experienced with Cukor came during the one love scene he had to play with Hepburn, set on the grounds of the estate (as is virtually the entire movie). Tracy and Connor meet the night before her wedding, both having had too much to drink, and Connor, who has fallen for Tracy, makes one final, ultimately futile plea to win her love. During rehearsals, Stewart, feeling somewhat intimidated by Hepburn, and unwilling to come too close to how he really felt about her, reverted to the familiar tic-rich mannerisms, something that Cukor would not have in his movie. He instructed Jimmy to stand completely still when he spoke, not to flail his arms or shake his foot, or stutter his words, or glance away, or do anything but look straight into Hepburn's eyes and tell her how he felt.

The filming of the scene practically left Jimmy undone, and it wasn't until Cukor's good friend Noel Coward, who had happened to stop by the set that day and during a break told Jimmy how wonderful he was in the scene, that he was able to finish it at all. When Cukor finally called "Cut," satisfied that he had gotten what he wanted, Jimmy, in a cold sweat, retreated to his private dressing area to pull himself together, while a smiling Hepburn turned to the director and told him how surprisingly good an actor Jimmy really was.

Grant thought so as well, impressed with what he took to be Stewart's carefully worked-out style of casual acting, in contrast to his own way of working, which was on a purely instinctive level, making sure his own screen image never veered too far from the public's expectation of "Cary Grant." Grant told director and film historian Peter Bogdanovich years later he found Jimmy's studied performance "fascinating."

Production wrapped on August 14, 1940, with Cukor managing to bring the star-studded movie in five days ahead of schedule. The following week Jimmy busied himself with appearances at various anti-Nazi benefits, including one he organized himself for the third weekend in August, held at the Coliseum in Houston, Texas, in support of Great Britain, now at war with Germany (America was still officially neutral, despite Roosevelt's then-controversial "lend-lease" program that helped arm the British). For the heady occasion, Jimmy invited his pal Henry Fonda and two actors he had more recently become friendly with, Tyrone Power and Mischa Auer (one of his co-stars from both *You Can't Take It With You* and *Destry Rides Again*). At the gala, Jimmy did some magic tricks he remembered from his youth, using Fonda as his able assistant.

He also invited Olivia de Havilland, who quite graciously accepted the offer. She was in the middle of making *Santa Fe Trail* at Warner for Michael Curtiz and also in a blazing, secret sexual affair with co-star Errol Flynn, whom she simply adored.[4] Nonetheless, her appearance at Jimmy's benefit refueled the rumors of their involvement, to the point where the gossip press ran stories of how they were about to get engaged ("the *real* reason de Havilland attended"). When the benefit was over, Jimmy flew alone to Canada and met up with his family for a brief vaca-

---

4. Her relationship with Flynn would end a year later when she fell in love with director John Huston, after being directed by him in the 1942 melodrama *In This Our Life*.

tion, after which he returned to begin making the first of three scheduled movies, nonstop, Clarence Brown's *Come Live with Me,* George Marshall's *Pot O'Gold* (while on loan to United Artists; Marshall had directed Jimmy in *Destry Rides Again*), and Robert Z. Leonard's *Ziegfeld Girl.*

There was a reason both he and the studio wanted to stockpile as much James Stewart product as possible. The buzz for *The Philadelphia Story* was enormous; the talk around town was that everyone in the film gave the best performance of his or her career. MGM, uncertain of what America's eventual entry into the war would do to its foreign distribution, and therefore its budgetary limitations, and with many of its leading men eligible for military service, wanted to ensure it would have as much product as possible for future domestic release. That October, while filming *Come Live with Me, Pot O'Gold,* and *Ziegfeld Girl* (the latter two simultaneously, with Jimmy shuffling back and forth between UA for *Pot O'Gold* and MGM for *Ziegfeld Girl,* causing him to come down with a bad cold and a rough cough that nearly sent him to the hospital but which were not considered serious enough by either studio to suspend filming)—James Maitland Stewart was officially notified of his induction into the United States Army.

On September 16, 1940, in preparation for what looked like the United States' inevitable entrance into World War Two, President Roosevelt had signed into law the Selective Training and Service Act—otherwise known as the draft. All American males between the ages of twenty-one and thirty-six had to register with their local boards. The first nine hundred to be inducted were chosen by a highly publicized national lottery broadcast throughout the nation on October 29. Jimmy Stewart's number came up 310 and he was given thirty days to report for his physical. "The only lottery I ever came close to winning," he said, "was the drawing for the first draft before Pearl Harbor."

In that short space of time, Jimmy finished shooting all his scenes for *Come Live with Me, Pot O'Gold,* and *Ziegfeld Girl. Come Live with Me* is a lame, unfunny comedy about a German immigrant (Hedy Lamarr, one of Louis B. Mayer's personal "discoveries") who needs to marry an American (Stewart) to stay in the country.[5]

---

5. Mayer signed Hedy Lamarr after she had made the controversial 1933 Czech film, Gustav Machatý's *Ecstasy,* in which she appeared nude, the only thing about the movie anybody ever remembers. Coming off the international scandal it caused,

Pot O' Gold, an independent musical pastiche intended to capitalize on the popularity of Horace Heidt and his Musical Knights, the hosts of a highly rated radio show at the time, was produced by President Franklin Roosevelt's son, James, in what turned out to be his only venture in Hollywood. To flesh out the band's appearance, Mayer also lent Roosevelt Paulette Goddard to play opposite Jimmy, who sang several vocals with the band, and appears on film at least to be avoiding Goddard at every turn, not only for plot purposes, because in the film he simply can't stand her (or she him), as much as for her real-life politics, which were extremely left-wing. The film's seltzer-bottle humor didn't help. (The name of the film was changed to *The Golden Hour* for foreign markets, where its stars were virtually unknown.)

According to stories that abounded during the filming of *Come Live with Me,* Lamarr was said to be turned off by Jimmy's awkward manner during their love scenes, accounting for their lack of screen chemistry. Lamarr, also being stockpiled, was, at the same time, shooting King Vidor's *Comrade X,* opposite Clark Gable, with whom she was having a blistering sexual affair whose heat carried over onto and all but ignited the screen. As for Jimmy, he grumbled that he thought Lamarr was not a good enough actress for the role she was playing and that her overall iciness toward him off-set did nothing for the picture.

He was right; it didn't.

Mayer somehow thought they were so good together, despite Jimmy's obvious distate for Lamarr, that he recast them opposite each other in *Ziegfeld Girl* (1941) because he thought rural Jimmy and exotic Hedy made the perfect couple, both as lovers and as international ambassadors of peace; a symbolic marriage between the old world and the new. The film itself was a very soft sequel to Leonard's 1936 highly successful *The Great Ziegfeld,* notable for having as its stars William Powell and Myrna Loy (as Ziegfeld and showgirl Billie Burke) in the midst of their great run of *Thin Man* movies. Mayer, looking to guarantee *Ziegfeld Girl's* being a hit, shoe-horned every available MGM star into the film, including Judy Garland, Lana Turner, Tony Martin, Jackie

---

Mayer grabbed her for MGM, announcing that he had signed "the most beautiful woman in the world." By the time she had starred in John Cromwell's *Algiers* in 1938, the initial novelty had, for the most part, worn off. Mayer, nevertheless, continued to use Lamarr and loan her out.

Cooper, Ian Hunter, Edward Everett Horton, Philip Dorn, Paul Kelly, Eve Arden, Dan Dailey Jr., and Fay Holden. The film itself follows the lives of three young Ziegfeld hopefuls and their boyfriends, and the effect on all of them after the girls have been chosen to join the most famous chorus line in history.

Stewart did not think he would actually be able to make the movie at all, as he was scheduled to take his physical the same day as principal shooting was to begin, until he received notice that, without his requesting it, he had been given a deferment. At first he suspected Mayer had pulled some strings to make that happen and was not happy about it. When he finally did take the exam, he was notified that he failed to qualify for induction on the basis of preset height-weight limitations. At six foot three and 130 pounds, the army said he was too skinny to defend his country.[6]

The news of his rejection hit the newspapers and as soon as Alexander read about it, he called his son on the phone and urged him to get on the ball and gain the necessary weight to keep the family tradition of service intact. If he didn't, he warned, he would personally come out to Hollywood and kick his butt.

Jimmy was shaken by both the army's rejection and his father's phone call. He had to deal with the fact that in all the history of the Maitlands and the Stewarts reaching back to the Revolution, every able male had always *volunteered* to serve his country. Just by having waited for the draft was bad enough; being rejected was unthinkable. The first thing he did after talking to Alexander was to appeal the notification and set a date for a second physical. He was to take it that February, giving him less than three months to put on ten pounds and make them stick. If he looked a bit distracted during the making of *Ziegfeld Girl,* it was because all of his concentration and energy went toward gaining weight. He was constantly eating fatty foods, lots of milkshakes, and fried chicken wings

---

6. There is physical evidence to suggest that Mayer actually tried to get many of his biggest actors out of the draft. Mayer had vehemently tried to convince the Culver City draft board not to take Mickey Rooney. He also met with Stewart every day to convince him not to contest the board's rejection, that to do so would mean throwing away a lucrative and important Hollywood career where he could do far more good for the cause of freedom as a screen hero than he could working as a clerk in some office, because the army would never dare send him out on active duty. Jimmy was not impressed with Mayer's arguments.

and trying his best to work out as often as he could at the studio health club to see if he could put some muscle on his thin-boned frame.

By any measure, Stewart should not have had to make the film at all. His role was far too small in what had turned into an ensemble production, and, besides, he was woefully miscast as a rough-and-tumble trucker. Everyone felt what the film's producer, Pandro Berman, finally said in public, that "Stewart deserved a much better part than he got."

All in all, Jimmy was miserable during the making of all three post–*Philadelphia Story* films, and as the new year finally arrived, the thing he most looked forward to was military induction.

— • —

Although *The Philadelphia Story* had completed production in August 1940, MGM, believing it had a smash on its hands, as well as an Oscar contender, held back its release until the day after Christmas in order to keep it fresh in the minds of audiences and Academy members. It became Jimmy's first film since *Mr. Smith Goes to Washington* to have its premiere at New York's prestigious Radio City Music Hall. In its initial six-week engagement (limited only by the theater's previous commitment to open Alfred Hitchcock's highly anticipated *Rebecca* that February), it grossed $594,000, an astonishing number for its day (more than half what the play's entire initial Broadway run had earned), and broke the previous Music Hall attendance record held by Walt Disney's 1937 animated classic *Snow White and the Seven Dwarfs*.[7] By the time its initial domestic run ended, *The Philadelphia Story* had earned a profit of $1.4 million, which made it the second-highest grossing film of 1940, behind Howard Hawks's *Sergeant York,* starring Hollywood's number one most popular actor of the day, Gary Cooper.

As everyone had anticipated, the film was showered with Oscar nominations. For the second time in two years, Stewart was nominated for Best Actor. The film itself was nominated for Best Picture, Cukor for Best Director, Hepburn for Best Actress, Ruth Hussey for Best Supporting Actress, and Donald Ogden Stewart for Best Screenplay. No-

---

7. The stage production of *The Philadelphia Story* opened on Broadway in February 1939, ran for 415 performances, and grossed just short of a million dollars. It played another 254 performances on a national tour that grossed more than $750,000. Twenty-five percent of the play's grosses went to Hepburn and Hughes.

tably absent from the list was Cary Grant, who got the girl but lost the nomination.[8]

Meanwhile, in February 1941, Stewart finally managed to pass his physical (with a little help from a friendly medical doctor who examined the still-too-skinny actor. Jimmy claimed years later the doctor had "looked the other way" and put him down as having just met the minimum weight requirements). As the date of his induction drew near, Jimmy sent his pet dog home to the family farm and arranged to lease the house he had just rented out for a year to Burgess Meredith. Mayer, meanwhile, told Jimmy he was doing him "a big favor" by not suspending his contract while he was in the army. In reality, induction was the out that Mayer had been looking for. Believing Jimmy was too old to regain the momentum of *The Philadelphia Story* unless he won the Oscar, which the studio head believed unlikely, there was no practical use in keeping him around. As long as he was serving his country and no other studio could use him, he might as well burn through his contract. It was a highly publicized gesture that made Mayer, in his own mind at least, for the relatively small salary he paid Jimmy, look as if he were making some sort of grand sacrifice by playing the patriot and doing the right thing.

— • —

On February 27, Jimmy attended the Academy Awards dinner held at the Biltmore Bowl of the Biltmore Hotel in downtown Los

---

8. The other Best Picture nominees that year were Anatole Litvak's *All This and Heaven Too*, Alfred Hitchcock's *Foreign Correspondent*, Hitchcock's *Rebecca*, John Ford's *The Grapes of Wrath*, Ford's *The Long Voyage Home*, Charlie Chaplin's *The Great Dictator*, Sam Wood's *Kitty Foyle*, William Wyler's *The Letter*, and Wood's *Our Town*. The other Best Actor nominees were Charlie Chaplin (*The Great Dictator*), Henry Fonda (*The Grapes of Wrath*), Raymond Massey (John Cromwell's *Abe Lincoln in Illinois*), and Laurence Olivier (*Rebecca*). The other Best Actress nominees were Bette Davis (*The Letter*), Joan Fontaine (*Rebecca*), Ginger Rogers (*Kitty Foyle*), and Martha Scott (*Our Town*). The other Supporting Actress nominees were Judith Anderson (*Rebecca*), Jane Darwell (*The Grapes of Wrath*), Barbara O'Neil (*All This and Heaven Too*), and Marjorie Rambeau in Gregory La Cava's *Primrose Path*. There were several writing categories, including Original Story, Original Screenplay, and Screenplay. The other Best Screenplay nominees were Nunnally Johnson for *The Grapes of Wrath*, Dalton Trumbo for *Kitty Foyle*, Dudley Nichols for *The Long Voyage Home*, and Robert E. Sherwood and Joan Harrison for *Rebecca*.

Angeles, where the ceremony had been moved, having outgrown the Cocoanut Grove. The evening was hosted by new Academy president Walter Wanger (Capra's replacement). Jimmy arrived with Ginger Rogers, his date for the evening, and Ruth Hussey, his fellow nominee; and as had been the case the previous year, no members of his family were present.

He sat at the MGM table, and was, interestingly, the only Best Actor nominee in the category to show up in person for the awards. There is reason to believe everyone knew who was going to win in advance, and that the losers simply chose to stay away. A week earlier, Jimmy had received a phone call from someone at the Academy asking if he was going to be at the Biltmore. Before he could answer, the unidentified voice on the phone said, "I know it isn't my place to say so, but I really think you would find it in your best interests to attend." Stewart told Fonda about it, and asked if he had been contacted as well. Fonda said he had not received any such call. At that point, believing he had lost, he told Jimmy that he had decided not to attend after all, that he was going to go to Mexico with John Ford and get in some fishing, adding, "You know my views on all the Oscar crap, Jimmy—all those movie people in one room. I don't mind the losing bit, it's all those gasps of 'not him' if you win."

Among the women, Bette Davis, Joan Fontaine, and Ginger Rogers all attended. Carmen Miranda, one of Stewart's favorites, the actress he had impersonated for Katharine Hepburn on the set of *The Philadelphia Story,* set off a round of murmurs with her outrageous costume, accented by a silver turban topped only by Carole Landis's embarrassing entrance down the grand stairway during which her slip fell from beneath her gown and landed at her ankles, nearly tripping her.

The ceremonies began precisely at 8:45, when President Roosevelt's familiar voice was piped into the room. Originally scheduled by Walter Wanger to make a personal appearance, the president had begged off, citing the worsening international conflict. Instead, over a closed-circuit wire, Roosevelt praised Hollywood for its fund-raising efforts, defended Lend-Lease, and singled out for special merit the heads of the studios who had so diligently promoted, as he put it, "the American way of life."

After a round of pleasantries by the evening's emcee, Bob Hope, the actual awarding of the statuettes began. David Ogden Stewart kicked things off with a Best Screenwriting Oscar for *The Philadelphia Story.* Best Director came next. Frank Capra opened the envelope and read aloud the name John Ford, for *The Grapes of Wrath.* Now it was time for Best Picture. Director Mervyn LeRoy came to the podium, opened the envelope, and read aloud the name of the winner: Alfred Hitchcock's *Rebecca.* The upset victory belonged to the film's producer, David O. Selznick, who had won the previous year for *Gone With the Wind,* and had now defeated the two heavy favorites, *The Grapes of Wrath* and *The Philadelphia Story.*[9]

The acting awards, considered the most important in terms of box office, were the last to be handed out. For the occasion, the theatrical husband-and-wife team of Alfred Lunt and Lynn Fontanne, both previous nominees, who happened to be in Los Angeles for the West Coast swing of their Broadway triumph *There Shall Be No Night* (both losers in 1932), were given the honor of handing out the honors.[10] The first award, for Best Supporting Actress, went to Jane Darwell for her performance as Tom Joad's (Henry Fonda's) mother in *The Grapes of Wrath,* over the heavily favored Ruth Hussey. The audience gave Darwell a standing ovation, in response to which, at the podium, she said that winning the award was great, but that she hadn't worked in six months and much preferred someone giving her a job.

Next came Best Supporting Actor, which went to Walter Brennan for his performance in *The Westerner,* a total surprise that added even more suspense to the remaining three awards. Everyone had expected either Jack Oakie, who had so perfectly satirized Mussolini in Chaplin's *The Great Dictator,* or James Stephenson, who played Bette Davis's lawyer in *The Letter,* to win. After a respectable round of applause and Brennan's acceptance speech, the room grew deeply silent, except for Oakie, who burst out in tears, his wails audible even as he sobbed into his handkerchief.

The emotional response was even stronger when Ginger Rogers

---

9. Best Picture is a studio and a producer's award, which is why Selznick, rather than Hitchcock, was given the Oscar.

10. They were nominated for Best Actor and Best Actress for their performances in Sidney Franklin's *The Guardsman* (1931). Lunt lost to both other nominees, who shared the Oscar—Wallace Beery in King Vidor's *The Champ* and Fredric March in Rouben Mamoulian's *Dr. Jekyll and Mr. Hyde.* Fontanne lost to Helen Hayes, who won for her performance in Edgar Selwyn's *The Sin of Madelon Claudet.*

won for *Kitty Foyle,* beating out Katharine Hepburn, who everyone felt was the surest bet of the night. Rogers, who was sitting at the RKO table, rushed to the podium and burst into tears as Fontanne handed her the Oscar. "This is the greatest moment of my life," she declared, and then went on to thank her mother, Lela Rogers, for having stood by her so faithfully. There were some who thought she looked directly at Stewart when she said that, but no one could be certain.

And then, finally, it was time for the Best Actor. As soon as the name "James Stewart" escaped Lunt's lips, the entire audience burst into a rowdy, stomping cavalcade of approval, complete with shrieks of approval and plates being rattled against tables. Although Jimmy had been the overwhelming favorite, many in the house thought that Fonda might pull off yet another upset, as the momentum seemed to be going away from *The Philadelphia Story.*

As he approached the microphone, Jimmy took a big gulp that sent his Adam's apple dancing up and down. When his words finally came, they slipped out slowly and steadily, in the familiar drawl that had become the actor's audible trademark. "I want to assure you," he began, as the room fell to a hush, with what sounded like a curious echo of Rogers, "that this is a very, very important moment in my life. As I look around the room a warm feeling comes over me—a feeling of satisfaction, pride, and most of all, gratefulness for the encouragement, instruction and advantage of your experience that have been offered to me since I came to Hollywood and with all my heart I thank you."

The *Los Angeles Examiner* reported in the next day's edition that "as he had done in many a wild motion-picture scene, [Jimmy] stumbled dazedly back to his table amid shouts and applause." That night, Jimmy uncharacteristically stayed out until well past dawn, roaming Hollywood and the Sunset Strip with the Oscar clutched in his hand, accepting the spirited congratulations of everyone, celebrity and civilian, wherever he went. When he finally did get home early the next day, he woke Burgess Meredith out of a deep sleep to show off his prize. "Look what I won," he said, with a big grin on his face, to which Meredith replied, "So you've been to Ocean [Amusement] Park again."

Although he remained beaming and appreciative for the next several weeks, Jimmy believed that he had really been given the award for what amounted to a supporting role behind Cary Grant, as payback for the Oscar he *should* have won—for the previous year's *Mr. Smith Goes to Washington*. Grant, who, it was whispered about, had developed something of a crush on the still youthful-looking Stewart (who bore a striking resemblance to Grant's live-in lover, Randolph Scott) remained annoyed for a long time that despite trading up for what he believed was the better role, he had not even been nominated, and told friends that Stewart had benefited from the "special attention" Cukor had lavished on him.

As if in response, Cukor told an interviewer shortly after Jimmy won the Oscar: "I wanted him to be his natural self, only I wanted to highlight and underline his boyishness, his spontaneity, his stunned wonder when love hits him during the scene when he and Hepburn take a midnight swim together. He followed along with my ideas and never regretted it."

Capra, on the other hand, was angered by what he considered Cukor's public self-aggrandizement, and went around telling people that *he* was the one who had taught Stewart how to act for the screen, a boast that added much credibility to the notion that the Oscar had been a belated acknowledgment of Jimmy's performance for Capra as Jefferson Smith.

As for Jimmy's own assessment of his Oscar-winning performance, he had this to say: "I never thought much of my performance in *The Philadelphia Story*. I guess it was entertaining and slick and smooth and all that. But *Mr. Smith* had more guts. Many people have suggested that I won [the Oscar] as a kind of deferred payment for my work on *Mr. Smith*. I think there's some truth in that because the Academy seems to have a way of paying its past debts. But it should have gone to Hank that year. That was one helluva performance he gave in *The Grapes of Wrath*." What he left out of this interview, and of most others for years to come, was that he had actually voted for Fonda, hoping his friend would get both the Oscar and a much-needed boost to his not-as-yet-superstar career.

Katharine Hepburn was also said to be upset that Stewart had taken the acting honors for what was "her" picture, tailor-made to bring her back into Hollywood's open waiting arms, with an anticipated Oscar to seal her victory. The next day a bitter Hepburn told reporters that she had, in fact, been offered Ginger Rogers's role in *Kitty Foyle* but had turned it down because she didn't think she could play a shopgirl in a soap opera.

Back on the RKO lot, Rogers erupted in the middle of rehearsals for her next film, William Wellman's *Roxie Hart* (that would eventually become the basis for the hit musical *Chicago*), when someone commented about what Hepburn had said. "She ought to keep her damned mouth shut," she screamed.

Neither Grant, Cukor, Hepburn, or Rogers ever made another movie with Jimmy Stewart.

— • —

The day after the awards, Stewart received a phone call from Alexander. "You won some kind of prize," his father said, by way of a greeting. "I heard about it on the radio."

"Yeah, Dad," Stewart replied. "It's a Best Actor award. They give 'em out every year. I won it for *The Philadelphia Story*. You seen that one yet?"

"Never mind about it," Alexander said. "What kind of prize is it?"

"It's a kind of statuette. Looks like gold but isn't. They call it the Oscar."

"Well, that's fine, I guess. You'd better send it over. I'll put it on show in the store where folks can take a look at it."

Stewart said he would send it off that day. When it arrived at the store, Alexander put it in a small glass display case with dozens of other awards, mostly military, that the Maitland and Stewart men had collected through the years.

Exactly seven days later, Jimmy was ordered to report for duty as a buck private. When a reporter called to ask how much weight Jimmy had had to gain to meet the official requirements, he replied rather briskly that that was "a military secret."

And so it was that Jimmy Stewart wound up his initial five-year, nine-month residence in Hollywood, during which he appeared in twenty-eight features and won the coveted Academy Award. If his career had ended here, he would have likely been remembered as one of those extremely conventional actors who played off their natural personalities to achieve a familiar screen persona that touched audiences' hearts.

But it didn't end there. His wartime good-bye to Hollywood was, in a very real sense, a farewell to his own innocence and youth as well, the most recognizable and beloved qualities of his persona that had taken him to the very top of his profession and won him worldwide fame. Now he was about to walk onto another stage, one of battle, in a world war that would deepen, darken, and complicate everything about him and the world he knew and loved. And when that terrible war would finally end, Jimmy Stewart would reemerge into a new and very different kind of spotlight.

One of brilliant, if tortured, cinematic greatness.

PART FOUR

— • —

Flying High into Hell

Receiving the Croix de Guerre for "exceptional service"
in helping to liberate France.

12

"I, James Stewart, do solemnly swear that I will bear true faith and allegiance to the United States of America and will serve them honestly and faithfully against all their enemies whomsoever; that I will obey the orders of the President of the United States and the officers appointed over me, according to the rules of the Articles of War. So help me God."
—JAMES STEWART TAKING THE OATH OF SERVICE OF THE UNITED STATES ARMED FORCES AT FORT MACARTHUR, MARCH 22, 1941

"I'm sure tickled I got in," Stewart said in reply to Colonel Robenson, who had just congratulated him and eighteen other new draftees on becoming a soldier of the United States. Freed from the gerbil wheel he'd found himself on making movies in Hollywood, the army was, if nothing else, the real thing. And it was a lot of something else as well, starting with the crucial ancestral inch taller Jimmy felt he'd grown. In the beginning, when he had, one way or the other, won his private battle of the bulge and qualified for duty in the armed forces, nothing was more important or meaningful to him than acceptance into the Maitland/Stewart World of Real Men, otherwise known as the United States Armed Forces, because in his family, gold-plated Oscars were nothing compared to brass balls. Indeed, ever since his induction, a new and powerful emotional bonding had taken place between Jimmy and his father.

— • —

Burgess Meredith and Bill Grady threw Jimmy a going-away party at Franchot Tone's house, where all of his friends could stop by to say farewell and wish him luck, among them Henry Fonda (preparing to serve as an Air Combat Intelligence officer in the Pacific), Spencer Tracy, and James Cagney. To add a touch of humor to the event, everyone dressed up as a Knight of the Round Table. And for extra good luck, Grady arranged for a Hollywood starlet originally from the Ozark Mountains of Missouri, known around the lot for her shapely figure and round heels, to give Stewart the kind of send-off that would, in the parlance of World War Two, make sure he never forgot exactly what it was he was fighting for.

If that event had been cloaked in privacy, the same could not be said for Jimmy's actual induction. MGM saw his military service as something for the studio to make the best of, meaning cash in on. Mayer turned on the publicity machine, seeking to make the most out of "the first American Hollywood actor to be drafted."[1] Mayer made sure that every newspaper and radio reporter knew exactly when and where it was to take place. Dozens of photographers and reporters greeted him that morning, taking rolls of pictures and barraging him with questions.

If Jimmy said little directly to the press, Meredith and Grady, too, made the most of the opportunity. "We'll be seein' you," Meredith shouted to Jimmy, to a roar of approval from the small gathering of fans that Mayer had also made sure were on hand. Grady dutifully told the reporters that MGM had amended its policy and generously "waived" (suspended) Stewart's contract and that they would definitely "pick it up when he is dismissed from service."

Just behind the reporters were a group of Jimmy's female fans squealing at the sight of him. Young girls flashed their smiles his way, while the older ones in the crowd were equally enthusiastic, if less demonstrative, about seeing Stewart. "I've followed Jimmy through all of his pictures," sixty-six-year-old Mrs. G. S. Carney told the *Los Angeles Examiner,* having traveled all the way from Milwaukee just to see her favorite "boy" take the oath of induction.

All of which bothered Jimmy. He thought he was entering the army, not shooting a new movie, that he was now James Maitland Stewart of Roster #35, Company B, not James Stewart, movie star. This was about a real war. Didn't anyone get that?

— • —

He spent his first few days at Fort MacArthur, in California, a holding camp where the aptitude of the draftees was tested before their

---

1. Clark Gable was actually the first American movie star to enter the European war theater on active duty, but as an enlistee, whereas Stewart, contrary to most previous reports, actually had been drafted.

assignments were handed out. He was subjected to the usual itinerary of new inductees: KP (close-order drilling, guard duty, and kitchen police, better known in the army as potato peeling). One afternoon during KP he was instructed to peel a small mountain of potatoes. The next day, after another, double dose of the same chore, Jimmy decided maybe he ought to try to transfer to the Air Corps, at the time a more elite branch of the regular army, where the grunts preparing potatoes took a backseat to the glamour boys who flew the B-17s and B-24s. He certainly felt qualified, having logged more than four hundred hours in the air as a private pilot.[2]

Despite Jimmy's desire to, however, there were obstacles that made it unlikely the army would let him. The first was his fame. If anything happened to him, it would be a public relations disaster. The second was his relatively slight frame. According to the military, combat flying required a certain ruggedness no one thought he had. The third was his age. At thirty-two, he was six years over the standard pilot ceiling. For the first time, he decided to use some of the considerable studio influence that he had to this point disdained. He made a few calls to MGM, and a day later, without explanation, he was allowed to transfer to Moffett Field in Sunnyvale, California, just south of San Francisco, where he began training for service in the army's Air Corps. At Moffett, Jimmy was housed in a small tent with four other soldiers, as the regular barracks were overflowing with wartime recruits. He was overjoyed, believing he had gotten around the army's rules. And for the moment, it appeared that he had.

The first couple of weeks, a steady stream of reporters came by to try to catch a glimpse of Jimmy, and get him to say a few words. The lucky few who did all wound up filing essentially the same story, the fish-out-of-water celebrity angle, with Jimmy modestly insisting he was "just one of the boys."

As these first weeks passed, he began to sense that something was wrong, that he was being given an especially easy pass through his basic training, that he was little more than a celebrity recruitment poster boy.

---

2. At this time, the Air Corps was not a separate branch of the military, but the flying division of the army. It was officially known as the Army Air Corps until 1947, when it became the United States Air Force, an independent branch of the United States Armed Forces.

It was a situation that reminded him of the plot of *Mr. Smith Goes to Washington,* only this time he was being made to play the dupe in real life. Even when it seemed every other soldier he knew was being assigned to immediate overseas duty, he remained stateside. With an increasing steadiness, he began to return to Los Angeles, in civilian clothes, to hang out with his friends and occasionally drop by the studio to see what was happening.

Meanwhile, the Hollywood PR machine rolled on. In April, Jimmy's salary, it was reported, had gone from a princely $3,000 a week to a soldierly $21. The facts, however true, were embellished with the "scoop" that every week he sent Leland Hayward a check for $2.10, representing his agent commission on the new salary. Cute, patriotic, and utterly false. Nevertheless, the army made sure the note to which Jimmy supposedly attached his first check somehow found its way into the national press:

> *Dear Leland:*
>
> *Enclosed find $2.10 which is commission owed you by me from my salary of the month just passed. Leland, I would like to go into a little matter with you. Matters have come to such a point that I must get in touch with you about the situation in the thing I am doing now.*
>
> *Now, Leland, you know me, I never complain about anything and no matter what the conditions are I don't make a fuss; but just go along and make the best of things without a kick. You know that Leland, and I don't think you could say that since you have been my agent, I have made unreasonable demands or in any way gotten that—that—well—star complex. I hate to use the word "star" because you know how I hate that word.*
>
> *But, Leland, to get to the point, I am not happy in this thing I am doing now. This is for several reasons. Now they seem very small unimportant reasons, but I assure you they are not, because you know me, Leland. I don't let little petty things bother me like some actors and actresses I could name. Now I'll just take one of those reasons I'm unhappy. Well—it's the dressing room they have given me over here. It's a great big barn of a place, but I wouldn't mind that because you know me, but the thing is that they have*

*put 30 guys in here with me. Thirty guys, Leland. I don't know
who they are—they aren't actors—and they have brought beds in
here and are lying around. I don't know. I was treated much better
than this when I was over at Warner Bros.*

*You can say what you want to, Leland, you have to put up a
front in this business . . . now the other reason is a bigger reason,
Leland. It's about the salary you got me for this job. Just look at the
commission I have enclosed—and think it over—two dollars and
10 cents!!! Now I could go up to the front office and raise hell
myself, but I remember when I signed with you, you said that any
time I had any problem to just come to you and you would go up
and talk to them about it, and get it straightened out. So I hope
you will attend to this at once.*

Well, fellow, I'll see you soon. Your client and pal.

JIMMY STEWART

The widespread May publication of the "note" turned Jimmy's personal irritation into a full-blown rash of annoyance, and a nasty one at
that, especially since it was most likely written by MGM's PR department, or the army, or even, possibly, Hayward himself, as part of some
overall plan to publicize and exploit Jimmy during his military service.

That June, he attended a party at Judy Garland's house.

Over Christmas he was given a two-week leave, when he went to
L.A. and stayed with the Fondas (Henry was also on leave); he dressed
up as Santa Claus on the big day to entertain the Fondas' two young
children, Jane, four, and Peter, a tender one.

In September, he was given special permission to travel to Indiana,
Pennsylvania, to appear at a weekend benefit for the Allied Relief Fund,
where he performed some magic tricks with childhood friend and
now professional magician Bill Neff. The local press had a field day, but
Alexander was not pleased that Jimmy had performed out of uniform. It
was, in fact, hard to catch Jimmy anywhere in his military uniform, a
conscious decision he made in the hopes that it would lessen the bar-
rage of photographers who were always skulking, hoping to get a PR
shot of him decked out in full military regalia. Not long after, Alexander
and Bessie came to California, to Moffett Field for a visit, and over
dinner Alexander pulled out a photo that he had ripped from the local

Indiana newspaper showing Jimmy in civvies at a local Hollywood nightclub with actress Frances Robinson. Despite his protest that the girl was an MGM starlet and that he had been asked by the studio while on leave to accompany her for the evening, Alexander was not satisfied. This was not soldiering, he told his son. It was something, but not soldiering, at least not the Stewart-Maitland way.

In December, he was ordered by the army to participate with Edgar Bergen and Charlie McCarthy, Orson Welles, Edward G. Robinson, Walter Huston, and Lionel Barrymore in an all-networks live radio propaganda broadcast entitled "We Hold These Truths." Ostensibly to commemorate the hundred and fiftieth anniversary of the Bill of Rights, it really was to focus the nation's anger on the Japanese for the bombing of Pearl Harbor and rally a united domestic front to support America's entrance into World War Two. Jimmy's contribution to the show came down to these words, referring to the famous McCarthy marionette: "In our efforts to make the Army Air Corps the finest in the world, we've enlisted men from the backwoods. We've enlisted men from the front woods. But this is the first time we've ever enlisted the woods themselves." Despite the frivolity of his comments, he was quite moved by the show's overall theme and he reportedly broke down in tears after it was broadcast.

In January 1942, a month after the Japanese attack, Jimmy attended a birthday party at Hollywood's famed Roosevelt Hotel in honor of President Roosevelt. Because it was now officially wartime, he was instructed by the army to show up in full military regalia and ordered to have his picture taken by any and all reporters present. The next day it was plastered on the front page of dozens of newspapers across the country.

That same month Jimmy received his commission as a second lieutenant, Army air force.

On February 26, 1942, he was asked by the Academy to present the Best Actor award at the upcoming annual Oscars ceremony. The organization's president, Walter Wanger, made one special request—that he show up in uniform. He felt he had no choice but to comply, amid a couple of other side skirmishes already taking place that night. The first was the battle between Joan Fontaine (nominated for Best Actress, Alfred Hitchcock's *Suspicion*) and her sister Olivia de Havilland (nominated for Best Actress, Mitchell Leisen's *Hold Back the Dawn*). This was one fight that Stewart was loath to take sides in. The other, even bigger story, at least within the walls of the studios, was between William Randolph Hearst and Orson Welles over the fate of *Citizen Kane*. Hearst, having failed to buy back the negative to destroy it, was threatening not only to withhold any advertising for the film in his all-powerful news organization, but to ban all ads from the studio, something that could conceivably bankrupt RKO.[3]

Amidst these internecine struggles, no one, it appeared to Jimmy, had any concern or made any reference to the war. The Academy had decided a banquet was perhaps not the best format in light of the current events, and wanted to avoid making it appear that Hollywood was fiddling while Hawaii burned. At the last minute, the banquet was called a dinner, and everything else went on as if Hollywood operated in a cultural vacuum. Once again, the site was the Biltmore Bowl, with Bob Hope officiating.

Jimmy appeared in full dress uniform, down to the same necktie he wore every time he flew, an old superstition that remained with him for the rest of his life. He was at the Biltmore only a few minutes when he ran into his pal Burgess Meredith, who, as it turned out, was Olivia de Havilland's official escort that evening. When Burgess told him he was being inducted into the army the following morning, Jimmy broke into a huge grin, shook his hand, and congratulated him. Only then did he turn and nod once, wordlessly, to de Havilland.

When it was Jimmy's turn to give out an award, traditionally announced by the previous year's winner, he strode up to the podium and received a standing ovation. Once the applause subsided, he quickly opened the envelope, looked up and out into the audience, and announced that Gary Cooper had won the Best Actor Oscar for his role as the reluctant war hero in Howard Hawks's *Sergeant York*. Not lost on Stewart was the confluence of ironies, as precisely overlapping as the rhythm section of an army band. Hawks's movie saluted a World War One draftee, played by Gary Cooper, a real-life civilian actor who had never served a day in the military now being awarded

---

3. Fontaine won over her sister, de Havilland, intensifying the sibling rivalry between the two that would last a lifetime. The winner of Best Picture of the year was John Ford's *How Green Was My Valley.*

for playing a soldier by a real-life one who was a temporarily side-lined actor.

Following Cooper's "aw shucks" acceptance speech, the two men walked off the stage, both of them forgetting to take the Oscar with them.

— • —

For the rest of 1942, Jimmy did little more than make personal appearances as required by the army—most of which took place in Hollywood, which was why, instead of assigning him flight duty over-seas, the powers-that-were stationed him in Stockton, California, at the military air field. On March 15, he appeared on a radio program called "Plays for Americans" broadcast nationally on NBC, in which he played a soldier who writes back home to his family to explain to them why he was fighting in a far-off land. Again, the irony was almost too much for Jimmy to bear. On April 4, he narrated an episode of the weekly war documentary *This Is War* on the radio.

In April, he was transferred to Mather Field, near Sacramento, California, for further classes in flight training. However, his duties were kept minimal, as the army still considered him a major PR tool. At some point while at Mather Field, before he made the actual move, he spoke at length to Leland Hayward about the increasing frustrations of being used as a military figurehead. Leland happened to know a couple of senior Air Corps officers, who in turn went to Gen. Kenneth McNaughton, who then helped arrange for Jimmy to be transferred from Mather to the Kirtland Bombardier Training School in Albuquerque, New Mexico, where he would have the opportunity to do hands-on training for bombardier students.

Throughout this time, Jimmy continually made visits to the Los Angeles home of Leland Hayward, Margaret Sullavan, and their newborn baby. One evening Hayward invited Dinah Shore to join them for dinner. A pop crooner and a minor movie star, she had become involved with the Hollywood Canteen, a social hangout for GIs frequented by celebrities who did all the serving. A romance between Shore and Jimmy began that night, serious enough for Shore to begin making regular visits to his base, often staying at a nearby hotel with him. Friends later reported that Stewart had intended to marry Shore in Las Vegas during an upcoming weekend leave, but supposedly when they got as far as Highway 15, the main link between L.A. and the gambling mecca, he got cold feet and called off the ceremony.[4]

In July, he appeared in the first of two military-funded propaganda shorts, *Winning Your Wings,* an Army Air Force training film made by the First Motion Picture Unit of the army, produced by Warner Bros. and the War Activities Board of the Motion Picture Industry, aimed at recruiting young men. Colonel Henry "Pop" Arnold, who would later become the Air Corps chief of staff, credited Jimmy's performance in the film with helping to recruit more than a hundred thousand enlistees. One of the technical advisors on it was a young actor Jimmy had gotten to know a little in Hollywood. His name was Ronald Reagan.

The second film, *Fellow Americans,* recapped the attack on Pearl Harbor, meant to remind America of why it had gone to war. By this time, Stewart was totally fed up with what he felt was the army's endless exploitation of him. When he had the opportunity during filming to speak directly with Colonel Arnold, he was, for once, told the truth: the War Department thought the actor too big a risk to send into action. Should anything happen to him, it could demoralize the entire nation. This filled Jimmy with an even deeper despair. He decided to make one last, desperate appeal to his commanding officer, who listened patiently at his desk as Jimmy stood before him and poured out his heart.

At the end of their meeting, Colonel Arnold promised the actor he would not have to make any more public-relations appearances. He kept his word; from that point on, Jimmy was not seen or heard again in any army promotional vehicles for the duration of the war. To underscore that promise, he personally assigned Jimmy to Hobbs Field, New Mexico, to learn how to fly the B-17 Flying Fortress and B-24 Liberator. Only those sent overseas were trained on these heavy bombers. Many

---

4. Later on, while Stewart was overseas, he reportedly received a "Dear John" letter from Shore, who had met actor George Montgomery and had decided to marry him instead. Actor Burgess Meredith dismissed the entire romance as the type of relationship soldiers often had during wartime, when they believed anything they did might also be the last thing they did, and Stewart apparently did not want to die in combat without having at least gotten married. Others insist that it was Hayward who had arranged the whole thing, hoping to spark a romance between Shore and Stewart. Still others have suggested it was Shore who first asked Hayward to invite her to dinner so she could meet the actor she found irresistibly handsome.

of those Jimmy trained with went directly into combat and died. The list of casualties was filled with men he'd gotten to know, men he'd personally taught how to fly the war machines. It unnerved him to the point where, despite the fact that he hadn't been inside any house of worship for years (except for weddings), he began attending regular Sunday-morning Protestant services.

He was officially billed as "Lieutenant James Stewart" on July 20, 1942, when the army granted him permission to reprise his role in *The Philadelphia Story* along with Cary Grant and Katharine Hepburn, as part of a "special victory show" radio version of the hit movie. Jimmy believed it would be his last acting assignment before being sent overseas, though instead of a combat assignment, he was sent to Gowen Field in Boise, Idaho, to instruct pilots of the 52nd Squadron of the 29th Bombardment Group. Filled with despair, Jimmy called Colonel Arnold, who told him he was being classified as "static personnel," army lingo for designated stateside duty. The truth was, the colonel told him, even if he wasn't going to be used for propaganda purposes, he still was far too valuable to the morale of the country to be sent into combat.

— • —

And then, in August, everything changed. Col. Robert Terrill, Commanding Officer of the 445th Bombardment Group (Heavy), a squadron that had been formed only four months earlier, was looking for a new squadron operations officer good enough to be able to lead his men into combat and get them home safely, even if their planes were hit. Colonel Arnold called Colonel Terrill, who was a close friend, and told him Captain Stewart was, without question, the best qualified man for the job. Not long after, Jimmy was officially transferred to the 445th, based in Sioux City, Iowa, and began preparations for active duty. A few weeks after his arrival in Sioux City, he had impressed Colonel Terrill enough to be placed in command of the 703rd Bomb Squadron division, consisting of a dozen B-24 bombers and 350 soldiers and fliers.

In October, just weeks before he was scheduled to leave the country, Jimmy received a surprise visit at Sioux City from his parents, Alex and Bessie. Unspoken words between father and son made it a difficult time but one that meant everything in the world to Jimmy. On the last day of their visit, just as he was preparing to leave for the airport, Alex handed his son a letter. That night, alone in his bunk, he read it. "My dear Jim boy," it began. "Soon after you read this, you will be on your way to the worst sort of danger. I have had this in mind for a long time and I am very much concerned . . . but Jim, I am banking on the enclosed copy of the 91st Psalm. The thing that takes the place of fear and worry is the promise of these words. I feel sure that God will lead you through this mad experience . . . I can say no more. I only continue to pray. Good-by, my dear. God bless you and keep you. I love you more than I can tell you."[5]

It was the first time his father had ever actually told Jimmy that he loved him. When he finished the letter, he cried himself into a deep and fitful sleep.

In November, Jimmy was given his first flying assignment. He was ordered to take his squadron on a B-24, a four-engine bomber nicknamed Liberators by the aces of the U.S. Army Eighth Air Force "Liberator" division, to Brazil, for an advanced training mission. Just before he left, Jimmy was given a three-day pass. He flew to Hollywood to visit with Clark Gable, whose wife, Carole Lombard, had been killed the previous January, along with her mother, when her plane crashed shortly after takeoff, following a war bond drive in Las Vegas. Gable was so grief-stricken that he had enlisted in the air force, graduated Officer's Training School (OTS), and was determined to see action, despite the fact he was forty-one years old. He and Jimmy spent a long night together, one that began at Chasen's and ended at Gable's estate, where Jimmy comforted and encouraged Gable, wishing him luck on his upcoming combat assignment, all the while wondering when his own time would come.

Upon his return to the base, Jimmy flew to Brazil. From there he flew the squadron to Great Britain, to join the more than 350,000 American military men and women already stationed there. Just before boarding, a reporter for the *Los Angeles Times* caught up with what he described as a "shy and taciturn" Stewart, who apologized but insisted he was "unavailable for an interview."

5. 91st Psalm: I will say of the Lord, He is my refuge and my fortress . . . His truth shall be thy shield and buckler. Thou shalt not be afraid for the terror by night; nor for the arrow that flieth by day; . . . For he shall give his angels charge over thee, to keep thee in all ways. They shall bear thee up in their hands, lest thou dash thy foot against a stone."

He arrived in Great Britain on November 25, 1942, and was immediately besieged by the British press, which was given full access to the American base. He and every other soldier had been ordered by the army to remain totally cooperative. "I found that infinitely more nerve-racking than the actual duties I understood I was to carry out on bombings. I used every trick in the book to escape them. I had a very kind and understanding senior officer who kept me in the air so much that those intruders came to seem like tiny specks down there on land."

A week later, the 445th joined up with the 454rd and 379th at the Allied air base at Tibenham, a small village in Norfolk about a hundred miles northeast of London that was to become the permanent base for Stewart's squadron. As the commander of a B-24 Liberator, Jimmy believed he was certain to see action, as every one of every four raids over Europe came out of one of these three squadrons.

Eventually, the British press picked up on his reluctance to serve as the army's PR person and spun it to their best advantage. Screaming front-page headlines told the British people that, despite their best efforts, Captain Stewart "JUST WANTS TO DO HIS JOB!" This headline quickly reached America and soon, much to his surprise, the British and U.S. papers were flooded with sympathetic letters from civilians asking that Stewart be given a break and left alone. Nonetheless, the army, angered by what it felt was an unnecessarily uncooperative officer, insisted that he and all others continue to meet with and answer questions from the press. Jimmy did as he was told.

1942 turned into 1943, and still he continued to wait. Nearly a year passed while he performed practice runs and training during the day and listened to the report of distant bombs being dropped on England by the Germans while the Allies drove the Axis land forces from Northern Africa and slowly back to Germany.

Finally, on December 19, 1943, two years and nearly two weeks after Pearl Harbor, and four years after World War Two had officially begun, Jimmy was assigned to his first actual combat mission. To celebrate the occasion, Captain James Stewart, of Hollywood, was introduced to the London press at the Officers' Club 8th Air Force Headquarters, against a background of deep leather lounge chairs, chefs, ham and roast-beef sandwiches, and double sherries—surely not the normal fare for either enlisted men or officers. According to the *New York Herald Tribune*, present among the press were three young British "women reporters." One, a young woman "in a tweed jacket, gray skirt, mauve scarf and pork-pie hat, leaned close and rolled her gray eyes. 'Oh Captain,' she purred. 'You do look sunburned.'

"At that point Colonel John Hay Whitney, of the 8th Air Force Public Relations Staff, rose and cleared his throat: 'It is my pleasure, ladies and gentlemen, to present to you Captain Stewart.' "

Jimmy, squirming in his seat, crossed and uncrossed his legs several times, said a few words, and then asked for questions. The session ended after virtually every inquiry imaginable was asked, not about the war but about Hollywood. Would he return to pictures, did autograph seekers bother him? What was it like to kiss a movie star?

None of the navigators, copilots, enlisted gunners, or radio men who would fly on Captain Stewart's first combat mission had been invited to the affair.

One day later, on December 20, 1943, Jimmy led the 445th on a blistering all-out attack on the German port cities of Bremen and Kiel. They were met with strong aerial resistance from the German Luftwaffe, and, after several passes, Jimmy led his men on a daring midnight raid as part of a double American offensive against Germany that originated simultaneously from both England and Italy. The cluster of planes from England succeeded in shooting down between about fifty enemy aircraft in what was later described as dozens of "blazing dogfights" that left Bremen in flaming ruin. The Allied forces, in turn, lost twenty-five bombers. A Nazi rocket missed Jimmy's plane by twenty feet. He could still hear the buzz in his ears as he landed safely back in England early the next morning.

Stewart's next mission was set for January 7, 1944. He spent a sleepless night-before rereading the 91st Psalm that his father had given him. The next day he took it along on the squadron's bombing of Ludwigshafen.

On the return flight, one of his fliers broke rank. Stewart went on his radio to try to bring him back, an act that violated the mandatory silence for all squadrons actively engaged in combat. *Padlock Red Leader to Padlock Green Leader . . . Padlock Red Leader to Padlock Green Leader . . .* When the other pilot did not get back on course, insisting *he* was on the right path and the rest of the squadron was off, Stewart signaled the other fliers to fall in line with Padlock Green Leader. "We're sticking with you," Jimmy told him over the radio.

The Luftwaffe picked up their tail from the radio and set about to wipe them out. Twenty-eight miles south of Paris, sixty Messerschmitt and Focke-Wulfs came straight on toward Jimmy's squadron and launched a vicious attack. The first of Stewart's men to be shot down was the same pilot who had taken them off course. A badly shaken Stewart, who watched helplessly as the plane fell in a dark downward plume, managed to lead the rest of his men safely back to England.

On a subsequent assignment, Jimmy's plane was hit with direct flak, just behind the nosewheel. His ship's tail shot up in the air and his fuselage cracked open like an egg. He nonetheless managed once again to get back to base safely, crash-landing left onto the runway and leaving aluminum skid marks behind him. No one believed anyone could have survived that landing.

Including Jimmy. Although he walked away without a scratch, the mission had instilled in him a fear he could not easily shake. The night before another particularly dangerous run, he lapsed into a fit of panic. Unable to sleep, he broke out in cold sweats, believing he would not survive that attack. As he later recalled, "I was really afraid . . . our group had suffered several casualties even before I knew I was going to have to lead the squadron deep into Germany . . . I feared the worst. Fear is an insidious and deadly thing. It can warp judgment, freeze reflexes, breed mistakes. And worse, it's contagious. I felt my own fear and knew that if it wasn't checked, it could infect my crew members."

As 1944 began, Stewart continued to lead missions over occupied France and the German mainland. Reporters had not been able to find out much from or about him once this round of missions had begun. According to the *Los Angeles Times,* war correspondents had "braved mud and the commanding officer at the Liberator base in pursuit of the elusive Jimmy Stewart, but not one so far has come within sight of him," although one unidentified wingmate did report on the physical condition of the actor. "If you think he is skinny in the movies, you ought to see him now."

In mid-January, he led a bombing raid on Frankfurt, followed in February by raids on Nürnburg and Galze Rigen, Holland. On February 20, he led an attack on Brunswick that took down six German fighter planes. Three of his squadron's planes were shot down during the dogfight; twenty-seven crewmen reported missing in action; four casualties accounted for.

On nights he wasn't engaged in combat, he occasionally played the piano at the Officer's Club. One who got closer to him than most was a young staff sergeant who went to all the briefings just to listen to Jimmy deliver them. "I watched the way the crews would relate to him. They used to relate to him as a movie star for a while then they'd forget about all that and realize he was one of the boys. He was marvelous to watch." The sergeant was a young, unknown, wanna-be New York actor by the name of Walter Matthau.

— • —

Jimmy was at the Officer's Club one night when he received word that he was being promoted to full major, and also that he was going to be one of the leaders of the much-anticipated obliteration-bombing of Berlin.

On March 22, 1944, Jimmy led the 445th on a mission to take part in the bombing of Berlin. He returned unscathed, only to find out that his days with the 445th had come to an end. Just before he had taken off, news came down that Col. Joseph A. Miller, commander of the 453rd, had been shot down in Fredershafen, Germany. His replacement, Col. Ramsay Potts, was given a free hand in putting together his squadron, and Jimmy was among the first he took.

On April 8, Major Stewart received the Air Medal in recognition of the ten successful missions he had flown into Germany.

On April 12, at his insistence, after being promoted to operations officer for the new 453 Squadron, he was assigned to lead a group of Liberators over Oberpfaffenhofen.

The night before the mission, he sat alone in the half-empty combat mess. Thirteen crews had failed to return that day. Alone with his thoughts and his fears, he wandered about in his small, cold, blacked-out headquarters, scooping what little coal was available into his iron stove. In the morning, he knew he was going to lead his squadron deep into enemy territory, accompanied for only part of the journey by cover, or protection planes. For the rest of the mission there would be nothing but the bloodred, puke gray, and shit brown color-of-death curtain of firepower that would rain down on his men from the barrel-chested FW-190s that the German fighter pilots were so proud of.

Jimmy slumped at his desk, wary and afraid, once again certain he would not survive the onslaught.

Outside, Jimmy could hear an engine growling to a roar, then subsiding into quiet as a night maintenance crew tested it for the upcoming mission.

"I turned off the desk lamp, and my chair scraped the cement floor as I pushed it back. Walking to the window, I pulled back the blackout curtains and stared into the misty English night. My thoughts raced ahead to morning, all the things I had to do, all the plans I must remember for any emergency. How could I have a clear mind if I were saturated with fear? What was the worst thing that could possibly happen? I asked myself. A flak-hit in the bomb tray? A fire in one of our wing tanks? A feathered propeller on a damaged engine that would bring the enemy fighters swooping in (they always singled out a crippled bomber)? One by one I hauled my worst fears out of the closet, as it were, and tried to face up to them. Was that the best way to conquer them? I wasn't sure.

"Closing the curtains, I returned to my desk, snapped on the light and pulled out a notebook. I began writing out a list of emergencies and how I would handle them. Everything I could think of. *If our ship is mortally hit, I will try to get the crew out before I bail out—provided it doesn't blow up first. If I'm shot down and captured, I will reveal nothing but my name, rank and serial number.* On and on all the grim possibilities.

"Finally I finished writing and walked over to my metal cot. The springs creaked protestingly as I sat down. I stared unseeingly across the room. The deep-rooted fear was still there. It wouldn't go away.

"I thought of my grandfather, who had fought in the Civil War, and my father, who had served in both the Spanish-American War and in the First World War. 'Were you afraid?' I'd asked as a youngster back in Indiana, Pennsylvania, when we talked about Dad's experiences in France. I could remember the faraway look in his eyes as he nodded. 'Every man is, son,' he said softly. 'Every man is.' But then he would always add something else. 'Just remember that you can't handle fear all by yourself, son. Give it to God. He'll carry it for you.'

"Somewhere on a distant farm a cock crowed; dawn would be early. I got up and once more drew back the blackout curtains. The mist had cleared and above the dark trees the sky was sparkling with stars.

"I had no illusions about the mission that was coming up . . . I had done all I could. I had faced each fear and handed it over to God. And now, no matter what might happen, I knew that He would be with me. In this world or the next."

He was. Jimmy returned safely and on May 3, Major Stewart was personally awarded the Distinguished Flying Cross by the legendary James Doolittle for his leadership in the American air raid on Brunswick in February. The accompanying citation read as follows:

✪

AWARD OF THE DISTINGUISHED FLYING CROSS TO MAJOR JAMES MAITLAND STEWART, 0-433210, Army Air Forces, United States Army. For extraordinary achievement, while serving as Deputy Leader of a Combat Wing formation on a bombing mission over Germany, 20 February, 1944. Having been briefed for instrument bombing with condition that should visual bombing be possible the deputy leader would assume command, the formation proceeded to the target, meeting heavy enemy fighter opposition. When the target was reached, it became apparent that visual bombing was possible and Major Stewart smoothly assumed the lead position.

In spite of aggressive fighter attacks and later heavy, accurate antiaircraft fire, he was able to hold the formation together and direct a bombing run over the target in such a manner that the planes following his were able to release their bombs with great accuracy. The courage, leadership and skillful airmanship displayed by Major Stewart were in a large measure responsible for the success of this mission.

Entered Military service from California.
By command of Lieutenant General Doolittle

✪

At Jimmy's request, no press was allowed to witness the ceremony. Afterward, he arranged to have the Distinguished Flying Cross sent to his father, in Indiana.[6]

On June 3, he was promoted to the rank of lieutenant colonel. His first order of business was to brief his squad for what their support role was to be in the historic Allied invasion of occupied France.

On his next assignment leading bombers into the heart of Berlin, a cadre of Luftwaffe put up a fierce battle that lasted for hours. When he

---

6. Jimmy was only the second flier in World War Two to receive this honor.

finally returned to the base, Stewart, although physically unharmed, got out of his plane and collapsed to the ground.

It was to be his last mission.

Although no official records reported it, according to General Arnold, "they shot [his men up] pretty badly. It wasn't ever official, but I just told him I didn't want him to fly any more combat. He didn't argue about it."

His nerves shot, his confidence shattered, Stewart experienced something as close to a nervous breakdown as a soldier gets, a condition commonly referred to as shellshock. He spent several weeks in a hospital suffering from emotional trauma, until his military doctors felt he was well enough to be released.

For the duration of the war, he remained grounded in Great Britain, conducting briefings while serving as wing operations officer and chief of staff. He never again flew into battle.

On May 7, 1945, the war in Europe officially ended. The next day, Stewart was awarded the prestigious Croix de Guerre from Lieutenant Gen. Martial Valin, chief of staff for the French Air Force, in a ceremony held in England. Among the American soldiers in attendance was Clark Gable, who, afterward, spent about an hour with Stewart in private, sharing stories about the war. Three days later, General Arnold was promoted to chief of staff of the Second Air Division, and gave Stewart the privileged position of command of the wing. It was an honor, if totally ceremonial, and one that the general felt Stewart had earned. That summer, along with twenty-eight thousand other American veterans of war stationed in England, he was given an honorable discharge and put aboard the *Queen Elizabeth* bound for America.

His adjustment back to civilian life was not easy. He took all due pride in having established himself as a Stewart-Maitland warrior, but had not counted on the bad dreams that kept coming, in the dead of night. Back in the States, he refused to talk about the war to reporters, answer any questions about his own experiences, the missions he flew, or his physical and emotional health. He also informed MGM that he would refuse to play soldiers in combat in any future films they might have planned for him. He also refused to allow the studio to make him the subject of any publicity stories or other promotional devices that in any way mentioned his service in the war. Privately, he told friends that he would never fly again, not as a pilot or, unless absolutely necessary, a passenger.

All he wanted now, he told Hayward, was to live a normal life. As Jimmy later remembered, from that point on "[Leland] was always trying to get me married. When I got back from the service, he came to me and said, 'Now look, you've been away for five years and the movie business is all changed and God knows what, you don't know what you're gonna do—what you ought to do is marry a rich girl and take it easy.'"

Stewart told a reporter from the *Hollywood Citizen-News* that he was eager to get back to the business of making motion pictures, but no movies about the war (not that MGM was banging down his door to put him, or any of the other aging actor veterans, on the big screen). "The country's had enough of them. I want to be in a comedy."

It took a year before he finally found one, a nice little laugher about suicide. In the script, hand-delivered to him by Frank Capra, the hero of the film decides to kill himself because he wishes he'd never been born. What could be funnier?

13

"*It's a Wonderful Life* sums up my philosophy of film-making. First, to exalt the worth of the individual. Second, to champion man—plead his causes, protest any degradation of his dignity, spirit, or divinity. And third, to dramatize the viability of the individual—as in the theme of the film itself. I wanted *It's a Wonderful Life* to say what Walt Whitman said to every man, woman, and babe in the world: 'The sum of all known reverences I add up in you, whoever you are . . .' I wanted it to reflect the compelling words of Fra Giovanni of nearly five centuries ago: 'The gloom of the world is but a shadow. Behind it, yet within reach, is joy. There is a radiance and glory in the darkness, could we but see, and to see we have only to look. I beseech you to look!'"

—FRANK CAPRA

"After World War II, Stewart somehow failed to regain his stride with critics and audiences. Although he wisely abandoned Leo and Lion for an ambitious fling with Frank Capra, his explosively emotional performance in *It's a Wonderful Life* was overlooked in a year galvanized by the classical grandeur of Laurence Olivier in *Henry V* and the sociological scope of William Wyler's timely *The Best Years of Our Lives*. As far as the critical establishment was concerned, Stewart was drifting more and more beyond the award-consideration pale to action pictures and wacky farce comedies."

—ANDREW SARRIS

*H*edda Hopper loved to tell this story about Jimmy Stewart and his battle experiences in World War Two: "In my files are copies of two telegrams that always amuse me. They were sent shortly after the German surrender in 1945. One from me to Alexander Stewart, Indiana, Pa., reads, 'Where is our Jimmy? Please wire me Hollywood collect.' The reply was, 'We don't know. If he does not show up soon, I may have to go after him myself. (Signed), Alex Stewart.'"

As much as he may have wanted to, there was no need for Alexander to rescue his son. He showed up that September in Indiana, on a brief stop-over on his way to Los Angeles. The entire town turned out to cheer for his hometown public appearance, after which the local newspaper called for him to run for governor.[1]

Three days later, a photo of him graced the cover of *Life* magazine.[2] It had been taken in Indiana by the magazine's legendary Peter Stackpole, who had covered the parade. In addition to the standard portraits, however, Stackpole wanted a more original, candid shot and asked if they might be able to go fishing together. Jimmy agreed, although he had never handled a fishing pole in his life. He quickly sent someone over to the hardware store for some tackle and the two went out in a boat on the small lake near the edge of town. As Stackpole snapped away, Jimmy became hopelessly entangled in his own line. Finally, ready for casting, he tossed it over the side and somehow managed to hook the photographer right under his left eye.

The magazine ran the standard photo of Jimmy posing on shore in his uniform.

— • —

By the time the magazine hit the newsstands, he was back in the warmth and comfort of Southern California. And, just as when Jimmy had arrived for the first time a decade earlier, Fonda was waiting at the station for his train to roll into Pasadena. This time, a handful of reporters had gathered for the occasion. "Hey Jimmy, where did you get the gray hair?" one shouted, to which he quietly and unsmilingly replied, "It got pretty rough overseas at times." Another apologized, warned he had a bad question, and asked if there was anybody "special" waiting for him. Again Jimmy answered with a grim, direct simplicity, "No. At least not yet. But you're right, it's a bad question."

---

1. Stewart's response to the local press was that he didn't think it was such a good idea. "It's only in pictures that I make a good office holder. I talk much too slowly for a politician." As for his being given a hero's welcome, he shrugged that off, too, reminding everyone that "thousands of men in uniform did far more meaningful things and got small recognition, if any."

2. *Life* Magazine, September 24, 1945.

After obligingly answering a few more, Jimmy tossed his duffel into Fonda's car and the two quickly drove off.

Jimmy's eight-room rented Brentwood house on Evanston was still occupied, but no longer by Burgess Meredith, who, upon being drafted himself in 1942, had subleased it to a single businessman. When Meredith was discharged, he married the actress Paulette Goddard and decided to buy a house to go along with his new life, letting the tenant remain. When Jimmy sent word that he was coming home, the tenant he had never met said he needed a few days to move out, and those "few days" stretched into three months, during which time Stewart stayed with the Fondas.

Henry and his wife, Frances, had built Tigertail, as they called their Dutch Colonial–style house just above Sunset Boulevard on Tigertail Road (a real "cat house," according to Jimmy). It was complete with a children's playhouse that was a miniature version of the main house, including a working fireplace, a refrigerator, and a record player. Tigertail was the perfect place for Jimmy to hang until his house was ready, with plenty of room and privacy while he contemplated the next phase of his life and career.[3]

Moving in with the Fondas proved providential for Henry, who had returned from the war far more depressed and insecure about his future in show business than Jimmy, whose presence helped cheer him, especially when several of the "boys" would come by for their weekly card game. John Ford was a regular, as were John Wayne and Ward Bond. Despite Fonda's lack of appreciation for the politics of Ford's "gang," and Jimmy's too for that matter, all of that was left at the door in favor of an evening of Pitch. They played it around a big card table in full movie-costume regalia, cowboy hats and gun holsters, with spittoons nearby. They'd light up stogies, take out their guns, lay them on the table and play as if they were in some local saloon, remaining in whatever character they had chosen to play for the entire night.

At Christmastime, Jimmy once again dressed as Santa Claus,

---

3. Jimmy loved being in a house with Fonda's children. Along with Johnny Swope and Josh Logan, he had agreed to be one of their three godfathers. On more than one occasion, Jimmy told Fonda that his home life was "just what I want in life, a family like that."

which Hank and Frances, as always, enjoyed as much as the children did. During the cool afternoons of the Los Angeles winter, Fonda and Jimmy loved to fly kites and reminisce about "the old days" or go to the golf course to try to improve their handicaps.

According to Hedda Hopper, who got the first in-depth postwar newspaper interview with Jimmy, every studio was "clamoring" for his services, eager to put the real-life war hero up on the big screen. In her nationally syndicated piece, she declared that "the whole town loves and admires him, and he can have had any picture he wants." As was usual with the machinery of studio-controlled gossip, the story also included the "news" that the "shy" Stewart (studio lingo for single and straight) was dating two actresses at the same time, Anita Colby and the luscious Martha Vickers, but that he slept alone in a large bed and always wore pajamas, both trousers and jacket.[4]

The truth about Jimmy's personal life and professional career was considerably more complicated than Hopper and MGM allowed the public to believe. To begin with, the status of his contract with MGM was unclear. Mayer let it be known, via Hopper, that although it had been voluntarily suspended by the studio while Jimmy was in the service (as a so-called favor to the star), he was willing to renegotiate it. In truth, he wanted to extend it in the studio's favor, with little in the way of a pay raise. Had he not suspended the contract, he would have had to make a brand-new and presumably far more expensive deal for Jimmy's postwar services. Mayer felt that he held all the cards. Like virtually every other prewar male movie star who had gone into the service, the five years spent away from the cameras had taken a visible as well as emotional toll. Those who went to war looking like young Adonises—the Clark Gables, the Henry Fondas, and the Jimmy Stewarts—all returned with the unspecified war marks of savagery on their faces. Gable, in particular, looked weathered and weary (the death of

---

4. Prior to being granted her interview, Stewart's advisors warned Hopper of the no-talk-of-war stipulation. The closest she got to discussing any of his military experiences was to break the news that he was planning to return to England at the completion of a memorial library being erected to honor the soldiers in his division who had been killed in action. When Hopper reminded Stewart that he was the last of the big-time Hollywood bachelors, he responded, "Frightening!"

Lombard written in every line that surrounded his sad eyes). Fonda had begun to lose his hair, the sockets of his eyes had hollowed, and his skin had taken on the consistency of a well-worn saddle.

Stewart's hair loss was even more dramatic, as if plucked out from the front strand by strand, accentuated by a washed-out grayness around the fringe. His face had tightened with age and was marked by the tension and fear of war; his eyes occasionally lapsed into a haunted stare. His body, though, like Fonda's (but unlike the paunchy Gable) was as lean as ever—he weighed the same 140 the day of his discharge he was supposed to have weighed the day of his induction. And these days if anyone had noticed that he was shouting a bit, they didn't mention it. He had lost some of his hearing as a result of all the bombs bursting he'd been exposed to on the many raids he'd led.

The studios, all too aware of what the country had been through, wanted to give audiences some escape from it. In that sense, Jimmy's mindset of not wanting to talk about his experiences as a warrior matched that of the moguls, only none of the veteran stars, including Jimmy, seemed especially predisposed or well suited to return to prewar everything-is-wonderful, isolationist comedies about an age of relative innocence that seemed lost now, forever.[5]

Even nights when he and Fonda, Bill Grady, and a couple of others would make the rounds of the nightclubs along the Strip, Jimmy appeared to have acquired a new wariness about being out in public, especially when women he didn't know approached. Grady took it as a look of loneliness, and determined to see if some "instant cure" might not make it go away, at least for a couple of hours. One night, when a provocative note was sent over to him by one of the local lovelies, complete with a request for an immediate answer, Jimmy turned to the waiter who had brought it and said, "Would you bring me a revolver, please?" tossing the note back at the silver tray on which it had arrived.

---

5. The most successful films used gunfights as a metaphor for battle or were new-style "psychological dramas," in which the damage of the war was brought home in less-direct fashion. Fonda's first film after three years of war duty was John Ford's *My Darling Clementine* (1946), the lyrical, if extremely dark, version of the famed gunfight at the OK Corral. Gable's was Victor Fleming's *Adventure* (1946), a noirish psychological drama co-starring Greer Garson, Hollywood's premier on-screen "war widow," a film best remembered for its memorable tagline that made oblique reference to the actor's wartime duty: "Gable's back and Garson's got him!"

— • —

Back in late 1944, while Jimmy was still stationed in England, Leland Hayward had sold his business, and its valuable A-list of movie stars, to Jules Stein and his burgeoning MCA talent agency. Stein had decided to try to expand his music management company into film production and needed a ready roster of top clients.[6] Hayward made the decision to leave Hollywood partly because his wife, Margaret Sullavan, had tired of the movie business (as had the business of her) and longed to return to Broadway, and partly out of a real fear that California was about to be bombed by the Japanese. When the opportunity came for Sullavan to star in *The Voice of the Turtle* and the show proved an enormous hit, running for more than a year, Hayward decided the time was right to divest himself of his West Coast affairs and relocate to New York City, to do business on Broadway and live in Connecticut.

Before he left Los Angeles, one of the last clients he had signed was the up-and-coming Gregory Peck, among the first of the new postwar crop of young, handsome male actors. Hayward had quickly secured a

---

6. According to Stein, quoted by Brooke Hayward in her memoir *Haywire*, "We bought his [Hayward's] agency in 1944 and his clients turned out to be our most important clients. He overshadowed everyone in the business . . . he was by far the outstanding man in the entire agency field in California." (See Notes for further information.)

According to Dennis McDougall, author of *The Last Mogul*, "For giving up his agency, Hayward got MCA vice presidencies for himself and Nat Deverich [his partner, after the death of Myron Selznick and Hayward's full acquisition of his agency], guaranteed by a ten-year employment contract calling for a base weekly salary of $500 plus half the commissions generated by every client the Hayward-Deverich Agency brought to MCA. Essentially, Hayward and Deverich didn't have to do anything for the next ten years to earn a minimum of approximately $100,000. In addition, MCA promised to help Hayward buy his Connecticut farm and a new home high up in the Coldwater Canyon section of Beverly Hills."

Hayward's client roster at the time of the sale included Myrna Loy, Greta Garbo, Judy Garland, Gene Tierney, Dorothy McGuire, Dame May Whitty, Ginger Rogers, Margaret Sullavan, Gail Patrick, Clifton Webb, Pat O'Brien, Andy Devine, Gregory Peck, Fredric March, Raymond Massey, Joseph Cotten, Van Johnson, Fred Astaire, Gene Kelly, Boris Karloff, Thomas Mitchell, Oscar Levant, David Niven, Barry Sullivan, Irwin Shaw, Dorothy Parker, Russel Crouse, Howard Lindsay, Edna Ferber, Lillian Hellman, Ben Hecht, Charles MacArthur, Dashiell Hammett, Waltern Van Tilburg Clark, Arthur Koestler, Walter de la Mare, Billy Wilder, Alfred Hitchcock, Arthur Hornblow Jr., Joshua Logan, Salvador Dali, Henry Fonda—and Jimmy Stewart.

one-picture deal for Peck at MGM, to appear in Tay Garnett's *Valley of Decision* (released in 1945). The success of that film led Mayer to offer Peck a seven-year exclusive contract, which Hayward advised Peck to turn down, which he did. Hayward believed, correctly, that exclusivity was a thing of the past, and that Peck should do what a lot of other newbies were doing, going freelance; picture-to-picture was where the real money was. A-liners working without exclusive contracts were routinely earning in the neighborhood of $750,000 a picture, not counting profit participation.

Mayer, in retaliation, barred Hayward from the studio's lot. When the time came, in the fall of 1945, for Jimmy to deal with Mayer's insistence on renegotiation, Hayward was, technically, no longer his agent; Jules Stein's MCA was. Nevertheless, Hayward participated indirectly, as "personal advisor," and informed Mayer, through Stein, that as far as he was concerned, there was nothing to negotiate. Forget about that "generous" suspension of time, Hayward said. Stewart's contract at MGM was up.

Mayer was furious. He had so magnanimously "suspended" Jimmy's contract for the five years during his military service so that it wouldn't run out while the actor was "away," as he liked to put it, and had recently on numerous occasions proclaimed publicly that he wanted to throw Jimmy a ticker-tape parade to celebrate his safe return (it never took place), while in private he insisted to Stein that James Stewart still belonged to MGM.

Bill Grady, meanwhile, told Jimmy off the record that Mayer was willing to forget the five suspended years that were technically left on Jimmy's original contract and that the president of the studio, Nick Schenck, had personally authorized a new deal at very favorable terms, but that it had to be for seven years. Jimmy, via Hayward, via Stein, said no. He insisted the money was far too low for a Best Actor Oscar winner. Schenck's best and final offer was $125,000 per picture, with a guarantee of one picture per year, no profit participation. Hayward considered that an insult, and indicative of the fact that MGM didn't really want Jimmy at all. At least not enough to pay him even close to what other stars were earning.

Mayer then pulled out all the vengeful stops. Articles began to appear in the studio-controlled "gossip" press about how much the actor had aged while being away, about the rumors of a "nervous breakdown" he had suffered as the result of combat, and, pointedly, that perhaps he had had it in Hollywood. One only had to look at how many of Stewart's prewar films had not made any money.

Among the most consistently negative of the studio mouthpieces was Jimmy's "friend" Hedda Hopper, who, at Mayer's directive, now wrote a series of "reports" about all the new faces in Hollywood, such as Van Johnson, whom she described as the new hot kid on the block, a cross between James Stewart and Gary Cooper, and younger by years than both. Mayer's campaign was effective. As a postwar freelancer, Jimmy did not make a movie for a year after returning home from the war.

Whenever he was asked about his absence from the screen, Jimmy would say only that he was thinking of leaving the film business altogether. In truth, he believed he could survive in Hollywood without ever shooting another foot of film. He had invested his earnings wisely, including buying part of Southwest Airways, a start-up venture of Leland Hayward's and his business partner Jack Connelly, with additional seed money from Cary Grant (whom Stewart had convinced to invest in the company while they were making *The Philadelphia Story*), Fonda, Johnny Swope (the company's secretary-treasurer as well as a flight instructor), songwriter and performer Hoagy Carmichael, and businessmen Gilbert Miller. As far as Stewart was concerned, if the film business didn't work out, he could pursue commercial aviation as a full-time occupation.

To stay active Jimmy starred in radio adaptations of several of his hit movies, a pre-TV style of home drama that had become the vogue. He did four the last two months of 1945 alone—*Destry Rides Again, No Time for Comedy, Vivacious Lady,* and *Made for Each Other,* plus one original script, *The Sailor Who Had to Have a Horse,* a noncombative comedy about a sailor whose shipmate was a palomino.

Then, in the winter of 1945, Frank Capra, also without a studio deal, decided to form his own production company and approached Jimmy about starring in an independent feature to be called *It's a Wonderful Life.*

— • —

Following the end of the war, Capra, like Jimmy, had not found a welcome committee for his services. His career had begun to stutter after he lost the Best Director Oscar for *Mr. Smith Goes to Washington,* his last picture for Columbia. He made only two more films before the war, both at Warner Bros., both in 1941: the dark, suicidal comedy/drama *Meet John Doe,* which starred Gary Cooper, and *Arsenic and Old Lace,* a drawing-room comedy about murderous aunts that starred Cary Grant (the release of which was delayed for two years due to contractual restrictions regarding the Broadway run: the movie could not open until the show closed). Underlying Capra's downturn was the fact that his dual roles as president of the Academy and head of the Directors Guild had, ultimately, backfired, leaving each side resentful of his role with the other. What's more, in the mushrooming chauvinism of America's suddenly united populace after Pearl Harbor, *Mr. Smith Goes to Washington,* and its star director, had lingered as more cynical than when it was first released, if not in the minds of general audiences then certainly with the studio heads (and, eventually, Congress), who wanted little to do with anything or anyone who had had something bad (i.e., anti-American, i.e., Communist) to say about how the government conducted its business.

Capra was not the only director, producer, or studio head to see the path of his career twisted by the war. Once America formally joined the Allied forces, the government wanted Hollywood to turn out fiercely anti-Axis films that would inspire not just those on the front (who were shown them regularly along with feature films) but their families back home, and it enlisted the services of some of the industry's most talented filmmakers, including Capra, John Huston, John Ford, Alfred Hitchcock, Anatole Litvak, Don Siegel, and the Walt Disney animation outfit.

Capra's six-part *Why We Fight* propaganda series, unsigned by the director, an enlistee given the rank of colonel for his filmic efforts, was among the most striking to come out of the war. And yet, upon receiving his discharge in 1945 and returning to Hollywood, Capra felt the distinct chill of the cold-war-conscious studios that had not forgotten what they considered the left-leaning politics of *Mr. Smith* or Capra's diminishing profit potential. In postwar America, no studio was sure if Capra was still employable, and none were willing to put up enough money to find out. The only real option the director had was to go into business for himself. "Four years ago Hollywood was my town," Capra wrote in his memoirs. "When I fiddled, people danced. I was president of everything. Now [after the war] the pip-squeaks with L.P.'s (Learners Permits) asked 'Frank *who*?'"

According to Capra, the idea to form an independent production company called Liberty Films had begun while he was still in the army. Working with other Hollywood pros to turn out propaganda movies, he'd started to think about what it would be like to commercialize this pool of talent, "uniting producer-directors in service into a post-war independent combine of independent filmmakers. The prime candidates were John Ford, Willie Wyler, George Stevens, John Huston, Garson Kanin, and Frank Capra." In 1945, Capra named himself president of Liberty Films. Its vice presidents were Wyler and Stevens, its secretary-treasurer was Samuel Briskin, and its trademark logo was the same shot of the cracked Liberty Bell that had adorned Capra's *Why We Fight* series.

After securing the right from RKO to use its facilities in return for a first look at anything he made, Capra put up $40,000 of his own money—each partner/investor was required to put up a proportionate amount, based on his stock holdings—(he was the company's largest share owner). He then began to search for what he considered the best commercial property he could get his hands on, a film that would provide the kind of escapist fare he believed audiences were looking for. He already had one piece, something whose working title was *The Flying Yorkshiremen,* that RKO wanted him to do, a film that would feature Barry Fitzgerald in the lead. Capra appeared willing to make it until Fitzgerald, for reasons that remain unclear, rejected the role (most likely political, as he was a Hollywood right-winger). Capra, through Liberty, then purchased a property called *It Happened on Fifth Avenue,* a comedy about a poor man who lives rich, which had been rejected by every studio because it was considered outdated, a Depression movie a decade too late. It went nowhere.

Charles Koerner, RKO's studio chief, suggested Capra look at a short story, "The Greatest Gift," based on a Christmas card that Philip Van Doren Stern had used as a private holiday mailing to his friends. RKO had purchased it for a relatively small amount, $10,000, with Cary Grant in mind for the leading role.[7] Trying to develop the story into a comedy, the studio had gone through several writers, including

---

7. According to film historian Jeanine Basinger, it was Cary Grant who first brought the project to Koerner.

Dalton Trumbo, Marc Connelly, and Clifford Odets, before Grant moved on and the film's development came to an end.

When Capra read it, he flipped. "It was the story I had been looking for all my life," he said later on. "Small town. A man. A good man, ambitious. But so busy helping others, life seems to pass him by. Despondent. He wishes he'd never been born. He gets his wish. Through the eyes of a guardian angel he sees the world as it would have been had he not been born. Wow!"

Capra paid RKO $50,000 for the rights to the story and made it Liberty Films Corporation's first official production. He then tried to sign Robert Riskin to write the script, but Riskin turned him down. He, too, had gone into business for himself and formed his own independent company. Capra's next choice was Sidney Buchman, who had written *Mr. Smith Goes to Washington,* but he was irrevocably tied to Columbia and Cohn would not allow him to work for Liberty. Capra eventually hired the writing team of Albert Hackett and Frances Goodrich and, with them in place, turned his attention to casting.

There was only one man he would even consider for the lead, and that, of course, was J.S.—"Jefferson Smith." Capra placed a phone call to Lew Wasserman, an agent at Stein's newly formed MCA-Universal. Wasserman, thus far unable to find any takers for Jimmy since the actor had gone freelance, told Capra that Jimmy, on Wasserman's advice, wouldn't even hear the story, because it sounded too confusing to him (Wasserman). Capra insisted he tell Jimmy about the movie in person, his own way. Wasserman finally agreed, if only to get rid of Capra, and set up the meeting.

Jimmy, however, was looking forward to working in movies again. While he'd been out flying kites with Fonda (until Fonda finally landed in Ford's *My Darling Clementine*), he felt more isolated and apart from the industry than ever. Indeed, several of the other "old-timers" who had returned to Hollywood and tried without success to go freelance had quietly re-signed with their former studios, churning out standard-issue contract-player pictures. Gable and Robert Taylor were the big two whom Mayer had successfully pressured into signing seven-year contracts.

Capra's enthusiasm about pitching directly to Jimmy was not the only reason he wanted a face-to-face. Rumors of the actor's wartime breakdown were everywhere, as was speculation that his absence from the movies was simply due to his not being ready to return to work.

Capra didn't believe it, but with his own company on the line, he wanted to see for himself that Jimmy was all right.

It was a shaky meeting, during which Capra stumbled his way through a story that made no sense and Jimmy said little, but after, he agreed to do the film. With Jimmy in tow as the hero, George Bailey, Capra now went after Jean Arthur to play Mary, George's high school sweetheart and eventual wife. Arthur, however, was in rehearsal for the Broadway show *Born Yesterday* and turned Capra down.[8] In retrospect, the failure to get Arthur was probably a good thing. The postwar James Stewart was no longer that same little boy with the cinematic (and real-life) adolescent needs as he was in *Mr. Smith*. The lack of chemistry between them would have likely ruined the film.

Capra then turned to Ginger Rogers, who said no, then de Havilland, who said no, then Ann Dvorak, who said no, then Martha Scott, who said no. He finally cast a relatively unknown twenty-four-year-old Donna Reed to play opposite the thirty-eight-year-old Stewart, after seeing her in John Ford's *They Were Expendable,* in which she played a wartime nurse. Prior to *Expendable,* she had appeared without much fanfare in nearly two dozen MGM films, including a couple of Dr. Gillespies, and an Andy Hardy.[9] What caught Capra's eye about Reed was her ability to project an intelligence that enhanced her slim body and wispy, wide-eyed face, with its beautiful dark eyes and hair. Despite her loveliness, there was a notable lack of heat about Reed, which had thus far prevented her from becoming a star. But it was just that coolness that Capra was looking for, as a contrast to Violet, the other woman in the film (and in George's life), the town "flirt," Hollywood cast-speak for slut. To find the right Violet, Capra turned to Bill Grady, who, when asked by the director if he knew of any actresses who could play that kind of a role, replied, "For crissake I'm up to here in blonde pussies!" The one who Capra chose was Gloria Grahame, an unknown who, like Reed, would emerge a star from *It's a Wonderful Life.*

---

8. Arthur would leave the production prior to its opening. She was replaced by an unknown actress by the name of Judy Holliday, whose performance in the play made her a star.

9. Harold S. Bucquet's *Calling Dr. Gillespie* (1943) and Willis Goldbeck's *Dr. Gillespie's Criminal Case* (1943) in the role of Nurse Marcia Bradburn, and as Melodie Eunice Nesbit in George B. Seitz's *The Courtship of Andy Hardy* (1942).

Filling out the principal cast was Lionel Barrymore as Mr. Potter, the skinflint and evil banker (borrowed from MGM), and Todd Karns as George's brother, Harry. For the rest of the townspeople, with few exceptions, Capra went to his regular "stock company" of players, including Thomas Mitchell, H. B. Warner, Beulah Bondi (again playing Stewart's mother), Frank Faylen, Sam Hinds, Mary Treen, and Frank Hagney. For the small but important role of the bartender, Capra used Sheldon Leonard, a newcomer to film who had made his reputation on Broadway as a "tough guy." And finally, for the key role of Clarence, George's guardian angel, Capra chose the lovably cartoonish Henry Travers.

Capra then went to work on the script, having seen during his pitch to Jimmy its many holes. Although it remains difficult to parse exactly who contributed what to the final shooting script, the film hardly resembles the original story. By the time Capra had finished with it, the film had turned into a modern retelling of Charles Dickens's *A Christmas Carol,* as if written by playwright Tom Stoppard, in the style of his *Rosencrantz and Guildenstern Are Dead,* in which audiences view Shakespeare's *Hamlet* from the perspective of two minor characters in the plays-within-a-play. In *It's a Wonderful Life,* Potter is the Scrooge-like character, but the story is told from the point of view of the Bob Cratchit figure, George Bailey, who, rather than Scrooge, is the one visited by "ghosts," in this case Clarence, and the one taken on the magic carpet ride to just-in-time redemption.

The story is a familiar one today, as the film has become a Christmas perennial on television. Only two other movies in Hollywood's history have remained as regularly revived, via annual TV playoffs—Victor Fleming's *The Wizard of Oz* (1939) and Cecil B. DeMille's *The Ten Commandments* (1956).[10]

The film opens at the gates of heaven, or so we are to presume from the shot of the diamond-and-black sky, where unearthly voices are in the midst of discussing the politics of how angels earn their wings. Clarence is then given the assignment of trying to save one George Bailey, who is about to commit suicide by jumping off a bridge, rather than face going to

---

10. The reason that today "children of all ages" know the names and faces of Judy Garland, Charlton Heston, and Jimmy Stewart over, say, Ginger Rogers, Victor Mature, and Clark Gable.

jail for embezzlement of funds from the family-owned Bailey Savings and Loan, a crime of which he is innocent and, through a series of unfortunate events, framed by his evil enemy, Potter. We learn via flashbacks and freeze-frames that George has a free spirit, and, while born and raised (and trapped) in the small town of Bedford Falls, he longs to see the world and take his place among the big-city boys as a professional architect. However, every time he is about to leave Bedford Falls, some disaster happens that keeps him from making his departure. It is as if some unearthly force has imprisoned him from which he cannot escape.

We follow George through his teens, his courtship and marriage to Mary (Donna Reed), and his restoration of an old house he dearly loves—itself a representation of the small-town life of Bedford Falls that is forever in danger of collapsing from the weight of economic development and profiteering under the greedy and illegal control of banker Potter (Barrymore). When George's simple-minded uncle (Mitchell) loses $8,000 in cash, which quickly falls into the hands of Potter (a crime that, by the way, goes unpunished), George is framed by Potter as an embezzler. With his arrest imminent, George becomes bitter and mean-spirited, gets into a fistfight with the husband of one of his daughters' teachers, and finally, alone and frightened on Christmas Eve, believing his life insurance policy will take care of the $8,000 shortfall with enough left over for his family, he decides he is worth more dead than alive. He staggers to the edge of town, stands on the bridge that he has never been able to cross over, the one that leads out of town, and jumps. Clarence then "saves" George and, to teach him a lesson, grants him his wish that he had never been born.

Clarence then takes George on a journey that revisits all the key events and the people involved in them whose lives he has, without realizing it, affected in so many ways. The lesson George (and the audience) learns is that his life was far more valuable to the townspeople, and therefore to himself, than he could ever have imagined. These scenes end with George at little Harry Bailey's grave, begging Clarence to give him back his life.

Having accomplished his mission, Clarence grants that wish. Snow begins to fall once more and Stewart retrieves from his pocket Zuzu Bailey's petals, which his daughter (Karolyn Grimes) had given him to hold for safekeeping, and which had disappeared when he no longer existed. Now they represent his return to life in the most dramatic and touching of ways. A triumphant George returns home, reunites with his family, and laughs at the prospect of going to jail. Just as things appear at their darkest, the entire town turns out with donations to save him. Finally, as George is holding Zuzu in his arms, surrounded by his friends and family, she tells him, "Every time a bell rings, it means an angel's got his wings." A book is found under the tree signed by Clarence with the inscription "No man who has friends is poor." A shot of bells ringing on the tree dissolve into the peal of the Liberty Pictures' logo of the Liberty Bell as the film ends.

It's a Wonderful Life opened in theaters on December 21 (at the Globe in New York City, and three days later at the Pantages in Los Angeles. The day after Christmas it went into nationwide release).[11] Reviews were mixed. The *New York Times* began its review with tongue firmly in too sugary a cheek when it said, "The late and beloved Dexter Fellows, who was a circus press agent for many years, had an interesting theory . . . that the final curtain of every drama, no matter what, should benignly fall upon the whole cast sitting down to a turkey dinner and feeling fine. Mr. Fellows should be among us to see Frank Capra's *It's a Wonderful Life* . . . He would find it very much to his taste . . . the weakness of the film is the sentimentality of it . . . a little too sticky for our taste . . ." The reviewer, the always pedestrian Bosley Crowther, did however, single out Jimmy for doing a "warmly appealing job, indicating that he has grown in spiritual stature as well as in talent during the years he was in the war." The *Hollywood Reporter* called it "just a wonderful picture." United Press's reporter wrote, "Never in all my years of covering Hollywood have I been so moved by a movie as by *It's a Wonderful Life*. The Capra film is the season's climax." The *New York Sun* called it movie-goers' "finest Christmas present." *Time* magazine declared, "Producer-Director Frank Capra and Actor James Stewart stage a triumphant Hollywood homecoming!"

Although it was not the complete box-office failure that today everyone believes it to have been, compared with Capra's earlier films, it was

---

11. The film's world premiere was a dinner-dance screening by invitation only, held at the Ambassador Hotel in Los Angeles, on December 9, 1946. The guest list of all the players and crew of the film also included Clark Gable, there in support of his friend Stewart, and one hundred other stars, all of whom had appeared, at one time or another, in a Capra feature.

a major disappointment and confirmed, at least to the studios, that Capra was no longer capable of turning out the kind of populist features that made his films the must-see money-making events they once were.[12] Moreover, the final budget of the film, originally set at $1.5 million, had ballooned to nearly $3 million (2.8), most of which came out of Capra's pocket. By the end of its initial 1946–1947 run, it had grossed a total of $3,300,000, a net loss of nearly $3 million.[13]

Nevertheless, the qualities of the film remain diamond bright. The entire structure may be seen as a recap of American movies itself, via a sentimental revisiting by Capra to his own career. In the first part of the movie, there is a high school dance in which the floor of the gymnasium opens wide and everyone falls into a hidden swimming pool. Shot on location at Beverly Hills High School, the entire sequence is reminiscent of Capra's (and Hollywood's) early silent comedies. The story then moves to an idealistic view of hope, as George prepares to enter "the real world." Here Capra recalls the populism of the thirties, followed by the run on the bank that takes the film to the far side of the Depression. The outbreak of World War Two becomes a reminder of Capra's (and Hollywood's) own experiences in making films about the war, and finally, George's descent into despair and darkness evokes the darker side of *Mr. Smith Goes to Washington* and forties film noir, with a climax that is, as critic Andrew Sarris noted, a "wildly melodramatic parable of near

---

12. *It's a Wonderful Life* received three Academy Award nominations (Best Picture, Best Actor, Stewart; and Best Director, Capra), but the awards all went to William Wyler's *The Best Years of Our Lives*. That film won Best Picture, Best Director, Wyler; and Best Actor, Fredric March. *It's a Wonderful Life* eventually made a $3 million profit by the end of its initial domestic release, and was the twenty-seventh highest grossing film of the year. (Nineteen forty-seven was not a good year for films; an unusually stormy winter kept ticket buyers at home.)

In its first week of domestic release, *It's a Wonderful Life* wound up ninth on the top ten grossing films. They were, in descending order, Alfred E. Green's *The Jolson Story*, George Seaton's *The Shocking Miss Pilgrim*, Richard Whorf's *Till the Clouds Roll By*, Robert Montgomery's *Lady in the Lake*, Richard Wallace's *Sinbad the Sailor*, Jean Negulesco's *Humoresque*, Clarence Brown's *The Yearling*, Wyler's *The Best Years of Our Lives*, Capra's *It's a Wonderful Life*, and John Farrow's *California*.

13. The film's break-even point for Capra's company was approximately 6.3 million dollars, double the production cost. In addition to shooting the film, Liberty's expenses included the manufacture of prints, newspaper and magazine advertising, coast-to-coast distribution (RKO), and exhibition—a large portion of admission went to the theater-owner or the distributor, often the same in the studio era.

crucifixion and redemption in the patented mode of *Mr. Smith* and *Meet John Doe*." Traces of Capra's cinematic brand of religiosity are scattered throughout the film, from the appearance of a guardian angel to the redemption of Violet, a rather transparent Mary Magdalene figure.

Without question, however, the single most remarkable aspect of the film remains Jimmy's performance, coaxed out of him by Capra, who, early on, became aware of the postwar differences in his favorite screen actor. "Jimmy didn't feel quite right being back in pictures. In the middle of *It's a Wonderful Life*, his first film after the war, he told me he thought maybe being an actor was not for decent people. That acting had become silly, unimportant next to what he'd seen [in the war]. He said he thought he'd do this picture and then quit."

A reporter on the set saw it differently. "Both Capra and Stewart are needlessly worried they might have lost the know-how during their military service. In consequence, the set of *It's a Wonderful Life* has hardly been a restful place. They worry about each other. 'There are two million dollars invested in this picture,' says Stewart. 'I just can't let Frank Capra down.' Capra, for his part, has been driving the not-unwilling ex-colonel without mercy, wringing the utmost out of him by methods that range from trickery to endless rehearsals. At times he has tossed Jimmy into scenes cold, saying, 'Make up your own dialogue as you go along. Just say whatever seems natural, the first thing that comes into your head.' In one of the longest, heaviest scenes in the picture, Jimmy, who plays the frustrated owner of a small-town building and loan company, is beating off with vigorous oratory the assault of depositors making a run on his company. To lend added realism, Capra, without warning, set off a fire siren in the midst of Stewart's speech. The startled cast abandoned Jimmy to rush to the windows to see the blaze, leaving him waving his long arms at their backs. Stewart gulped, matched the siren, roar for roar, and actually won his audience back while the camera ground on. Tactics like this have left Jimmy bushed, but they give him tremendous satisfaction. . . . His main regret is that he has to waste Sundays on relaxation."

The film spans George Bailey's life from a teenager to a middle-aged suicidal depressive. Approaching forty, Jimmy was able to effectively play a teenager, without spoof or farce, and make the transition to populist hero as a middle-aged man filled with despair. Sarris described this most remarkable performance as expressive of "the pain and sorrow so eloquently expressed. Stewart's angry, exasperated, anguished [marriage] 'proposal' to Reed is one of the most sublimely histrionic expressions of passion mingled with the painful knowledge that one's dreams of seeing the world outside one's small town were vanishing before one's eyes."

Despite its richly textured and thematic complexities, the film did not capture the imagination of the public and, despite its respectable numbers, was considered a failure at the time. Frank Capra Jr. offered this explanation as to what went wrong: "The film was released very late in the year, understanding that it was never intended as a 'Christmas or holiday picture.' RKO apparently had another film they had wanted for its big Christmas release that had run into technical problems.[14] *It's a Wonderful Life* was originally intended as a 1947 release, probably for the early spring. As a result, the film was rush-released, in time for Christmas, but actually missed getting wide release before the holiday. By then it had gotten the reputation of being a 'holiday' picture, and once January hits, they're as relevant as Christmas trees. So it didn't have very much time to find and build an audience, despite some pretty good reviews and an o.k. public response. I think coming out of the war, the audiences weren't expecting, or wanting this kind of a movie."

— • —

Even with the commercial and artistic success of the other picture Liberty had a financial interest in, William Wyler's *The Best Years of Our Lives*, the failure of *It's a Wonderful Life* put Liberty into bankruptcy and effectively ended Capra's film career. Into the fifties, he would be dogged by accusations of Communist sympathies by HUAC, and for the most part shunned by the paranoid heads of the crumbling Studio system for having led at one point or another the pro-union movement that, as they saw it, helped destroy Hollywood as they knew it.

As for Jimmy, he was both disappointed and disillusioned by the film's failure. He feared what one critic eventually wrote was true, that "it was when Stewart became too old to be fashionable he became too good to be appreciated."

---

14. Richard Wallace's remake of *Sinbad the Sailor,* delayed several months due to Technicolor processing problems.

14

Alexander Stewart: They had him out in Hollywood ten years, and none of the girls seem to like him, so I'm going to bring him home to marry a country girl. I can dig up a girl for him.

Jimmy Stewart (in response): I'll get married one of these days.

—WILLIAM MILLER, *PIC* MAGAZINE, NOVEMBER 1947

*F*ollowing the brief period of euphoria that came with the end of World War Two, Frank Capra's prediction that the American public would want escapist movies, which he actually believed *It's a Wonderful Life* was, proved not to be so. The new Communist occupation of Europe, the Rosenbergs spy case, and the so-called fall of China in 1949, all combined to introduce the notion of a cold war to American society that was soon reflected in the type of pictures Hollywood began to turn out. Themes such as anti-Semitism (Elia Kazan's *Gentleman's Agreement,* 1947, and Edward Dmytryk's *Crossfire,* 1947), wide-spread corruption (Robert Rossen's *Body and Soul,* 1947, and again in his *All the King's Men,* 1949), uncontrollable greed (John Huston's *Treasure of the Sierra Madre,* 1948), and social paranoia (Anatole Litvak's *The Snake Pit,* 1948) dominated the postwar big screen.[1] Even John Wayne, the cinematic strongman of World War Two, was not immune to the cultural shift, reemerging in 1948 in Howard Hawks's *Red River* as an aging, angry father figure, whose son, played by newcomer Montgomery Clift, was the first of the next generation of actors to personify the onset of what would later come to be known as the generation gap. Clift's pained, neurotic persona in *Red River* served as the linchpin for a group of Broadway-bred "sensitive" actors that included Marlon Brando and James Dean. Virtually every good-looking actor under thirty summarily rejected the stylis-

---

1. All were Oscar nominated for Best Film in their respective years of release.

tic acting ways of the Duke, and by extension the entire "Greatest Generation." The new breed could and would do things differently. It was the dawn of the Method, '50's Hollywood style, along with the youthful fervor of rock and roll and the paranoia spawned by the notorious blacklist, that, with the exception of Howard Hawks, damaged the careers of every one of the directors mentioned above, including Frank Capra.

All of which, following the commercial disappointment of *It's a Wonderful Life,* left Jimmy Stewart, for the moment cinematically adrift, occasionally touching shore in a stream of meaningless movies that the public reacted to with what at best may be described as indifference. Increasingly desperate for work, Stewart hoped MCA powerhouse Lew Wasserman could guide him back into the movie fast lane. Wasserman quickly managed to line up five films for Stewart, each one, notably, an independent production, and each with a different studio serving as distributor. The situation made it painfully clear to Jimmy (and Wasserman) that since his acrimonious split over his contract extension with MGM, the other studios were united with Mayer against him (and any actor who tried to thwart the hitherto ironclad system). While, clearly, the grip of the studios was beginning to weaken, with actors from Cary Grant to Bette Davis increasingly seeking their creative freedom by staying independent, Jimmy was different from them in that he *liked* the studio system. He had been discovered by it and depended upon it for his livelihood. He did not see himself as a rebel or a troublemaker. He simply wanted to work, but when the studios rejected him—for whatever reason, either solidarity with Mayer or, at least as likely, the difficulty in casting the once-tender, boyish leading man fast approaching middle age—he had no other choice but to join the growing ranks of the acting independents.

While Wasserman continued to try to line up films for him, Jimmy, on Hayward's advice, continued to make frequent goodwill public appearances in military uniform at such events as the Forest Lawn monthly sunrise services to honor the war dead. It wasn't until 1947, a full year after *It's a Wonderful Life,* that the first of Jimmy's Wasserman-generated movies finally made it to the big screen: William Wellman's *Magic Town,* made from a script by Robert Riskin for Wellman's newly formed independent film company (distributed by RKO). Unfortunately, the film failed to find an audience, with a badly miscast Stewart in the role of a public relations man who discovers the perfect demographic town, Grandview. Cast opposite Jane Wyman, who offered him zero chemistry, the film, a mishmash of redemption, remorse, and Americana, was an irrelevant comedy without laughs that left both critics and audiences ice cold.

Stewart decided it might be best to leave Los Angeles for a while after *Magic Town's* less than magical opening. When Princeton announced an honorary degree for him that spring, he decided to accept it in person. While at an on-campus reception, he met Brock Pemberton, the producer of the Mary Chase Broadway hit *Harvey*. At some point in the evening, Pemberton offered Jimmy the opportunity to take over the title role when the play's original star, Frank Fay, now in the hundred and forty-first week of the show's run, went on what Pemberton described as a much-needed vacation.[2]

Harvey had been around for quite a while even before it landed on Broadway, opening first on London's West End in 1944, at the height of the war when audiences desperately needed a bit of humorous escapism. Jimmy happened to have been stationed there, saw the show and fell in love with its leading character, Elwood P. Dowd, an alcoholic bachelor (a "funny drunk" in vaudeville parlance); his nutty sister Veta Louise Simmons; and his best friend, an invisible six-foot rabbit who answered to the name Harvey.[3]

— • —

Based on the British production, Universal had purchased the film rights for what was then an astoundingly high sum of $1 million— more than it cost to make most movies at the time, with an additional $25,000 earmarked for Chase to write the screenplay.[4] The studio originally intended it as a star vehicle for Bing Crosby, who was then Holly-

---

2. Or so the carefully scripted press releases read. Actually, Fay flew to Colorado to do *Harvey* for a special limited run that played to sold-out audiences, an unofficial test run for the future national touring company.

3. The comic conceit of *Harvey* was not a new one. Its title character takes the form of a "pooka," a large fairy sprite in animal form that populated many of the Irish folktales that its author, Mary Chase, had grown up reading and hearing.

4. The breakdown of the deal was $750,000 for the rights, an additional $250,000 to be paid on the first day of principal shooting. Chase's $25,000 writing fee was paid at the time of the initial purchase.

James Maitland Stewart at four years of age. He gave this photo to his favorite restaurant, Chasen's (Beverly Hills), where he frequently dined with his wife, Gloria, and often with the Reagans. Throughout his lifetime, until Chasen's closed, it hung above his favorite table.

Young Jimmy (far right) stands alongside his father, Alexander's (rear) Hardware store, in Indiana, Pennsylvania.

Two versions, about twenty years apart, of the Stewart family. Left to right: Elizabeth, Jimmy's mother; Mary, his younger sister; Alexander; Virginia, Jimmy's youngest sister; Jimmy.

In the earlier photograph, wearing a "dress-up" army uniform, Jimmy is approximately twelve. In the later, he is approximately 32.

Left: James Stewart, in his senior year at Princeton, in costume for the 1932 Triangle Club production of "Spanish Blades."

Below: 1934, on Broadway in *Yellow Jack*. Left to right: John Miltern, Sam Levene, James Stewart, Myron McCormick, Edward Acuff, Katherine Wilson.

With Margaret Sullavan in the early 1930s.

Left: Lobby card for *Destry Rides Again* (1939).

Below: Rosalind Russell and Jimmy fooling between takes on the set of *No Time for Comedy* (1940).

Below: In dress uniform, on leave during the war. Left to right: Clark Gable, sister Mary, mother Elizabeth, father Alexander (hugging Bill Grady, standing next to an unidentified woman), sister Virginia, Jimmy.

Above: In England, 1941. "Just one of the boys."

Right: A member of the elite Army Air Corps.

BOTH: COURTESY KELLY STEWART HARCOURT/THE ESTATE
OF JAMES STEWART

Lobby card for Frank Capra's
It's a Wonderful Life (1946).

FORTY-EIGHTH STREET
THEATRE

FIRE NOTICE: Th exit indicated by a red light and sign nearest to th seat you occupy is the shortest route to the street. In the event of fire please do not run—WALK TO THAT EXIT.

Thoughtless persons annoy patrons and distract actors and endanger the safety of others by lighting matches during the performance and intermissions. This violates a city ordinance and renders the offender liable to a summons from the fireman on duty. It is urged that all patrons refrain from lighting matches in the auditorium of this theatre.

Frank J. Quayle,
FIRE COMMISSIONER

THE · PLAYBILL · A · WEEKLY · PUBLICATION · OF · PLAYBILL · INCORPORATED

Week beginning Monday, August 18, 1947   •   Matinees Wednesday and Saturday

BROCK PEMBERTON

presents

JAMES STEWART

in

HARVEY

THE PULITZER PRIZE PLAY

a new comedy by
MARY CHASE

with
JOSEPHINE HULL

Directed by
ANTOINETTE PERRY

Settings by JOHN ROOT

CAST

(In the order in which they first speak)

MYRTLE MAE SIMMONS .... JANE VAN DUSER
VETA LOUISE SIMMONS .... JOSEPHINE HULL
ELWOOD P. DOWD .... JAMES STEWART

BETWEEN THE ACTS...

GILBEY'S
GIN

GILBEY'S
DISTILLED
LONDON DRY
GIN

90 Proof. Distilled from 100% grain neutral spirits
National Distillers Products Corp., New York, N.Y.

Left: Program title page from the 1947 Broadway production of *Harvey*.

Below: February (Friday the) 13th, hand- and footprints implanted at the legendary Grauman's Chinese Theatre, on Hollywood Boulevard.

Left: With former roommate and lifelong friend Henry Fonda, in a publicity still from King Vidor and Leslie Fenton's *On Our Merry Way* (1948).

Below: As Robert Caddell in Alfred Hitchcock's *Rope* (1948).

August 1949. The outside of Chasen's decorated for Jimmy's "stag" party.

Left: Spencer Tracy and Jack Benny "console" their friend at the party.

Below: Honeymooning in Hawaii.

Jimmy starring as Elwood P. Dowd in the 1950 film version of *Harvey*.

At home with the children. Gloria's two boys from a previous marriage, and the Stewarts' twin girls. Left to right: Ronald, Michael, Gloria (holding Judy), Jimmy (holding Kelly).

Jimmy and Gloria, with Henry Fonda, having drinks at the Stork Club. Taken in the early 1950s while both Jimmy and Fonda were appearing on Broadway (in *Harvey* and *Mr. Roberts*, respectively).

With Hitchcock and Grace Kelly on set during the filming of Hitchcock's *Rear Window* (1954).

Above: Grace Kelly and Jimmy in
Rear Window.

Right: Jimmy with his frequent co-star
June Allyson (who was always cast as his
wife), in a publicity still from Anthony
Mann's *Strategic Air Command* (1955).

Below: With *the* Alfred Hitchcock in
Marrakesh, while filming the director's
second version of his *The Man Who
Knew Too Much* (1956).

A clever publicity shot of Jimmy in *Vertigo,* surrounded by Kim Novak as Madeline/Judy (1958).

On set during the filming of Mervyn LeRoy's *The FBI Story* (1959).

Playing his beloved accordion in a scene from Henry Koster's *Dear Brigitte* (1965). Glynis Johns, as Jimmy's wife, Vina Leaf, is playing the flute.

Congressional Record

United States
of America

PROCEEDINGS AND DEBATES OF THE 90th CONGRESS, SECOND SESSION

Vol. 114   WASHINGTON, TUESDAY, JUNE 25, 1968   No. 109

Senate

RETIREMENT OF BRIG. GEN. JAMES STEWART FROM U.S. AIR FORCE RESERVE

Mr. MURPHY. Mr. President, on May 31, 1968, James Stewart, formally retired as a brigadier general in the U.S. Air Force Reserve. Gen. J. P. McConnell, Air Force Chief of Staff, conducted the retirement ceremony, during the course of which he presented to General Stewart the Distinguished Service Medal "for exceptionally meritorious service to the United States." This is only the second time in history that an officer in the Air Force Reserve has been so honored.

As one who has long considered Jimmy Stewart his friend, I am proud of the matchless record he has compiled of service to our Nation and to the motion picture industry.

In the course of his exceptional acting career, Mr. Stewart has appeared in 73 motion pictures. His face and his voice have become known to people in every country of the world and he has, through his profession, become one of the best international ambassadors of good will we could present abroad. An Academy Award winner and one of the world's most admired and respected actors, Mr. Stewart has still found time to perform noteworthy service in many other fields. He served for 4 years as a member of the board of trustees of his alma mater, Princeton University. Presently he is a trustee of Claremont Colleges and of Project Hope. He has been active for many years in the Presbyterian Church and the Boy Scouts of America, among many other worthy causes.

General Stewart's military career be-gan during World War II, when he served on active duty from March of 1941 until October of 1945. During that time he rose from the rank of private to colonel, flying 20 missions over Germany with the 8th Air Force.

Mr. President, I congratulate our good friend, Gen. Jimmy Stewart, on his outstanding contribution to our people and our Nation. In closing, I ask unanimous consent that there be printed in the RECORD the citation which accompanied the award of the Distinguished Service Medal to James M. Stewart.

There being no objection, the citation was ordered to be printed in the RECORD, as follows:

CITATION TO ACCOMPANY THE AWARD OF THE DISTINGUISHED SERVICE MEDAL TO JAMES M. STEWART

Brigadier General James M. Stewart distinguished himself by exceptionally meritorious service to the United States in his mobilization assignment as Deputy Director, Office of Information, Office of the Secretary of the Air Force from 17 July 1959 to 31 May 1968. During this period, General Stewart selflessly devoted his time, knowledge and broad experience in a concerted effort to publicize the Air Force contribution to our nation's security. As a result of his personal efforts he has brought about a greater awareness, throughout the nation, of the significant contributions Air Force personnel have made toward our country's defense. His sincerity, dedication and ability to communicate to people young and old, were significantly responsible for the general public's appreciation of the Air Force role in safeguarding freedom throughout the world. The singularly distinctive accomplishments of General Stewart culminate a long and distinguished career in the service of his country, and reflect the highest credit upon himself and the United States Air Force.

Above: On safari in Kenya. While filming Robert Aldrich's *The Flight of the Phoenix* (1966), Jimmy left the location (Phoenix, Arizona) and flew to Kenya to spend one day with his family. Left to right: Jimmy, Ron, Gloria (in car), Mike, Judy, and Kelly.

Left: The *Congressional Record* acknowledgment of Jimmy's being awarded the Distinguished Service Medal.

Jimmy's signature hand-gesture style of acting, on display in Gene Kelly's *The Cheyenne Social Club* (1970).

With Orson Welles on *The Dean Martin Show* (circa 1970).

With Gloria on one of their many safaris to Africa (circa 1970).

Looking not very happy while standing with producer and long-time friend William Frye and Gloria, at a publicity function during the making of Jerry Jameson's *Airport '77*.

The Reagan White House years.

DAILY ◉ NEWS

NEW YORK'S HOMETOWN NEWSPAPER

50¢   http://www.mostnewyork.com   Thursday, July 3, 1997

A WONDERFUL LIFE
Jimmy Stewart 1908-1997

SEE PAGES 2 & 3

At the end of a wonderful life.

wood's popular male movie star, thanks to his Academy Award–winning performance as Best Actor in Leo McCarey's *Going My Way* (1944), a wartime Jesus-walks-among-us drama that broke all box-office records and in doing so revived the radio crooner's movie career. He considered the role in *Harvey* for quite a while before turning it down after winning the Oscar, claiming his fans would be offended if their favorite "priest" were seen as being tipsy all the time and talking to an invisible rabbit (invisible God conversations that dotted *Going My Way* and its sequel, McCarey's 1945 *The Bells of St. Mary's,* were apparently okay).

The show's long-delayed journey to Hollywood was due to a similar clause that had kept Capra's *Arsenic and Old Lace* from opening for several years after it had been made, the same reason that Hepburn had closed *The Philadelphia Story* while it was still filling houses on Broadway. In each instance, the producers of the stage production withheld film release rights until the Broadway runs ended. Universal opted to wait before filming began (unlike Warner with Capra, who made *Arsenic and Old Lace* and then had to wait two years before the film could legally open).

It has often been written that Stewart's "retreat" to Broadway was proof of the old (and continuing) adage that the New York stage, the Great White Way, serves as either a training ground for new Hollywood talent or the graveyard of those whose film careers have worn down and have no other option but to return to the boards.[5] Indeed, it certainly looked that way to the *New York Times,* which promptly dispatched reporter Gladwin Hill to interview Stewart, after informing him that the newspaper intended to write a major piece on the order of "The Rise and Fall of James Stewart," on the failure of *It's a Wonderful Life* and *Magic Town,* combined with Stewart's coming in to a major hit show as a substitute for Frank Fay.

The newspaper, the adage, and everyone else couldn't have been more wrong. Jimmy's reason for taking the role was to let it serve as a public audition for what he wanted most—to play Dowd in the film version. When he'd first approached Jimmy, Pemberton guessed that he couldn't pay anything like he assumed Jimmy was used to in film.

---

5. Stewart's Hollywood friends tried to put the best face on the move. Fonda threw a farewell dinner in which the main dish served under a platter turned out to be a giant, live rabbit. Bill Grady sent Stewart two live rabbits a day for ten days, up until the day of his departure for New York City.

Jimmy responded by offering to do the entire seven weeks for free, with the show having to cover only his hotel and day-to-day expenses. That idea actually came from Lew Wasserman. MCA also owned Universal Pictures, and once Crosby proved unavailable, Wasserman wanted Jimmy to star in the movie.

Fay played the role for 1,351 of its 1,775 Broadway performances. His first vacation, in 1946, saw him replaced by legendary song-and-dance eight-a-day, red-nosed vaudevillian Bert Wheeler, who knew how to win over the hearts of his audiences and milk the role for every laugh it had. Jimmy, on the other hand, played it much more realistically, with the droopy-eyed style of drawl acting that had gotten him so far in his early days of theatrical performing. Although he hadn't been on a live stage in twelve years, he took to the part naturally, and New York theatergoers fought over the limited amount of seats available to see him play the part. The hard-nosed New York theater critics, with some caveat, accepted him as Dowd. According to the *New York Times*'s Brooks Atkinson: "Although the structure of Mr. Stewart's performance is much weaker than Mr. Fay's, his honesty as a human being gives the climax of the play warmth and emotion. In every way that counts, Mr. Stewart is thoroughly admirable."

Opening night, Stewart graciously thanked Fay from the front of the proscenium for letting him take over the role for a while, prompting a second standing ovation. Afterward, the stage-door crowd was so large, special security had to be installed on subsequent nights to ensure Stewart could get through it.

The *New York Times* profile that had originally intended to chart the actor's ups and downs was rewritten as a "star" interview and retitled "Jimmy Stewart Prepares to Meet a Rabbit," a far more positive, even genial recap of Stewart's career, with liberal quotes from the actor.

The *Daily News* was the only paper in town to talk about the elephant in the room. Columnist Erskine Johnson started off his rather fanciful August 21 column this way:

> They say Jimmy Stewart is a forgotten man. I'd like to argue about it, but the box-office data on the last Stewart picture, *It's a Wonderful Life*, makes that "forgotten" business hold water.
>
> It was a good picture. It had comedy, home-townness, good entertainment and a lot of good supporting players around Jimmy.

But now that it has played all around the country, they added up the shekels on paper and Jimmy's agents said, "Sorry, Jimmy, they've forgotten you. You'll have to start all over again." . . .

That Jimmy Stewart and many others have to stage a comeback just because they've been out of sight for a while seems a regrettable situation. The only proof that counts with the studios, however, is that box-office take, which is the public's voice.

Jimmy's highly successful, if brief, run in *Harvey* ended on August 30, when Fay returned, but it was a thoroughly revitalized Stewart who returned to Hollywood to enthusiastically begin work on a new film Wasserman had gotten for him. Something of a departure for Jimmy, especially after *Harvey,* the docu-bio drama was based on the exploits of Chicago journalist Jim McNeal, who'd won a Pulitzer prize for his series of articles that helped to clear the name of Joseph Majczek, an innocent man convicted of killing a cop. *Call Northside 777* was written by Jerome Cady and Jay Dratler, and produced under the strict guidance of Darryl F. Zanuck at 20th Century Fox.

Jimmy's role in *Call Northside 777* was, in every way, different from the type audiences had come to expect from him. Zanuck had personally selected the ham-fisted Henry Hathaway to direct. Because of his harder, adventurous edge, which the producer felt the film needed, his film work had all the finesse of a barroom brawl. The script itself was tough, no-nonsense, and edgy, and the role of McNeal demanded a certain gritty brusqueness. Wasserman had to convince Zanuck that Jimmy could do it, and he was right. By the time the film had finished shooting, the dailies revealed that all remaining traces of the familiar, charmingly boyish James Stewart were gone, replaced by a toughness and a manliness no one had seen in him before. Both audiences and critics alike were duly impressed.

Upon its release in February 1948, Bosley Crowther, in the *New York Times,* singled out Jimmy for special praise, calling his performance "winningly acted." The *Herald Tribune* said, "The performances, from James Stewart's characterization of an inquisitive reporter to the merest bits, have honesty and persuasion." While no one called *Northside 777* a great film, which it wasn't by any means, Jimmy had shown enough in it to get the doors of Hollywood to crack open for him once more.

His next movie was King Vidor and Leslie Fenton's *On Our Merry Way* (aka *A Miracle Can Happen,* 1948), yet another product of Wasserman's relentless wheeling and dealing on Jimmy's behalf, this time with United Artists. The film centered around a roving reporter who asks a series of randomly selected "people in the street" what child has had an influence on his or her life. The film was made up of three segments, each starring a duo of actors—Fred MacMurray and William Demarest (who would reteam again twenty years later on the TV sitcom *My Three Sons*), Dorothy Lamour and Paulette Goddard (Burgess Meredith's wife at the time), and Henry Fonda and Jimmy Stewart, working together on-screen for the first time.[6]

In the film, Fonda and Stewart are a couple of musicians who rig a talent contest as a way to pay for the repairs on their broken-down bus. The influential child is the daughter of the mechanic, who brings out the latent moralists in them. To get help with their part of the film, Stewart and Fonda placed a call to John O'Hara, another old friend from the New York days, and privately commissioned him to write their segment. O'Hara finished it in ten days. Satisfied with their written parts, they then asked John Huston to help direct their sequences. Huston accepted at first, only to change his mind at the last minute, citing a project about to go into production that he said he had somehow "forgotten about" (Huston was drinking heavily at the time). In a panic, they turned to George Stevens, Jimmy's director in *Vivacious Lady,* who agreed to do it as long as he didn't get any on-screen credit, which explains his absence from the official director's line.[7]

During production, the magazine *Woman's Home Companion* dispatched feature writer Barbara Heggie to do an on-set profile of Jimmy, which she titled "Penrod in Hollywood." The fact that she misspelled his name throughout the entire piece said a lot about the still-wavering,

---

6. It would not happen again for another fourteen years, until *How the West Was Won* (1962), directed in segments by John Ford, Henry Hathaway, and George Marshall in which they appeared in separate sequences.

7. Stevens did not want to be seen as a second choice, nor did he like the concept of multiple directors. Also, Huston had initially agreed to do it without credit, and Stevens would have had to accept the same offer. The other two segments were directed by King Vidor and Leslie Fenton, respectively.

if misconceived, perception by Heggie of her subject: "All the engaging awkwardness of a Booth Tarkington boy—but what else is it that gives Jimmie [sic] Stewart the power to tie the American woman into emotional knots?"

That was a terrific question, if it were asked of Clark Gable or Cary Grant. Jimmy's career was unique in more ways than one, not the least of which was that while he was often classified a leading man, he was never a sex symbol—just the opposite, in fact; he represented the very epitome of on-screen Puritanism Americana. That was his stock and trade. Henry Fonda may have played Abe Lincoln on-screen, but in real-life it was Jimmy who was far more Lincolnesque—tall, awkward, soft-spoken, real-life heroic; the very definition of the lean, wise American loner. These qualities and his war experiences, although he refused to talk about them, had actually elevated his stature, if not his box office, among American men. Women still remembered him as that nice boy, but not one capable of tying them into emotional knots.

Among the "revelations" of Ms. Heggie's article was that "Jimmie" *loves* coffee and spaghetti for lunch, wears his tweed off-set jackets with sleeves that are perennially too short, has startling steel blue eyes, and has stopped reading Flash Gordon because "the poor guy has taken up fighting giant beetles." All in all, a neat little basket of condescending tidbits that did nothing to fuel Jimmy's resurgence, until the reporter moved to an area that was supposed to be off-limits. "Later, over coffee, the subject of marriage came up," Heggie reported, "and Stewart immediately became depressed. [Ever since] his bachelor pal John Swope married Dorothy McGuire there is scarcely a friend at whose house Jimmie [sic] can drop in without disturbing some snug domestic tableau. This makes him feel unwanted. But marriage is not a week end [sic] in Mexico; it is serious business and he is a cautious man.

" 'I don't want to marry one of these actresses and have it last a month,' he told me moodily, 'and if I find some nice girl and bring her out here what would Hollywood do to her? I'm not so conceited that I think I can buck what a lot of others guys haven't been able to buck.' "

Meaning what? Lose your wife to another man? Or fail to please your parents? Ms. Heggie did not follow up on one of the most revealing statements Jimmy had ever given to the public.

Shortly thereafter, as if to deflect all the unexpected attention the

Heggie piece was getting, Jimmy sat with Hedda Hopper and tried to keep the focus on business. He said he was thinking of starting his own repertory company for actors who wanted to tour the country performing live before audiences, because "something has to be done to relieve the employment situation here." Hopper listened politely, then brought up the marriage question, to which an exasperated Stewart replied, "Well, I've been thinking about it. I don't aim to be rushed." Jimmy was forty at the time of the interview.

— • —

On Our Merry Way actually opened two weeks before *Northside 777*, and, perhaps not surprisingly, did nothing at the box office. Reviews were generally poor, and both pictures faded quickly from the screens of theaters and the memories of audiences everywhere.

And then came *Rope,* Jimmy's first opportunity to work with Alfred Hitchcock, one of Hollywood's top directors, his first since Capra, one who was capable of understanding precisely what it was about Jimmy that made him so extraordinary and unique, both as an actor and as a man, and who would use it in the four unforgettable features they would make together over the next decade.

15

"Stewart claimed that *Rope* was the toughest job an actor ever had . . . as it was, he had to hang around the set eighteen days before making a bona fide entrance for the rolling camera. It was the final dress rehearsal for reel 3 in which Jimmy makes an entrance while Farley Granger is playing the piano. The piano stopped and silence ensued, as all eyes went to Stewart. He just made it into the room and was ready to open his mouth. 'Just a minute,' I said. 'I'd like you to make your entrance differently.'

"Jimmy punched the air in a defeated gesture. 'Hey, look,' he complained, 'I've waited three weeks for this!'" —ALFRED HITCHCOCK

The famed British director had come to America in 1939 to be able to continue making movies. With England officially at war, the industry there had all but shuttered, the film company he'd worked for, Gaumont-British, had gone under, and he was deathly afraid that Hitler was going to successfully invade Great Britain. Hitchcock's arrival in Hollywood in partnership with David O. Selznick set into motion one of the most contentious creative alliances in film history. Their stormy relationship nevertheless produced several near-great movies: *Rebecca* (1940), *Suspicion* (1941), *Spellbound* (1945), and one undisputedly great one, *Notorious* (1946). Hitchcock completed his obligations to and partnership with Selznick in 1946 with *The Paradine Case*, one of the few American failures Hitchcock made in the forties, and one that pointed him in the same independent direction as Capra and so many others. Tired of working for the always-difficult Selznick, he decided instead to form his own film company, appropriately titled Transatlantic, and began searching for his first property.

He chose *Under Capricorn*, a vehicle intended for his then-favorite leading lady, Ingrid Bergman. However, when her schedule proved too difficult for Hitchcock to work around—she was making two other movies while appearing on Broadway—he shifted gears and settled on adapting a play he had seen and enjoyed in London's West End some twenty years earlier, one that had remained at the back of his mind and would be eminently workable, and probably superior, when made into a movie. The play, *Rope's End* by Patrick Hamilton, was to be the continuation of an experiment Hitchcock had tried once before—shooting an entire film in a single, confined set.[1] The first, *Lifeboat*, in 1944, took place completely on a raft, and was good enough to earn Hitchcock an Academy Award nomination.[2] With *Rope,* all the film's action was to unfold, as on stage, in the various connected rooms of a Manhattan penthouse.

In the film, a murder has taken place. Two homosexual student lovers have killed a friend simply for the thrill of it—a killing based loosely on the sensational true-life bloody Leopold and Loeb child abduction and murder case of the 1920s. Eventually the crime is (literally) uncovered by their professor, whose philosophical teachings may have, in fact, unwittingly inspired the slaying. The dead body is hidden in an antique chest, the closed lid of which serves as the table for a buffet supper. The buffet was placed at the forefront of the set, looming large in the screen's mise-en-scène.

The trick that Hitchcock wanted to perform was to shoot the entire film in single ten-minute magazine takes, in real time.[3] To enhance the atmosphere and open up the set, a picture window with a panoramic view of the city dominated the background, growing continually darker as day turned to night. The film was shot in Technicolor—a first for the previously unrelenting black and white the director loved.

For the screenplay, Hitchcock turned to old friend Hume Cronyn, an odd choice, but one the shrewd director knew would not interfere

---

1. Hamilton had also written the play *Angel Street,* which had been turned into the classic suspense film *Gaslight,* directed by George Cukor, starring Ingrid Bergman and Charles Boyer.

2. The director, who never won a competitive Oscar, lost that year to Leo McCarey (*Going My Way*). The film also earned a nomination for Writing—Original Story, for John Steinbeck, who also lost to McCarey.

3. At the time, 35-mm film came in ten-minute "magazines," or reels, the maximum amount of footage allowable for a single, uninterrupted "take."

with his specialized vision of what he wanted to accomplish. Cronyn provided less a complete script than an expansion on the original play, changing very little of it. For the finessing, the gloss, and the deeper abstract connections, Hitchcock hired Arthur Laurents, a young, talented, up-and-coming playwright. Laurents had first been discovered by Irene Selznick, David's ex-wife (he had by now left her to marry movie star Jennifer Jones), who had since gone on to become a Broadway producer. While Selznick and Hitchcock often clashed during their years together, the director always had strong positive feelings for Irene, and did not hesitate when she recommended Laurents, who had just done a successful uncredited screen rewrite of Anatole Litvak's *The Snake Pit* (released in 1948), good enough to eventually earn it Oscar nominations for Best Picture, Best Actress, Best Director, Best Sound Recording, and Best Screenplay (for Frank Partos and Millen Brand).[4]

The other thing about Laurents that Hitchcock liked was that he was gay and currently involved with Farley Granger ("Fah-Fah" to Hollywood insiders), an actor the director was interested in for the part of Phillip, the weaker-willed of the two killers. Hitchcock loved that kind of "doubling," believing the resonance of those actual relationships deepened the reality of those on the screen. For the role of Brandon, the other killer, Hitchcock wanted Montgomery Clift (another known-to-the-industry homosexual). And for the role of Rupert Cadell, the professor, Hitchcock assumed there would be no problem getting Cary Grant, who had had the biggest and most successful film of his career two years earlier starring in Hitchcock's *Notorious*. Grant, who had also had gay relationships in the past, would, for Hitchcock, complete the "doubling" aspects of the film—three homosexuals played by three homosexuals, in a screenplay written by a homosexual, based on a real-life murder committed by two infamous homosexuals. The very thought of all this made the always mischievous, devious Hitchcock salivate.

Granger quickly accepted. Then, one by one, problems began, beginning with the cast, having mainly to do with the still-taboo subject of homosexuality in American commercial movies. Cary Grant was the

---

4. It won one, Best Sound Recording (20th Century Fox Sound Department). Best Picture went to Laurence Olivier's *Hamlet*, Best Actor to Olivier, Best Actress to Jane Wyman for Jean Negulesco's *Johnny Belinda*, Best Director to John Huston for *Treasure of the Sierra Madre*, which also won Best Screenplay.

first to drop out. Not long after, Clift said no, telling Hitchcock he couldn't do the part because he was afraid it would "raise eyebrows." According to Laurents, "Both Cary Grant and Montgomery understood [the characters were gay] and both were leery. Since Cary Grant was at best bisexual and Monty was gay, they were scared to death and they wouldn't do it."[5] Grant's loss in particular was a difficult one for Hitchcock to accept, and it caused a rift that prevented the two from forming their own independent production company. Grant returned to making mostly easy comedies and conventional romances, such as Howard Hawks's *I Was a Male War Bride* (1949) and *Monkey Business* (1952), before announcing his first retirement, one that would end seven years later when he reunited with Hitchcock to star in *To Catch a Thief*.

It was only after Grant declined that Hitchcock was forced to turn to an alternative list of actors for the two remaining leads. Casting Brandon was easy. John Dall was a social acquaintance of Hitchcock's, a frequent dining companion at the director's favorite Beverly Hills restaurant, Chasen's, the most famous celebrity eatery in town (originally called Chasen's Southern). In addition to Hitchcock, it was the home away from home for such stars as Clark Gable, Errol Flynn, W. C. Fields, Cary Grant, Gary Cooper, Jack Benny, Howard Hughes, James Cagney, Alan Ladd, and writer F. Scott Fitzgerald. Dall was Ivy League educated (Columbia) and, perhaps most important, had scored big in his film debut a few years earlier in Irving Rapper's *The Corn Is Green* (1945), opposite Bette Davis, for which he was nominated for a Best Supporting Oscar. Dall, who was also gay, was nonetheless willing to allow himself to go in that direction on the screen.

The path to Jimmy Stewart was much more complicated. Wasserman, eager to keep Stewart working, had a working relationship with Hitchcock, born out of the director's loose bond with Irene Selznick's talent agency prior to its being folded into Hayward's, which was then sold to MCA. Although Hitchcock was still intrigued with the idea of using a homosexual as an unwitting accomplice (an intellectually superior man who was unaware of his own darker sexual desires appealed to

---

5. Both Grant and Clift would work with Hitchcock on other projects. Grant, who had already made *Suspicion* (1941) and *Notorious* (1946), would go on to do *To Catch a Thief* in 1955 and *North by Northwest* in 1959. Clift would play an ultra-straight priest in Hitchcock's *I Confess* (1953).

Hitchcock—"You've given my words meaning I never dreamed of," Cadell says at one point), he changed his mind quickly when he discovered that the Bank of America, Transatlantic's underwriter (along with Warner, which had agreed to distribute), had based its funding of *Rope* on the international box-office strength of Cary Grant, something that Jimmy Stewart could in no way match. The only way the deal could still go down, Hitchcock told Wasserman, was if Jimmy took less salary than the $300,000 Grant had agreed to up front (plus a percentage of the profits). He offered $175,00 for Jimmy's services, and no profit participation.

Wasserman would have none of it. He held firm and Hitchcock, eager to start filming (and stop running up costs at his own company), agreed to give Jimmy the same terms he had offered Grant. To get the bank to agree, he personally guaranteed any losses that might be incurred as the result of having Jimmy in the film (although how such a thing could be proved no one was ever able to explain).[6]

It was a major financial victory for Stewart, although, as he would admit later on, he thought it was a mistake to take the part. "*Rope* wasn't my favorite picture," he told Fonda and others whenever anyone asked how it was going. He was annoyed at the trickery of the single-take shoots that seemed to totally preoccupy Hitchcock. "The only thing that has been rehearsed around here is the camera."

Another problem for Jimmy was Farley Granger, who had signed on because he wanted to work with the sophisticated and beautiful Cary Grant, whom he had a crush on, not the unsophisticated and decidedly unbeautiful Jimmy Stewart (with whom he was less than enamored). As Laurents so succinctly put it, "Jimmy Stewart was not sexual as an actor, while Cary Grant was always sexual."

Playing one of three gay leading characters in *Rope* only caused Jimmy's lack of inherent cinematic hetero heat to be seen by some as clear evidence that he was, in fact, homosexual. Conceding he was

---

6. The deal wasn't an entire mystery. Hitchcock agreed to the $300,000 with a built-in "safety net," meaning that there would be little or no money up front for Stewart, as there would have been for Grant, with most of it payable on the back end. Hitchcock guaranteed Wasserman and Stewart that if the profits fell short, he would make up the difference to $300,000 for Stewart. When the film did not earn back its negative cost, Hitchcock remained true to his word, seeing to it that Stewart was paid exactly that amount for his work on *Rope*.

"miscast" in *Rope,* a defensive Jimmy told Louella Parsons after the film failed at the box office that it had been nothing more than "an experiment. I'm glad I did it and I'll go on record as saying I'll make a picture for Alfred Hitchcock anytime."

— • —

A month after production on *Rope* wrapped, in the winter of 1948, Jimmy traveled east by train, to New York City, where he had signed on to take over the role of Elwood P. Dowd in *Harvey.*

PART FIVE

— . —

Man, Marriage, Mann

Jimmy and Gloria's wedding day — August 9, 1949.

16

"The American dreamboat is Jimmy Stewart. Sure, sure, they're also mad about Clark Gable, Eddy Duchin and Victor Mature . . . but it's Jimmy they burn to mother and smother in the oven of their lovin'. That's because he's a bachelor and never been snagged by any of these mantraps." —SYNDICATED COLUMNIST EARL WILSON, CIRCA 1940s

*T*wo days after his second New York run ended in *Harvey,* Jimmy began filming Hank Potter's *You Gotta Stay Happy,* a so-called airport comedy shot mostly at Newark Airport in New Jersey. It was yet another independent movie, this one under the auspices of Rampart, a company owned by his co-star, Joan Fontaine, and her husband, William Dozier. Wasserman had urged Jimmy to take the part, even though it gave him only second billing under Fontaine. After the failure of *Rope,* Wasserman thought it was important just to keep Jimmy's name out there and he hoped a light comedy would remind audiences of the "nice," i.e., "straight" James Stewart.

Because the thirty-one-year-old Fontaine was pregnant at the time, she had an especially difficult shoot with a script that attempted to recapture the lost art of physical screwball comedy.[1] Jimmy, having worked with stodgy journeyman Potter before (with Margaret Sullavan in *The Shopworn Angel*), did the best he could in a plot with distinct echoes of Capra's *It Happened One Night.* The nonsensical tale (based on a serialized novel by Robert Carson that ran in the *Saturday Evening Post* while the film was being made) centers around Dee Dee Dillwood (Fontaine),

---

1. Fontaine nearly miscarried during production due to an on-set accident involving her jumping off a hay wagon; inexplicably, she performed it without a stunt double, but managed to carry the baby to term. This prompted a brief hospital visit in which the only representative from the film to visit her was Stewart. When she was released, she baked a fortieth-birthday cake for him.

a "wacky" heiress on her honeymoon, unsure if she has, after all, married the best fellow for her, Henry Benson (Willard Parker). Her uncertainty causes her to hide in the bedroom of the adjoining honeymoon suite that happens to be occupied by Marvin Payne (Stewart), the owner/operator of a small flying cargo business. An attempted suicide on Dee Dee's part gets her taken along with Payne and his copilot, Bullets (Eddie Albert), on a run to California. Also on board is an embezzler who has paid them to get him out of town (Porter Hall), a GI (Arthur Walsh) and *his* new bride, a corpse, a shipment of whitefish, frozen lobsters, and a cigar-smoking chimpanzee. As if this wasn't enough, during the flight, an emergency forces them to land in a field, where they are met and assisted by a farmer (Percy Kilbride). By the end of the film, Dee Dee and Payne have found true love—with each other.

The film proved Wasserman right, and actually fared better than any of Jimmy's other postwar efforts to date, including *It's a Wonderful Life*. Following its November 1948 release, the *New York Times* agreeably proclaimed, "James Stewart, to our mind, shows up much better in *You Gotta Stay Happy* than in any of his previous post-war efforts." *Time* magazine was positively effusive: "This is the kind of role that Jimmy Stewart could play blind-folded, hog-tied and in the bottom of a well. He gives it all the best Stewartisms." These reviews read better than the picture played. In truth, it dragged when it should have soared, schlumped when it should have stretched, and, despite a perky box office after its first run, quickly left the consciousness of the American filmgoing public.

Still, *You Gotta Stay Happy* succeeded where *It's a Wonderful Life* had failed; it was an independent picture that showed a healthy profit. This was not an insignificant turn of events, for Jimmy or the industry.

The studio system continued to crumble into disarray, with successful competition from independents the least of its postwar problems. Like a prehistoric monster in a B movie, the ugly head of paranoid anti-Communism had begun to stomp its jackboots. The formation of the Hollywood Alliance in 1941 by studio-head Walt Disney; directors Sam Wood, Clarence Brown, and King Vidor; stars John Wayne, Robert Taylor, Ginger Rogers, Barbara Stanwyck, Clark Gable, Gary Cooper, Adolphe Menjou, Ward Bond, and Richard Arlen had all but invited HUAC (the House Un-American Activities Committee) to come in like some heroic gunslinger to "clean up" the town, with every breathless victory reported by "journalist" Hedda Hopper, who used her syndicated Hearst column in unwavering support of Hollywood's far-right movement.

Because of his long military service, Jimmy, no less a right-leaning performer than the others on the list, had been gone for most of the early days of the first wave of anti-Communism. Throughout much of the first half of the forties he was off fighting a real enemy rather than a suspected one. By the time he had returned to Hollywood, HUAC had begun a new and very blunt probe to "investigate" the political affiliations of many of the postwar industry's most famous actors, writers, producers, and directors, not coincidentally the majority of whom happened to have gone the independent route. Jimmy, as red, white, and blue as they came, had no problems with HUAC or the Motion Picture Alliance.

The same could not be said for Frank Capra. He was brought before HUAC and testified before the committee in what amounted to a last, desperate effort to salvage his career.

Although Jimmy was aware of all that was going on between Capra and HUAC, he did not come out in public support of him. It wasn't that he didn't believe in the director's innocence, he just did not think it was right for him to take sides in what he felt was Capra's battle. Keep your nose clean and mind your own business was one of the earliest lessons learned by young Jimmy from his father. It was a credo he chose to live by, one that would eventually cause an even deeper rift than the one currently developing between him and his best friend, Henry Fonda, intensified by Jimmy's refusal to publicly come out in defense of Capra.

In the spring of 1947, the ultra-liberal Fonda publicly aligned himself with Humphrey Bogart, Lauren Bacall, John Huston, and a host of lesser Hollywood lights in signing an open letter to HUAC, complaining of its tactics and rather brazenly telling the committee to get lost. The letter was later repudiated by most of these same names, none of whom suffered any loss of work, except for Fonda. Before he put his signature to the page, he and Jimmy had a long and at times heated discussion about whether or not either one should get openly involved with the increasingly political polarization of the film industry. Jimmy vehemently opposed Fonda's intention to sign and privately warned him of the consequences to his career such an action might bring (it was a warning that was meant as cautionary rather than threatening).

Fonda, however, had made up his mind. Despite Jimmy's pleas, he went ahead and put his signature on the document. Stewart was angry at him, but this did not, as has been written elsewhere, signal the end of their friendship. Precisely the opposite; it was their concrete closeness that gave each of them the strength to disagree, even passionately, over any and everything, always in the spirit of helping each other. Fonda thought it was his patriotic duty to take a stand. Stewart did not disagree; he just feared that that stand might effectively end Fonda's film career. As things turned out, he wasn't far from wrong.

Except for an unbilled cameo in Fletcher Markle's independent feature *Jigsaw* (1949), Fonda did not star in another Hollywood movie for seven years following John Ford's brilliant *Fort Apache* (1948) until Ford's 1955 *Mr. Roberts,* the film version of the hit show that had run during that same period of time on Broadway—starring Henry Fonda for much of the time.[2] In 1948, the same year Jimmy put his footprints in the cement at the fabled Grauman's Chinese Theatre on Hollywood Boulevard, Fonda relocated with his family back to their East Coast home.[3] He then accepted the title role in his old pal and one-time director Joshua Logan's stage version of *Mr. Roberts,* the best-selling autobiographical novel by Thomas Heggen, produced by Leland Hayward, about an idealistic officer who, in the days preceding the onset of World War Two, seeks a transfer to another ship rather than deal with a bullying captain. He does eventually confront his captain for the sake of his men, and, through an unfortunate (but not strictly coincidental) series of events, loses his life for it. The reluctant hero taking on an increasingly out-of-control bully holds the drama together in both the novel and the play. The theme had a strong appeal to Fonda, who regarded the story as a metaphor for the madness and tyranny that he believed had gripped Hollywood.

Mr. Roberts would go on to win five Tony awards.[4] On the strength

---

2. *Jigsaw* is also known as *Gun Moll.* During filming, Ford was replaced on *Mr. Roberts,* reportedly due to illness (although some still believe the politically conservative director didn't want to work again with Fonda), by Mervyn LeRoy, who shared directorial credit. LeRoy, in his memoir, claimed he shot 90 percent of the film.

3. Stewart's footprint (and handprint) ceremony took place on February 13, 1948. Fonda's had actually gone in six years earlier, on July 24, 1942, the same day as Rita Hayworth, Charles Laughton, Edward G. Robinson, and Charles Boyer.

4. In 1948, Henry Fonda won the Antoinette Perry (Tony) Award for Best Actor, Joshua Logan and Thomas Heggen (Heggen had written the original novel the play

of his Broadway popularity and the waning of the blacklist (which no one ever officially admitted or could prove had ever officially included the actor), Fonda eventually returned to making movies in Hollywood, but the memory of the aging Academy remained long and characteristically vengeful. He would not win Oscars for some of the strongest roles of his career until his sunset performance in 1982's *On Golden Pond*, a year after a younger and more liberal Academy had already granted him its traditional consolation prize (referred to in the industry as the graceful losers' award), an honorary Lifetime Achievement Oscar.[5]

— • —

In 1948, Jimmy made his next movie for MGM, the first project he had done for the studio in nearly a decade, playing the title role in *The Stratton Story*, directed by one of the MPA's founders, Sam Wood.

During production, Jimmy started dating a pretty, young starlet by the name of Myrna Dell, and after two months—an eternity by Hollywood standards—rumors began to appear in the gossips that they intended to marry, something Dell later denied they ever talked about in all the time they were together. At least part of the problem, she later told one interviewer, was another woman. Not Rita Hayworth, Mitzi Green, or Helen Walker, all of whom the press had recently linked him to. No, she said, it was Jimmy's apparent ongoing love for Margaret Sullavan. According to Dell, she was all he ever talked about.

After his forty-first birthday passed, a depressed Jimmy confided to Dell that he was thinking of giving up acting and returning to the family business and the inner Pennsylvania folds of the Episcopalian Church. This did not come out of the thin, smoggy L.A. air. While reading in the local paper about his son going out with Dell, Alexander had come across a quote in which Jimmy said although he was still religious, he no longer felt the need to attend services every Sunday. That sent Alexander straight to the phone, to find out if his son had completely lost his mind as well as his faith. All of this angered Dell, who

---

was based on) won both as playwrights and for Best Play, Logan won for Best Director, and Leland Hayward for producing.

5. Fonda had been nominated for a Best Picture Oscar (as producer, with Reginald Rose) in 1958, for Sidney Lumet's *12 Angry Men*. They lost to Sam Spiegel, who won for *The Bridge on the River Kwai*. In 1941, he lost for Best Actor in John Ford's *The Grapes of Wrath*, to Jimmy Stewart (*The Philadelphia Story*).

had strong feelings for Stewart, and who told friends that his father had Jimmy acting like he was turning twenty-one rather than forty-one.

Regardless, there was no way that Dell could have turned around Jimmy's life. She simply did not have the emotional arsenal or any real opportunity to try to somehow make Jimmy fall in love with her. And anyway, another woman had already fixed her sights on him with a determination that would not allow for failure.

That July not long after he finished shooting *You Gotta Stay Happy,* Jimmy, glowingly referred to by Hedda Hopper in her columns as the "Great American Bachelor," accepted an invitation from Gary Cooper and his wife, Rocky. Jimmy had maintained a casual friendship with the right-wing-, MPA-, and HUAC-friendly actor after presenting him with his Academy Award in 1942. They had a lot in common—both were Oscar winners, both were disciples of Frank Capra, and both personified the long, lean, quiet ways of Lincolnesque Americana in their early films. Later on Capra recalled the special, nonverbal bond that had grown between the two actors: "One morning I was watching Jimmy mow his lawn when Gary drove over. They waved greetings. Then Coop raised his hands and made some shooting signs. Jimmy nodded. Coop held up two fingers. Jimmy shook his head. Instead, he raised three fingers. This time it was Gary who was negative. He held up four fingers. Jimmy nodded; Coop nodded. Friday—four days away. Nothing had been said. Nevertheless, an invitation to go hunting had been made and accepted. They waved good-by as Coop drove away."

Cooper and Rocky, both having decided that Jimmy's extended bachelor life did not appear to make him especially happy, decided to introduce him to one of Rocky's good (and eligible) friends, Gloria McLean, by inviting them both to a dinner party in their home.

Also present at the Coopers' that evening were Ronald Reagan, newly separated from his wife Jane Wyman, actress Ann Sothern, and Margaret Sullavan and Leland Hayward. It was Leland who had to convince a reluctant Jimmy to come along in the first place, despite the fact that he didn't have a date for the evening, having stopped seeing Dell.

Although Jimmy wasn't aware of it at the time, he had already, if fleetingly, met Gloria the year before, during the Christmas holidays, when, along with Bill Grady and Johnny Swope, he had decided to crash the actor Keenan Wynn's party and help himself to some imported, hard-to-get hundred-proof holiday cheer. Gloria, who happened to be one of the invited guests, was not at all impressed with the invaders' sloppy demeanor.

This time, during dinner at the Coopers', while chatting with Jimmy, Gloria realized they had a lot in common. They both loved to play golf and go sailing, were interested in animal conservation, and, perhaps most important, both loved movies—he making them, she seeing them. Later on that evening the party moved to Ciro's, the famed night spot on the Sunset Strip, where Nat "King" Cole was appearing.

During the show, Jimmy asked Gloria if she would like to go golfing with him. She would indeed, most definitely. He then asked her to dance.

The next day she beat him handily on the links.

— • —

Gloria Hatrick McLean was born in 1919 in Larchmont, New York, to Edgar B. and Jessie Hatrick. Edgar Hatrick had made his career by introducing newsreels to movie theaters to be played after the coming attractions and before the double feature. His efforts got him promoted to vice president and general manager of the Hearst Metrotone News, after which he moved the family to the tony suburbs just north of New York City.

While still a teenager, Gloria's good looks landed her a variety of local modeling jobs, and a stint as a dance instructor at the then-popular Arthur Murray Dance Studios and Schools. She thought about becoming an actress and took acting lessons for a while, but eventually rejected show business, preferring the more tangible pleasures of hunting, fishing, and golf.

With her quick wit and intense green eyes, she quickly joined the ranks of the most eligible young women in New York's registered social set. One evening, at a social function for Cosmopolitan Pictures, a Hearst subsidiary, Gloria met Edward Beale McLean II. Not long after, they married. Ned, as friends called him, was from a wealthy publishing family. His mother, Evelyn Walsh, owned the legendary Hope diamond.[6]

---

6. According to an interview conducted by the author with Jimmy Stewart's daughter, Kelly Stewart Harcourt: "The diamond was in the possession of the McLean family. It had a kind of 'evil eye' connotation to it, that we believed was some kind of curse. There was a bit of insanity that plagued the McLeans ever since they got the diamond."

Gloria and Ned moved to a ranch in Colorado, where she gave birth to two boys, Ronald in 1943, and Michael, three years later. By 1947, the marriage was over. Gloria divorced Ned in Sun Valley and moved with her boys to Los Angeles.

Single motherhood did not suit her and she let it be known among her social set, which included the Coopers, that she was interested in the possibility of remarriage. That was when Gary and Rocky Cooper decided that despite the more than ten-year difference in their ages, she and Jimmy were perfect for each other. They set up the dinner and let the dance take on a life of its own.

— • —

That October of 1948, only weeks after they had started dating, rumors of a new Jimmy Stewart romance began to appear in the pages of the gossip press. The *Los Angeles Times*, the paper of record for the film industry, covered the story in headlines:

JAMES STEWART LINKED WITH GLORIA McLEAN—

Hollywood Agog Over Latest Romance Rumor Concerning Its No. 1 Bachelor

———

James Stewart, Hollywood's No. 1 bachelor, is still rolling with Cupid's punches, it seems. But Cupid is still in there swinging, this time reportedly in the charming person of Gloria McLean, former wife of Edward B. McLean II.

The question furrowing Hollywood's brow nowadays is: Is Stewart serious with a girl at last?

Jimmy last night gave an answer—of sorts:

"I've had Mrs. McLean out to dinner several times. If that be romance, make the most of it."

Rumors of the romance stirred months ago when Stewart and Mrs. McLean were reported "engaged." That—as sometimes happens to Hollywood rumors—proved wrong.

Agent Pooh-Poohs

But the rumor didn't die. It popped up again, this time in a Denver newspaper report that said Stewart and Mrs. McLean were to have met in the fashionable Hotel Broadmoor in Colorado Springs last week. The meeting, the report said, was called off because Jimmy had some screen chores to do.

His agent pooh-poohed that one.

"If that's so," Jimmy retorted, "I guess every time I take a girl out to dinner, there's grounds for thinking there's a romance, eh?"

Who could have said it better?

Only, of course, a romance was exactly what it was, and a serious one at that.

It had really begun the instant Jimmy had laid eyes on Gloria. The spark he felt was unlike the usual instant heat zap he got from starlets, the ones who always, if temporarily, lit him up inside the forbidden zone. This was something else, more of a cool, sharp beam that didn't go away. (It did not hurt at all that Gloria physically resembled Jimmy's mother, Bessie, or, more accurately, the way she looked when he was a little boy.)

She had a lot of Alexander in her as well. She was into sports, physical fitness, was smart, articulate, haughty, and just a bit controlling. All of which Jimmy loved about her. "I could tell right off that she was a thoroughbred," Jimmy later told friends. "For me it had been love at first sight. She was the kind of a girl I had always dreamed of. The kind you associate with open country, cooking stew and not fainting because it was made of cut-up squirrels. She'd look at home on a sailboat or a raft; in a graceful swing from a tree branch into the swimming pool."

"The romance very nearly broke up before it got started," Gloria later recalled. "At the time, I had a beautiful big German police dog named Bellow. When Jimmy saw me to the door [that first night], Bellow took one look at the strange man and went for his jugular."

Jimmy: "I realized that I first had to woo the dog. I bought him steaks at Chasen's. I prattled baby talk to him. Patted him. Praised him. It got to be pretty humiliating, but we finally got to be friends. I was free to court Gloria!"

— • —

During that year, Jimmy concentrated as much on revitalizing his career as he did igniting his love life. Returning to MGM to star in Sam Wood's *The Stratton Story* was a big deal for him, as much as it was for the studio and for all of industrial Hollywood. In those uncertain times, performers not suspected of being Communists were, by *reductio ad absurdum,* loyalists, and were easily forgiven for all past industrial sins. Although Mayer still held a vengeful attitude toward Jimmy over their contractual differences, Sam Wood was eager to get *The Stratton Story* made, and, when Cooper proved unavailable, wanted and got Jimmy to play the lead.

Wood's previous baseball film, *The Pride of the Yankees* (1942), the very softly focused biography of New York Yankee Lou Gehrig, who'd died at a young age of the disease that would eventually bear his name, had starred Wood's good friend and politically correct actor Gary Cooper. Wood then lobbied for Cooper to play Monty Stratton, a ballplayer who, at the peak of his pitching career, had shot himself in the foot and wound up losing his leg. Mayer believed that despite the success of *Pride,* baseball pictures almost never made money, and at first agreed to green-light the feature only if Van Johnson played the part. As far as Mayer was concerned, Johnson, one of his favorites, epitomized perfect all-American youth, with his curly red hair and winning smile, and would bring the film the kind of warmth it needed to offset the grim saga of Stratton's blowing off his own leg.

Johnson, however, was prevented from being in the film by the real Stratton, who personally rejected him for the role. The ballplayer had somehow gotten casting approval over who would play him on the big screen, and after inviting Johnson to his home and working out with him, decided the actor, a professional song-and-dance man, wasn't a good enough ballplayer to be convincing as a major league pitcher. (It probably didn't hurt Jimmy any that Wood worked on Stratton to convince him the only actor besides Cooper who could do justice to playing him was Stewart.)

At the direct urging of Lew Wasserman and the indirect lobbying of producer Dore Schary—a relative newcomer to the scene who had come to MGM via RKO and who would eventually rise through the corporate ranks to lead the successful coup that ousted Mayer in 1951— Jimmy got the part.

Schary then ordered Wood to cast June Allyson as Stratton's wife, who had previously become something of a team with Van Johnson and had expected to be working with him again on the picture, but Wood had other ideas.[7] He wanted Donna Reed, though when Jimmy heard that, he vetoed her. He still had a bad taste in his mouth from *It's a Wonderful Life,* and didn't want to go through another round of movie-making with her. At that point, Wood, desperate to start shooting, went with Allyson, thereby creating one of the most successful "marriages" in all of Hollywood history.

Allyson and Jimmy's on-screen chemistry was real. They had known each other before either of them was married to their current spouses— Jimmy to Gloria, Allyson to actor Dick Powell. Jimmy and Allyson had dated, and at one point they actually considered marriage. Allyson recollected, "I knew Jimmy before he married Gloria. With my cooking, it's a good thing he didn't marry me. The poor dear weighed only 154 pounds before he was married and he was all of 6 feet 2 or 3 inches tall. Jimmy hated being photographed when he was out with a girl and he seldom took his dates to nightclubs. Instead, he fed them steak that he grilled himself in his own backyard. If they didn't like that and wanted the limelight, they were not for him . . . Gloria was the perfect choice. They were both so suited to each other—both slim and dignified and both with the same sense of humor."

Without question, on screen at least, the key to the successful pairing of Jimmy and June lay in their wholesomeness rather than any sexual chemistry. It was that wholesomeness that audiences wanted to see in Jimmy when he starred in films such as *The Stratton Story,* about a married man whose moral stamina allows him to overcome any and all obstacles, with, of course, the unwavering support of a good woman.

The Stratton Story became the first unqualified hit of Jimmy's postwar film career, the movie that finally restored him to the front ranks of Hollywood's A-level stars. His portrayal of a ballplayer with a life-threatening injury who overcomes it reverberated with American audiences as a clear metaphor for a generation of soldiers seriously wounded on the battlefield and now struggling to return to normal civilian life. To achieve the effect of having an artificial leg, Stewart wore a leather-and-steel device that kept one knee stiff and forced him to walk with a limp.[8] As he had in *Mr.*

---

7. Sometimes billed as June Allison. Her real name was Ella Geisman.

8. His second "limp" role in a row. In *Rope,* his character also had one, but, unlike Stratton's, which signified the struggle for a return to physical normalcy, the one in Hitchcock's film denoted a physical imperfection that personified a moral one.

Smith, when he used an external method—throat painting—as part of his acting technique, Stewart employed a physical prop to help him find the character's interior.

The Stratton Story was also the first of a series of films in which Jimmy portrayed a living American cultural hero. In the next decade he would enact the lives of such uncomplicated (or so they were thought to be at the time) American iconic figures as Charles Lindbergh and Glenn Miller, polishing up the luster of their "perfect lives," while adding his own performance's sheen to their legends.

Immediately after *The Stratton Story* wrapped, Jimmy went right back into the MGM studios to make Richard Thorpe's *Malaya,* an uncomplicated star vehicle for Spencer Tracy.[9] Tracy was at the height of his postwar popularity, and Jimmy was eager to work with him again.

Malaya revolves around a rubber-smuggling scheme during World War Two. The Allies need it, the Japanese have it on occupied Malaya, the Americans intend to smuggle it out. Royer (Stewart) is chosen to help Carnaghan (Spencer), a smuggler currently serving a life prison in Alcatraz looking for a pardon by completing the mission. Their mysterious but knowledgeable middleman, The Dutchman, was played by Sydney Greenstreet, in a variation of The Fat Man from John Huston's *The Maltese Falcon* (1941).

The film, a so-so, rainy-Saturday matinee adventure yarn, came and went fairly quickly. It was released in the shadow of another Tracy film, George Cukor's hilariously urbane *Adam's Rib,* one everyone at MGM loved, with its unbeatable chemistry between Katharine Hepburn and her co-star. Audiences much preferred Spencer's Adam to his Carnaghan, and proved it at the box office.

In real life Tracy was nothing like either Adam or Carnaghan, neither a man-o'-war adventurer or a domesticated intellectual. He was, rather, a bad drunk, frustrated by marital difficulties, his off-screen relationship with Hepburn, health problems, and money woes. This time around, in *Malaya,* unlike years earlier, Tracy was anything but kind to Jimmy, no longer the wide-eyed boyish innocent, but someone who was about to overtake him (again) in the popularity polls. For his part, Jimmy was turned off by Tracy's star-power demands, and the nickname his co-star

---

9. *Malaya* is also known as *East of the Rising Sun* in foreign distribution.

had assigned him: "son of a bitch," as in "Listen to me, you son of a bitch, . . ."

Neither said good-bye the last day of production, and they never again spoke directly to each other.

The Stratton Story held its premiere at New York's prestigious Radio City Music Hall on May 12, 1949, to coincide with the onset of the baseball season. It went on to become MGM's biggest hit of the year and the sixth highest-grossing film of 1949, earning an impressive $4 million in its initial domestic run. The *New York Times* once more singled out Jimmy for praise: "*The Stratton Story* was the best thing that has yet happened to Mr. Stewart in his post-war film career . . . he gives such a winning performance that it is almost impossible to imagine any one else playing the role." The *New York Herald Tribune* agreed: "The redoubtable James Stewart has turned baseball player in *The Stratton Story*. Thanks to his engaging and artful performance, a sentimental and inspirational screen biography has more than a little power."

— • —

However, Jimmy had far more important matters on his mind than how the movie was received. Shortly after *Stratton's* release and during production on his next film, Delmer Daves's *Broken Arrow,* Jimmy asked Gloria, whom he'd been seeing now for a year, to help celebrate his forty-first birthday. He spent the entire day rehearsing his proposal speech to her. She said yes even before he finished stammering through it on one of his narrow, bended knees.

As he loved to tell friends later on, whenever he recounted the story, "I, I, I pitched the big question to her last night and to my surprise she, she, she said *yes!*"

17

"If the prewar Stewart stood for something essentially American, the postwar Stewart stood for something truly universal. It's difficult to think of another American star who remade his own image so thoroughly, or so bravely."

—MARTIN SCORSESE

roken Arrow (1950), which shot for nine weeks in northern Arizona, not far from the Grand Canyon, was a real departure for Jimmy, the first real Western he had ever been in (not counting the jocular *Destry Rides Again*). His wedding to Gloria was scheduled to take place at the completion of the principal photography.

Had Jimmy not been so caught up in real-life romance, it is likely he never would have agreed to appear in the film at all, especially not one as artificially romantic, idealistic, and blatantly liberal as this one (as opposed to the unabashedly patriotic *The Stratton Story*). *Broken Arrow*'s script and leading role were, in truth, far more suited to the rough-hewn looks, talents, and sensibilities of a Henry Fonda. The brainstorm of Selznick executive Julian Blaustein, the film tells the story of a relationship between an Apache chief, Cochise (Jeff Chandler), and Tom Jeffords (Stewart), based on the novel *Blood Brother* by Elliott Arnold. It was the first postwar, post-Holocaust picture in Hollywood to deal with the nineteenth-century plight of the Indians, from their point of view, a film in which they spoke educated "American" English. Because the chosen screenwriter, Albert Maltz, had by now made it to the blacklist as part of the notorious Hollywood Ten, a particularly vociferous group that refused to cooperate with the committee, he was forced to use a "front." In this instance, it was Michael Blankfort who was given screenwriter credit, for a payoff, for the movie.[1]

---

1. The Hollywood Ten were cited in 1947 for contempt by HUAC, and all served up to a year in prison. They were Herbert Biberman, Albert Maltz, Lester Cole, Dalton

The whole project was another specially bundled deal from Wasserman, who represented not only Jimmy but also Blaustein, Daves, and secretly, Maltz, and sold them together as a "package" to 20th Century Fox.

To play the part of (white) Jeffords's Apache love interest (a mixed pairing that pleased no one, from the studio heads to the FBI to the Apache tribe to mainstream audiences), a young, white contract player by the name of Debra Paget was chosen. She was only sixteen years old, twenty-five years younger than her toupeed leading man.

— • —

On the last day of two weeks of additional filming on Fox's backlot in Los Angeles, in anticipation of their upcoming nuptials, Jimmy and Gloria were surprised by a shower of wedding gifts consisting of fifty-two Indian blankets, forty pairs of beaded moccasins, thirteen turquoise necklaces, eleven deerskin blouses, thirty-seven hand-woven baskets, and one papoose carrier. All of it had come from the three hundred native Apaches Blaustein had hired to give the film an added sense of authenticity; it was a gesture that deeply moved Jimmy, who had come to know and admire the culture of the Native American tribe.

Their first night alone back in Los Angeles, Jimmy presented Gloria with a solid gold compact he had had custom made to match a similar cigarette case he had previously given to her. The next morning he took his bride-to-be to get their marriage license.

— • —

No one could have been happier than Jimmy, who proudly proclaimed to anyone within earshot, reporters included, that he had found his "perfect" bride, "the right girl," "an absolutely beautiful girl," "a funny girl," one with a "great sense of humor" who was "devoted," and "just about everything you could think of." This mountain of public praise was lovely and heartfelt, but the parts he left out told the truer tale. By finding someone suitable to marry, he was finally ready to take his place alongside, rather than below, Alexander in the hierarchy of Stewarts. And what

Trumbo, John Howard Lawson, Alvah Bessie, Samuel Ornitz, Ring Lardner Jr., Edward Dmytryk, and Adrian Scott. In several other biographies of Stewart, Maltz is not even mentioned. His proper accreditation for *Broken Arrow* was restored in 1991 at the behest of the Authors Guild. By then, both Maltz and Blankfort were dead.

was it he loved most about her? In 1970, for an interview with *Modern Maturity* magazine, Stewart described Gloria this way: "She's a little like my mother, who was somewhat domineering but always got what she wanted in a very kindly way."

Gloria, in fact, had been the aggressor, one of the reasons the marriage had a chance of working. "When I first met Jimmy at Gary Cooper's dinner party, I wasn't divorced yet, just separated, so I was in no hurry to get married," she told one reporter. "And all my friends told me I was making a large mistake marrying a bachelor; they're too hard to train!" Privately, Gloria had been disillusioned by the events of her first marriage. Her husband, a trust-fund brat, was an inveterate womanizer and a bad alcoholic, whose skirt-chasing and drinking both increased after they were wed. The marriage didn't last long but the heartbreak did, and while love may have been the motivating force the first time around, this time Gloria was more realistic. She told friends, including the Coopers, that she was looking for a decent man with a strong character, a proper father who could help raise her sons, and someone with enough money to keep her in the style to which she had become accustomed. The extremely trainable, naturally domestic, wealthy, and never-married Stewart perfectly fit her bill as much as she did his.[2]

Their relationship was not considered as perfect by Jimmy's family. For all her good qualities, Gloria was also a divorcée, a Maitland-Stewart no-no. The unspoken family credo was you got married and stayed married. She smoked, which to Alexander signaled a certain type of woman in which Hollywood specialized. And she was not a particularly good cook, housekeeper, or a regular churchgoer. The fact that she seemed capable of actually making Jimmy happy registered low on the scale of the Stewart family's initial evaluation of his chosen bride.

To stay on good terms with them, Gloria had no objections when Jimmy insisted, at Alexander's urging, that he and Gloria go before a committee on marriage and divorce at the Presbytery of Los Angeles. After a careful review of all the "facts," it was decided by the powers that be that a Presbyterian minister would not be guilty of any impropriety in officiating at the ceremony.

---

2. McLean, meanwhile, went east, married a hat-check girl who worked at the Stork Club in New York City, and eventually drank himself to an early death.

The decision held meaning and importance only to his parents. Jimmy had not been a regular churchgoer since leaving Princeton. As far as he was concerned, they could be married at City Hall. But to keep peace in the family he and Gloria agreed to this ritual of consent and tried to look pleased when the committee gave them its blessing.

The date of the wedding was set for August 9, at the Brentwood Presbyterian Church, to be followed by a reception at the Brentwood home of Peggy and Jack Bolton, Bolton being one of Wasserman's assistants and a good friend of Jimmy's. Three days before, Alexander and Bessie arrived in Pasadena by train from Pennsylvania (Gloria's parents were unable to attend the wedding because her mother was hospitalized in New York. Her father, also ill and living in Colorado Springs, died a month after the ceremony).

A raucous, good-natured "stag," or bachelor, party was thrown by John Swope and Myron McCormick at Chasen's, where a FAREWELL sign hung over the front door and two midgets appeared dressed in diapers. Several, but by no means all, of Jimmy's friends turned out for the occasion, and they drank until they were plastered to the walls. Everyone except Jimmy, that is, who had a few that caused his already flip-flopping stomach to churn like a nervous volcano.

He arrived at the church dressed in a blue suit, looking a bit pallid, and, as one witness recalled, "rather bewildered." His best man was Billy Grady, a choice that surprised some and shocked others who had been in his close circle for years. Grady was certainly a friend, but everyone asked why it wasn't Henry Fonda. For that matter, where was Fonda? Not at the wedding, that was for sure. Nor was Dore Schary. Nor was Guthrie McClintic. If the bachelor party had been meant as a farewell, Jimmy apparently took it literally and attempted to leave single life, and those still living it, behind.

The bride, dressed in a ballerina-length gray satin dress with push-up sleeves and a square neckline, had a band of flowers that looked like a halo on her curled brown locks. Her sister, Ruth Draddy, was the matron of honor, and her brother-in-law, Gregg, gave her away. Those who did attend from Jimmy's world were the Coopers, Frank Morgan, the David Nivens, the George Murphys, an unaccompanied (separated) Spencer Tracy, Ann Sothern, Mary Livingston, Mrs. Van Johnson, Dorothy McGuire, Johnny Swope, and Margaret Sullavan and Leland Hayward, who traveled to Hollywood especially for the ceremony and

headed directly back east the next day. The ceremony took twelve minutes, after which Jimmy kissed his bride, then they walked through the
doors of the church into the bright Southern California sunshine where
he kissed her again for the photographers, press, and the thousand fans
who had gathered behind the barricades to catch a glimpse of their favorite star.

Two days later, the couple left for Akron, Ohio, where Stewart was the
grand marshal of the National Soap Box Derby, after which they traveled
on to Cleveland to attend the convention of the Disabled American Veterans as personal guests of Gen. Jonathan Wainwright. Their next stop was
a brief one, in Indiana, to visit some relatives and say a quick hello/good-
bye to his parents. They then visited Gloria's mother in New York City, followed, at last, by a two-week honeymoon in Honolulu.

Upon their return to Los Angeles, Gloria convinced Jimmy to move
into her spacious house up on Coldwater Canyon, rather than she into his
smaller place, mainly because of the boys. There simply wasn't enough
room in Jimmy's one-bedroom pad in Brentwood for everyone. Having
settled in at Gloria's, and happily assuming the role of father as well as
husband, Jimmy was, at last, ready to get back to making movies.

— · —

Lew Wasserman was waiting for him with welcome arms and a
new deal, one he felt was "perfect" for the actor, a movie called *Winchester '73*. The film would change the direction of his career. The deal
behind it would change his life.

The seeds of the negotiations for *Winchester '73* lay in Wasserman's early forties "million-dollar contract" with Warner Bros. for their
second-tier player Ronald Reagan, the "Errol Flynn of the B's," as he
was then known in the industry. Wasserman had managed to secure for
Reagan $758,000 from the studio for forty weeks of guaranteed work a
year, for seven years. During this time Reagan appeared in twenty-nine
films, including William Keighley's *Brother Rat* (1938) and Lloyd
Bacon's *Knute Rockne, All American* (1940—in which he said the im-
mortal line, "Win one for the Gipper!"), before giving what is generally
considered his best on-screen performance, in Sam Wood's *Kings Row*
(1942), which was nominated for Best Picture, Best Director, and Best
Black and White Cinematography (James Wong Howe). After the critical and commercial success of *Kings Row,* Jack Warner believed Reagan

was at last ready to make the leap to A-list stardom. To prevent him from signing with another studio, as Wasserman implied was about to happen, Warner bumped up Reagan's contract to a cool million a year, breaking that glass ceiling for contract players.

Wasserman was now looking to make the same kind of spectacular money jump for Stewart at Universal, only not as a long-term deal, but within the limits of per picture framework. Wasserman set up a gross-percentage deal for Jimmy to appear in *Winchester '73*. While not unprecedented, only a handful of stars had ever been awarded this golden goose. Most of those who bargained for back-end money usually wound up settling for the illusory promise but not the money of *net* profits.[3]

The key to making the deal happen was Jimmy's phenomenal success on Broadway in the title role of *Harvey* at a time when his film career had been at a low. Although the show had already been a hit before he filled in for Frank Fay, it was nothing like the smash it became with Jimmy.

During the run, Wasserman quietly negotiated a series of well-planned moves to ensure that Jimmy would be offered the title role in the screen version. First he brokered the sale of *Harvey*'s film rights to William Goetz, the head of production at Universal, in what today might look like a suspiciously inside deal, as every other studio had wanted a chance to get their hands on the property. Goetz (who happened to be Louis B. Mayer's son-in-law), paid the playwright Mary C. Chase, also represented by Wasserman, $150,000 for the rights to her play. Once he had the rights, Goetz offered Jimmy $200,000 plus a share of the film's net profits if he agreed to star in it. To get him, Goetz had to make the offer through Wasserman, who wanted a second movie for Jimmy built in to the deal, with terms that sounded irresistible to Goetz on every level. Wasserman offered Jimmy no salary, but, sight unseen (meaning the property), *half the gross profits*. Starring in the film version of *Harvey*, a role Jimmy very much wanted (despite Frank Fay's

---

3. *Gross percentage* is the money a film earns *before* any and all expenses, including salaries, negative cost, distribution, and advertising are paid back to the studio. Net profits are what is left over *after* all expenses are deducted. Obviously, a studio would rather spend its profits on more advertising to generate more revenue, which are then listed as expenses, than pay much, most often nothing, in so-called net earnings.

spirited effort to get it), was the part of the deal that helped Wasserman convince him to take it.[4]

Wasserman also insisted that, since he was, in a way, subsidizing it, Jimmy have considerable control over the making of that second film, which was *Winchester '73*. No other cast member (including his popular co-star Shelley Winters) could have the same-size star billing; Jimmy's name had to come first in the credits. He also had to have director approval and approval of the rest of the cast.

The deal so angered Mayer, who was already far along the process of being eased out at MGM by Schary but still quite vocal in his opinions on how the film business was now run, that he declared James Stewart and Lew Wasserman the two men most responsible for destroying what was left of the crumbling studio system. And he cut Goetz out of his will.[5]

The last and most important business at hand for Jimmy (and Wasserman) was finding the right director for the second film, and after finally getting around to reading the script, Jimmy realized for the first time just how important that choice was.

Because, for a change, this one was a genuine work of art.

---

4. The original studio memo, dated February 15, 1950, actually guarantees Stewart 50 percent of the film's profits, defined as all monies left after a maximum 25 percent of the gross was deducted for distribution, production of the original negative, and general studio overhead, including advertising and distribution pay out.

5. Mayer and Goetz never spoke to each other again.

18

*A*nthony Mann was a Jewish-American careerist loner who vicariously experienced the horrors of the Holocaust while trying to assimilate himself into the great American dream, a cultural and artistic conflict that cast a long shadow on his life and work. He was born Emil Bundsmann, a name he eventually abandoned, some claimed because it sounded too Nazi-Germanic, while others believed he thought it was "too Jewish," and was more than willing to leave the *bund* and keep the *man* in order to pass into the mainstream of the all-American WASP ideal.

Mann was born in 1906 in San Diego, California, where both his parents taught philosophy at the university. Early on, his family moved to the more culturally diverse boundaries of New York City where, when young Emil was ten, he developed an intense interest in stage performing. He frequented a Manhattan branch of the YMHA (Young Men's Hebrew Association) and while still in high school acted and directed plays for it. He dropped out at the age of sixteen to earn money, lying his way into a night watchman's job at Westinghouse Electric in order to be free to spend his days looking for acting work. When he found none, he quit his $35-a-week job for one that paid $10, serving as a messenger boy for the Stagers acting troupe. Shortly thereafter, he joined the Triangle Theater in Greenwich Village, then worked his way through a number of theatrical groups until he formed his own stock company, the Red Barn Playhouse, which traveled the Northeast corridor, before taking up permanent residence in Long Island.[1] Eventually he landed a leading role in the Broadway production *The Squall* (in

---

1. No relation to the Logan Triangle Players.

which he did double duty as the assistant stage manager) and made his directorial debut helming Christopher Morley's *Thunder on the Left*, which was followed by a series of successful Broadway shows he directed as the newly anglicized "Anthony Mann."

He was introduced to film while serving as a New York auditions runner for David O. Selznick, and eventually helped cast many of the supporting roles in Victor Fleming's *Gone With the Wind*, Gregory Ratoff's *Intermezzo* (1939), and Alfred Hitchcock's *Rebecca*, because Selznick wanted his films fleshed out with Broadway caliber talent. From Selznick, Mann moved on to Paramount, where he became an assistant to the great Preston Sturges. When the studio felt he was ready, it gave Mann a chance to direct a movie of his own, *Dr. Broadway* (1942), which is where the public caught its first glimpse of what was to become, in a series of distinctive films, the Mann-ish style of forties noir. As the decade drew to a close, Mann caught a career break when Austrian-born Fritz Lang, another *noiree,* and Jimmy's first choice, dropped out as director of *Winchester '73* after concluding that the forty-two-year-old slim-Jim actor was just not strong enough to handle the part of tough-guy totem Lin McAdam.

In the winter of 1950, Jimmy screened movies and Mann's body of work, and was especially impressed by *Devil's Doorway* (1950).[2] He thought the not-yet-released film was a darker, rougher, and altogether more period-specific Western than his own *Broken Arrow* and that it had exactly the atmospherics that *Winchester '73* needed. By choosing Mann, Jimmy began what was to become one of the most dynamic, if darkest, creative partnerships to emerge in postwar Hollywood.

Winchester '73, a delirium of auteurist vision, is a Freudian nightmare played out in the time code of adolescent America, wherein one brother, Lin McAdam, is in a rage of revenge against the other, "Dutch" Henry Brown (Stephen McNally), for the killing of their father, although we do not learn of this aspect of their sibling relationship until the end of the film. Undoubtedly, the idea of "avenging his father's death" was a notion that appealed to the newly married Stewart, perhaps feeling for the first time able to compete with Alexander on every

---

2. The film, released the same time as *Broken Arrow,* which came out after *Winchester '73,* was overshadowed by *Broken Arrow*'s enormous popularity.

level. The idea of playing his rescuer slipped along the curvy edge of their longstanding, if unacknowledged Oedipal rivalry, doubled in the film by a brother Jimmy did not have in real life.

Added to the story is a layer that at first glance teeters dangerously close to gimmickry, the passing along of a rifle, the eponymous Winchester '73, a talisman that here actually serves as an astonishingly bold phallic symbol. Its long barrel, fiery ejaculations of bullets, and blood-battles for ownership are pure Mann, nuanced in a stylishly explosive way. He made Jimmy, for the first time in films, walk tall, ride hard, and act tough, and indeed he did. He shot to kill and seemed quite at home doing it.

The film, budgeted at a modest $850,000 for a thirty-day shooting schedule, escalated to $918,000 before production was completed. Most of it was shot in Tucson, Arizona, with the opening sequence—the contest for the rifle—taking a full four days before Mann was satisfied that he had captured on film what he wanted, and the final dizzying, dazzling dialogue-thick shootout between brothers on location as well. To appear skillful as a sharpshooter, Stewart spent hours every day for weeks, until his knuckles were red sore, on the firing range taking lessons from Herb Parsons, an expert dispatched from the Winchester movie (and who did most of the trick shots performed by Stewart in the film).

Audiences were shocked at the James Stewart they saw in *Winchester '73*, a film that pushed back the noir of the forties to another century to better (and more safely) examine the paranoia that had split Hollywood brother against brother in the crackling fury of the blacklist. In every way this was a political, psychological, emotional, adventuresome, and wholly satisfying thriller.

— • —

Shooting on *Winchester '73* began on February 14, 1950, one day after Stewart received the Photoplay Magazine Gold Medal for being the screen's most popular male performer of 1949, in acknowledgment of his portrayal of Monty Stratton.[3] Similarly, *The Stratton*

---

3. Jane Wyman won Female Most Popular performer for her Academy Award–winning (Best Actress) role in Jean Negulesco's *Johnny Belinda*, released in 1948. Male photoplay runners-up were Kirk Douglas, Cary Grant, Bob Hope, and William Bendix. Female runners-up were Olivia de Havilland, Ingrid Bergman, June Allyson, and Loretta Young.

Story won for Best Picture, with medals going to producer Jack Cummings, coauthors Douglas Morrow and Guy Trosper, and, posthumously, to director Sam Wood, who had died of a heart attack at the age of sixty-five the previous September. Appearing in person at the ceremonial dinner and adding a touch of genuine emotion was the real Monty Stratton.

The film opened in June to spectacular reviews, with critics noting the emergence of this James Stewart, a tough, strong, hard killer without a conscience who, at one point, pounds bad guy Dan Duryea's head to a near pulp on the hard wood of a saloon bar, a scene that anyone who sees it for the first time is not likely to forget. According to screenwriter Borden Chase, "When the picture was given a sneak preview, there had been some titters in the audience at seeing Stewart's name in the opening titles of a western. This was before *Broken Arrow* was released. But once he smashed Duryea in the bar, there was no more snickering." The *New York Herald Tribune* said that "Stewart takes to horses and fast shooting as though he had been doing nothing else throughout his illustrious career."

Indeed, this was the first film to showcase the so-called "mature" Stewart, although hints at his deeper and darker side could be found as early as *Mr. Smith* and throughout *It's a Wonderful Life*. However, whereas Frank Capra had used those qualities in neoreligious fantasies of sacrifice and resurrection, Mann put them into a far more complex psychological context that, as critic Richard Jameson wrote, "was not only a rock-ribbed Western revenge saga—Stewart on the trail of brother Stephen McNally, who had murdered their father—but an amazingly encyclopedic cross-section of a genre Mann was about to set his own brand to." Without strain, *Winchester '73* manages to incorporate a talismanic weapon, an epic marksmanship contest, a cavalry-and-Indians battle, a shady lady on a stagecoach (Shelley Winters), a stalwart sidekick for the hero (the great Millard Mitchell), a crazy outlaw (Dan Duryea in excelsis), a tin-horn gambler-gunrunner (John McIntire), a bank holdup, a poker game at a halfway house, miscellaneous chases and contretemps, and Wyatt Earp (Will Geer). Stewart and McNally's sibling rivalry is a study in controlled frenzy from the moment they sight each other and slap empty holders (they're in Earp's domain) to a cliffside climax wherein Mann's direction notes call for the "screaming trajectory of every ricochet." Critic Elliott Stein went even further, highlighting the link between Stewart's postwar desires (and combat traumas) to the kind of movies he chose throughout much of the new decade, when he declared that "Mann's reputation rests principally on the series of classic westerns he made in the 1950s, five of them starring James Stewart . . . one of the great actor-director partnerships, with few precedents in American movies . . . with Stewart's characters nearly always haunted by the past and the action triggered by a reaction to a traumatic incident that took place before the story begins." Critic Terence Rafferty echoes this interpretation: "The Westerners played by Stewart in *Winchester '73* [and the other Mann Westerns he starred in] are, like noir heroes, mighty ambiguous characters, motivated either by ignoble emotions like the desire for revenge or by the urge to distance themselves from an unsavory, violent past."

In every way, *Winchester '73* was a triumph and a turning point for Stewart. Overlapping with his new life as a married man, it signaled the emergence, the reinvention really, of a more steely maturity and an emotionally complex, edgier Jimmy Stewart, whose vulnerabilities in real life and on the screen became the basis for many of the twenty-four films he would make in the fifties. The depth of range, emotional upheaval, romantic exploration, and compulsive dramatics in that remarkable run remains unequaled in the history of modern movies.[4]

Jimmy had already displayed his toughness to the world in wartime, even as he proved to himself, beyond any doubt, that he was once and forever a Maitland and a Stewart. The challenge for him now was to find a way to reconcile the emotional toll hard combat had taken on him with the image of the youthful innocent the American public (and Hollywood) still thought he was.

Beginning with *It's a Wonderful Life,* Jimmy's characters took on a dimension that had not been evident in any of the prewar characters he had portrayed. Even in Capra's 1946 throw-back glorification withcracks of small-town Americana, these differences began to show. In simpler times, as Jefferson Smith in *Mr. Smith Goes to Washington,*

---

4. The twenty-four films Stewart made in the fifties are out of an astonishing total of the eighty feature films he made during his lifetime, plus more than fifty appearances as himself in various documentaries, two TV series, and forty-two TV appearances as himself, including eight on the *Jack Benny Program,* six on the *Dean Martin Variety* series, and nine on *The Tonight Show Starring Johnny Carson.*

Jimmy's heroism had been less complex because it was purely external, the hoarse throat a metaphor for democracy's struggle to be heard, while the character simultaneously (and quite predictably, in formulaic Hollywood fare) falls in a goofy swoon-love with his secretary. In *Life*, it's a different story. George Bailey never even gets as far as the edge of town before his character drops into a despair that turns hauntingly inward; it is the emotional suffering more than the social injustice that pumps the blood through the temples of this movie.

With Mann, Jimmy found something Capra could no longer supply for him, a suitable mise-en-scène, a dynamic correlative to the real horrors of war, a physical turf that extended the mental terrain. Whatever it was that Mann tapped in to, Jimmy's performances in these films come across as less acting than acting out, less sentimental than psychosomatic, less intellectually plotted than emotionally scarred. Making *Winchester '73*, Jimmy found a fitting outlet for his shell-shocked sensibilities, and in it and the rest of the Mann Westerns he would set the stage for his grand emotional leap into Hitchcock's *Vertigo*, in which Jimmy, as Scottie Ferguson, does not merely react to the nightmarish circumstances in which he finds himself ensnared, he remains trapped within them, unable to escape, the haunting no longer distinguishable from the haunted.

— · —

Broken Arrow opened three months after *Winchester '73*, due at least in part to the problem of Albert Maltz (if word got out that he had actually written the film, it might suffer at the box office), and also because Fox had recently released several films that could be classified as "liberal" (Anatole Litvak's *The Snake Pit*, Elia Kazan's *Pinky* and *Gentleman's Agreement*) in an atmosphere of committee hearings and witch hunts. However, it benefited from the success of *Winchester '73* and the crest of a wave of Stewart popularity.

The "gurrrlll," meanwhile, as Jimmy liked to refer to Gloria in private ("my wife" in public, almost never referring to her by name), was eager to get away with him as soon as possible to take a vacation. Prior to the opening of the two films and the start of production on *Harvey*, she persuaded her husband to take her and the two boys to England. While there, Jimmy took her around to the places he remembered from his wartime days, and the press, at his request, let them alone as much as possible. It was a fun trip, one he would remember fondly, coming as it did at a time when he had managed to resurrect his career and felt he was once more flying high.

— • —

Back in time for the premieres of his two Westerns, he was ready to resume work, and the first order of business was the second part of the Wasserman-conceived *Winchester '73* deal, the shooting of the film *Harvey.*

Jimmy brought his rabbit act to the big screen under the creative auspices of Henry Koster, in charge of transforming the stage play into a film. The plot of *Harvey* is light as the head of the foam at the top of a beer, if not quite as frothy or substantial. Elwood P. Dowd (Stewart), a gentle, always inebriated philosopher of life, who enjoys bringing happiness to others, spends most of his days down at the local pub engaged in conversation with his favorite drinking buddy, an invisible rabbit he calls Harvey. A bachelor at forty, his sister Veta (Josephine Hull) and niece Myrtle Mae (Victoria Horne) are concerned their well-to-do brother and uncle, despite his all his money, will never find a wife. When Veta decides to have her brother committed, Elwood manages to get her taken away while he walks out scot-free. Not only that, but the admissions director of the hospital begins to believe that "Harvey" is real, as do several other staff members, all of whom undergo a transformation into much nicer people. Eventually people come to accept Elwood and Harvey and decide the world is a better place when both the man and his six-foot rabbit are in it.

Harvey opened on October 13, 1950, to less than spectacular reviews. The film left critics and audiences alike scratching their heads, wondering what all the fuss was about (a few who had seen Fay in the Broadway show lamented his absence), and the film was quickly pulled from release. While he never liked to respond directly to critics, Stewart admitted to friends that the film had been a mistake, that he shouldn't have done it, especially after *Winchester '73*. Nonetheless, if *Harvey* proved a financial and/or popular success (*Harvey's* eventual acceptance, like that of *It's a Wonderful Life,* came much later, due mostly to repeated showings on television), the trajectory of his career might have taken a different turn. Because it was *Winchester '73* that proved the big film of the three, Stewart wanted to continue to work with Mann, and to discard the slow, drawling comedies that once made him seem purist and altruistic, but now, as a grown man in his forties, something like brain-damaged. For much of the rest of the fifties, he would appear in offbeat, darker films, culminating in the most offbeat, darkest film of the decade, perhaps of all time, Alfred Hitchcock's *Vertigo*. But that was still a long way off.

Despite *Harvey's* financial failure, it was part of a film deal that finally gained Stewart entrance into the millionaires' club, thanks in large part to Lew Wasserman's adjusted gross clause. After the studio recouped its original production costs, Stewart received 50 percent of the two films' profits with net limited to 25 percent for distribution and studio overhead. While this may not seem like much today, it was revolutionary at the time. For a film that cost a little over $900,000 to make—the so-called negative cost of *Winchester '73*, Stewart eventually earned more than $600,000, a figure that would have been inconceivable as a prefigured salary on a film with that kind of budget. With the added $200,000 plus percentage he earned for *Harvey*, the two-picture deal for the first time put him over the magical million-dollar figure in earnings for a single year.[5]

Shortly after completing *Harvey*, Stewart shot another quickie, Walter Lang's *The Jackpot*, a goof-ball comedy without laughs about the woes of sudden inheritance. He did it for Fox, and for the money.

To make his final film of the year, Jimmy went to Great Britain where, on September 25, at the Fox affiliate Denham Studios, he began filming Henry Koster's *No Highway in the Sky* (aka *No Highway*), written by acclaimed novelist Nevil Shute, whose novel *On the Beach* would thrust him into the front ranks of popular fiction writers. The film is an airplane drama about a plane in danger of exploding due to structural defects, paranoia a popular theme in fifties films when commercial flying increased dramatically. Stewart did it for his love for flying and a chance to return yet again to England with his wife and sons.

---

5. According to Lew Wasserman biographer Dennis McDougal, "Stewart's [contract] success launched a full-blown actors' revolt. Every star on and off the MCA client list now wanted Wasserman to swing the same kind of profit participation deal for him." Those who successfully renegotiated their contracts were Tyrone Power, Tony Curtis, and Clark Gable, all of whom became millionaires for the first time by virtue of aligning themselves with MCA, Lew Wasserman, and his new team of aggressive agents who used Jimmy's two-picture deal as their contract model.

His co-stars were Glynis Johns and Marlene Dietrich, who made it clear she was unhappy to be co-starring with the much younger Glynis Johns, or to be reunited with her former co-star and one-time lover Stewart, with whom she had made *Destry Rides Again*. This time around, Dietrich was relegated to a character role, while the much younger, sexier Glynis Johns got all the attention. On top of that, the happily married Stewart was not at all interested in the aging German movie star.

As a result, the tension between the two stars was palpable, and the production was not at all aided by the fact that during filming on November 15, Stewart had to be rushed to the hospital, doubled over in pain. His emergency appendectomy and week-long stay in the hospital added to the problems of getting the film delivered on time. Production was completed on December 29, and that same day Stewart and the family flew back to America.

One other significant and much happier event took place at the end of 1950. Just before they left for England, Gloria found out she was pregnant. On November 11, Hedda Hopper broke the story in the *Los Angeles Times* that Jimmy Stewart and his wife, Gloria, were expecting a baby.

Two weeks later, Louella O. Parsons, writing for the *L.A. Times*'s chief rival, the Hearst-owned *L.A. Examiner*, scooped Hopper and everyone else when she revealed that Gloria Stewart was going to have twins.

"It's the best Christmas present either of us could have," she told the reporter over the phone, just before Jimmy's emergency surgery.

"That's my gurrrrrl," Jimmy told friends back in the States, with the biggest grin they'd ever seen riding side-saddle atop his gently rounded jaw.

19

"I played Jimmy Stewart's wife so often that Dick Powell once rose at a banquet and introduced him as 'My wife's husband.'"

—JUNE ALLYSON

*T*he first order of business for Jimmy and Gloria Stewart was to find a new home large enough for a family of six. Jimmy's first choice was to build a place from the ground up on a little piece of property he had had his eye on for some time, just off the coast of Pacific Palisades above Malibu, but Gloria rejected that idea because she felt the steep cliffs, endless beaches, and the warm waters of the inviting ocean were too dangerous for small children.

She favored a two-story, ivy-covered Tudor house on North Roxbury Drive in the heart of Beverly Hills that she initially described as looking more like a dormitory than a home, something that made Jimmy laugh, before realizing that a dormitory might be exactly what they were going to need.

They bought the Tudor in January 1951 and moved in later that month. The interior was plain and spacious, with non–show business furnishings more likely to be found in Indiana than Beverly Hills. Gloria was in charge of the décor, and she chose a combination of muted beige and green tones as her basic color scheme. She had the living room built around a large fireplace at one end, and put Jimmy's grand piano on the other. Several family-oriented oil paintings were hung, including their collection of Rouaults alongside paintings by disabled veterans that Jimmy was especially fond of. Upstairs were five bedrooms, one for each child and one for the Stewarts, with two rooms ready and waiting for the expected twins. The lower level of the house was finished with a TV/family room, a kitchen, a breakfast room (where most of the meals were eaten), and a formal dining room, used mostly for entertaining guests.

Gloria gave birth on May 7, 1951, at Cedars of Lebanon in Beverly Hills to twins, Kelly and Judy. "Where Gloria and I got so fortunate was that we got girl twins to go with the two boys. We had decided, when we expected just one child, that it would be named Kelly. We wanted to use a family name, and Kelly was a name for either sex, and this represented my father's side of the family. Kelly Jackson Stewart, that's her name, Jackson being a name from my mother's side." They named the other girl Judy. "Judy Powell Stewart was what we named her. The Powell part was for Gloria's family. But the Judy—well, that was plain sentimentality on both our parts. Hoagy [Carmichael] wrote a song years ago that I could play on the piano and sing, and Gloria remembered that I used to play it to her before we got married."

The actual birth had been an unexpectedly difficult cesarean because of the size of the twins, further complicated by what was believed to have been an unrelated intestinal condition discovered during the operation that grew progressively worse in the hours immediately following delivery. The girls were perfectly healthy—Kelly weighed in at 5 pounds 14 ounces, Judy at 6 pounds 2 ounces—but that same day Gloria underwent first minor, then what was described by her doctor, Mark Rabwin, as major surgery.

The next few days were tense, punctuated by a series of improvements and relapses, then more surgery, before Gloria was suddenly rushed to intensive care and Jimmy was told she was gravely ill. He remained at her side as much as the doctors would allow, and when he wasn't, he either paced nervously outside her room, chain-smoking, or sat on a bench in the hallway, his head buried in his hands or his fingers bent under his chin as he looked up and silently prayed to God.

Two days later, Gloria was declared officially out of danger. After that, she made a rapid recovery and on June 6 was released from the hospital. What happened next was something Jimmy could never completely explain, other than to attribute it to what he liked to call his absent-mindedness, perhaps understandable after all the drama of the past several weeks. "I remember painfully the day I was to bring her home from the hospital after giving birth to our twin girls. I had gone there to help her gather her things and said to her, 'I'll get the car and bring it around to the ambulance entrance. Take the elevator and I'll meet you there.' Well, I went down, but somehow I forget and went by a photographer's to pick up some pictures. He asked how Mrs. Stewart was, the light turned on in my head and I dashed back to the hospital. I never lived that one down."

After Gloria's release, Stewart spent several days with her at home assisting his wife's long-time governess, a well-trained French-Canadian by the name of Irene Des Lierres who had cared first for the boys and was now assigned the task of minding the twins. Only when he felt that Gloria was safely on the road to recovery did Jimmy go back to work, to join the production of his newest film, *The Greatest Show on Earth*. Directed by Hollywood pioneer Cecil B. DeMille, this was an old-fashioned action-adventure-mystery spectacle, the kind DeMille could do in his sleep (some thought he actually did) in which Jimmy played Buttons, a warm and friendly troupe clown who is secretly a fugitive doctor, speaks as little as possible, and never takes off his white-face makeup, because, we finally learn, he is, in fact, a murderer on the run. To hide from the law, he has somehow gotten himself hired onto a traveling circus where, predictably, tragedies like fires, high-wire mishaps, and train derailments strike as often and as regularly as the cymbals in the house band, and where the clichés of melodrama pile up like fresh-popped corn in a tub full of fake butter. This film had a lot of artificial flavor.

Because DeMille was such a stickler for a kind of detail he believed brought a heightened reality to his movies, shooting didn't actually begin until April. Before that, the director had several of his actors join up with Ringling Bro. and Barnum & Bailey to soak up some "real" circus atmosphere. During this stage of production, in the scenes where Jimmy's presence was required for rehearsals, because he wasn't as yet available, DeMille simply doubled him, using a tall, thin actor in clown white-face wearing the same fedora that Jimmy would don upon his arrival.

Many observers in the industry, some gossips, and even a few film critics wondered why Stewart, who had made a spectacular career recovery and was now back at the top of his game, would take such an odd little supporting role that buried him (without a face and no dialogue) inside a cast that included such fifties icons as Charlton Heston, leading the circus train across the country in what appears to be nothing so much as a warm-up for his leading the Hebrews out of Egypt, Betty Hutton at her smiling wackiest, a smoldering Cornel Wilde, an overacting Dorothy Lamour, and a thin-lipped, quivering Gloria Grahame (a good friend of Jimmy's ever since they'd both appeared in *It's a Wonderful Life*). In a movie cast so decidedly ensemble, with a director nowhere nearly as noir as Anthony Mann; as redemptive as Frank Capra; as compelling as Hitchcock; or even as clever about circuses as Chaplin (*The Circus,* 1928), or the Marx Brothers (Edward Buzzell's *At the Circus,* 1939), no one could quite figure out exactly what the attraction was for Jimmy. Whenever asked why he had taken such a bizarre role, Jimmy always said the same thing, that he had been inspired by the great silent film star Lon Chaney's ability to completely disguise his physical self with heavy makeup and colorful costumes while still letting the character he was playing emerge. Stewart insisted he had wanted to try that for the longest time and, to a certain extent, succeeded in his goal with *The Greatest Show on Earth.* To accurately capture the essence of a clown, Stewart had, on his own, hired the great circus clown Emmett Kelly to tutor him in the ways of great, silent circus entertainment.

The film opened on January 10, 1952, tellingly, after the big Christmas season was over. Most critics pounded the film, spraying uncomplimentary verbal buckshot that hit everyone, including Jimmy. *Newsweek* pulled no punches when it said, "Undoubtedly the most foolish aspect of the narrative casts James Stewart as a sweet, sad clown." *Variety,* on the other hand, seemed to like his performance a bit more: "James Stewart is woven into the picture as an extraneous but appealing plot element." And the *New York Herald Tribune,* taking the high, if bumpy, road, said: "James Stewart has a minor role as a clown with a dark past hiding his identity behind the grinning make-up which he never takes off in the picture. He is good enough in his make-believe job to tour with the circus this spring." Faint praise, indeed—be a clown, be a clown, be a clown.

However, despite its cool critical reception, the film proved a big hit at the box office, displaying enough of the old DeMille grandiosity to pull in the crowds. Early in 1952, when the nominations for Academy Awards were announced, *The Greatest Show on Earth* picked up several, against such formidable competition for Best Picture as Fred Zinnemann's towering *High Noon,* John Ford's spectacular *The Quiet Man,* Richard Thorpe's *Sir Walter Scott's Ivanhoe,* and John Huston's *Moulin Rouge.* Although the overwhelming favorite (and far superior movie) was *High Noon,* due to writer/producer Carl Foreman's ongoing problems with the blacklist (his name appears only as the writer in the film's credit roll), and John Wayne's public denunciation of it as "un-American," the conservative Academy gave the trophy instead to ultra right-winger DeMille's circus of a movie.[1] Jimmy was not even nominated, for Best Actor or Best Supporting Actor, in what shaped up to be an unusually strong roster of Oscar-worthy performances.[2]

The Greatest Show on Earth would go on to be the top-grossing film of 1951.

— · —

Stewart, despite his newly enlarged family, remained immersed in the unreal world of filmmaking. Five weeks after *The Greatest Show on Earth* finished production, Jimmy was back at work to begin *Bend of the River,* his second Mann collaboration, and one in which Stewart again worked for a percentage, rather than a salary, this time a full 50 percent.

In *Bend of the River,* Stewart plays the role of Glyn McLyntock, a wagon-train leader with a dark and hidden past. The rest of the cast included the sultry Julie Adams, an up-and-coming Universal contract player, and Arthur Kennedy, fresh from his Tony-award-winning role on Broadway as Biff in Arthur Miller's searing *Death of a Salesman.* The film was made on location at Mount Hood National Forest, in the north-central rugged terrain of Oregon, and proved an extremely difficult, physically challenging shoot.

---

1. John Ford's *The Quiet Man,* starring John Wayne, was nominated for Best Picture. Wayne was also nominated for Best Actor.

Gary Cooper, a well-known Hollywood right-winger and one of the so-called Friendly Witnesses before HUAC, won for Best Actor in *High Noon.* Gloria Grahame won, but not for her role in the DeMille film. She was nominated in the Supporting Actress category for her part in Vincente Minnelli's *The Bad and the Beautiful.* John Ford, another Hollywood conservative, but one with integrity, broke with DeMille over what he saw as that director's unsavory actions in support of the blacklist, and won Best Director for *The Quiet Man.* The only other award *The Greatest Show on Earth* won was for writing, with Oscars going to DeMille, Fredric M. Frank, Theodore St. John, and Frank Cavett.

2. Best Actor nominees included Marlon Brando in Elia Kazan's *Viva Zapata,* Gary Cooper in Fred Zinnemann's *High Noon,* Kirk Douglas in Vincente Minnelli's *The Bad and the Beautiful,* José Ferrer in John Huston's *Moulin Rouge,* and Alec Guinness in Charles Crichton's *The Lavender Hill Mob;* Best Supporting Actor nominees included Richard Burton in Henry Koster's *My Cousin Rachel,* Arthur Hunnicutt in Howard Hawks's *The Big Sky,* Victor McLaglen in John Ford's *The Quiet Man,* Jack Palance in David Miller's *Sudden Fear,* and Anthony Quinn in Kazan's *Viva Zapata.* Jimmy was voted *Look* magazine's "Actor of the Year," an award he said meant just as much to him as any Academy Award.

Filmed in magnificent Technicolor, *Bend of the River* tells the story of two ex-mercenaries, McLyntock and Cole (Kennedy), looking to start fresh in the years following the Civil War. After they realize they have been swindled, they employ an extra gunslinger, Trey Wilson (Rock Hudson), and steal back their own goods. On their way to their new settlement, McLyntock realizes that Cole intends to keep all the goods for himself and sell them to the highest bidder. He confronts Cole, who beats him bloody and leaves him for dead. From that point on, the film turns into a manhunt, with McLyntock knocking off the members of Cole's gang one by one, until he finally confronts Cole by a riverside in a climactic, brutal battle, after which a victorious McLyntock, along with Wilson, Laura (Adams), and Baile (Jay C. Flippen), Laura's father, move on to the promised settlement.

It is easy to see the attraction in this film for Stewart, as it seems to recall so clearly the pioneering and warrior spirit of the Maitland/Stewart clan. Increasingly rugged in his visage, Stewart exhibited the new toughness that Mann had instilled in him with *Winchester '73*. And with the stylistic and thematic echoes of Howard Hawks's *Red River* (1948) and Zinnemann's *High Noon* (1951), the film contained all the crucial elements of a box-office smash, which it became. It is *Bend of the River* that led Howard Teichmann to declare, in his collaborative biography of Henry Fonda, that "Fonda, his long-time friend Jimmy Stewart, and Gary Cooper . . . played cowboys better than any other actors."

Upon the film's completion, Stewart went immediately into Richard Thorpe's *Carbine Williams*, the biography of the inventor of the rifle that played a crucial role in the Allied victory in World War Two. Marsh Williams (Stewart) is a Prohibition-era North Carolina metalworker who doubles as a moonshiner. When he is busted by the government, one of the federal agents is killed. Wracked with guilt, although it is unclear who did the actual killing, Williams gives himself up and is sent to prison for thirty years. While incarcerated, he invents the M-1 carbine rifle. Eventually he is pardoned, after serving eight years in jail, a reward for his help in creating a weapon that saved millions of Allies' lives.

The film was the inspiration of Dore Schary, who discovered the story as part of the ongoing series in *Reader's Digest*, "The Most Unforgettable Character I Ever Met." Schary, now the sole head of MGM, chose Thorpe to work with Stewart because of the good relationship they had had making *Malaya*. Jimmy, for his part, was hesitant to make

the movie for two reasons: he didn't want to violate his pledge to himself not to do anything that glorified war, no matter how indirectly, and
he didn't want to play a true-life ex-con. However, the latter seemed to
cancel out the former when the real Williams was brought in as a technical advisor, Stewart found in him something ultimately redemptive.
The film did moderately well.

Carbine Williams was immediately followed by yet another Mann
Western, *The Naked Spur.* In this one, Howie Kemp (Stewart) is a bounty
hunter tracking killer Ben Vandergroat, played by veteran actor Robert
Ryan, a master of the twisted personality (and one of the most overlooked
leading men of the forties and fifties). There is a suggestion in the course
of the manhunt that the two used to be friends. Traveling with Vandergroat and apparently unaware that he is a killer is Lina Patch (Janet Leigh,
luscious and lovely in her early studio-contract-player period). What follows is a roundup of good guys and bad guys, good girls and bad girls, with
no one ever sure which is which, supplemented by Mann's dizzyingly
sharp camera angulation to help us understand who is who and which is
which. The film's climax involves an incredibly well-staged fight between
Kemp and Vandergroat. Mann's camera makes sure the audience knows it
is really Stewart and Ryan, not doubles, doing the action. After a near-
maniacal Kemp decides to abandon the reward and accept instead a true
and higher reward from Lina, her hand in love (and presumably marriage),
the two ride off into the sunset to start a new life.

The film premiered at Loew's State on March 25, 1953, and while
Jimmy received great reviews—"One of the best roles of his career" according to the *New York Herald Tribune*—the film was lost among the
more overtly psychological Westerns of the day. Despite a tight structure, great performances, razor-sharp direction, and an edgily redemptive story, it was soon forgotten.

In the midst of Jimmy's energetic early fifties burst, a strange and
menacing real-life incident occurred when a fifty-five-year-old Los Angeles truck driver named Clyde Davis tried to extort a thousand dollars
from Stewart. Davis, a disgruntled ex–MGM employee, had been
driving through Pittsburgh, Kansas, and happened to see a poster on
the highway for one of Stewart's movies. He pulled over to the side of
the road and wrote a note threatening to harm Stewart and his family
unless a thousand dollars in cash was sent to J. B. Small at Carthage,

Missouri. Stewart promptly turned over the note to the FBI and hired a private security team to guard his house until the extortionist was captured. Before that happened, however, Davis gave himself up, confessed that he never intended to harm anyone, and was just looking to get himself arrested so he could have a permanent home in a federal penitentiary.

Afterward, Jimmy sent Davis a note thanking him for sparing him, and the family, any further unwanted fear and anxiety.

— • —

In late August 1952, Stewart reported for a month of required duty with the Air Force Reserve. He was still not cleared for piloting (something that did not bother him in the least) and was assigned instead to the Pentagon, where he reported to Andy Low, a good friend who had been his assistant during the war. Upon the end of his brief tour, instead of returning to Southern California, he flew directly to Morgan City, a small fishing community in southern, Cajun, Louisiana, to begin production on his next film, *Thunder Bay,* his fourth collaboration with Anthony Mann.

Both Jimmy and the studio had agreed that after the lack of box office for *The Naked Spur,* another Western wasn't in Jimmy's best interest, and instead decided that he and Mann should next tackle the world of oil drillers, a "new" subject for Hollywood, although three years later George Stevens's *Giant* would do it bigger and better (with Rock Hudson in the Stewart-type role, and the explosive James Dean in his final screen performance before his sudden, early, and tragic death in a car accident just prior to the film's release).

It had become clear to the studio that Mann's Westerns were of the highest quality, comparable to anything coming out of Hollywood, they were not able to sustain an audience. With each progressive pairing of Jimmy and Mann, the box-office returns were less than the previous collaboration. At least one of the reasons was a virtual blizzard of Westerns being cranked out at Universal, so many that the studio had a permanent Western set built on its back lot, to $^{11}\!/_{12}$ scale, meaning everything was one inch smaller per foot than actual size, to make all the performers seem all that much bigger, heroes more heroic, villains more formidable. They were made on minuscule budgets with mostly B actor casts, and almost always played as the second film on a double feature.

Shot on location in the Louisiana bayou town of Morgan City, in Technicolor (by the great color cinematographer William Daniels), *Thunder Bay* came off as a modern-dress Western, less cow, more boy.

Thunder Bay opened in August 1953, a time usually reserved for the third, and least important, tier of summer films, following the Memorial Day blitz and the July 4 weekend. It was a wise move. Audiences were increasingly turned off as well by the escalating violence in Mann's oeuvre and by the notion of Jimmy playing grizzled, wild-eyed maniacs in ever more stylized landscapes of a metaphorical moral wasteland.

Part of film's uniqueness is that actors grow old in real life and must always and forever compete with their younger selves in the minds and the imaginations of their loyal followings. Inevitably, the reflection of mortality begins as a speck in the distance and continues to grow relentlessly larger, much to the displeasure of moviegoers forever in search of the allure, if not the illusion, of immortality through the evergreen images of their favorite movie stars. Unquestionably, while working with Mann, Jimmy had turned a generational corner. Once the eternal, pure youth who could survive anything in the name of eternal fill-in-the-blank—love of life, American democracy, family, baseball, the right woman, a good horse, etc.,—now, in Mann's incarnation, the older man was being pursued by his own past, ultimately by his own ravaged youth, and death loomed ever larger against a backdrop of longing and limbo.

Interestingly, it was Henry Fonda, having not made a movie in years, who observed during Jimmy's Mann period how awkward the young/old persona was that he had developed. "When Jim stops pretending to be so young," Fonda said, "he'll become an artist."

— • —

Fonda was right and Jimmy knew it. Even before he finished shooting *Thunder Bay*, it was clear to him that a change of directors and direction had to be made. He thought he was on to something when he came up with the novel idea of acknowledging the maturation of his image by appearing on live TV. In May 1953, Stewart and Gloria appeared on the *Ed Sullivan Show*, a cultural mainstay of fifties variety television, as part of a tribute to Josh Logan in which Jimmy filmed a recreation of his bit in the Triangle Club's 1930's production of *The Tiger*

Smiles.[3] In December of that same year, he showed up on, of all things, the *Jack Benny Program,* the popular half-hour show-within-a-show format that the great comedian had devised, one of the early, classic achievements of television before the medium ceased being a stage-based technological marvel that yielded such a wealth of highly original comedy. In that episode, Jimmy and Gloria's Beverly Hills neighbor, Benny (also their neighbor in real life) inadvertently ruins the Stewarts' plans for a quiet New Year's Eve at home. As a "middle-aged couple" Jimmy and Gloria (who played herself) enjoyed the experience so much that they consented to appear once a year on the show, essentially doing the same skit over and over.

— • —

Early that July, Stewart agreed to make one more movie with Mann, as long as it wasn't Western. He had long admired the work and the life of bandleader Glenn Miller, whose plane disappeared somewhere over the English Channel on December 15, 1943. Miller's death shocked the nation, put a belovedly human face on the countless military dead, and plunged America into the type of mourning usually reserved for heads of state. Miller, like Stewart, had been a part of the Army Air Force, and, although he was supposed to be protected from seeing real action nonetheless died in the service of his country, something Jimmy could well identify with. Miller, an off-the-farm Iowa boy, happily married and altogether altruistic, was someone Stewart had wanted to make a movie about for some time. Now, when the opportunity finally came, he jumped at it. It came as close as any film he would ever make to dealing with the American military heroics of World War Two.

Although Mann was going to direct, the film had little to do with his brand of filmmaking. The studio insisted it be music heavy, featuring original Miller recordings and "real-life" cameos by Frances Langford, Gene Krupa, the Modernaires, and Louis Armstrong. To implement and slightly update the arrangements, Universal hired a then-unknown Henry Mancini to work on the score. To play Miller's wife, the studio once more called upon June Allyson, whose role in the film was, essen-

---

3. Stewart received no fee for the appearance. In return, Sullivan agreed to air promotional clips from *Thunder Bay.*

tially, to gush at her husband's talent, encourage him when things were rough before the high tide of fame came in, and to mourn in place of America when he, at the peak of his popularity, dies.

And then, on August 2, 1953, one day after production on *The Glenn Miller Story* wrapped, real-life tragedy visited the life of Jimmy Stewart, when seventy-eight-year-old Elizabeth was stricken with a heart attack. As soon as the news reached Jimmy, he and Gloria flew to Indiana, where he sat by his mother's side until she slipped quietly into eternity.

That night, cloaked in the shroud of irreplaceable loss, he wept like a baby in his wife's arms.

PART SIX

—·—

Venus, Veritas, Vertigo

Hanging on by his fingertips. Jimmy Stewart as John "Scottie" Ferguson
in a studio publicity shot for Alfred Hitchcock's *Vertigo* (1958).

20

"Hitchcock saw in Stewart an American different from the George Bailey of *It's a Wonderful Life* . . . his was not the dark opposite of Stewart's usual character, as some critics have written, but a much more complex figure—a George Bailey whose guilt and confusion were uniquely Hitchcock's creation. The Hitchcock male was complex—the hero, yet reluctant; the lover, yet confused and restrained; the innocent, yet menaced as if guilty. They were men drawn reluctantly to women— Cary Grant in *Notorious* and *To Catch a Thief* and Jimmy Stewart in *Rear Window* and *Vertigo*."

—DAN AUILER

The Glenn Miller Story opened on February 11, 1954, to rave reviews, especially for Jimmy's performance in the title role. It would go on to become the third highest-grossing film of that year, just behind Michael Curtiz's musical *White Christmas*, starring Bing Crosby; and Edward Dmytryk's *The Caine Mutiny*, based on the Herman Wouk novel, starring Humphrey Bogart, yet another postwar '50s film that reflected with dark uncertainty on military and political authority.

The *New York Times*'s Bosley Crowther summed up the critical and popular reception of *The Glenn Miller Story* this way: "Mr. Stewart and Miss Allyson in their roles—the gentle ease, the solid form of their strong acting—puts the living throb into the film. It is they who make genuine the tender sentiments that are worked in behind the songs. This is a wonderful achievement, of which they and their associates may be proud. . . . Not since [Michael Curtiz's] *Yankee Doodle Dandy*, the film about George M. Cohan, have we seen as appealing and melodic a musical biography as this charmer . . . and not since Jimmy Cagney's spirited playing of Mr. Cohan have we seen as likeable and respectable a portrait of a show-world personage as James Stewart's genial performance in this picture's title role."

The film proved so popular with audiences that Jimmy agreed to go on what was a relatively rare national live tour to local movie theaters for standing-room-only in-person promotional purposes. He had a significant financial stake in the picture, and knew that he could make a big difference in attendance just by showing up in person at certain key theaters around the country. In an era before television and radio talk shows revolutionized the way a film was promoted by its star, he tirelessly pursued the public appearance route, taking his wife and father along with him—Gloria for company, Alexander to attempt to raise the old man's spirits, or at least keep him busy so that he wouldn't swallow himself in grief and loneliness following the death of beloved Bessie.

When the tour passed through Coral Gables, Florida, Jimmy's sixth-grade teacher, retired, showed up to congratulate him on all his success. It was a gesture that touched Jimmy deeply. However, it was Alexander's brief appearances that always stole the show when he would tell audiences "I used to keep Jimmy's Oscar [for *The Philadelphia Story*] in the window of my hardware store. But it's no longer a conversation piece. So I moved it to one of my knife case counters. It's out of balance and needs another Oscar for the other end of the counter." This always got a big laugh while Jimmy would smile and pretend to look sheepishly at his dad.

— . —

Nevertheless, by the time he hit the road, Stewart had relatively little remaining interest in the movie, Glenn Miller, or Anthony Mann. Even before its release, he had quietly decided to take his career in yet another direction, surprising everyone (except Wasserman) by accepting an offer to work again with Alfred Hitchcock, despite *Rope*'s having been an unhappy and unsatisfying experience that nearly ended the actor's career.

The reteaming of Stewart and Hitchcock would result in the most inspired, moving, darkly mysterious and beautiful trio of films of the decade, surpassing in sum even the four the great director would make over the course of his career with Cary Grant. As with the suave, urbane, British sophisticate in whom Hitchcock used to project his own dark side on-screen, the director saw something similar within Jimmy that he felt had not yet been sufficiently brought to the surface of the screen by any other director.

While previously Capra had played upon Jimmy's easily identifiable idealism, and Mann brought out his repressed wartime fear and rage, in Hitchcock's view neither had come close to revealing the true greatness of Jimmy's talent: his ability to act out the profound inner, emotional tragedy of unrequited love. *That* was the side of Jimmy that Hitchcock was after, and, in classic fashion, the side of Jimmy he got, in the three movies in the fifties that chronicled, in loose sequential progression, the devastating emotional consequences of the risks, the dangers, and the disappointments of love, marriage, and loss. All three featured iceberg Madonnas unrelentingly beautiful and ultimately unattainable.

Hitchcock's greatness may be defined as his ability to bring to the surface of the screen, i.e., the world, whatever it was his characters felt on the inside, to visualize both the implications and the consequences of their internal hopes, desires, wishes, and dreams. When, in most instances, someone might think in a moment of anger, "I'd like to kill my wife," Hitchcock's characters more often than not find a way to externalize, or act out those impulses. This surfacing of a character's psychological subtext, of their inner, often subconscious feelings shown on-screen as if they were ordinary, everyday actions, placed Hitchcock's best movies in a world of hard and deep moral consequence, not to mention intensely exciting cinematic action. As the director, he presented a moral view of the world that was as universal as it was Hitch-specific. In it no one is completely innocent, and therefore no one ever truly escapes the fate of the guilty. Villains are sympathetic, and heroes are imperfect.

Hitchcock's two favorite on-screen projections of his own inner and idealized self were Cary Grant, whose physical beauty served as an ironic, transparent cover (for both his and Hitch's real-life darkness as much as the darkness of the characters Grant portrayed), in *Suspicion* (1941), *Notorious* (1946), *To Catch a Thief* (1955), and *North by Northwest* (1959); and Jimmy, whose ordinary, medium-cool down-home looks masked a faulty nuclear reactor of repression, of unexplored desires and of staring-into-the-face-of-death fear. The first intimations of Hitchcock's Jimmy are glimpsed in *Rope*. Phillip and Brandon have acted out their inner desire to murder, but have not directly, or consciously, seen it as an extension of their homosexual desires for each other (they are gay, but do not "see" that erotic connection to the motivation of killing together for the sake of killing). Caddell (Stewart), the teacher, serves as their moral guide as he eventually discovers the truth behind their actions (but not their feelings). Thus, what links Caddell to the students, a link that allows him to "solve" the case, is also what separates him from them. He is consciously repulsed by their actions, but subconsciously drawn to their homosexuality, the link to his deeper wish to have participated, at some thrillingly dark level, in the crime itself. That Caddell never makes that connection, or even suspects (or senses) it, is what limits the film's Hitchcockian-style power of suggestion. Jimmy's characters in *Rear Window* (1954), *The Man Who Knew Too Much* (1956), and most disturbingly in *Vertigo* (1958) have no such blind spots. It is, in fact, their awareness, at varying levels of recognition, of the effects of their own repressed desires (usually coming full blown during the climax of the movie), that makes the characters and the films so dramatically compelling.

— • —

Rear Window was the first picture Hitchcock made under a new nine-picture deal with Paramount, put together by Lew Wasserman, with five to be directed and produced by Hitchcock and four to be produced by the studio, with Hitchcock only directing. He was to earn $150,000 per picture, plus 10 percent of the profits (adjusted for prearranged, agreed-upon budgetary limits), and given eventual outright negative ownership of the five pictures he produced and directed, among them the three that starred Jimmy, *Rear Window* (1954), *The Man Who Knew Too Much* (1955), and *Vertigo* (1958).[1]

The film was based on a short story titled "It Had to Be Murder," which first appeared in the February 1942 edition of *Dime Detective* magazine, written by William Irish, a pseudonym (one among many he used) for the great Cornell Woolrich. *Dime Detective*'s pulpy stories had long supplied Hollywood with noirish material for B-movie thrillers. Woolrich happened to be one of Hitchcock's favorite writers. The screen rights to "Murder" had originally been sold to producer Buddy DeSylva, and then to Leland Hayward and Joshua Logan, both

---

1. The dates cited are years of release. The other two films were *To Catch a Thief* (1955) and *The Trouble with Harry* (1955).

of whom immediately saw it as the perfect vehicle for Jimmy. Both would remain with the picture as noncredited but well-paid coproducers, a stipulation Jimmy insisted on when Hitchcock offered him the part.

To adapt the story to film, Hitchcock called upon the talents of the brilliant John Michael Hayes (another Wasserman client), whom he had met at Warner while the director was filming *Dial M for Murder*. One of the key ingredients Hitchcock wanted Hayes to add to the story was a girlfriend for L. B. Jeffries, or "Jeff" (whose character was loosely based on the *Life* magazine photographer Robert Capa), confined to a wheelchair while nursing a broken leg, the result of his having gotten too close to the action of a race-car crash, which has left him in a toe-to-hip plaster cast.[2] Grace Kelly was the only actress Hitchcock would consider for the girlfriend role, Lisa, a high-fashion model desperate to marry the seemingly confirmed bachelor she has fallen in love with. Jeffries's reluctance to marry, or to "settle down," is a clear sign of his emotional unavailability. To Hitchcock, the broken leg signals at once Jeffries's immobility (impotence, really, a symbol of his fear of commitment), keeping him confined to a wheelchair (that happens to resemble a director's chair), and at the same time a state of constant erection (a sign of sexual energy without accompanying intimacy). The notions sexual fear and arousal are underscored several times in the film, by the binoculars and huge telephoto lens Jeffries uses to spy on his neighbors' lives during his convalescence, his excitement heightened whenever he zooms in for a round or two of sexual voyeurism that will lead to mayhem, murder, and more—and eventually his own rescue of and subsequent marriage to Lisa.

Lisa at first vehemently disapproves of Jeffries's spying, implying her dislike for what she sees is a perverse form of nothing less than masturbation (looking at other people's most sexually private moments), until she too, is "turned on" by the forbidden nature of it, discovers her own capacity for perversity, and becomes an all-too eager player in the grim psychosexual murder follies that ensue. Jeffries has

---

2. Stewart's ongoing persona by surname continues—Jefferson Smith in *Mr. Smith Goes to Washington*, Thomas Jefferson Destry Jr., in *Destry Rides Again*, Tom Jeffords in *Broken Arrow*, Jeffries in *Rear Window*.

defined the players in the various panorama of rear windows morally, as either good and bad, victim or killer, lover or loser. They all share one thing in common, one aspect or another of his own fantasies and fears of marriage, including murder, his own darkest, unrealized fantasy of how to get rid of Lisa for good. Or bad.

At one point during the film, after he has turned her on to what he believes has been taking place in an apartment across the courtyard, Lisa leaves Jeffries, climbs up the fire escape, and literally enters the room of the suspected killer (all seen from Jeffries's point of view, meaning ours—we watch him as he watches her, making us just as projection perverse as both he and Lisa and, for that matter, Hitchcock). It is as if she has entered one of the eroticized sexual fantasies that has been playing on the screens of Jeffries's imagination.

This stylistic touch was not invented by Hitchcock; Buster Keaton did the same thing, ostensibly for laughs, in his altogether brilliant *Sherlock Jr.* (1924) when a projectionist falls asleep and imagines that he has walked down the theater's aisle and taken a literal leap of faith— into the movie he is showing.[3] What makes Hitchcock's use of it so terrifying is when, later on, during the film's climax, the killer, Thorwald (Raymond Burr), played with a devastating mixture of vicious menace and pathetic self-mockery, after discovering that he is being spied on by Jeffries and realizing Jeffries has uncovered the matricide, travels back across the yard to Jeffries's apartment. He has, in effect, left the movie in Jeffries's mind and entered his real world—*to kill him.*[4]

Ultimately, *Rear Window* is less about murder than it is about movies, and the ability they have to draw in the viewer, the profound sense of identity they invoke in us for the heroes in which we invest our

---

3. Woody Allen uses variations on this stylistic touch in several of his movies, most notably in *Zelig* (1983) and *The Purple Rose of Cairo* (1985).

4. One of the "jokes" of the film is that Stewart's character winds up with two broken legs—double the arousal, double the impotence—Hitchcock's commentary on Jeffries's succumbing to the temptation of marriage, even to Grace Kelly. "That wasn't in the script," Stewart told *New York Times* interviewer Janet Maslin in 1983. "On the day we were going to shoot, Hitchcock came up to me and said, 'What would you think about breaking another leg?'" During production, both casts had hinges on them so Stewart could get out of the wheelchair and walk around in between shooting his scenes.

emotions, and the power they have to reach into our very soul. As *Rear Window* so beautifully reminds us, life truly passes in the shutterlike blink of an eye, often hangs by a thread (in this case a bedsheet), and is best redeemed by the power of belief in one's own ability to survive, endure, and hopefully, if unrealistically, to love.

Jimmy Stewart was perfectly suited for the role of Jeffries, one of the reasons he initially signed on to work again with Hitchcock. Another was that he had fallen hopelessly in love with Grace Kelly. Perhaps not so coincidentally, this surge of romantic feelings for his co-star came not long after the death of his mother. It signaled an emotional return to form for Stewart, whose chaste infatuations for his co-stars had somewhat diminished with his postwar marriage and return to the screen in films that were, for the most part, male-dominated action features. It is safe to say that the maternal June Allyson did not set off any emotional or erotic sparks in Jimmy from within. Grace Kelly, however, was a whole other story.[5]

The closest he ever came to admitting that he was attracted to Kelly came years later, in 1987, when he told her biographer, James Spada, "A lot of things impressed me about her. She seemed to have a complete understanding of the way motion picture acting is carried out. And she was so pleasant on the set; she was completely cooperative. She was really in a class by herself as far as cooperation and friendliness are concerned. In filming that movie with her I got the feeling that they were real scenes. She was very, very special." That same year he told *USA Today*, "I was absolutely smitten by Grace Kelly, a wonderful, wonderful girl." In Patrick McGilligan's biography of Hitchcock, he quotes Jimmy as saying, "We were all so crazy about Grace Kelly. Everybody just sat around and waited for her to come in the morning, so we could just look at her. She was kind to everybody, so considerate, just great, and so beautiful." And, according to assistant director Herbert Coleman (also quoted in McGilligan), "Every man who ever was lucky enough to work with Grace Kelly fell in love with her, me included. Even Hitchcock."

---

5. In an interview with the author, June Allyson claimed she greatly enjoyed playing Mrs. Miller and all the other Stewart wives, and that her favorite of their movies together was *The Glenn Miller Story*, primarily because of all the great music.

Up until this time, Stewart had been very careful not to discuss his feelings for his leading ladies in any but the most objective terms, if for no other reason than to spare his wife from any embarrassment he imagined that might result from some unintended private revelation. For her part, Gloria understood the nature of Stewart's work, and behaved more like a political wife than an actor's spouse. In public, she took all the gossip column implications in stride, understanding that her husband had been a bachelor until his forties and that his work called for him to interact with some of the most beautiful women in the world.

But, in 1977, she gave a rare interview to Clive Hirschorn in which, after twenty-seven years of marriage to Jimmy, she talked about her difficulties dealing with the emotional complexity of her husband. Not being one to act upon his emotions and attractions often made her rivals far more important than they might have been if he had gone with them and gotten them out of his system. "It gave me a lot of cause for anxiety, because during [the early years of our marriage] Jimmy was working with some of the most glamorous women in the world, women such as Kim Novak, Joan Fontaine, Marlene Dietrich and Grace Kelly. And, of course, my constant fear was that he would find them more attractive than me and have an affair with one of them. A lot of men in Hollywood constantly became involved with their leading ladies—and as Jimmy was a red-blooded American male, naturally I thought it could happen to him too. I was convinced that it would only be a matter of time before the phone would ring and it would be James telling me he had to work hard at the studio, or that he would be out playing poker with the boys. Well, no such phone call ever came. And I can honestly say that, in all the years we've been married, Jimmy never once gave me cause for anxiety or jealousy. The more glamorous the leading lady he was starring opposite, the more attentive he'd be to me! He knew the insecurities I was going through, and made quite sure that they were totally unfounded. His consideration was incredible and one of the reasons why our marriage has lasted so long and is still so good."

At the time of *Rear Window*, then, Gloria obviously chose to look the other way as her forty-six-year-old husband remained for weeks in close proximity to the gorgeous twenty-five-year-old Kelly, more alluring for him than any other actress he had worked with since Margaret Sullavan.

To make matters worse, at least for Gloria, Kelly had a reputation in Hollywood for sleeping with every one of her leading men, without regard for their age (Crosby, Cooper) or marital status (Frank Sinatra, William Holden) or anything but her own desires. As for Jimmy, all he would say on the matter at the time was that while he appreciated Grace's attributes, he was a happily married man. Contrary to all rumors and reports, Jimmy did not succumb to Kelly's considerable charms. If he had, he likely would have told Gloria, or Kelly surely would have, as she and Mrs. Stewart, who met during the filming of *Rear Window,* became close friends for the rest of Kelly's life.

One of the things that made Stewart such a great actor, and the quintessential Hitchcock antihero, was that in *Rear Window* he came across a bit diffident but in the end morally unshakable. And what makes Jimmy's performance so gratifying is that he manages to combine all of Hitchcock's subrosa sadistic, obsessive, voyeuristic fantasies and still make Jeffries someone the audience strongly identifies with, and deeply roots for.

Jimmy always credited the quality of his acting in the film to Hitchcock's direction. "When you think about *Rear Window,*" he told Roger Ebert years later, "you'll remember my role largely consisted of reacting. First Hitchcock would show what I was seeing through my binoculars. Then he'd show my face, and I'd reflect what I saw. I spent an astonishing amount of time looking into the camera and being amused, afraid, worried, curious, embarrassed, bored, the works."

— • —

A poll taken in 1955 by the *Motion Picture Herald,* an influential trade magazine that reflected the previous year's total box office, named Jimmy Stewart the "king" of Hollywood, for having earned the most money of any single actor in 1954.[6] The list also included Grace Kelly (number two), William Holden, Gary Cooper, Marlon Brando, Dean Martin, Jerry Lewis, Humphrey Bogart, June Allyson, Clark Gable, and John Wayne. It is noteworthy that Allyson and Kelly, the only two

---

6. Stewart earned the title via profit-percentage deals he had negotiated for *Winchester '73, Bend of the River, Thunder Bay, Harvey, The Glenn Miller Story,* and *Rear Window.*

women on the list, had both co-starred with Jimmy, in, respectively, *The Glenn Miller Story* and *Rear Window.*

That same year, *Look* magazine named forty-seven-year-old Jimmy Stewart the most popular Hollywood movie star in the world, putting him for the first time on the top of their immensely popular list, moving John Wayne, the holder of the crown the previous three years, to second place.[7]

---

7. Whenever asked about replacing Wayne at the top of the list, Stewart always had the same, rather telling answer. "Maybe what it is," he said, "is that people identify with me, but dream of being John Wayne." Missing from the list was Cary Grant, who had appeared on it with regularity but had temporarily retired. He appeared in no movies in 1954 but would return to the screen and the list in 1956 after he starred in Hitchcock's *To Catch a Thief,* opposite Kelly.

21

"I've never got much out of rehearsing because the camera isn't going. I need to hear lights-camera-slate-speak to trigger me. All these fellows talk about why so many takes. Well, it's giving you a chance to stumble upon that moment that works. I'm suspicious when somebody says, 'We rehearsed three weeks, shot in ten days.' "

—JIMMY STEWART

Stewart took some of the earnings he had made with *The Glenn Miller Story* and *Rear Window* and bought out his neighbor on North Roxbury Drive. He then tore down the existing house and turned the property into an enormous planting garden for Gloria to use as her retreat, especially when he was off on location and she wanted some privacy from the children and their governess.

He also bought himself a new Volvo, his modest preference over a Mercedes, the usual *auto de rigueur* for someone of his stature in Beverly Hills. He preferred the boxy, cranky Swedish car, he said, because it had a high roof that accommodated his height and lots of legroom. He drove this first one for six years before finally and reluctantly replacing it—with another Volvo.

— • —

After the fevered, curved-wrists-and-darting-eyes display he had put on for *Rear Window*, Jimmy wanted to turn down the heat a bit and deal with a subject he was (at least consciously) more familiar with. The film was to be about the Strategic Air Command, a vital new addition to the nation's military forces during the early years of the cold war. Jimmy was an impassioned supporter of SAC, as it was known, and said so to *Newsweek*, declaring, with what was for him unusually hyperbolic fervor, that it was "the biggest single factor in the security of the world." He managed to convince Paramount to make the film on the basis of its political importance (although the studio, riding the crest of Stewart's success, would likely have made a film out of the phone book if he had asked them to).

In subsequent interviews before, during, and after the making of the movie, Jimmy continually stressed its political importance as a way to convince the public of the necessity of spending millions of dollars to develop weapons delivery systems. He was always careful to differentiate between what he called a service film, which, as everyone in Hollywood and the government knew, was code for "propaganda," and an out-and-out war film, which he still steadfastly refused to do: "For a long time I wanted to make a service film, but it was tough. There's been so many good pictures about all branches of the army and navy and marines and air force. And I didn't want to do another war story. Then I thought about SAC. Nobody knew anything about SAC, the air arm entrusted to deliver the atom or hydrogen bomb. The bomb's no good if it can't be delivered."

Jimmy had other reasons for wanting to make this film, one of which had to do with his strained relationship with Fonda. It had not been overlooked by Jimmy that Fonda had been away on Broadway for years playing the ultraliberal Mr. Roberts in the play of the same name, and had received raves in the Josh Logan production that now seemed headed for the movies. On one of the few times they had gotten together during Fonda's New York run, Jimmy had told him the play was too preachy, too political, and wouldn't make a good movie, to which Fonda scoffed. Also, as early as 1951, against Jimmy's advice, Fonda, in New York, led and spoke at a series of Times Square rallies urging people to vote for liberal Democrat nominee Adlai Stevenson in the 1952 presidential campaign, which added a few degrees to the chill between them. Jimmy was an ardent supporter of the Republican nominee, Supreme Allied Commander Gen. Dwight Eisenhower. After the election, Jimmy believed there was no need for direct celebrity campaigning on the issues of the day, which is why his military movie, unlike the play *Mr. Roberts,* dealt with programs he felt were necessary to fight the cold war. The result was what amounted to a two-hour Technicolor, wide-screen piece of propaganda to show off the American military might, carrying the not-so-subtle title *Strategic Air Command.*

The film contained echoes of many of Jimmy's previous postwar hits, in its attempt to humanize a story that was essentially mechanistic in nature. Once again he was a major league baseball player, recalling his portrayal of Monty Stratton, only this time a reservist with both legs intact recalled to active duty. The script was written by Beirne Lay Jr., a longtime friend who was, like Stewart, a colonel in the Reserves, and Valentine Davies, who had cowritten *The Glenn Miller Story*. June Allyson was drafted to service once again as his devoted, if decidedly maternal, let-me-fix-your-collar Protestant housewife.

Sensing the film would need some heft to hold up the integrity of its preachy message, Jimmy prevailed upon Anthony Mann to helm it, which Mann agreed to do, providing that Jimmy, continuing hot as a six-gun at the box office, promised to return the favor and appear in at least one more movie for him. Jimmy said yes immediately. When producer Sam Briskin went to the air force to get its permission and cooperation, Gen. Curtis LeMay enthusiastically assured him everything would be done to make the film as authentic as possible, that is, as long as the military had final say over the script. As for Jimmy, his only proviso was that the film have heroic combat scenes that glorified war.

The film, released in the studio's new wide-screen Academy Award–winning screen process VistaVision, appeared to be about little more than a bunch of planes, its human characters practically afterthoughts in the majestic presentation of American military might.

The critics were united in their feeling that the film had no blood, no emotion, no story, and no drama, and that both its leads were far too old for the parts they were playing (Jimmy was forty-seven when he made it and looked every day of it, despite the fact that his character was supposed to be an active major league pitcher; Allyson, at thirty-seven, was still playing the young, sweet, childless housewife). Nevertheless, America's preoccupation with the cold war was supercharged with enough high-test to jet-propel *Strategic Air Command* to the sixth-highest-grossing-picture spot of 1955.

The ongoing screen "affair" between Jimmy and Allyson became something of a joke in both the Dick Powell/June Allyson and Jimmy Stewart/Gloria Stewart households, a joke, that is, with a slight pinch. This is how Allyson recalled that period: "When Richard [Powell] and I got together with our friends Jimmy and Gloria Stewart, Richard kidded Jimmy and me about the string of hit movies that had made us the reigning romantic team in Hollywood. As Gloria put it, jokingly, but with just a bit of an edge, 'June is Jimmy's perfect wife—in movies—

and I'm his imperfect wife.' And one time Richard [at a banquet] said in front of our whole table, 'June here must be a good wife. Jimmy Stewart has married her three times.' "

— • —

That same year, 1955, Ernest Borgnine won Best Actor for the title role in Delbert Mann's *Marty,* which also won Best Picture. A young, up-and-coming comic performer by the name of Jack Lemmon won a Supporting Actor Oscar for his work in John Ford's screen version of *Mr. Roberts,* which starred Henry Fonda, who re-created his award-winning Broadway performance for the screen. Neither Fonda, back in Hollywood after seven years on its "gray" list, nor Jimmy Stewart, voted the most popular actor in Hollywood, were nominated for anything.[1]

— • —

Bill Goetz left Universal late in 1954 to pursue what he believed were the greener pastures of the movement toward independent production, wherein a feature was produced with little or no financing from a studio, and then leased back at a profit, gaining distribution by giving to the studio a piece of the action. Goetz then struck a deal with Columbia to distribute two films that would prove to be the final collaborations between Anthony Mann and Jimmy Stewart. It was Mann who discovered the source for the first, a novel by Thomas T. Flynn called *The Man from Laramie,* which, at least to his way of thinking, had distinct echoes of *King Lear,* the Shakespearean play he had long wanted to bring to the screen. In *Laramie,* Jimmy once again plays a Mann-sized, grizzled, embittered loner out for vengeance, this time as a cavalry officer in mufti looking to avenge his brother's death. As critic

---

1. Fonda was never officially blacklisted. He remained on the so-called gray list of actors who were available but almost never hired. He did appear once during that period, in Fletcher Markle's *Jigsaw* (aka *Gun Moll*), made in 1949. Cheaply produced on locations in and near New York City, the plot revolves around a secret, unnamed organization in which it is strongly hinted there are Communists. Many of those who appeared in the film did so as a way of "proving" they weren't Communists and should not be blacklisted. Among the stars were Franchot Tone, Myron McCormick, Jean Wallace, and Hester Sondergaard. Fonda's appearance is uncredited. The last Hollywood mainstream movie he made prior to *Mr. Roberts* was John Ford's 1948 *Fort Apache.*

Richard Jameson described the film, "The classical base of the drama remains strong as bedrock, and no one who witnesses it ever forgets the most striking moment of physical agony in all Westerns: Stewart's horror and rage as [Alex] Nicol deliberately shoots him through the palm of the hand."

Much of the film, yet another of Mann's Oedipal-sibling rondos, was shot on location in the New Mexico town of Coronado, on land owned by the Pueblo Indian Nation, and in Santa Fe. In it, Jimmy and Mann appeared to be in a macho sibling rivalry–like dueling contest to see who was going to outlast the other. Mann's sadistic streak, always lurking just below the surface, hit its peak during *Laramie,* complemented by Jimmy's willingness to please. As Elliot Stein pointed out, "In *The Man from Laramie,* the last of the Mann-Stewart Westerns, Stewart isn't from Laramie, or anyplace else in particular—he's as rootless as all of Mann's other heroes and has come to town to track down the man responsible for his brother's death. There are more warped sadistic characters and Freudian tangles here than anywhere else on Mann's map of the West— Stewart is humiliated, lassoed, dragged through salt flats, and in the most brutal scene in any '50s western, shot in the hand point-blank."

Mann told one interviewer that *The Man from Laramie* was his grand summation of the five-year collaboration with Jimmy as he described with great relish what he had put him through this time around: "That [film] distilled our relationship. I reprised themes and situations by pushing them to their paroxysms. So the band of cowboys surround Jimmy and rope him as they did before in *Bend of the River,* but here I shot him through the hand! . . . I benefited from CinemaScope and from a perfectly harmonious crew . . . [and was gratified that at the end of our run] Jimmy wound up . . . in first place in the Top Ten!"

Jimmy, for his part, had little to say about the grueling experience. Approaching fifty, he could hear as well as feel his bones begin to creak, and upon completing *The Man from Laramie* graciously surrendered the chance to play in the next scheduled film of Mann's two-feature deal for Columbia, *The Last Frontier.* (After trying and failing to get Jimmy to change his mind, a disappointed Mann then turned to Victor Mature for the part. When the film opened, without Jimmy's chemistry to ignite Mann's explosive vision, it slipped quickly into oblivion, where it remains to this day.)

The Man from Laramie finished production in November 1954;

three weeks later, after what was for him a disturbing phone call from his eighty-two-year-old father back in Indiana, Jimmy immediately packed up the family and headed home. Over the phone, Alexander had, almost matter-of-factly, as if he were ordering a barrel of roofing nails, informed his son that he was getting remarried.

The news shocked Jimmy, who listened silently as his father described his bride-to-be, a seventy-six-year-old Canadian widow by the name of J. J. Stothard of St. John, New Brunswick, Canada. Barely a year had passed since Bessie's death, and here was his father taking another woman. And one whom he had known for at least six years. Why? Jimmy wondered. What was the reason? What was the point?

As was his way, he kept his feelings to himself, said nothing to Alexander, and even agreed to serve as best man at the small reception planned for later that month. If he felt a sense of betrayal in the air, Jimmy wasn't really certain who was being betrayed.

— • —

Jimmy, Gloria, and the kids left for Indiana on December 12, and had hardly had any time to meet the bride before the ceremonies. After the wedding, Alexander announced to one and all he was going to take his new wife to Hollywood for Christmas, so she could spend time with his boy's family.

Jimmy said nothing, just nodded his head up and down in apparent agreement.

Also invited both to the wedding and the reception that followed were Leland Hayward and Margaret Sullavan. Although divorced, they remained on friendly terms. Hayward, eager to get back into the picture business, had just acquired the rights to the story of Charles A. Lindbergh's historic 1927 solo flight across the Atlantic, which had become the greatest media story of all time, one that transformed the skinny kid from St. Louis into an international icon. After selling his agency and moving east to accommodate his wife's desire to play on Broadway, Hayward once more wanted to produce movies, and he felt that the Lindbergh saga was a can't-miss vehicle.

As soon as Jimmy arrived back in Hollywood, he had Wasserman get Jack Warner to approach Hayward about the possibility of his playing the lead. There was a reason Jimmy didn't go directly to Hayward; in reality, there was little chance he could get to play the part of a charac-

ter twenty-five years his junior, once nicknamed the "flying fool" because of his idealistic youth and the folly of his dream. Jimmy wanted to
spare Hayward (and himself) the embarrassment of what was almost
certain to be a turn-down.

He was right; it was. Wasserman then urged Jimmy to talk directly
with Hayward, which he reluctantly agreed to do. Hayward dealt
straight and tough with Jimmy, telling him that he was approaching
fifty, looked it, and that there was no longer anything dreamlike about
him. Sorry, impossible.

"Lindbergh's flight was a great event in history," Jimmy told an interviewer. "But my good friend Leland was dead set against me because
of my age. Then, last fall, when my eighty-four-year-old dad came out to
Hollywood on his honeymoon, he busted everything wide open."

A few days later, with Alex and his bride still in town, Hayward invited them, Jimmy, and Gloria out for a dinner in Beverly Hills, during
which, to Stewart's mixed feelings of pride, hurt, and embarrassment,
Alexander continued to lobby for Jimmy to get the part. "My dad had
found out that I wanted to play Lindbergh, but there wasn't a prayer of
it. You can imagine how I felt when he suddenly whispered to me in the
middle of dinner, 'Son, I'm going to fix things for you.' Then, before I
could stop him, he asked Hayward his plans for the coming movie, and
listened only until Hayward said he was looking for a young, unknown
actor to play the role.

"Dad acted as if someone had shot him out of a cannon. Smacking
his fist on the table, he leaped to his feet and began shouting at Hayward, 'Unknown young actor, indeed! What's the matter with my boy
Jimmy? You've been his best friend for years, and now you're deserting
him! There's only one man who can play Lindbergh—my son!'

"Of course, I was dying with embarrassment throughout all this
commotion. I kept muttering, 'Now Dad . . .' But he went on ranting."

It was an altogether humiliating evening for Jimmy, and everybody
knew it. The next day, Leland quietly took him to lunch with Billy
Wilder, the director and co-writer already hired for the film. Jimmy remembered his throat feeling as if a vise had it clamped shut, with every
bite of food he took having to fight its way down to an already queasy
stomach. They talked about everything that afternoon except the film
and who was to play young Lindbergh. And with good reason. At the
time Lindbergh was lobbying hard for Hayward to cast John Kerr to play

him in the film; he was a young, good-looking actor just breaking into bigger films and far closer in age and temperament than Stewart was.[2]

Alexander, meanwhile, continued on in Hollywood, taking up one cause after another. As Jimmy later recalled, "One Sunday morning, he got up and said, 'Where's the church?' He could only mean the Presbyterian church, of course. I stalled, saying, 'It's a long way over that direction. I—I haven't exactly located it yet.'

"He left the house with a purposeful step. Two hours later, he returned, trailing four men behind him. They entered the living room, and Dad said briskly, 'I guess you didn't search in the right direction, Jim. The church is two blocks to the north.'

" 'Oh,' I said, unable to think of any other reply.

" 'These gentlemen are the elders,' Dad continued. 'And they told me they are having difficulty raising funds for a new church building they need. I told them I had a son who was a movie actor and making a lot of money and might be willing to discuss their problem with them.' Thereupon, Dad marched out of the room, leaving the embarrassed elders and me facing each other. We did discuss the problem, and I joined the fund drive; and I joined the church."

In March 1955, eager to get away from everyone and everything having to do with the movie, entitled *The Spirit of St. Louis,* Jimmy took Gloria and the kids and flew to Tokyo to attend the opening of *Rear Window.* He was surprised and delighted at the reception he got there, considering his strong war record (even though he had fought exclusively in the European theater). When asked by a reporter if he felt any resentment from the Japanese, Jimmy replied, "None whatsoever. The United States was very wise in letting Japan keep its Emperor and not imprisoning him or putting him to death . . . and they all adore General MacArthur, who did such a magnificent job for our country and for Japan. The Japanese people realize the United States wanted to do its best for them. When General MacArthur first took over, they thought they'd probably all be killed."

The Stewarts also made stops in Macao, Hong Kong, and the Philip-

---

2. Lindbergh had enough clout to actually get Kerr considered for the part before Stewart, but the young, liberal actor had turned it down for political reasons. He did not wish to portray the aviator due to Lindbergh's isolationist, soft-on-Hitler activities prior to World War Two. Anthony Perkins and Martin Milner were two other actors Lindbergh preferred for the role instead of Stewart. Both turned it down.

pines. In Macao, Jimmy was able to look over the border into what he called "Red" China, and spoke of Mao's Communist revolution having done nothing so much as renewed his and the free world's belief in democracy, and how important it was to continue to spread the message of freedom to the four corners via American movies.

"You can hardly compare Hong Kong and Japan," Gloria told Louella Parsons, who had accompanied the family on the trip to report on it for the *Los Angeles Examiner*. "Hong Kong is completely cosmopolitan and is made up of all races and nations. In Japan there are only Japanese, but in Hong Kong you see Arabs, Chinese, Africans, Americans and English. There is a great air of mystery and intrigue about it, too." Turning to her husband, she then urged Jimmy to tell Louella "about the self-appointed spies who come from Red China with secrets to sell!"

Jimmy smiled in agreement but said nothing.

— • —

Upon his return to the States, Jimmy accepted an offer to appear on TV as a guest on the struggling Ronald Reagan–hosted *G.E. Theater*, a half-hour anthology of the old West whose stories always carried a message underscoring individualism, freedom, and democracy. Jimmy, among the hottest actors in the movies at the time, always maintained that he did the appearance as a personal favor to Reagan, one of his oldest and dearest friends, who happened to be the coldest actor anywhere at the moment, his last gig prior to the TV series a nightclub act in Las Vegas.[3] Just the mere acceptance of a dramatic part on the tube (as opposed to

---

3. Following movies like *Bedtime for Bonzo,* in which he co-starred opposite a monkey, Reagan's film career had hit rock bottom. On February 15, 1954, MCA booked Reagan for the first and only time into Las Vegas, as a headliner and stand-up comic in a show at the ironically named Last Frontier. Also on the bill were vaudeville duos, a singing quartet called the Continentals, and several leggy and bosomy Vegas showgirls. Reagan maintained he took the gig to pay back taxes and a new mortgage for the house he had bought for his second wife, actress Nancy Davis. Despite good reviews, he declined to go on the road with the Continentals. He never again played Vegas as a performer. Prior to the engagement, he had begged Wasserman and Stein to get him anything—magazine ads, personal appearances, testimonial dinners. There are many who feel that the Johnny Fontaine character in *The Godfather* is not really based on Frank Sinatra, but on Ronald Reagan and the dealings with MCA that led to his comeback TV series. Dennis McDougal discusses this in detail in his biography of Lew Wasserman.

the jokey guest shots on Jack Benny's show or the journalistic Sunday-night Sullivan hour) was enough to trigger talk in the trades that Stewart was having career problems as well. He was, after all, never a conventional leading man, those marshmallow bags around his delicate WASP eyes had begun to thicken and droop, those veins in his complexion had become more visible, and his cheekbones looked to have exhaled, sending billows to his jaws like coming attractions of jowls. His shoulders, never broad, began to ever so slightly stoop. The diminutive TV screen, whether intended or not, regularly reduced flaws like these, which is why it became the perfect cosmetic for many of the aging male and female stars of Hollywood, who found second wind for their fading film careers and became huge TV stars on the smaller-than-life medium (among them Dick Powell, Ward Bond, George Montgomery, Loretta Young, Lucille Ball, and dozens of others). Those able to resist the tube did, including Henry Fonda, John Wayne, Humphrey Bogart, Lauren Bacall, Bette Davis, Marilyn Monroe, and Cary Grant.

However, career-arcing had nothing to do with Jimmy's decision to go on dramatic TV. The real reason was far more complex, and had its roots in Jimmy's 1950 precedent-shattering, profit-participation deal to make *Winchester '73*. Thanks to Wasserman, it made Jimmy a millionaire, but, as all those who did business with Wasserman sooner or later learned, such monetary reward came with long, gripping tentacles.

Ever since purchasing what was left of Leland Hayward's talent agency, Wasserman, along with Jules Stein, had had an eye on creating an agency that would not only handle the biggest talent in Hollywood, but produce films, and later TV shows and series for them. Prior to World War Two, when television was first set to burst onto the social conscience and popular culture of America, before Pearl Harbor forced what would be a seven-year delay in setting up and putting the networks into operation, Wasserman was a big believer in television. He always liked to tell people that when it came to TV, he was a true visionary, because he had bought one of the first two television sets sold in Southern California.[4]

Meanwhile, in the early fifties, the only aspect of show business

4. The other was purchased by Don Lee, an L.A. Cadillac dealer who also operated the West Coast division of the CBS radio network.

that Reagan drew the line at was television, which he thought would forever prevent him from returning to the big screen, and which mostly came out of New York City, a town he particularly disliked. Almost everything on the tube came from there, including Westerns. CBS often used the rooftop of Grand Central Terminal to film running packs of horses.

This brought a lot of tension among the clashing studio heads of the two coasts, as Hollywood watched while a mass medium that had begun in the East before migrating to Hollywood seemed to be returning to its roots. The studio moguls went so far as to ban the broadcast of any of their movies by the big three TV networks (for this and other reasons, including competition and royalty discrepancies). The film studios, already in disarray, feared that television was going to destroy the industry by giving away entertainment for "free."

Wasserman and Stein then had a brainstorm. Rather than fighting the inevitable, they decided that MCA could be a part of the new revolution in home entertainment by creating a TV subdivision, producing TV fare out of Hollywood to sell directly to the networks. Both coasts immediately took to the idea. The East was running out of train-station rooftops, while the West had acres of studio space going unused.

Ironically, the only people opposed to the idea were those who had the most to gain from it—the performers; more specifically, their unions. The Screen Actors Guild (SAG) had, since its inception in the thirties, absolutely forbidden its members to work for any agent who also produced films. The conflict of interest was obvious. An agent wants to get the most for his client's services; a producer wants to pay the least. This rule was rarely bent, and only by individual waiver after much lobbying for specific events the guild deemed reasonable.

Not to worry, Wasserman told Stein, he would appeal directly to the president of SAG, who at the time happened to be Ronald Reagan, who had stepped into the top position after the resignation of Robert Montgomery (he'd resigned when he became the part owner, or producer, of several of his own movies, thereby placing him in conflict with the very rules of the guild of which he was the head). Reagan, on the other hand, had no connection in any way to producing or ownership, and eagerly stepped into the position as the head of the guild that nobody with any real earnings potential and therefore inevitable studio/guild conflicts wanted.

When approached by Wasserman and Stein, Reagan was loath to turn them down, as these were the very men who had saved his hide. But he was also smart enough to know it was an extremely dangerous career move to go against SAG precedent and grant such a sweeping exemption.

After much consideration, Reagan came up with the idea of a necessary quid pro quo, that the guild would have to somehow benefit in a broad and sweeping way from any exemptive grants. Following several meetings with various guild officials and Wasserman's people, the notion of residuals for actors was introduced.

For the longest time—until independent production contracts included participation clauses—actors were paid once for their performances on film, no matter how many times that film was played, anywhere around the world. The first of the new contracts was Cary Grant's, with his two simultaneous, nonexclusive deals with Columbia and RKO in 1936, which opened the floodgates to profit participation. Residuals were meant to make this practice standard, so that any actor who appeared in any movie or TV show would be paid a set amount whenever that product was replayed, in theaters or on TV. The guild loved the idea; the studios hated it. While the debate over whether or not to grant residuals and how to dispense them dragged on, Reagan, through SAG, granted Wasserman's MCA (and its TV subsidiary, Revue) a blanket waiver that allowed them to represent its roster of talent and to hire them to appear in programs Revue produced for TV, with residual payments for their work.

Following the granting of that waiver, Reagan's career experienced one of the most incredible comebacks in the history of show business. Revue became a major player in fifties television, and Wasserman became the most powerful mogul in Hollywood. Revue's *General Electric Theater* premiered February 1, 1953. A year later, Reagan was the host of the popular Sunday-night show, at a starting salary of $120,000 per episode, plus separate salaries for occasionally appearing in the episodes. To ensure the show remain a top ratings draw, Wasserman ordered his A-line stars to make special guest appearances in the half-hour episodes. The performers really had no choice. Refusing Wasserman meant risking his ire and potentially damaging their own careers.

In 1954, the first year G.E. *Theater* was on as a weekly show (its second year of production; it had been biweekly), Wasserman ordered

Joan Crawford, Tyrone Power, Henry Fonda, Joseph Cotten, Jane Wyman, Fred Astaire—and Jimmy Stewart—to accept roles on the show. They all said yes without protest. Jimmy's episode, "The Windmill," was the highest-rated one of the season, and ensured Reagan's show would be picked up the following fall.[5]

For his part, even though he had more or less been forced into it, shoved by Wasserman's kid gloves, so to speak, Jimmy discovered he enjoyed doing TV very much—the speed, the efficiency, the disposability of it all, and the people associated with the new medium. In particular, he liked the show's producer, William Frye, who was to become a lifelong friend. He considered making the one-time move a permanent career shift, and likely would have, if one of his favorite directors had not come knocking again, delivering the future in the form of a brand-new and, to Jimmy, irresistible screenplay.

— • —

The director was Alfred Hitchcock and the project was an intended American remake of the director's 1934 Gaumont production of *The Man Who Knew Too Much*, produced by Michael Balcon, Hitchcock's primary British producer. While the original version was received popularly, and made Hitchcock a brand name in America, he had been dissatisfied with the limitations the financially struggling studio had necessitated upon the production. He had always had it in the back of his

---

5. The episode starred a veritable roster of MCA talent, including Stewart, Barbara Hale, Donald MacDonald, Cheryl Callaway, John McIntire, Walter Sande, James Millican, and Edgar Buchanan. It first aired April 24, 1955, on CBS.

In the early sixties, MCA came under federal investigation for its business practices and possible relationship to organized crime. Dozens of Hollywood's top stars testified; MCA clients mostly in support of Lew Wasserman, including Jack Benny, Rita Hayworth, Rock Hudson, Bob Cummings, Cary Grant, Tony Curtis, and Danny Kaye. Of particular interest to the government was the deal that Reagan had brokered that changed forever the way Hollywood did business with talent, namely the introduction of residuals on top of freelance contracts. According to Dennis McDougal in his biography of Lew Wasserman: When Fricano, the lead interrogator of the grand jury, zeroed in on the blanket waiver that Reagan helped engineer for MCA as president of the Screen Actors Guild, the actor's memory failed. "I think I have already told you I don't recall that," said Reagan . . . Later on, grand juror Ruth Ragle said, of Reagan's testimony: "The only thing he knew was his name."

mind to remake it, American-style, in color, wide screen, and with top-of-the-line American movie stars in the leading roles.[6]

In January 1955, riding the crest of the popularity of *Rear Window,* for which he had just been nominated by the Academy for Best Director, Hitchcock began to actively work on a new screenplay for *The Man Who Knew Too Much,* using *Window*'s writer John Michael Hayes, who had also been nominated.[7] He wanted to expand the characters, and also to focus on what would become the middle of a three-part trilogy of fifties films, beginning with *Rear Window,* which would chronicle the joys—or more accurately, in Hitchcock's world, the nightmares—of the rituals of romance, marriage, and loss. Having more or less dealt with the first aspect in *Rear Window,* Hitchcock wanted to keep the same actor for all three parts, while rotating the leading women. The idea was ingenious, the effect extraordinary.

He went to Wasserman to sign Jimmy, and immediately agreed to the same participation deal he had given the actor for the first film.

Finding a leading lady would prove far more difficult. Hitchcock did not want to use any of his normal repertory of gorgeous ice blondes, because it would defeat the notion that he was trying to explore: what happens in a marriage when children serve as the vacuum for the heat, and the parents are no longer attracted to each other? The underbelly of all this fell into familiar Hitchcock-style Freudian turf; what happens when a wife turns into a mother? How do you continue to regard her as your lover? To explore this, Hitchcock needed an attractive American movie star whose heat was not readily apparent, whose sultriness could be sublimated into a maternal visage, and whose acting could complement the

---

6. The rights to the British film had been purchased by Selznick early on, intended as a gift to Hitchcock for signing with Selznick International Pictures. However, once their relationship broke down, which it did during their very first film, *Rebecca,* Selznick, looking to recoup, offered the project in 1941 to John Houseman, who tried but ultimately failed to put together a remake. Eventually Hitchcock bought the rights back from a cash-strapped Selznick.

7. The 1954 Best Director Oscar went to Elia Kazan for *On the Waterfront.* Other Best Director nominees that year were George Seaton for *The Country Girl* (also starring Grace Kelly, who was nominated for and won for this performance rather than the far superior one she gave in *Rear Window*), William Wellman for *The High and the Mighty,* and Billy Wilder for *Sabrina. Rear Window* was also nominated for, but did not win, Best Screenplay (Hayes), Color Cinematography, and Sound Recording.

equally sexless meowing of Jimmy's character, Dr. Ben McKenna. That actress was Doris Day. According to Day: "Hitchcock and I met accidentally at a party. Neither of us had a reputation for being partygoers, and I think we were both surprised to meet in that setting." Hitchcock then complimented her on her performance in a little-known film, Stewart Heisler's 1951 *Storm Warning*, a noirish melodrama about the Ku Klux Klan, no less, in which she played the sister of the heroine (Ginger Rogers). Taken aback but nonetheless impressed by his knowledge of the movie, she was unaware that Hitchcock was also a fan of her singing style. As it happened, singing was crucial to the role he was setting her up for.

That initial meeting between them took place late in 1951, just after Hitchcock's spectacular return to form with *Strangers on a Train*. *I Confess*, *Dial M for Murder*, and *Rear Window* had all followed, in rapid succession, after which Hitchcock convinced his other favored fifties doppelgänger, Cary Grant, to come out of retirement to make *To Catch a Thief*. In that film, he cast Kelly, Jimmy's lover in *Rear Window* a year earlier, as a character strikingly similar to Lisa, Frances Stevens, a young beauty chased by an older man. This time, in contrast to the confines of a Greenwich Village back alley, Hitchcock shot his film in the wide-open spaces of Monaco and southern France. The drabness of the former mise-en-scène was in profound contrast to the latter's glamorous one that reflected the difference between how Hitchcock saw Jimmy in his marriage-bound world and Grant in his single, emotionally unattached one, and Kelly's reaction to both men in them.[8]

The entire Hitchcock oeuvre is made up of these kinds of cinematic crossword puzzles, as his leading men get caught up in adventures aided and abetted by beautiful marriage-minded women, or get caught up with beautiful single and exciting women who then play crucial roles in saving the day before they kill the thrill with marriage. In *The Man Who Knew Too Much*, Dr. McKenna makes his wife give up her career

---

8. "The ultra Hitchcockian performances are those of James Stewart in *Rope*, *Rear Window*, *The Man Who Knew Too Much*, and *Vertigo*; and Cary Grant in *Suspicion*, *Notorious*, *To Catch a Thief*, and *North by Northwest*. Stewart and Grant gave Hitchcock the means he could not have got from any other actors. In return, Hitchcock gave Stewart and Grant meanings they could not have got from any other director." (Andrew Sarris, *The American Cinema*, pages 60–61.)

as a singer (her own adventure) for the sake of their marriage (his). In effect he enslaves her to unwanted domesticity, yet it is her singing "Que Sera, Sera" at the climax of the plot that not merely saves the political day but also suggests the ultimate failure of their rigid prefeminist, anti-individualist marriage.[9]

The story centers around Dr. Ben McKenna, his wife and young son on vacation in Marrakech, Morocco. On a visit to a marketplace, they witness a murder, the dying man whispers something to McKenna, and shortly thereafter his boy is kidnapped, "inadvertently" involving McKenna in an international assassination plot scheduled to take place at the Royal Albert Hall. The assassination gang has kidnapped McKenna's child to ensure the doctor's silence.

The plot is patently ridiculous—the best way to silence McKenna, of course, is simply to kill him. The details of the assassination are never disclosed, reducing the entire murder scenario to the familiar "MacGuffin," the meaningless points and objects of the plot that Hitchcock's movies are hung on (the radiation dust in *Notorious,* the jewels in *To Catch a Thief,* the entire Raymond Burr subplot in *Rear Window,* etc).[10] What does count, and mightily, is how the endangerment of the McKennas' son brings to the surface the suppressed but very real absence of his parents' passion for each other, and in doing so reveals the

---

9. "Que Sera, Sera" was written by veteran movie songwriters Jay Livingstone and Ray Evans. It won the Oscar for Best Song, over "Friendly Persuasion" from the movie of the same name, "Julie" from the movie of the same name, "True Love" from *High Society,* a musical remake of *The Philadelphia Story,* and "Written on the Wind" from the movie of the same name.

10. "[The MacGuffin] is the device, the gimmick, if you will . . . a term we use to cover all that sort of thing—to steal plans or documents, or discover a secret, it doesn't matter what it is . . . it's beside the point. The only thing that really matters is that in the picture the plans, documents, or secrets must seem to be of vital importance to the characters. . . . You may be wondering where the term originated. It might be a Scottish name, taken from a story about two men in a train. One man says, 'What's that package up there in the baggage rack?' And the other answers, 'Oh, that's a MacGuffin.' 'What's a MacGuffin?' 'Well,' the other man says, 'it's an apparatus for trapping lions in the Scottish Highlands.' The first man says, 'But there are no lions in the Scottish Highlands.' And the other one answers, 'Well then, that's no MacGuffin!' So you see that a MacGuffin is actually nothing at all." Hitchcock, quoted in François Truffaut, *Hitchcock/Truffaut,* New York: Touchstone Books, 1985, p138.

dormant, inner strength of Mrs. McKenna—a mother's indomitable spirit—strong enough to rescue her boy and prevent the assassination. The real tragedy in the film is not the attempted assassination and kidnapping, but the realization of the death of love. The climactic, and in many ways primal, scream, as Hitchcock biographer Donald Spoto astutely points out, not only prevents the assassination but, with the force and fury of all that has been churning inside of Mrs. McKenna, "interrupts the harmony and order of the concert . . . the inevitable result of the clash of external and internal forces." In this light, it is possible to see Ben and Jo McKenna as the projected nightmare of Jeffries's fears of what marriage to Lisa will do to their relationship and their lives.

Day, not used to the distant silences used by Hitchcock as a way of nonverbal consent for his actors' performances—he was not of the school that showed actors how to play a scene, but of the one that assumed they were skilled workers who knew how to do what was expected of them—early on wanted to quit the film, but was talked out of it by Jimmy, who took great pains to convince her she was doing really well in her portrayal of his screen wife. Day: "The first time I saw Hitchcock on *The Man Who Knew Too Much* I was with [costume designer] Edith Head, talking about my costumes. Hitchcock came in, wanting to see the sketches and discuss them. On that day he threw some of them out and was very precise about exactly what he wanted for my wardrobe." It was a meeting that caused her a lot of turmoil because of Hitchcock's distance, what she took as his uncaring attitude, apparently more interested in what she wore than how she performed.

"[Hitchcock] was very generous and lavish at the hotel dining room, ordering food from Paris and London, and insisting on the right wines for each course, but when we were shooting the exterior scenes in Africa I began to become very upset. He never said anything to me, before or during or after a scene, and so I thought I was displeasing him and I was crushed. . . . I told my husband it was obvious I should try to get out of the picture. . . . Hitchcock was astonished! He said it was quite the reverse, that he thought I was just doing everything right—and that if I hadn't been doing everything right he would have told me."

At Hitchcock's urging, Jimmy took over the job of reassuring the actress that she was doing a terrific job. "In the beginning," he said later, "it certainly threw Doris for a loop. She surprised a lot of people with her acting in *The Man Who Knew Too Much,* but she didn't surprise Hitchcock, who knew what to expect from her. A singer's talent for phrasing, the ability to put heart in a piece of music, is not too far removed from acting, in which the aim is to give life and believability to what's on paper . . ."

"Hitch believed you were hired to do your job. You were expected to know your lines and carry your part. In Marrakech in Morocco I could see Hitch in the square amid complete confusion with all those extras in 110 degrees heat, in a blue suit and tie, sitting in a chair, waiting for the cameraman to get ready. Everything quieted down, and people did what they had to do. He then said, 'Let's move over here now.' You know, I really don't think he cared much for the spoken word. He was interested in getting those 'pieces of time' and he just used the words as little as possible. For example, the scene in Albert Hall. You remember the last part with the cymbal. The assassin was going to kill this man while the London Symphony is playing. During all this I'm charging up the stairs trying to tell Doris Day what's happened to our kidnapped child. It was a long speech, and I had done it a couple of times. I had memorized about three pages of dialogue. Well, Hitch came up to me and said, 'You're talking so much, I'm unable to enjoy the London Symphony. Why don't you just not say anything? Try to hold Doris and whisper something.' Well, the audience was way ahead of the people we were playing in the film anyway. Hitch didn't want words to get in the way. Words have their place, but you have to know when to use them."

The film, a difficult shoot in the oppressive heat and with an unrelenting schedule, tension between Day and Hitchcock, and a forty-seven-year-old Stewart huffing and puffing to keep up with all the physical action of the filming, finally wrapped on August 24, 1955.

— • —

The Man Who Knew Too Much opened nearly a full year later in New York City's Paramount Theater, in May 1956, due to the studio's desire to space out what had become a deluge of Hitchcock product. Although the critics were not blown away by it, many comparing it unfavorably to the original, much of what praise there was for the film went to its two leads. *Variety* singled out Jimmy for "ably carrying out his title duties," while *The Nation* said that "James Stewart and Doris Day, faultlessly groomed and as smooth as marbles, earn their high pay with perfect studio performances."[11]

The film wound up eighteenth of the year's highest-grossing films.[12]

By then, Hitchcock and Jimmy had their eyes on their next project together, something the director wanted to call *Vertigo*. In the interim, for a variety of reasons, mostly having to do with contracts and money, Hitchcock went off to make *The Wrong Man*, a depressing neonoir nightmare based on a true story of a musician wrongly accused of a series of neighborhood robberies, starring, of all people, Henry Fonda in a film about a good man wrongly identified as an evil one.

Jimmy, meanwhile, thirty days after *The Man Who Knew Too Much* wrapped, flew to New York to attend a meeting with Billy Wilder arranged by Leland Hayward about that Charles Lindbergh film that Hayward was going to co-write and produce, and Wilder was set to direct.

Hitchcock's and Stewart's interim ventures would prove problematic, but in the end it wouldn't matter. When they finally did get together one last time, the dizzying heights of cinematic transcendence would once more revisit both their houses, higher and brighter than it ever had before.

---

11. Upon its 1987 reissue, critic Andrew Sarris assessed the film this way in his weekly column for the *Village Voice*: "It is a thrilling piece of cinema for anyone who can appreciate the working out of formal problems as a means of stirring the murky depths of the unconscious . . . if you come out of the movie relieved that Stewart and Day are back together and happy again with their surprisingly sissyish little boy, then you have missed the whole point of Stewart's implacability and Day's delirium. This is no ordinary nuclear family."

12. Not everyone, however, was pleased with its critical reception or the financial windfall it produced. Day was sufficiently distressed to want to turn her career in an entirely different direction, to the comedies she would make in the late fifties and early sixties opposite mostly lighter-weight actor/comedians, such as James Garner and Rock Hudson. She also developed a lifelong interest in charity work to relieve poverty, after her firsthand experience while making the film on location in Africa.

22

"Leading my list of leading men is most definitely James Stewart. For me, he encompasses all the things I appreciate in a man. He always has been—and always will be—my ideal. Setting him apart is his endearing shyness, an innocence that I found irresistible. He was the sexiest man who played opposite me in thirty years." —KIM NOVAK

*I*n subsequent talks with Billy Wilder, without Jimmy's knowledge, Leland Hayward had dangled the notion of casting Jimmy in a role half his age, where youth was the key to the character, as something daring, original and . . . *doable*. The more Hayward had thought about it, the more he believed the film called for an experienced actor who could *play* youthful, rather than a youthful actor who might not be able to project sufficiently Lindbergh's depth of courage and derring-do. As much of the film was going to be shot in a cockpit, with a leather helmet and goggles, Jimmy might actually be able to pull the thing off. He was so unnerved when he got the word from Hayward that he called Gloria and asked her to fly in for moral support; in case his legs gave way, she could grab him under one arm and keep him on his feet. Gloria laughed and made arrangements to catch the next flight east.

During the next dinner, which Margaret Sullavan and Mrs. Lindbergh also attended, Jimmy and Lindbergh talked at great length about their mutual lifelong passion for flying, until eventually, guided by Lindbergh, the discussion came around to Jimmy's heroic war record. That was when Jimmy first believed the part was going to be his, that Hayward and Wilder had agreed that, despite the huge gap in ages, he could play it. As the dinner ended, Jimmy turned to Lindbergh and said, "I hope I can do a good job for you," to which Lindbergh replied, in the shy, quiet manner that had so endeared him to the imagination of the American public, "I hope so too." With that, good-byes were made and the Stewarts left.

What Jimmy did not know was that the battle had already taken place, behind the scenes, between Wilder, whose other casting choices had all fallen through, either because he couldn't convince the actors he'd wanted to do it or Lindbergh had vetoed them. Nonetheless, Jack Warner, always prone to hyperbole, was furious at Wilder's decision to go with Jimmy (he had no way of contractually overruling it) and predicted that if the film were made with him, it would result in the greatest disaster in Warner Bros.' history.

This is how Hedda Hopper, writing in the *Los Angeles Times* in the spring of 1955, officially announced the project: "James Stewart will forever consider March 22, 1955, as the luckiest day of his life, for on that day he got his heart's desire—the role of Charles Lindbergh in *The Spirit of St. Louis*."

Filming began in September 1956 in a Santa Maria, California, airplane hangar reconfigured to pass for the ground site at Long Island, New York's original Roosevelt Field landing strip. Interiors were shot on the Los Angeles Warner Bros. backlot and at Platt Ranch, a facility the studio often used for exteriors. Problems with the shooting script became apparent early on, but because Lindbergh had approval over everything, from the smallest dialogue change to the shifting of a preset camera angle, Wilder wound up beating his head against a cement wall when anything he or Wendell Mayes, his screenwriter, suggested wasn't literally in the original book, and was therefore immediately rejected by the aviator. This posed special problems when it came to the thirty-three-hour solo flight, forcing Wilder to rely on excessive character voice-overs and flashbacks. And Wilder came up against that cement wall once more when he tried to include a reference to what had long been rumored, that Lindbergh had dallied with a local waitress in the hours before his historic takeoff. None of that made it into the movie.

To prepare for the role, Jimmy had spent much of his time watching newsreels of Lindbergh, and decided that in order to get the part he'd better *lose* five pounds: "I wanted to watch that newsreel because while it would be impossible for my face to look exactly like Lindbergh's, I wanted to catch his mannerisms. For instance, I noticed he has a very distinctive walk. He has a habit of swinging his left arm in front of him, even when he only takes three steps; I tried to imitate that. Then I went through the horrible ordeal of having my eyebrows dyed reddish-blond, like Lindbergh's, and my hair colored the same."

Every Sunday morning Jimmy and Gloria would join the children for an early breakfast, then drive them to the Presbyterian church in Beverly Hills where Gloria taught Sunday school and both her boys sang in the choir. Late in the afternoon, Jimmy liked to fly a duplicate of the *Spirit of St. Louis,* the small monoplane in which Lindbergh had flown nonstop across the Atlantic to Paris, one he and Hayward had completely refurbished. "Like Lindbergh, I couldn't see straight ahead because the whole front of the plane, where the pilot would normally sit with fine vision, was used for fuel storage. Lindbergh had sat way back in the plane, in a wicker chair. When he wanted to see where he was going he had to lean out the window or look through the periscope he'd rigged up. It was a strange experience to fly that old plane. But having done it I felt I had a better knowledge of how he felt, and moved, and flew."

The film was released on May 20, 1957, Jimmy's forty-ninth birthday and the thirtieth anniversary of the start of Lindbergh's historic flight. There was the usual self-generated excitement of dual-coast klieg light premieres, one in Hollywood and one in New York City, but despite all the advance publicity, the natural tie-in with the flight's anniversary, and Stewart's seemingly invincible box-office clout, the film proved a financial dud. Its grueling nine-month shoot had caused its budget to balloon to triple its original $2 million, and it grossed just over $2 million in its initial domestic release.[1] As Jack Warner had predicted, it was an unqualified financial disaster for Warner Bros., and Jimmy's first out-and-out flop after a run of ten straight moneymakers.

Despite its poor reviews and indifferent audiences, Jimmy continued to champion the film, calling it one of the best of his career. While the privilege of playing Lindbergh had been, he said many times, the chance of a lifetime, the hard truth was, the age factor mattered. It was difficult for audiences to understand the youthful exuberance of a character who looked as if he was approaching forty (makeup managed to knock off ten years). The film had other problems as well. Most of the drama took place in a small cockpit with no dialogue and what seemed like an endless series of Lindbergh leaning into swirling clouds to see

---

1. Lindbergh was paid $1 million for the rights to his story; $5 million went into the actual production.

where he was going, which never appeared to be anywhere so much as deeper into those Hollywood manufactured "skies." And it was long— two hours and eighteen minutes, which effectively cut down the play schedule by one showing per day. Wilder, whose direction in this film lacked the dry, wry wit and sophistication of his best work, said later that he should have made the picture bigger (meaning scope, not length), and included Lindbergh's courtship, wedding, the infamous kidnapping, the resultant reclusiveness and swerve to the conservative right. Jack Warner thought Sam Wood or William Wellman or, ideally, Michael Curtiz, could have made a better picture in their sleep.

However, the biggest personal disappointment remained Stewart's. After his spectacular comeback with *Winchester '73* and *Rear Window*, he now began to sense that Hayward and Wilder had been right all along, that he had made something of a laughingstock of himself by attempting, at his age, to play a world-famous character barely out of his teens. (He had been able to pull off this kind of stretch once before, in the early scenes of *It's a Wonderful Life,* but he was nearly ten years younger when he made that film.) Later on, critic Andrew Sarris would describe the miscasting as an embarrassment.

Following the failure of *The Spirit of St. Louis,* Jimmy felt every day of his forty-seven years etched onto his face, behind his eyes, in his knees. For the next several months, he retreated from filmmaking and concentrated on family and fatherhood, taking the children to school, puttering around the house, making phone calls, and watching his old movies on TV. The closest he came to doing business was his daily monitoring of his various financial investments. It all added up to a lot of nothing.

The hard truth was, he might have returned much earlier if someone had offered him a decent role. Unfortunately for Jimmy, parts had grown increasingly lean, and there was little for him to do except wait for word from Hitchcock that production was to begin on *Vertigo.* He was ready, but it had already been postponed once from the spring of 1957, due to Hitchcock having taken ill.

One day during lunch, Hitch's face suddenly went pale as he grabbed his big stomach with both hands. He had suffered from a navel hernia for years that doctors warned could strangulate without warning. After having put off the surgery numerous times, due to his morbid fear of operations, this attack made him finally agree to have it done. During it, the doctors discovered Hitchcock was also suffering from colitis. His recovery from that necessitated an even longer delay, into September.

In the meantime, Hitchcock had his second unit do some background shooting and begin wardrobe tests for Vera Miles, cast in the dual role of Madeleine/Judy. When she became pregnant soon after marrying Gordon Scott, a former movie Tarzan, the start of principal photography was once again delayed.[2]

The young and lovely Vera Miles—whom Hitchcock had previously used in an episode of his *Alfred Hitchcock Presents* TV series and in the feature film *The Wrong Man* (1956) as Rose, the wife of Emmanuel Christopher Balestrero (Henry Fonda), who ultimately loses her mind over the injustice done to her husband—was not, in fact, the director's first choice for the part. He had originally wanted Grace Kelly, the favorite of all his leading ladies, for Rose, but her marriage to Prince Rainier of Monaco had put a halt to her film career with a royal finality.

While Jimmy impatiently waited for production to begin, Gloria thought it best that they get away for a while, out of the country, as far from the press and pressures of Hollywood as possible. She set up a trip to Africa with close friends Fran Kirk and Bess Johnson. Kirk was a businessman from Fort Worth whom Jimmy had first met regarding the family cemetery plot, which Johnson's investment firm handled (along with other related Stewart estate matters). Jimmy and Kirk had since become partners in several successful real-estate business ventures; the two couples became an inseparable social foursome and eventually a regular traveling unit. It was the Johnsons who taught the Stewarts

---

2. Although Hitchcock had initially been quite enthusiastic about Miles, a former Miss Oklahoma, and signed her to a personal contract, after her pregnancy he used her only once more, in the overlooked supporting role of Lila, Janet Leigh's sister in *Psycho* (1960). There is some question as to whether or not Hitchcock was willing to delay the start of *Vertigo* to accommodate Ms. Miles. Some reports suggest that Hitchcock was overruled by Paramount, others that he became obsessively smitten with Ms. Novak, and used Miles's pregnancy as a way to tactfully remove her from the film. In his book-length study of *Vertigo*, Dan Aulier suggests that Hitchcock indeed originally planned to shoot around Miles's pregnancy until he saw Novak in *The Eddy Duchin Story* at an October 1956 screening and may have used Miles's condition as an excuse to recast the dual roles of Madeleine/Judy with Novak. Peter Brown, who has written extensively about Novak, confirms this version of the story.

how to travel in style and introduced them to the pleasures of an African safari. The continent, with its rich history, landscapes, climate, and wildlife, would eventually become Gloria and Jimmy's favorite vacation spot.

— • —

That summer, still waiting for *Vertigo* to get the green light, at the request of Lew Wasserman, Jimmy returned to work in yet another Anthony Mann Western, *Night Passage*. While he was antsy to get in front of a camera again, Jimmy looked upon the assignment with dread, as it became apparent to him the first day of shooting that Mann was going to be more contentious than ever.

Upon his initial arrival, Jimmy had come upon Mann in a heated verbal battle with longtime collaborator Gordon Chase over the shooting script. This time, Mann insisted to Chase, he wanted to push the violence envelope further than he ever had before. Jimmy said nothing, but agreed with Chase. He would have preferred a softer Western, one in which his character might even get to play the accordion.

Eventually, after a series of physically exhausting and often dangerous action shots that Mann insisted his increasingly exhausted and aching star do, Jimmy told Wasserman he wanted Mann off the film. Wasserman reluctantly complied, and Mann was fired. (He left the production and immediately signed on to direct *The Tin Star*, a vehicle he had long wanted to make—with Henry Fonda.)

After Mann's departure from *Night Passage*, Jimmy felt set adrift by the uncertain guidance of the director's replacement, first-timer James Neilson, who had gained a solid reputation as a war photographer, and had worked for a while as an assistant director on live-action features at the Disney studio. On the brighter side, for Jimmy, his character got to play the accordion, accompanied by a score by the inspired musical genius Dimitri Tiomkin, but nothing was enough to salvage this orphaned mess of a film, Jimmy's second outright disaster in a row. The unwritten rule in Hollywood (then as now) is three strikes and you're out. Jimmy, now more than ever, wanted Hitchcock to start production on *Vertigo* as soon as possible, hoping the rotund director could save his career from falling off the ledge.

— • —

During this time, a series of bizarre events ensnared Jimmy in public partisan politics, the one place he had carefully avoiding going. It began in February, when President Eisenhower decided to promote Jimmy, now a colonel in the Air Force Reserve, to the rank of brigadier general and deputy operations chief of the Strategic Air Command. The news was initially met with what might be described at best as casual press attention, single-paragraph blurbs buried in the middle sections of the nation's newspapers, until rumors began to float that the real reason the medal was begin given was that Jimmy had asked for it as a way to gain some publicity to rejuvenate his failing career.

The rumors were in reaction to a series of industry-driven columns by various gossips, who gushingly recalled Jimmy's World War Two heroics as a way to remind everyone what a war hero he was and how much he truly deserved the promotion. In response to the persisting whispers that it was all a cleverly designed attempt to help his flagging career, Vincent X. Flaherty wrote in the March 21 *Los Angeles Examiner*, "Col. James Stewart isn't seeking publicity or campaigning to be a general or anything of the kind. He completely deserves the rank and honor of a generalcy [sic]. There isn't a member of the Air Force Reserve better qualified . . . just thought I'd try and set something straight about a man who not only was a hero but was long ago recognized as a great flyer and leader of men."

On April 17, 1957, the Senate Armed Services Committee announced it planned to hold public hearings on the air force's decision to promote Jimmy and ten other active reservists, including his one-time commanding officer, Gen. Ramsey Potts, after Senator Margaret Chase Smith, a Republican from Maine, officially questioned the motivation behind the promotions, thus delaying what would ordinarily have been a pro forma vote, and causing the Senate committee to go forward in public. Even before the hearings could begin, Smith grabbed headlines of her own when she held a press conference and announced, with much gravity, that "there is some doubt as to what degree some of the nominees are truly active reservists." She then went on to request detailed records on all the nominees, including those of Col. Jimmy Stewart. Her inquiry had to do with the actual time Jimmy had served in the reserves, a question to which she already knew the answer. Before going public, she had done considerable research into Jimmy's postwar record and discovered that he had done only one fifteen-day stint as a reservist in the eleven years following the end of World War Two. And, during all that time, he had officially worn his uniform a total of eight days. Finally, because he had been stopped from flying after Berlin, she wondered if he even qualified as a pilot on any craft developed and used by the air force since the B-29. Holding her cards close to her vest, she waited for the right time to put her hand into play.

The public hearings before the Senate Armed Services Committee began May 7. None of the nominees themselves showed up. Instead, they were all represented by one Lt. Gen. Emmett (Rosie) O'Donnell, who vigorously defended all ten of them, but none more vehemently than the best-known of the lot. "Colonel Stewart is qualified for the promotion and a very positive inspirational force to the young men of the country," O'Donnell told the committee. When it was her turn, Senator Smith pointedly asked for more specific justification for the promotions. A stunned and apparently unprepared O'Donnell said he would need more time to gather that information, and at that point the hearings were adjourned.

The story then exploded, with photos of Jimmy in uniform splashed across the front page of virtually every newspaper in the country. The next day, Senator Smith, for reasons no one could fathom other than she wanted to keep the pressure up and the publicity high, gave a public scolding in the press to Air Force Lt. Gen. O'Donnell, accusing him of misrepresentation and extensive false testimony in an effort to promote Col. James Stewart, *actor*, to reserve brigadier general.

General O'Donnell angrily responded, via the press, that he had done nothing of the sort. Senator Smith then issued the following statement: "Stewart's normal civilian pursuit is that of the motion picture actor. Obviously he can't maintain his proficiency for deputy director of operations of the Strategic Air Command by being a motion picture actor. Past national presidents of the Reserve Officers Association have complained bitterly to me that the Stewart nomination was destructive to the morale of the Air Force Reserve." Then she dropped the big bomb. Colonel Stewart, she declared, had not put in sufficient reserve time to qualify for the promotion.

Stewart was shocked and depressed by Smith's statements. Was he being punished for being an actor? He began to wonder if he had, despite all his efforts to avoid it, been caught up in the web of 1950s paranoia that had made Hollywood a hotbed of political opportunism, fakery, glamour, and mistrust. Was he a victim of "guilt by association," while the real heroics and patriotism of his military service were being ignored? Despite being bombarded by reporters, and urged by Wasserman to say something in his own defense, he steadfastly refused to make any public comment.

— • —

Not so quiet was General Potts, who publicly accused Senator Smith of favoritism and said that Smith was angry because she had wanted one of the ten available slots to go to her instead of her own administrative assistant, William C. Lewis Jr., also a reservist, who had somehow made it onto the preliminary list of nominees. Her response to Potts was that her only motivation was to maintain the high standards and therefore the morale of the United States Air Force. How would it be, she asked, if an actor, someone who plays heroes on the screen, is passed over those who actually are heroes, like Lewis? It was this kind of comment that not only ignored Stewart's war record but appeared to belittle it.[3]

In July, Stewart made a highly publicized, fully uniformed appearance in his Reserve unit. For the first time since the war, he was allowed to pilot a B-52 jet bomber across the U.S. skyways, performing various feats that showed off his still-considerable flying skills.

On August 22, the Senate Armed Services Committee reconvened and rejected Jimmy's nomination thirteen to zero, along with that of one other nominee.[4] General Potts and the rest were approved. Afterward, in a statement to the press, Senator Smith suggested that if Colonel Stewart were to give up his acting career and devote all his time to the Air Force, she might be willing to reconsider her position. Once again, Jimmy chose not to respond publicly, although he remained at a loss as to how being a full-time actor disqualified him from being a brigadier

---

3. *Newsweek* reported in its September 2, 1957, issue that Senator Smith had indeed personally lobbied on behalf of Lewis.

4. The other person to be rejected that day was not one of the original ten nominees. Dr. Paul D. Foote, a sixty-nine-year-old retired Gulf Oil Company scientist, had been put up for assistant secretary of defense in charge of research and engineering. Foote was turned down after he told the committee he was unwilling to give up his oil company pension or to sell his stock in Gulf Oil and Standard Oil Companies of California.

general, a rank that had been part of his ancestry all the way back to 1863, when his mother's father, Samuel Jackson, had earned it for his valor at Gettysburg. Was his own bravery during World War Two somehow devalued because he made movies? His worst fear was that, perhaps, just being part of the Hollywood community had, in the minds of Congress, somehow left the Red taint of the times on him too, and that the conditions of giving up his acting career for "full-time devotion" to the military were really code words that challenged his loyalty and his commitment to his country.

President Eisenhower was also shocked at what he considered to be an unseemly turn of events. In February 1959, a full two years after the incident, in the last year of his second term, he once again nominated Stewart for promotion to brigadier general "for his great contribution to the Air Force." This time the Senate unanimously approved the promotion, although not for the same position of SAC deputy chief of operations. Instead Jimmy was given the title of public information officer at the Pentagon, a far less important and less prestigious appointment. When questioned by a reporter after the approval vote why Senator Smith did not oppose the lesser assignment, she sniffed, "That's more like it," meaning the relatively minor position he had been awarded.

Jimmy maintained his silence for two more years, until 1961 when responding to Pete Martin of the *Saturday Evening Post* about why he thought the whole unfortunate mess had taken place. Jimmy said, with an air of reconciliation and a sense of wanting to put the whole thing behind him, "The promotion was approved [the second time around], leaving me to wonder whether Senator Smith [the first time] was mad at me personally. I didn't think she was. She was protesting against giving a movie actor an important rank because she didn't think I had done enough recent flying to qualify for a star. I'm not sure that the senator fully understood that nobody was expecting me to climb into a modern jet bomber and fly it. Anyone who knows that my next birthday will be my fifty-third will agree that jets have made the pace too hot for my slowing reflexes. . . . Even before Senator Smith squared her jaw at me, I was in line for more suitable assignment—deputy director of the Office of Information."

Twenty years later, in 1980, when Jimmy was seventy-two, his friend Ronald Reagan, who had never seen a day of combat of any sort (except in the movies), was elected by an overwhelming majority as president of the United States, a position that automatically made him commander-in-chief of the armed forces.[5]

— • —

        In September 1957, one month after his original rejection by the Senate for his promotion to brigadier general, Jimmy reported to the set of *Vertigo*, where a still-frail Hitchcock was at last ready to start production on the movie. Both director and star were eager to begin a new film they could bury themselves in.

        Just before production began, Hitchcock confirmed that Kim Novak, the gorgeous, tempting, full-figured blond actress whom he had once considered for the role of Jennifer Rogers in *The Trouble with Harry* (1954) before going with Shirley MacLaine, was set to play Madeleine/Judy. Audiences, it seemed, couldn't get enough of Novak. *Box Office* magazine named her the number one female film star of 1956, on the strength of her consecutive star turns in Josh Logan's *Picnic* (1955), Otto Preminger's *The Man with the Golden Arm* (1955), and George Sidney's *The Eddy Duchin Story* (1956).

        Novak, however, had not been all that easy to get. Harry Cohn had first caught sight of her as Marilyn Novak when she was touring the country as "Miss Deepfreeze" (a job description Hitchcock especially loved), to promote a new type of refrigerator, after which she landed a bit part in a Jane Russell vehicle, Lloyd Bacon's *French Line* (1954). Cohn then signed her to an exclusive contract, renamed her, redressed her, and reinvented her as "Kim Novak" in public, and referred to her as "that fat Polak, Novak," to anyone he knew in person. Once the crude but shrewd studio head had Novak under contract for $150 a week, he convinced Otto Preminger to pay Columbia $100,000 to let her appear in the director's controversial heroin-addiction movie. (Just before making *Vertigo*, Novak starred in the title role of George Sidney's *Jeanne Eagels* [1957], for which she was paid a bonus of $13,000 from Cohn, money she had to fight for, while her co-star, Jeff Chandler, received

---

5. Reagan was thirty years old when World War Two began, making him ineligible for the new draft. He enlisted, but was turned down for combat duty due to poor eyesight. In May 2002, he and former First Lady Nancy Reagan were awarded the United States Congressional Gold Medal for his role in ending the cold war.

$200,000—and no one recalls his even being in the film once they see Novak's spectacular star turn.) When she found out how much Chandler had gotten, she fired her agent and—at the urging of none other than Frank Sinatra—signed with the William Morris Agency. (Cohn punished her for doing so by placing her on suspension, until *Time* magazine put her on its cover and he realized she was worth more to him working than not and renegotiated her contract through the agency.)

That was when Hitchcock had decided he wanted her for *Vertigo.* Cohn agreed to let her appear in it only if Wasserman, who represented both Hitchcock and Jimmy, would agree to have Jimmy make his next movie for Columbia.[6] All four men—Hitchcock, Wasserman, Cohn, and Jimmy—then met for lunch (without Novak, who no one thought important enough to invite) and came to terms on Jimmy's reciprocal appearances in the two pictures.

— • —

The story of *Vertigo* was taken by Hitchcock from the popular French novel *D'entre les morts.*[7] He was attracted to it because the main character falls in love with a dead woman. In the film version, *Vertigo,* this premise defines the agitated, flawed, ongoing nightmare of John "Scottie" Ferguson—the obsessive longing for irretrievably lost love in a beautiful, living woman who becomes, to him, an idealized version of an irreplaceable dead one. Wracked with desire, guilt, and remorse over the death of a client, Madeleine Elster, Scottie eventually goes insane, blam-

---

6. It was a purely commercial move. Novak recalled in a July 2005 interview with the author that when she first read *Vertigo,* she loved it and went to Cohn, begging him to let her make it. Cohn's reaction was to say it was "a piece of crap," but let her do it anyway because Hitchcock was an important director in the midst of a solid commercial run, and thought it would be good for Novak to appear in one of his films. After its release, when it did only moderate business at the box office, Cohn read aloud the negative reviews to Novak and told her that he still thought the film was crap.

7. The literal translation being "From Among the Dead," or the more idiosyncratic "Between Deaths," or "Those Between Death," by the writing team of Pierre Boileau and Thomas Narcejac, who had also written the novel *Celle qui n'etait plus,* a successful French suspense thriller on which the even more popular 1955 Henri-Georges Clouzot French movie *Les Diaboliques* (aka *Diabolique* and on TV, *The Friends* [U.S.] or *The Devils* [U.K.]) was based.

ing himself for her demise. It is the power imposed by the loss of that love—of the nature of lost love itself—that Hitchcock suggests is the deeper cause of Scottie's emotional undoing and what gives the film much of its dark and powerful beauty. Hitchcock's own well-documented sexual fantasies written about by others, his lifelong obsession with the untouchable blondes he repeatedly cast in his movies, are reflected to a remarkable degree in his use of Jimmy Stewart and Kim Novak in *Vertigo,* more so, perhaps, than even he might have realized (although he rarely acknowledged any emotional connections to his biographers). Jimmy's Protestant roots, his childhood experiences with his disappearing and then reappearing father, during which time he took over his role and, in a sense, "became" his father, his natural shyness around women, and the recent death of his mother were all elements of his history and personality that made him so profoundly perfect a choice to play Scottie Ferguson. (Hitchcock's other '50s leading man of choice, Cary Grant, had many appealing qualities but excluded the very one that Jimmy's acting projected better than anyone else at this point in his career—that of repressed-rage morbidity.) An open, warm smile almost never crosses Jimmy's face in any of his Hitchcock films, although we see him in close-up to a startling degree in the various nonverbal scenes where he is trailing Madeleine (whereas a smile almost never leaves Grant's face in *North by Northwest*).

As for Novak, her experiences in Hollywood closely resembled that of the character of Judy, without, of course, any of the streetwalking or hustling Hitchcock's movie suggests as a substantial part of the character's young life. Novak's manipulations by Harry Cohn, who chose what roles she was to play, his continual "loan-outs" and the fact that each film found her in a different "role," vividly resonate in a film where a young and beautiful woman is controlled and manipulated by at least two powerful male figures—Ferguson and Elster—and possibly a third, her father, whom she suggests at one point in the film (as was true in her real life) she had a more complex relationship with than either of the two men are aware, and who may be the source of her criminally infused moral vulnerability.

In that sense, the entire film may be taken on some level as a feature-length dramatization of the devastating fallout from a series of unresolved Oedipal-based conflicts in which the two leads, Madeleine/Judy and Scottie, the actors who play them, the two supporting characters,

Midge and Elster, *and* the film's director are all playing out variations of a similar, if romanticized (or at least eroticized) scenario involving love, loss, replacement, and idealization to a degree in which no other film (certainly no Hollywood studio film) ever had. In that sense, *Vertigo*, like Scottie at its chilling climax, stands alone.

— • —

In 1955, a first-draft screenplay had been commissioned by Hitchcock from Maxwell Anderson for a flat fee of $65,000, and he was dissatisfied with almost everything about it. Hitchcock then hired a little-known screenwriter, Alec Coppel, who had worked on a film called *No Highway in the Sky* while he was at Fox, and who now was under contract to Paramount. Hitchcock worked with him closely from September through the end of 1956 on an entirely new draft.[8]

Sensing something was still missing, Hitchcock next brought in Samuel Taylor, a writer he particularly liked (after he couldn't get Ernest Lehman, one he loved and who would, later on, write the screenplay for *North by Northwest*). It was at this point that Hitchcock took ill. While lying in bed believing he was near death, he realized the real underpinning of his lost-love screenplay in a single, compelling visual motif—a man literally hanging on to life by his fingertips, who won't or can't let go.

During Hitchcock's hospitalization, Sam Taylor met with Jimmy numerous times, finding in the actor, as Hitchcock assured Taylor he would, a willingness to go where he hadn't before. While Taylor commiserated with Jimmy over the loss of his military promotion, he began to formulate the character of Scottie as a man consumed with loss. After conferring with Hitchcock, Taylor developed Scottie into someone trying desperately to retrieve the sense of romance from his youthful past, while being irrevocably propelled into the emotional banality of his aging future. The illness of vertigo, both director and screenwriter

---

8. Coppel was paid $1,500 per week to work on *Vertigo*. Coppel's only previous solo screenplay (he had worked with R. C. Sherriff and Oscar Millard on *No Highway in the Sky*) had been for Anthony Kimmins's *The Captain's Paradise* (1953), a story about a sea captain who changes his personality to please a different girl in every port. Hitchcock may have been attracted to the way multiple personality was portrayed by Coppel in *The Captain's Paradise*.

agreed, could be defined as a condition that stretched a person's heated emotions like passionate taffy, only to have them shrink from the brute coldness of lost love.

The now-famous opening rooftop sequence introduces John "Scottie" Ferguson (Stewart) and his inability to keep up with both a thief and a pursuing uniformed officer during a rooftop chase that inadvertently leads to the uniformed officer's death. As Ferguson dangles from an infirm gutter high above a darkened alley, he stares into the darkness of eternity.[9] The movie begins and ends literally and figuratively with Ferguson on the edge, and all that comes between—the dangling body of the movie—may very well take place all in Scottie's mind while he hangs by his fingertips suspended between life and death.

Scottie is temporarily suspended from the force while he recuperates from his near-death experience (we never see how he gets off the roof). He frequents the apartment of his former college sweetheart, the overly maternal Midge (Barbara Bel Geddes, who wears unattractive glasses, no makeup, has washed-out blond hair that droops unflatteringly, and designs cantilevered bras). Scottie explains to her how his vertigo has manifested itself in a fear of heights.[10] He also mentions that he has heard from one of their college classmates, Gavin Elster (Tom Helmore), who wants Scottie to pay him a visit. Midge urges him to go, which he reluctantly does.

At Gavin's magnificent waterfront offices (so elegantly designed by Henry Bumstead that Hitchcock had his own home office made into an exact copy, minus the raised floors and a sloped ceiling that gave audiences the illusion that the much shorter Helmore "towered" over

---

9. This rooftop reverie may very well have been influenced by Chaplin's set piece in his 1922 *The Kid*, during which he performs one of the most extraordinary rooftop-to-rooftop sequences ever imagined on-screen. Hitchcock's version is, of course, sexually charged. The pain and fear on Scottie's face will, during the course of the film, take on erotic under- (and over-) tones and take a masochistic twist. Scottie's damaged sexual lust, his fetishism, eroticizes the pain of his emotional suspension to make it tolerable.

10. That Midge and Scottie were supposed to have been classmates makes the casting of the brilliant Bel Geddes somewhat problematic, as, despite her inherently maternal presence, she appears to be at least ten years younger than Scottie. In real life, during the filming of *Vertigo*, Bel Geddes was thirty-five years old, Stewart forty-nine. Novak, Stewart's love interest, was only twenty-five.

Jimmy), Scottie listens as Elster, who has read about Scottie's "misfortune," offers him some private detective work until he gets back his job with the police. It is a scene reminiscent of the hook-baiting opening of *Dial M for Murder*, as Elster tells Scottie he wants to hire him to follow his wife. Scottie asks if she is having an affair. No, Elster says, nothing as simple as that. She thinks she is possessed by a woman who has been dead for more than a hundred years.[11]

Scottie tries to back off, but allows himself to at least check out the situation, partially out of friendship but also, he says, because he needs something to do with his time while he recuperates. But the look on his face reveals something else. He has become intrigued by the notion that a dead person could somehow come back to life.

Scottie goes to Ernie's restaurant that night, where he knows Elster and his wife will be dining, to catch his first glimpse of Madeleine. Sitting at the bar, he sees her with Elster as they leave the dining room. Ravishingly wrapped in a green satin dress, her platinum hair twisted into a provocative swirl, Scottie is stunned by her beauty and reacts as if he has been struck by emotional lightning. So powerful is his attraction to her that when she pauses near him, he has to turn away. She passes him, then turns and looks back; he dares to glance directly at her, then once more turns just as she does. This broken-backed circle of head turning, accentuated by Madeleine's almost hypnotic stare, marks the beginning of something strange, balletic, and beautiful, although no one—the audience, Scottie, or Madeleine—can possibly yet know what.

Several minutes of brilliant silent filmmaking follow, Hitchcock style, with no dialogue, only the beautiful, haunting masterpiece soundtrack of Bernard Herrmann (conducted by Muir Mathieson). It is the follow-

---

11. In *Dial M*, this very scene is seen from the "Elster" character's point of view, when Tony Wendice, played exquisitely by Ray Milland, invites *his* old college chum for a visit, and winds up convincing him to kill his, Tony's, wife (Grace Kelly). Although the perspectives are different, the circumstance not as clear so soon into the movie, and we do not yet know Elster's real motives, he does, in fact, duplicate Tony's goal, to get an apparent stranger to kill his wife. This was a favorite plot ploy of Hitchcock's, seen in variations reaching all the way back to his *Rebecca* (1940), with echoes in *Suspicion* (1941) and most vividly in *Strangers on a Train* (1951). The similarities in Hitchcock's plots led to his reputation as a director who had made not fifty-two different feature films, but one film fifty-two times.

ing day. Scottie is tailing Madeleine's Rolls-Royce in his Plymouth as she drives around, apparently in circles, through the ups and downs of the streets of San Francisco (an apt visual metaphor for the mood swings of both characters, his real, hers faked). Scottie follows her to a flower store where she buys a bouquet, to a museum where she sits before a portrait of the long-dead Carlotta, whose hair is also tied in the same peculiar swirl as Madeleine's, to a cemetery where Madeleine leaves the flowers, to a rooming house where she appears to vanish into thin air. Scottie questions the proprietress, who tells him the place once belonged to Carlotta Valdez.

To this point, Hitchcock has led Scottie and the audience on a bit of a wild-goose chase and a fraudulent one at that. Just as he would do three years later in *Psycho*, he has set up a false plot, a lot of good old-fashioned ghost story hokum, although it will soon become all too apparent there is nothing good, old-fashioned, or ghostly about Madeleine. The next day Scottie reports to Elster, who encourages Scottie to keep following his wife, who, he says somberly, is no longer Madeleine at all, but the living embodiment of . . . *Carlotta Valdez*.

Scottie agrees, no longer reluctant but enthusiastically immersed in the case. Back at Midge's studio, he tells her what's been going on, and she immediately suspects this is something more than a mere "case." She has recognized what is already there, the growing obsessiveness Scottie has for Madeleine. He dismisses her suspicions as nonsense, but Midge knows better, and by now so does the audience, although still neither knows exactly what. What everyone can plainly see on both sides of the screen is that Scottie is a goner. He has fallen, and hard, for Madeleine. Or Carlotta. At this point it apparently no longer makes any difference.[12]

The next day is filled with more lineless auto surveillance, up and down those hilly avenues, around in circles, until Madeleine leads him to, of all places, the base of the Golden Gate Bridge, that *can-*

---

12. Hitchcock's playful use of names is highly engaging: John "Scottie" Ferguson— John as both romantic everyman and phallic pursuer, Scottie as in scot-free, Fergu-son, the "son"; Madeleine, as in Proust's madeleine, the cake whose taste evokes "memories of things past." Midge sounds like an unerotic, shrunken version of Madeleine.

tilevered wonder of San Francisco, where he watches in horror as she throws herself into the cold bay waters. Without hesitation, he dives in after her and pulls her to safety. While she remains unconscious, he throws his arms around her and says her name, over and over again. He has rescued her (he thinks) from being possessed by the dead and "delivered" her back to the living. By doing so, he has reignited his long-dormant desire for romance. This, finally, is where *Vertigo* really begins.

That evening, back at his home, Madeleine is in his bed, naked. Her clothes hang around the kitchen, drying. It is clear that while she was unconscious, Scottie stripped her, put her to bed, and, appropriately (to him), lit the fireplace to greet her when she awakens. The unseen stripping will be echoed in reverse in a key scene later on in the increasingly fetishistic nature of Scottie's growing and decidedly unhealthy obsession with Madeleine. Just as vertigo has prevented him from being able to keep his mind clear when looking down from great heights, so has Madeleine's beauty clouded his ability to think clearly about her, and ultimately about himself. In other words, she is the living manifestation of his vertigo.

Madeleine disappears while Scottie is on the phone with Elster, telling him she is okay. The next day she pulls up to his front door, intending to leave a note of apology for her "bad behavior." Jumping into the bay is not something she is proud of, she tells him. They decide since they are both wanderers, they may as well "wander" together for the rest of the day. He takes her across the bridge to Muir Woods, the location of the giant-sequoias forest. There they discuss the meaning of life in front of a gigantic crosscut of one of the trees. Scottie sees in the circle the continuum of life, while Madeleine sees in it only death, including her own, as she points to the exact spot in the tree's time line when she, meaning Carlotta, was born, and when she, Carlotta, died.

As they spend more and more time together, she relates to Scottie a series of disjointed memories, symbols really: a long dark corridor; an empty, open grave; a tall tower. As Scottie desperately tries to make sense of it, he saves her from yet another suicide attempt by the bay, this time taking her into his arms before she has a chance to hit the waters. Waves smack, music swells, Madeleine says she doesn't want to die and begs him to never leave her. He promises he won't. They kiss, a deep, long, powerful embrace that ends in a long, dark fade.

The movie then shifts back to Midge's apartment, where she is busy working on a new painting. She has summoned Scottie in order to check up on him, and offers him a drink and a night out at the movies. Things seem fine, if a little stiff. Scottie is calm, though preoccupied when Midge shows him her latest painting—a portrait of Carlotta, but with her own face on it. The effect on Scottie is devastating. She knows about his obsession with Madeleine because she has been following him (a grim but clever joke on Hitchcock's part—while Scottie has been tailing Madeleine, who has aroused his emotions, Midge has been tailing him, and is now in fear of losing him from her maternal clutches). "Not funny," he mutters, canceling their date and leaving in an angry huff. Alone, Midge breaks down as she realizes the extent of her own moral dilemma. She desperately wants to be Carlotta, or Madeleine, whichever one Scottie is really obsessed with, but knows she just doesn't fit the physical mold of his erotic fantasies. To Scottie, Midge (Margaret? Mother?) has been consigned by him to play the maternal, noneroticized role, and consciously, at least, he has no desire to resurrect anything with her.

Now it is night. Scottie is half drunk and generally disheveled when Madeline appears at his front door. She has had "the dream" again. This time she remembers more details. Scottie figures out she is describing an old Spanish mission; he insists on taking her there to show her it's real and exists in the present. There, in the barn next to the mission, Scottie logically explains to Madeleine the apparent meaning of the dream, pointing out objects that she had previously described to him; then he suddenly embraces and kisses her, before declaring his love. She says she loves him too, but "it wasn't supposed to happen this way!" With that, she breaks loose and heads for the church. Scottie follows. To his horror, he realizes she is going up the tower; she is going to kill herself. He desperately tries to follow, but the height of the stairs makes his vertigo, the physical manifestation of all his guilt, fear, and repressed pleasure, kick in stronger than ever. He looks down and can't tell if he is coming or going. As he tries to continue up the stairs, he falls behind, looks again down the shaft, which, from his perspective, appears to be stretching and shrinking.[13] He is torn between the compulsion to keep looking down (back) and trying to go up (forward), until he hears a scream, and sees, through the tower window, Madeleine falling to her death. Scottie's face breaks out in a sweat. His head turns from side to side, his cupped wrist goes to his chin, he screams but nothing comes out. His eyes bulge and dart. As nuns rush into the church, he manages to slink away.

Scottie has now caused two deaths in the first hour of the film, the detective's and Madeleine's, by his inability to keep up during a pursuit. An inquest is held, in which Scottie is viewed as technically innocent but morally guilty, his weakness having allowed ("once again") someone to die (from falling). He is also criticized for having "run away" from the scene of the crime.

At home that night he has an astonishing dream, in which all the un-joined pieces come together. Elster is there with a living Carlotta, not "Madeleine," presumably his real wife. There is the open or unfilled grave that Madeleine talked about. He imagines it is himself falling from the top of the tower. Only Scottie doesn't land (a wet dream without the climax). Instead, he floats in vertigo-like suspension. The truth is too horrifying—that Madeleine is not dead, at least not the Madeleine he knows, that somehow he has been duped by her and used as a pawn, and that most likely Elster is behind it all. The truth—that there was something wrong about his love for Madeleine, and her death—awakens him from his sleep. He then lapses into a conscious state of total, im-mobilizing catatonia. Asleep he was awakened, awake he is asleep.

He is committed to an asylum and cannot be brought around, surely not by Midge, who tries her own patented "Mozart" cure supple-mented by her own brand of maternal care ("Mother is here . . ."). Eventually Midge gives up on Scottie (and her own maternally driven rescue fantasy) and walks out of the hospital and out of Scottie's life,

---

13. The creation of the shot was by Robert Burks, the director of photography, and Irmin Roberts, the second-unit cameraman (who didn't get screen credit on *Vertigo*). Roberts simply combined a forward zoom with a reverse track, something that henceforth became known as "the vertigo shot," according to Dan Auiler, author of *Vertigo: The Making of a Hitchcock Classic,* "one of the most innovative and imitated effects in film history."

disappearing down a long hospital corridor that resembles nothing so much as the open grave in Scottie's dream. We never see her again.

A year passes. Scottie is freed (but not free), crazy (as in not cured), and apparently unable to remember the context of the dream that paralyzed him.[14] As a result he reverts to his favorite habit of "wandering (in circles, on foot, driving apparently aimlessly along the streets of San Francisco)." But the wandering this time is pointed. Everywhere he goes he thinks he sees Madeleine—leaving her apartment house, at Ernie's, in the flower shop window, inside the museum. He has, in effect, become possessed by Madeleine, just as she supposedly was by Carlotta.

Then one day, while walking along a boulevard, he is suddenly taken aback by a beautiful young, dark-haired, full-figured, big-breasted girl in a skin-tight sweater who bears a strong resemblance to . . . *Madeleine*! All at once, the erotic illusions are revived, and the pursuit begins yet again. He follows her up to her drab rooming house flat and literally forces himself into her room. He quickly realizes she is a hooker—she confesses as much—and convinces himself that despite her miraculous resemblance to Madeleine, she really is who she says she is, Judy Barton (also Kim Novak) from Salinas, Kansas. He asks her to go to dinner with him and she reluctantly agrees. He gives her an hour to get ready. As soon as he leaves, she flashes back on what really happened that day at the tower, that Elster was waiting at the top of the stairs, knowing Scottie's vertigo would prevent him from being able to make it all the way up in time (to climax), with the body of his already murdered wife, the one he throws out the window to her "death."

Judy writes a note of confession. She finishes, tries to leave, realizes she can't—she is as helplessly in love with Scottie as he is with her—tears the note up, and prepares for his arrival.

He takes her to Ernie's, where he begins what becomes the film's final, fatal, phenomenal depiction of Scottie's obsession. He begins to slowly but relentlessly and fetishistically turn Judy back into Madeleine, and she, however reluctantly (and masochistically), allows him to do so.

---

14. By eroticizing his pain, he had made his loss/replacement bearable. The dream removed this protective, if illusory, self-deception.

He makes her wear the same corsage Madeleine wore, buys her the same gray suit and the same black, shiny high heels, and finally, forces her to dye her hair platinum blonde (what harm would it do? he asks). He leaves her at the beauty parlor and waits for her back at her hotel room. When she arrives, everything is nearly perfect—except her hair is down. Scottie insists she put it up in a swirl—in Madeleine's (and Carlotta's) swirl. It is the final link, and, with great reluctance but helpless to resist, she goes into the bathroom, only to reemerge in a ghostly green light (the reflection of the neon outside her window, and the dress she wore the night Scottie first saw her at Ernie's). She is, at last, Madeleine.[15]

They stare at each other. They embrace. They kiss. As their lips press together, Scottie is, to his horror, overcome with one last bout of vertigo, only this time it comes on not in shrink/stretch form, but as a spiral, the same shape of the swirl in Judy's hair. The room begins to turn, and suddenly he is back at the mission the day Madeleine died. It is Madeleine, not Judy, in his arms. He remains locked in her embrace, but his eyes look away, trying to find an escape, an explanation, a reason.

The kiss ends, and Judy, or Madeleine, decides to put on her necklace, the same one that Madeleine wore, the same one that hung around Carlotta's neck in the portrait at the museum. For her, the kiss ended the game. They can both come clean now and start over. She will be his Madeleine and he will be her Scottie. They'll be able to laugh about it all one day.

For Scottie, however, the necklace holds a far different meaning. Because of it, he finally understands the last, missing piece of this maniacal puzzle. Nothing is real anymore except the deception that has

---

15. In his book-length conversation with Truffaut, Hitchcock described Judy's transformation as a specialized form of a striptease, only in reverse: "Cinematically, all of Stewart's efforts to recreate the dead woman are shown in such a way that he seems to be trying to undress her, instead of the other way around. What I liked best is when the girl came back after having had her hair dyed blond. James Stewart is disappointed because she hasn't put her hair up in a bun. What this really means is that the girl has almost stripped, but she still won't take her knickers off. When he insists, she says, 'All right!' and goes into the bathroom while he waits outside. What Stewart is really waiting for is for the woman to emerge totally naked this time, and ready for love." Truffaut: "That didn't occur to me, but the close-up on Stewart's face as he's waiting for her to come out of the bathroom is wonderful; he's almost got tears in his eyes." (From François Truffaut's Hitchcock/Truffaut, page 244.)

been put over on him. He understands now that he cannot ever resurrect lost love, *even if he believes that love is never truly lost.*

A wicked, frightening smirk crosses his face. He decides to teach Judy a *real* lesson in calculated rage, revenge, and reclamation. He forces her into his car and drives her back to the mission. Judy grows ever more agitated while he talks about having to go back into the past "for the last time." He pulls her into the church and forces her up the steeple. He literally drags her by her arms to the top; Judy begs for her life. In the belltower in her last desperate attempt, she throws her arms around Scottie and kisses him. This time, however, there is no swirling delirium. Instead, a curious nun appears out of the darkness ("Mother Superior"?) and so frightens Judy that she backs out of one of the tower's openings and falls to her death.

It is this third and final death that "cures" Scottie. Ironically, it is his resurrected ability to scale the heights that leaves him physically alive but emotionally alone. He walks to the edge of the tower, his arms outstretched in Jesuslike supplication. As the film enters its final fade, the audience does not know what to think. Has he finally been freed of his primal, displaced obsessions, or is he about to dive after them, to join Carlotta, Madeleine, and Judy and all they represent to him, in eternity? This final suspension suggests that Scottie's vertigo can never be truly "cured," that the true definition of his illness is and always will be his twisted desire to go forward in his life by trying, however impossible it may be, to travel backward into the past.

— • —

In a decade whose most popular films were defined and dominated by youth, the best performances were done by veteran actors in what might arguably be the greatest roles of their careers—John Wayne in John Ford's *The Quiet Man* (1952) and Ford's *The Searchers* (1956), Gary Cooper in Fred Zinnemann's *High Noon* (1952), Alan Ladd in George Stevens's *Shane* (1953), Cary Grant in Hitchcock's *To Catch a Thief* (1955) and Hitchcock's *North by Northwest* (1959), and arguably the best of all, Jimmy Stewart in *Vertigo,* a bravura display of tortured and timeless emotion, controlled as expertly as a jet plane in the hands of an ace pilot. At once mature, erotic, manly, and vulnerable, Jimmy's work in this film stands alongside the best and most complex acting ever captured on screen. For so many reasons, both personal and professional, no actor was ever more perfectly suited to play the role of the middle-aged, damaged, sexually repressed voyeur Scottie Ferguson than Jimmy Stewart.

Without question, his performance is enhanced immeasurably by the astonishing duality of Kim Novak (whose chemistry with Jimmy makes Hitchcock look like even more of a genius), an actress who never looked lovelier, or more mysterious, or more alluring, or sexual, in a film whose distinctive, singular, signature style no one has ever been able to duplicate.

While today *Vertigo* is routinely ranked by scholars, critics, historians, and audiences (if sales and rentals are any indication of the latter) as one of the greatest movies of all time, in 1958, while both Novak and Jimmy received terrific notices, the film did not, and was subsequently met with both critical and box-office indifference;—not enough *nouvelle,* too much *vague.* That year the Best Picture Oscar went to Morton DaCosta's antique *Auntie Mame;* Best Actor went to David Niven and Best Actress to Wendy Hiller for their performances in Delbert Mann's dour *Separate Tables;* Best Director went to Vincente Minnelli for his splashy, if inane, wide-screen musical *Gigi.* Except for two technical nominations, Best Art Direction and Best Sound, *Vertigo* was shut out at that year's Academy Awards.[16]

Because of it, *Vertigo* became something of a curio, a speed bump along the otherwise smooth highway of Hitchcock hits, coming as it did after *Rear Window, To Catch a Thief, The Trouble with Harry,* and *The Wrong Man* and before *North by Northwest,* all of which were far more commercially successful. Disappointed with the film's initial critical and box-office reception, Hitchcock, who owned the negative to *Vertigo,* pulled it from general circulation in the seventies (along with four other of his Paramount movies). In truth, although it didn't do anything like Hitchcock believed it would, the film was not a financial failure. By

---

16. Hal Pereira, Henry Bumstead, Sam Comer, and Frank R. McKelvy were nominated for Best Art Direction, Set Direction, Black and White or Color. They lost to William A. Horning and Preston Ames, Henry Grace and Keogh Gleason for *Gigi.* The Paramount Studio sound department and George Dutton, sound director, lost to Joshua Logan's *South Pacific,* recorded in Todd-AO, Fred Hynes, director.

the end of 1958, its first year of domestic release, it ranked as the twenty-first highest-grossing Hollywood film, having earned a respectable $3.2 million, good, not great; $2 million less than his previous Stewart venture, *Rear Window* (*Vertigo*'s final negative cost was $2,479,000, about a million dollars more than what it cost to make *Rear Window*).[17]

Jimmy, too, was deeply disappointed by the film's apparent failure. He had banked on the strength of his name above the title and the power of his performance to push *Vertigo* into major profits (that he had a piece of) and when it failed to do so, he believed it signaled nothing less than the end of the arc of his big-budget movie-making career. From that point on, he feared, he would recede into the archives of Hollywood history and legend, along with the studio era itself and the other glorious stars it had produced who, like him, had once dominated the kingdom of Hollywood-style greatness.

He was not entirely wrong.

---

17. *Vertigo* had a second, limited theatrical release in the late sixties, then was sold to television, after which the negative rights reverted to Hitchcock. In 1974, it was pulled from distribution, along with *The Trouble with Harry, The Man Who Knew Too Much, Rear Window,* and *Rope.* After Hitchcock's death in 1980, the film was rereleased by the estate and eventually was given a meticulous restoration by two film historian preservationists, James Katz and Robert Harris. In 1998, a full-size VistaVision-proportioned negative print was released in theaters and subsequently on video and DVD.

In one final twist to the rereleases, in 1990, the Supreme Court ruled on a case involving the copyright of *Rear Window.* A 6-to-3 ruling written by Sandra Day O'-Conner (*Stewart vs. Abend, #88-2102*) affirmed a 1988 decision by the United States Court of Appeals for the Ninth Circuit, in San Francisco, declaring that a literary agent had the legal subsidiary rights to "It Had to Be Murder," by Cornell Woolrich. The story was first published in *Dime Detective* magazine in 1942. The case involved the nature of the length and origins of copyrighted material, and acquisition rights and control to derivative works based on it. Woolrich had died before he could renew the story's copyright, and ownership of the rights were eventually sold by his estate, via Chase Manhattan Bank, to New York literary agent Sheldon Abend for $9,250. When *Rear Window* was rereleased in theaters, TV, and on video in the eighties, Abend sued the Hitchcock estate, Jimmy Stewart, and Universal, each of whom owned a piece of the film, for copyright infringement. The court agreed and unspecified damages and a significant portion of the movie's $12 million profits were eventually awarded to Abend.

23

"Ford, Hitchcock, Wilder, Wyler, Capra, DeMille, Hathaway—they all base their work on one primary theory, and that is that movies are primarily pictorial—not words."

—JAMES STEWART

Four months after *Vertigo* was released, Jimmy broke the sound barrier.

It was a brisk morning in September 1958 that Colonel Stewart and Maj. Tom Hart, liaison officer at Palmdale for the Air Defense Command, climbed into a jet headed for Dallas to attend the annual Air Force convention. During the thirty-two-minute flight the jet climbed to 38,000 feet and reached supersonic speed. Newspapers described the incident as "breath-taking." When asked why he'd done it, Jimmy just smiled and told reporters, "It was the most amazing flight I've ever made." Unfortunately, he did not feel the same way about his next movie.

Richard Quine's *Bell Book and Candle* was a tangy, if wispy venture, but one with far-reaching consequences to Jimmy's career. From the start, Jimmy had utterly no interest in the film, whose supernatural (and superficial) overtones satirically echoed the fakery suggested in the plot of *Vertigo*—in *Bell Book and Candle,* Gillian (Kim Novak) is a witch who tries to put a spell on Shepherd Henderson (Jimmy). Any further comparison of the two films would be like comparing Shakespeare's *Hamlet* to television's *Bewitched.* What had been a bit of enjoyable neo-Cowardian fluff on the West End and Broadway stages, written by John Van Druten and starring Rex Harrison and Lilli Palmer, landed with a thud as loud as Carlotta's body off the top of the mission tower. This despite Jimmy and Novak's great on-screen chemistry and solid supporting cast that included Jack Lemmon, Ernie Kovacs, Hermione Gingold, and Elsa Lanchester.

Screenwriter Daniel Taradash, who was also the producer (along with his partner, Julian Blaustein), had a multiple-picture deal with

Columbia and had brought the play to the studio with the idea of using its original stage cast, a plan vetoed by Harry Cohn because he felt Palmer was too old to play the part on the big screen. Taradash's next dream cast was Cary Grant and Grace Kelly, but Kelly had since married and retired from the screen; and Grant, although interested, wanted certain changes made in the script to make it better suited to his particular style of cinema suavity—he could not appear to pursue Novak in any way, shape, or form; she would have to pursue him. Taradash knew that wouldn't work, as Novak's character had all the magic powers. His next choices were handed to him by Cohn, who still held the option on Jimmy's services as part of the agreement to let Novak do *Vertigo*. He suggested to Taradash that he use both of them in *Bell Book and Candle*.

Jimmy, meanwhile, had hoped to return to form in Hitchcock's next production, *North by Northwest* (a loose remake of his own highly successful 1942 *Saboteur*, which had starred Robert Cummings and Priscilla Lane). Because of that, he kept delaying the start of *Bell Book and Candle*, waiting for the call from Hitchcock.

It was not going to come. Hitchcock later told François Truffaut that part of the reason he felt *Vertigo* had not done better was because the lead actor looked too old for the part, the primary reason he would never use him again in any film.[1] Instead, the part in *North by Northwest* went to Cary Grant. Hitchcock, as was his nature, did not tell Jimmy there was no way he was going to get *North by Northwest*, even as he was having the screenplay finessed by the great Ernest Lehman to Grant's persona until it fit him as perfectly as one of his custom-made Savile Row suits. Once Cohn announced that Jimmy and Novak were going to make *Bell Book and Candle*, Hitchcock used that as his excuse, allowing him to diplomatically avoid confronting Jimmy and maintaining their personal friendship, which both valued.

As for Jimmy's acting in *Bell Book and Candle*, the best that may be said is that he was no Rex Harrison. Never good at playing sophisticates (as he had unsuccessfully attempted in *Rope* and *The Philadelphia Story*, in which, despite his Oscar, he remains to this day the forgotten

---

1. Truffaut revealed Hitchcock's feelings toward Stewart's performance in *Vertigo* after the director's death.

player in what is essentially a Katharine Hepburn/Cary Grant two-seater), in *Bell Book and Candle,* his performance was so flat that the only sign of life was his familiar slow stammer, hardly the stuff of seduction for a witchy sex kitty as sassy as Kim Novak.[2]

There were many in Hollywood, both behind the scenes and at the head of the columns, who were convinced the only possible reason Jimmy had agreed to star in the film was to remain in close contact with Novak, with whom, it was believed by many then (and still today), he was romantically involved. Here is what noted filmmaker and critic Peter Bogdanovich wrote about what he presumed to know of Jimmy's married love life, regarding not only Novak but Grace Kelly as well: "The common wisdom is that Ms. Kelly had already been through Gary Cooper and Clark Gable and that Stewart (in *Rear Window*) had no escape. Hitchcock hinted to me that Stewart also could not resist Kim Novak on *Vertigo* and the director's longtime assistant and dear friend, Peggy Robertson, confirmed this romance; and a good friend of mine heard about it directly from a still-fond Kim Novak. Evidently the affair continued, because immediately after *Vertigo* the two of them co-starred in a pretty weak *Bell Book and Candle.* Of course, this occasional occupational hazard could have caused some private grief to Gloria, which Jimmy would no doubt have profoundly regretted after her passing."

This lively but uninformed scenario suggests that Jimmy and Novak made *Bell Book and Candle* because they were in love. Bogdanovich apparently was not aware of the contractual obligations regarding Novak and Jimmy, agreed upon before they had even met, prior to the making of *Vertigo.* And Hitchcock was a notoriously gossipy and unreliable source for anything but film technique and theory.

Finally, when Novak was asked directly about the alleged affair, she denied it with a laugh that suggested the utter absurdity of such a thought: "First of all, at the time I made *Vertigo,* Jimmy was twice my age, married, and I was in love with another man, Richard Quine, although [Jimmy] may not have known it at the time. Richard would direct both Jimmy and me in *Bell Book and Candle.* Yes, I found Jimmy

---

2. "Any role requiring a formal wardrobe is [my] pet peeve!" Stewart, in a Paramount press release for *Bell Book and Candle.*

attractive, and he had a crush on me, I think, but I didn't have one on him. I liked him in the way high school kids like each other. What he saw in me was the same thing I did in him, that I was not in any way a 'Hollywood' person. I had come out of the Midwest, so did he I think, and we retained those qualities. I can remember whenever we were together, and had to do a kissing scene, he would blush beet-red.

"During the making of *Bell Book and Candle,* there was a scene where we were both bare-footed, our feet up on a coffee-table. We did the scene all morning, and when Richard called 'Cut' and everyone went off to lunch, Jimmy and I stayed right where we were, the whole time, our feet barely touching each other. It was quite a sexy moment, but that was it, the only time we ever had any non-filmed contact. Years later he did write a letter to me in which he admitted that during the making of *Vertigo* and *Bell Book and Candle* he had had an enormous crush on me, but had been afraid to admit it at the time. Then, when I did that cover story for *TV Guide,* that I wrote, during the period I was appearing on *Falcon Crest,* I said that Jimmy Stewart was 'the sexiest man I ever knew,' or something like that, and ever since then, people have thought we might have had an affair. That is uncategorically untrue. I won't deny that I had a number of relationships in my day, I have never denied any of them, but in this instance it just isn't true. For Mr. Bogdanovich to quote Hitchcock is laughable, since his whole body of work was about that fantasy, of his leading ladies being sexually available. I never told anyone, 'happily' or otherwise, that Jimmy and I were romantically involved, because it just wasn't true."[3]

— • —

When Jimmy completed *Bell Book and Candle,* and Grant was announced as the lead in *North by Northwest,* Jimmy decided that perhaps it was time he returned to television, after he received an invitation to do so from his North Roxbury Drive neighbor Jack Benny, who wanted Jimmy to make another appearance on his highly popular *Jack Benny Show.* The brief but hilarious star turn he did was received by critics better than any movie he had made in years, and was the subject of choice the next morning at water coolers across America.

---

3. In an interview with the author, Bogdanovich responded to Novak's denial this way: "If it's not true, then everybody lied. Everybody lies in Hollywood, anyway."

Nonetheless, it did little in the way of jump-starting his film career. Jimmy's negative reaction to the critical and commercial failure of *Bell Book and Candle* lingered and he began to focus on the coming demise of the studio system as the main reason films like it were being made at all (*Bell Book and Candle* was an independent venture by Taradash's company, funded and distributed by Columbia). Nevertheless, at a time when nearly every major star was setting up independent production companies and taking charge of his or her own movies, Jimmy steadfastly maintained that his only film talent was acting, and steadfastly refused to produce, direct, or write anything.

Later that same year he signed on with Warner to make *The FBI Story,* directed by Mervyn LeRoy, a film about the venerable institution whose dictatorial leader, J. Edgar Hoover, happened to be one of LeRoy's closest friends.[4] So close, in fact, that Hoover assigned two agents to the production of the film "to make sure of the technical details."

The film shot five weeks' worth of footage inside the FBI Building in Washington, D.C., and a couple of scenes in the Bronx, New York. Episodic in nature, *The FBI Story* is based on the best-selling book of the same name by two-time Pulitzer-winning Don Whitehead, the former Washington bureau chief for the *New York Herald Tribune*. It tells the history of the FBI through the eyes and life of Chip Hardesty (Stewart), a member of the first generation of federal agents in the pre-Hoover FBI, a disheveled law enforcement organization with no leadership, focus, or power. Engaged to young Lucy (Vera Miles, in the usually thankless June Allyson "wife" role), he agrees to leave the Bureau and become a lawyer if she will marry him. Just prior to their wedding, Hardesty (hard work and honesty?) is invited to Washington to meet the Bureau's new chief, J. Edgar Hoover, and agrees to take part in the overhauling of the FBI. A disappointed Lucy nevertheless goes through with the marriage, and stoically stands by as Hardesty helps take on the Ku Klux Klan, Indian murderers in Oklahoma, all the big-name gangsters of the thirties, suspected Nazis in South America, and, later on, Communists

---

4. LeRoy's filmography begins in 1928 at First National with *No Place to Go,* after which he worked for virtually every major studio, for nearly four decades, turning out such classics as *Little Caesar, I Am a Fugitive from a Chain Gang, Anthony Adverse, The Wizard of Oz* (producer), *Random Harvest, Madame Curie, Thirty Seconds Over Tokyo, Mister Roberts, The Bad Seed, Gypsy,* and dozens of others.

in New York City. Although the pressure becomes too much for Lucy and she takes their children with her when she leaves Hardesty, by the last reel she returns to the nest happily, fifties-housewife style.[5]

The week *The FBI Story* opened, on September 24, 1959, at the prestigious Radio City Music Hall, in an interview with *Variety* that appeared on October 3, Jimmy defended its "classic" style of storytelling by publicly ripping into the growing independent movement: "Hollywood's horde of independent film companies have fallen far short of their promises; that they have in most cases failed to deliver quality product. As a result, it's up to the major studios to exercise leadership. [Independents] are cutting corners and cheating, clipping expenses and shoestringing things. That's at the sacrifice of quality . . . the industry should also clamp down on those performers who come here [to Hollywood] to do one picture and go back to Broadway for a play, or to the South Seas to write the story of their lives." Something else he said in that interview would, years later, reverberate through his own career: "I don't see why the studios shouldn't sell their post-1948 [movies] to TV . . . they didn't make a mistake with their vintagers [pre-1948]."

He was referring to a specific issue that was currently dividing what was left of the old studios and the unions over what to do with their most valuable asset, their inventory. At the time, selling films to TV was a major issue because of the question of residuals. The unions wanted them for their actors, directors, writers, and technicians; the studios felt they owned the properties and had no obligation to pay for them again. Jimmy's harsh comments about the new generation of filmmakers, combined with his implied support for releasing newer, competitive product to TV for free, turned much of independent Hollywood against him, and likely cost him a shot at another Oscar for the two pictures he made in 1959, *The FBI Story* and the far superior *Anatomy of a Murder* for Otto Preminger.[6]

---

5. Henry Fonda had nothing but disdain for this project. When Mervyn LeRoy, who had for the longest time wanted to work with the actor, offered his daughter, Jane, a small part in the movie (as Jennie Hardesty), despite the novice actress's excited reaction, Fonda made her turn it down, telling her, "You don't want to start your acting career as Jimmy Stewart's daughter." She reluctantly agreed, and instead enrolled in the Actors Studio.

6. Production for *Anatomy of a Murder* began one week after filming for *The FBI Story* was completed.

— • —

After finishing *The FBI Story*, Jimmy took Gloria and the kids on a five-day vacation to Europe before starting production on *Anatomy* (Hoover arranged for around-the-clock "protection" for Jimmy and his family, as a "courtesy," in appreciation for his having made the film). The ostensible reason for the trip was for Jimmy to receive an award at the Berlin Film Festival, after which he took the entire brood on a quick jaunt through Switzerland, Italy, and Spain, making lightning-fast stops in small towns along the way. The twins were now seven years old and Jimmy felt the time had come for them to see the world the way the boys had. Ever the commander, Jimmy was constantly changing rooms, and making sure that every last detail was the way he wanted it, sometimes staying up well into the night to ensure the following day's itinerary.

The story goes that on the flight back to the States, one of Hoover's agents told Jimmy the Bureau was on the hunt for a jewel thief and thought he might be on that very plane. Jimmy nodded, got up, quietly walked the aisles, came back, and told the agent who he thought the thief was. How did he know? the agent asked. The size of his diamond stickpin, Jimmy said. The agents arrested the fellow when the plane landed. He was later convicted, after which Hoover sent Jimmy a personal letter of congratulations. Did it really happen? Perhaps some version of it is true, although it smacks of old-Hollywood precision promotion, the days when apocryphal acts of heroism and bravery were the very fodder upon which a hungry-for-details press relied. In truth, no one in "new" Hollywood believed the ridiculous story, and used it as an excuse to put even more distance between themselves and Jimmy's old-time style of studio-controlled "self-promotion." It was just at this time that Jimmy finally won his long-sought promotion to brigadier general. The congratulatory silence coming out of pendulum-swinging, now-liberal-leaning Hollywood was deafening.

— • —

Anatomy of a Murder (1959) was based on a best-selling novel written by Michigan Supreme Court Judge John D. Voelker writing under the pseudonym Robert Traver. The story revolves around a soldier with an extremely short fuse (played by a frighteningly ferocious

Ben Gazzara, a Broadway actor whose performance in the film made him a movie star) who is married to a woman with an extremely short sense of morality (the hot and sexy Lee Remick, a last-minute replacement for Lana Turner, who walked out on the film after production had already begun, claiming she couldn't get along with Preminger. Moreover, the material seemed far too risqué to her. In fact, on-screen at thirty-nine, Turner looked too old and Preminger fired her. Gazzara was at the time only twenty-three.)[7]

The young, trigger-tempered soldier is accused of killing a tavern owner after he's raped his wife. The equally short-fused prosecutor, Assistant State Attorney General Claude Dancer, was played by George C. Scott, whose film career was also made by this film. Joseph Welch, the Boston attorney-turned-folk-hero for having taken on Sen. Joseph P. McCarthy during the nationally televised *McCarthy vs. the United States Army* hearings, played presiding Judge Weaver. And Jimmy was cast as Paul Biegler, the small-town lawyer who defends the seemingly undefendable Lt. Manion. What is most notable about the film is that, for the first time, Jimmy played crotchety—an aging lawyer whose country-bumpkin ways appear to be no match for the tight-collared, red-necked angry young prosecutor, until a brilliant defense move turns the entire case upside down.

The film was prime Preminger, who loved to push the limits of what he felt was an overly restrictive Production Code. His *The Moon Is Blue* (1953) was the first Hollywood film to use the word "virgin." *The Man with the Golden Arm* (1955) was the first Code film to deal directly with heroin addiction and to explicitly show the horrors of heroin withdrawal. And his *Porgy and Bess* (1959) was racially controversial. *Anatomy of a Murder* was about a sensational rape and murder trial complete with visible panties on display as Exhibit A. It proved not only daring and provocative but highly successful at the box office.

Casting Jimmy as the defense attorney was a shrewd, if risky move on Preminger's part. The always-wholesome actor gave the film the necessary moral heft it needed to balance out its increasingly sordid plot developments, but nevertheless resulted in a vicious letter-writing campaign aimed at both Preminger and Stewart—the director for making

---

7. "I'll get an unknown and make her a star," Preminger announced after firing Turner.

such a "disgusting" film, and the actor for appearing in it. Nevertheless, Jimmy was so good in the role that he created a prototype of the "small-town lawyer," which Andy Griffith would capitalize on for television series fare, first as a sheriff and justice of the peace in *The Andy Griffith Show* and later on as a lawyer in *Matlock*.

There were many who thought the temperamental Preminger and the veteran Stewart would prove to be a bad mix, but it turned out not to be so. They enjoyed each other's on-set manner, Jimmy appreciating Preminger's formality, the director respecting the actor's professional approach to his role. Jimmy also was impressed with Preminger's use of wide-screen black-and-white cinematography, which gave the film at once a classical and contemporary feel.

Anatomy of a Murder opened three months earlier than *The FBI Story*, due mainly to Preminger's being able to get the film cut, scored, and printed in less than a month after filming was completed, and it opened to raves: *The Saturday Review* said "the marvelously equivocal portraits provided in *Anatomy of a Murder* by James Stewart, Lee Remick, Ben Gazzara, and George Scott reveal complexities in character such as rarely are seen on the American screen." The *New York Times* raved about how "magnificently [it] hews to a line of dramatic but reasonable behavior and proper procedure in a court," and singled out Jimmy for special praise. "Most brilliantly revealed is the character of the lawyer for the defense, a part that is played by James Stewart in one of the finest performances of his career. Slowly and subtly, he presents us a warm, clever, adroit and complex man—and most particularly, a portrait of a trial lawyer in action that will be difficult for anyone to surpass."

Time magazine was one of the few major publications that did not particularly like the movie, apparently put off by its frank sexual nature, calling it "a courtroom melodrama less concerned with murder than with anatomy . . ."[8]

---

8. The *Time* review went on to say that "even the least bark-bound of the spectators may find himself startled to hear, in his neighborhood movie house, extended discussion of what constitutes rape." Mayor Richard Daley of Chicago banned the film, and Preminger had to get a Federal District Court order declaring the film did not undermine morals to open the film there. Nor was this the only Hollywood film of its time to have such problems. The state of Kansas banned Wilder's *Some Like It Hot*, not for having two men masquerading as women, but for some of Marilyn Monroe's more risqué moments.

Anatomy of a Murder grossed more than $2 million in the first six weeks of its initial domestic release, prompted major Oscar buzz, and went on to become the seventh biggest earner of 1959. For his work in it, Jimmy won the New York Film Critics Award and the Venice Film Festival Award for Best Actor, and an Academy Award nomination, his first since 1950's *Harvey.* He believed he would win the Oscar, despite the powerful juggernaut for MGM's $15 million biblical extravaganza, William Wyler's *Ben-Hur* (whose script had been masterfully doctored by British playwright Christopher Fry) and the other unusually strong acting performances that won Best Actor nominations, including Laurence Harvey for Jack Clayton's *Room at the Top,* Jack Lemmon in Billy Wilder's hilarious *Some Like It Hot,* Charlton Heston for *Ben-Hur,* and Paul Muni in Daniel Mann's *The Last Angry Man.*

— • —

The annual award ceremonies were held on April 4, 1960, at the Pantages Theater in Hollywood. The host was Bob Hope, and the event was broadcast live on the ABC television network. The drama of the night boiled down to the competition between *Ben-Hur* and *Anatomy of a Murder. Ben-Hur,* made by MGM, one of the studios that, ironically, Jimmy had singled out for praise in his criticism of the independent movement, was, in fact, struggling to remain afloat, and had put all its chips on *Ben-Hur,* a copycat of Paramount's hugely successful 1956 DeMille Old Testament bibliopic *The Ten Commandments.* MGM owned the property (so to speak) and had decided to remake its silent version much the same way Paramount had owned the first Moses epic and even went so far as to hire Charlton Heston, DeMille's hand-chosen Moses, to play the title role.

The three-and-a-half-hour film didn't disappoint, at least not at the box office, grossing an astounding $80 million, worldwide, in its first year of release. The Academy, at the time made up of older, more conservative, studio-loyal members, loved nothing more than a money-maker, and for its earnings alone, the smart money said *Ben-Hur* was the film to beat.

On the other hand, young Hollywood had thrown its support behind *Anatomy of a Murder,* because of its willingness to stretch the boundaries of its provocative content and for its lively display of acting. As the evening wore on, and it became apparent that *Ben-Hur* was going to sweep, there was little tension left when Susan Hayward approached the podium to announce the Best Actor awards. She opened the envelope, smiled, and said in her famously husky voice, "And the winner is . . . *Charlton Heston!*"

A respectable round of applause followed. No one in Hollywood ever thought Heston was much of an actor, with his blustery, pompous style and his granite, immovable face. But he was the star of the biggest film of the year and to the voters of the Academy, that mattered.[9]

As it happened, Heston and Jimmy and their wives arrived at the Pantages at precisely the same moment, and graciously agreed to pose together for photographers. Heston later remembered, "As the flashbulbs finally petered out and we turned to go to our seats, Jimmy took my arm and said, 'I hope you win, Chuck, I really mean that.' I don't know another actor alive who would've said such a thing. He's an extraordinary man."

And an extraordinarily disappointed one when Heston's name was called, even if he chose not to show it in public. Instead, he remained gracious, stayed at the proceedings until the very end, skipped all the post-festivities, and went straight home with Gloria. He had had a lot riding on *Anatomy,* the last of his films released in what had been an incredible decade of filmmaking. He had wanted to end the '50s on a climactic, high-note flourish. Instead, he did it by losing a two-man chariot race to God.

— • —

A year later, as Cary Grant smoothly traversed the countryside in *North by Northwest,* a film that not only outgrossed *Vertigo* three to one (in its initial domestic release) but was hailed as the finest work of both Grant's and Hitchcock's careers, a dispirited Jimmy was finishing up a minor and quickly forgotten Daniel Mann feature for Columbia, *The Mountain Road,* in the type of role he once swore he would never

---

9. *Anatomy* was also nominated for Best Picture (it lost to William Wyler's *Ben-Hur*), Best Supporting Actor (Arthur O'Connell and George C. Scott, both of whom lost to Hugh Griffith in *Ben-Hur*), Best Director (Preminger lost to Wyler for *Ben-Hur*), Best Screenplay (Wendell Mayes lost to Neil Paterson for Jack Clayton's *Room at the Top*), Best Editing (it lost to *Ben-Hur*), and Best Black and White Cinematography (it lost to George Stevens's *Diary of Anne Frank*).

play—a U.S. army commander fighting the Japanese in southern China during World War Two. When it opened, in June 1960, the *New York Times* dismissed it as a "mild little war sermon."

The next thing fifty-two-year-old Jimmy Stewart did was to appear as an aging cowboy on an episode of one of NBC's hour anthologies, *Ford Startime*. He followed that by playing himself, with Gloria at his side, on yet another hilarious episode of the *Jack Benny Program*.

PART SEVEN

— . —

Valor and Death, Disillusionment and Resurrection

As Sam Burnett, the aging cowboy, in Andrew V. McLaglen's
The Rare Breed (1966).

24

"Of the westerns, I did one with John Ford, *Two Rode Together,* that I liked . . . there was one very long sequence of Widmark and me by the river, done all in one take. It was early in the morning and [Ford] was sort of grouchy and he walked out and for some reason put the camera in the river. . . . [The actor-director relationship] is a very good one when it works, when you get the thing working." **—JIMMY STEWART**

*T*he woman many considered to have been the only true love of Jimmy's life, Margaret Sullavan, died by her own hand in the early hours of January 1, 1960. The official cause was listed as an overdose of barbiturates, the intention left purposely vague on the death certificate. Later on it was revealed that she had lost most of her hearing, which made acting live on stage all but impossible. Toward the very end, desperate to get back on the stage, she had taken up lipreading and had landed a part on Broadway in *Sweet Love Remembered,* a bittersweet title for the movie star who had been unhappily married four times.[1] Finally, when she could no longer hear the other actors, she took an overdose of sleeping pills and never woke up.

The news of Sullavan's passing devastated Jimmy. As was his style, he said nothing about it to the public.

— • —

"I love him. That's . . . that's first of all. And that is, of course, intermixed with respect and admiration. He's just a genius. The way he'll do a script. Gets it across visually. Hates *talk.* I just wish there were more people like him . . . I think he is the best man doing the job."

---

1. Henry Fonda (1931), William Wyler (1934), Leland Hayward (1936), Kenneth Wagg (1950).

Jimmy was speaking to Peter Bogdanovich, not about Alfred Hitchcock, as one might expect, or Frank Capra, not even Anthony Mann. He was, instead, referring to John Ford. He had come relatively late to Ford (in both their careers), and was profoundly attracted by what Andrew Sarris later described as the director's poetic melancholia: "In accepting the inevitability of the present while mourning the past, Ford is a conservative rather than a reactionary." This perceptive description of the director goes a long way toward explaining how both he and Jimmy were perceived in Hollywood at the dawn of the sixties. Both were aware their star time was nearly over, and yet neither made an attempt, as so many others did, to repeat earlier success, to recapture "the good old days." Ford especially, but in his way Jimmy as well, made films with an increasing sense of graceful aging about them, as a way to remain dignified in an industry and the culture it reflected that tended to shove the aged to the side like the fallen dead leaves of a season gone by.

When it finally did come to him, Jimmy jumped at the chance to work with Ford, among the most talented of all the directors to emerge during Hollywood's golden age. He had six Oscars, more than any other director, and in his body of work managed to create a world on the screen in which the action on the screen represented the world, populated with his famous stock company, led by John Wayne, and at various times Ward Bond, Henry Fonda, Harry Carey (Senior and Junior), and John Carradine, among others.

Although each had made dozens of movies, Ford's and Jimmy's paths had never cinematically crossed, mostly because of studio restrictions, and that was probably not a bad thing. In retrospect, "Pappy" was a filmmaker for whom physical toughness represented spiritual strength, with the sensitivities of his rugged leading men protected, even if sometimes buried, beneath their actions. One thinks of the fistfight between John Wayne and Victor McLaglen in *The Quiet Man* (1952) as much a revelation of love as the moment when Wayne sweeps Maureen O'Hara into his arms against the howling winds. Jimmy's characters, meanwhile, were for the most part just the opposite, men with quiet exteriors, all the rage buried deep within their souls.

In 1960, an independent, low-budget producer by the name of Stan Shpetner had made his reputation by putting out a cheap quickie film built around the Kingston Trio hit song "Tom Dooley." After two or three more nondescript films, all of which showed a profit, Shpetner acquired the rights to a Will Cook Western novel, *Comanche Captives,* and brought it to Wasserman and MCA for packaging. Wasserman promptly turned it into a vehicle for the currently out-of-work Stewart and the aging but still viable Ford. He then added Richard Widmark to the mix and sold the film, retitled *Two Rode Together,* to Columbia, the only studio willing to take a chance on the project, the same studio that had successfully produced Shpetner's *Tom Dooley.*[2]

"I remember the first day I was ever on a set with Ford," Jimmy later recalled. I was the sheriff in an old Western town and I'm in front of the bar that I own. Ford said, 'Put your feet up on the bar and put your hat down. You're sort of snoozing.' And he didn't say anything else. He went back and said, 'Are you ready?' And this is all there was. I didn't have anything else to do so I yawned, but I did an immense yawn. My hat almost fell off. Then he said, 'Cut!' And I waited for something, and I looked; but he was gone. The cameraman was gone. They went somewhere else to shoot something else. Three days later we were in a different location—I was on a horse or something—Ford came up and said, 'I liked the yawn,' and went away. All I ever heard."

The main problem with the film was Ford's general lack of interest in it. Jimmy had a conversation with him during production when this first became apparent. "I went up to his office to see him about costume," he later recalled. "For this first picture we did [together], and of course, he didn't talk about costume at all. He talked about the Navy . . . about the war . . . then a little about . . . the Navy . . . and a little more about . . . the war . . . he mumbled, and that handkerchief he's always chewing on . . . then finally he asked what I oughta wear in this picture. I thought, and he said, now, before you say anything I'll *tell* you what you're going to wear! And he sent the wardrobe man out, brought back a costume and this, this *hat!* . . . He asked me what I thought. I said I don't know and he says, do you have hat-approval in your contract? I said I didn't know and everybody [started] looking for the contract and they couldn't find it 'cause I didn't have one. . . . [A]fter a while I went out and I brought *my* old hat, the hat I'd worn in every Western . . . old when I got it. So, I put it on. He kinda looked at it for a few moments and then he says, you *have* hat-approval."

---

2. Aka *The Legend of Tom Dooley.* The film was directed by Ted Post.

Ford never felt completely comfortable working with Jimmy, and even less so with Widmark, whom the director considered one of the new generation of too-liberal-leaning actors who had, in his opinion, taken over and subsequently ruined Hollywood.

Two Rode Together was a self-imitative meditation on Indians as seen by those who have suffered at their hands; it paled in comparison to the many films it superficially resembled, including Ford's own *The Searchers* (Ford, like Hawks, was fond of doing vague remakes of his favorite movies over and over again). Lacking in *Two Rode Together* was the majesty, the scope, the depth, and the sense of justice that fueled the emotions of *The Searchers'* existential heroes as they wandered through the wilderness looking for spiritual redemption in the form of physical rescue. In *Two Rode Together*, the motivation is bounty money.

Halfway through production, word reached Ford that his good friend Ward Bond had dropped dead of a heart attack, after which he quickly wrapped the film.

It didn't open until almost a year later, the end of July 1961, tradition-ally a time when those films not considered prime summer blockbuster material are released. It was met with critical indifference and generally ignored by audiences, which was fine with Ford, who responded to a critic's query about it by describing the film as nothing but "a load of crap."

Stewart was, perhaps not surprisingly, less than enthralled with his experience on the film, and insisted his entire salary be given in his and Gloria's name to St. John's Hospital in Santa Monica, a nonprofit health care center in which they were heavily involved. He had little more to do with movie-making the rest of the year, until November, when he was honored by the Screen Actors Guild for his "outstanding achieve-ment in fostering the finest ideals of the acting profession." The award was presented by Charlton Heston.

Jimmy finished out the year working on the narration of a docu-mentary salute to former President Dwight Eisenhower, *Tribute to a President*, broadcast on NBC.

— • —

Later in 1961, Jimmy participated in a Cinerama triptych called *How the West Was Won*, with each of its three segments helmed by a dif-ferent director, George Marshall, John Ford, and Henry Hathaway. Jimmy did a cameo in Hathaway's segment, playing the fictional Western pioneer Linus Rawlings (at thirty-four, twenty years younger than Jimmy was at the time) who courts and marries the symbolically named Eve, played by thirty-year-old Carroll Baker, and starts a family whose history parallels the so-called conquest of the West.[3] Until production actually started, Jimmy devoted much of his time to the air force. He spent most of February in Washington, D.C., at the Pentagon, amidst all the pageantry and fresh-air optimism of Kennedy's "Camelot."

He returned home in April, and even before he had fully unpacked his bags, the Academy asked Jimmy to accept Gary Cooper's Honorary (noncompetitive) Lifetime Achievement Award "for his many memorable screen performances and the international recognition he, as an individual, has gained for the motion picture industry" because, they said, the actor was too ill to attend. As Jimmy had presented Coop with his Best Actor Oscar in 1942 for his performance in *Sergeant York,* the Academy thought it would be a nice gesture to have him accept the honorary Award for him.

Although the public did not know it, it was no secret to anyone in Hollywood, including Jimmy, that Coop was on his deathbed. The tall, lean, still-handsome actor, unlike most "honorary recipients," had actually won two Best Actor Oscars, one for *Sergeant York* (1941) and another for his portrayal as Sheriff Will Kane in Fred Zinnemann's *High Noon* (1952). On-screen he had come to typify the All-American, tall, silent, righteous fellow who would never start a fight but never lose one when provoked. In real life he had been a legendary rabble rouser, a ladies man par excellence (known throughout Hollywood as the actor who talked softly and carried a big dick), and early in his career a paramount-sized headache for Adolph

---

3. Cinerama was a big-screen novelty, using three projectors and a curved screen to give the illusion of a gigantic, glasses-free 3-D effect to viewers. Because of its prohibitive production costs, and the necessity to reconfigure theaters to play films in this mode, only about a hundred theaters ever did so, and the two ever-present and always annoying visible lines that ran vertically between each third of the screen, the intended effects of Cinerama was rarely experienced. Most films shot in the process were of little consequence, with producers not wanting the content to overshadow the gimmickry of the wide-screen presentation, which was the major attraction of most Cinerama films. Those that survived were quickly reprocessed into 70 mm, or the more common 35 mm. *How the West Was Won* was actually the first Cinerama film with a dramatic narrative. Most were simply glorified travelogues or front-row rides on roller coasters.

Zukor, yet no one either in the industry or out of it (except Zukor) ever had a bad word to say about him.

The ceremonies were held on April 17 at the Santa Monica Civic Auditorium, thanks to the many televised industry events, the most famous high school assembly hall in the world. Thousands of "civilians" circled the grounds outside to see what was promised to be Elizabeth Taylor's first appearance since her near-death the year before following an emergency tracheotomy (that assured her a Best Actress Oscar for her phone-in on Daniel Mann's adaptation of John O'Hara's risqué story of a New York City prostitute, *Butterfield 8*).

After Billy Wilder won Best Director for *The Apartment,* William Wyler was introduced by the show's familiar and always funny host, Bob Hope, and somberly walked to the podium. He was there, he explained, "to give an Honorary Oscar to the kind of American who's loved in the four corners of the earth." Everyone present knew who he was talking about. When the applause died down, Wyler informed the audience, that "a close and worthy stand-in" would accept the award in Coop's stead. When Wyler said the name "James Stewart," an even more thunderous round of applause came forth.

Jimmy walked slowly to the podium, took the Oscar from Wyler, made the usual thanks, then looked directly into the camera, which closed in tight on his face, revealing tears streaming down from both eyes. In a cracked voice, Jimmy said, "I am very honored to accept this award tonight for Gary Cooper. I'm sorry he's not here to accept it, but I know he's sitting by the television set tonight, and, Coop, I want you to know I'll get it to you right away. With it goes all the friendship and affection and the admiration and deep respect of all of us. We're very, very proud of you, Coop. . . . We're proud of you, Coop . . . all of us are tremendously proud . . ." Unable to continue, Jimmy lifted the statuette over his head, turned, and walked off the stage, leaving the audience in stunned silence, as the network faded silently to a commercial break.

During his final weeks, Cooper was visited by a host of friends, including Audrey Hepburn and her (then) husband Mel Ferrer, Sam and Frances Goldwyn, Jack Benny, Danny Kaye, Bill Goetz and Jerry Wald, Robert Stack, Billy Wilder, and Gloria and Jimmy. After delivering the award Jimmy spent nearly all day, every day, at Coop's bedside, talking, reading the Bible to him, and listening to classical music, right up until the end. Less than a month after he had won his Honorary Oscar, Gary Cooper was dead.

— • —

Production on *How the West Was Won* was completed in July 1962 and Jimmy decided to take Gloria and join Fran Kirk and Bess Johnson on safari in Africa.

The trip proved an enormous delight even though the Stewarts insisted they would, at no time, bag any game, as neither believed in sport hunting for blood. This wasn't the case with the Johnsons. Bess took down a leopard, water buck, and elephant, and Fran killed an eland, a rhinoceros, and an elephant of his own.

What appealed to both Gloria and Jimmy was the sheer beauty of the wild. He loved being so close to nature, with all its dangers, both natural and man-made. Safari also allowed him to forget, a least for a while, about Hollywood and all its bottom-line tensions, and next-picture paranoia. It also permitted him to go about freely, without his obligatory movie toupee, which, whenever he had to wear it, annoyed him to no end. By the end of the safari, Jimmy had told Gloria that from now on, Africa would be the place they would come to whenever they wanted to get away from everything and rediscover themselves.

On June 29, in Nairobi, Kenya, the private plane Jimmy had commissioned for the group crash-landed in Nigeria, near the site of a former Mau Mau death and torture camp. Miraculously, all four aboard escaped serious injury. Jimmy was shaken up, and there were momentary flashes of the worst of what he had gone through during the war, but in the end he managed to slough off the damage as if it were nothing more than surface dust on his safari jacket.

Back in Hollywood that fall, Jimmy started work on what would prove to be his last great motion picture, the fascinating, enormously complex, beautifully shot, and powerfully affecting *The Man Who Shot Liberty Valance,* John Ford's elegiac view of the old West, his not-so-fond farewell to the Hollywood he knew.

The film was a powerful return to form for Ford, who, this time, had been actively involved in putting together the project from its inception, raising half the film's initial budget—$1.6 million—to match Paramount's share, the kickoff to a new multipicture contract he had signed with the studio. He then quickly acquired the rights to the original short story by Dorothy M. Johnson, first published in *Cosmopolitan* in 1949. He supervised all the script rewrites, and cast John Wayne and Jimmy first, in the two pivotal roles of the film. He later chose Vera Miles to play the woman they compete for, and finally (and superbly) he cast Lee Marvin in the ironically named title character, a role so unforgettably menacing that Marvin would find himself parodying it three years later in Elliot Silverstein's *Cat Ballou* (1965). Filling out the cast were various members of the Ford family of fine actors, including Andy Devine, Woody Strode, John Carradine, and Edmond O'Brien. Ford chose to shoot the film in black and white, to further link it to a time and a place firmly set in the past.

The casting of Wayne and Jimmy was no accident. Ford was after the opposing balance the two offered—Wayne (Tom Doniphon), the gentle giant, hulking, street-smart; and Jimmy (Ransom Stoddard), diminutive in build, tall, slight, with a sharp, well-educated mind. One was all brawn, the other all brain, and both would have to eventually, if somewhat begrudgingly, work together to conquer the brute force of Liberty Valance, who represented all that was evil, lawless, rough, and tough in an American frontier on the verge of civilizing itself.

The film is so gorgeously ambiguous that the interpretation as to what happens during it varies widely from critic to critic. To Bogdanovich, for instance, the film holds elements of assassination and conspiracy, as in the death of Marilyn Monroe and the murder of John F. Kennedy, and of what he refers to as Robert Graves's "single poetic theme": a triangular love story of two men in love with the same woman. Surely there are elements of this, as well as echoes of Fred Zinnemann's *High Noon*: two protagonists, one old (Cooper in *High Noon*, Wayne in *Liberty*), one young (Lloyd Bridges as the hot-headed sheriff in *High Noon*, Jimmy Stewart as the young lawyer in *Liberty*); both in love with a chaste, antiviolence blonde (Kelly in *Noon*, Miles in *Liberty*); and a romantic triangle upset by the looming threat of a showdown with the town's most evil citizen (Frank Miller, menacingly played by Ian MacDonald in *Noon*; Liberty Valance, Marvin in *Liberty*). Both films are shot in high-contrast black and white, and both films deal with political agendas that will heavily affect the future, all of which—money, power, industry, and lawfulness—is threatened by the misanthropic villainy of their respective antagonists that represents the hard-dying past.

That, however, is where the similarities end. The difference between Zinnemann and Ford lies in the invisibility of the town, i.e., the extended family of man; in *High Noon,* Marshal Kane realizes he must go it alone, while in *Valance,* the entire town rallies around the opportunity to stand up and be counted. Because of it, *Valance's* Doniphon, who personifies the old and ossifying West, all that was good about it and all that was bad, is slowly eliminated from the town's plans for its future, in favor of the smarter, more "civilized," if decidedly calculating Stoddard. Also, unlike the resolution in *High Noon,* in *Valance* it is the younger man who wins the girl away from the older one, even though he was the one who saw her and had her first.

Ford's meditation on politics becomes, finally, his statement on Hollywood. Although conservative, he had no use for the opportunists who abounded, particularly Cecil B. DeMille, whose well-documented anti-Semitism Ford could not stand, and who saw in DeMille a user of the difficult political times of the fifties to promote himself through hollow biblical epics that were thinly disguised calls for unquestioned allegiance. Ford would take no part in what he considered the hypocrisy that had become the by-product of politically paranoid Hollywood, and a large part of what *Liberty Valance* is about has to do with the nature of those forced to sacrifice themselves, along with their times, to make the future a better place.

For students of film, all of this comes down to an even higher truth— the poetic veracity of "the shot." When Stoddard is finally called out by Valance, he "miraculously" wins the duel, and subsequently marries the girl, runs for office, becomes a senator, and lives off the fame and fortune riding the town of Valance has brought him. At first, to the audience, it appears that Stoddard somehow did outdraw Valance, but in flashback we learn the terrible secret behind Stoddard's entire career, the lie that he has kept alive all those years: that it was Doniphon, standing down the road, who actually killed Valance but took no credit for it, unselfishly letting Stoddard get the glory and all that went with it, for the good of the town. To Stoddard, the feud between him and Valance was personal, mano-a-mano, and none of anyone's business. Only by showing the audience the scene from another angle does Ford allow the truth to be seen. The art of this film, then, lay in its literal vision of God, while its mise-en-scène is a description of deception, Hollywood style, the truth defined as not what actually happens, but as how the camera sees it from where the director has placed it.

In *Liberty*, Jimmy performs yet another of his amazing aging acts. At the age of fifty-four, he begins the movie as a young tenderfoot lawyer who can be no more than twenty-five, then manages to pull off the youthful part of his role far better than he does the "old" Stoddard. His performance is filled with all the nuances, edgy rawness, and subtle soft-spoken qualities that were the essential elements of his star power, something that Jimmy still had in abundance.

In every sense, then—cinematically, narratively, in the precision of the performances, the film's direction and its powerful themes—*The Man Who Shot Liberty Valance* ranks among the best work of Ford's and Jimmy's careers.

— • —

The Man Who Shot Liberty Valance was released in the fall of 1962 to mixed reviews. The *Los Angeles Times* said it was "old hat," the *New York Times* called it "creaky," and Brendan Gill, writing in *The New Yorker*, dismissed it as a parody of Ford's best work. The film proved a box-office dud, was quickly pulled from release, and remains to this day rarely seen, one of the forgotten moments of sixties-movie greatness.

For Jimmy, the film's failure made him see clearly that he could no longer play the energetic, youthful (if no longer young) idealist that had sustained him for so long. What to do next became a personal as much as professional existential dilemma. As an actor who defined the days of his life through the roles he inhabited, film was his true life's blood; to Jimmy, it was beginning to feel terribly thin.

To try to stop the bleeding, he signed a multiple-picture deal with Darryl F. Zanuck's 20th Century Fox to star in a series of films, the first of which was a Nunnally Johnson–written domestic comedy, directed by old friend Henry Koster. *Mr. Hobbs Takes a Vacation* was the brainchild of independent producer Jerry Wald, his eighth and final project under a multiple-picture deal he had with Fox.[4] Apparently, Wald had trouble attracting talent to the film. After purchasing the rights to the

---

4. But the first of a series of films at the studio for Jimmy, including *Mr. Hobbs Takes a Vacation* (1962), *Take Her, She's Mine* (1963), *Dear Brigitte* (1965), *The Flight of the Phoenix* (1965), and *Bandolero!* (1968). In Stewart's trilogy of family comedies

original novel, *Mr. Hobbs' Vacation* by Edward Streeter, he offered it to writers S. J. Perelman and James Thurber for adaptation to the screen. They read the book and turned him down. Wald then gave it to Johnson. Directorial duties were offered to Leo McCarey, who was willing to helm it but became unavailable due to illness. Jimmy, who had already signed on, suggested Koster, his director for *No Highway in the Sky.* Wald then decided that Maureen O'Hara was "wrong" for the domesticated housewife opposite Jimmy. He offered to buy her out of the film and give her another one, then offered the role to virtually every older leading lady in town, including Loretta Young, Polly Bergen, Lucille Ball, Olivia de Havilland, Ginger Rogers, and Rosalind Russell. When they all turned thumbs down on the project, Wald went back and re-hired O'Hara, at a considerable increase in salary.

Hobbs was a fat but hollow comedy, in which, like the three others to follow, Jimmy's character would disappear into the lush Technicolor backgrounds, making faces of befuddlement over the behavior of his children/teenagers/wife, as he gently crinkle-eyed his way into the fabric of film-fare middle age—fathers in cardigans who no longer work, have no career or interests in anything but the weather, have lots of kids but no sex, and seemingly endless amounts of money.

Mr. Hobbs Takes a Vacation went into production that November, just days after *Valance* had wrapped. At least in *Hobbs,* Jimmy was allowed to play a realistically close-to-his-own-age character (he was fifty-five when production started). His screen wife, Maureen O'Hara, was forty-one at the time. They go away for a quiet vacation and family chaos ensues. In a performance that seemed phoned in from the sleep ward, Stewart's special ability to show up quietly and at the same time be noticed on-screen came into full use.

He understood well the limitations of *Hobbs,* but at this stage of his career, it was less important to him what film he was making than the fact that he was making a film at all. He cranked his performance out smoothly, like a well-oiled machine, and it seemed to please him, until, in the middle of production of *Hobbs,* tragedy struck.

The call came from Gloria while he was on *Hobbs'* Carrillo Beach.

(*Hobbs, Take Her, Brigitte*), to attract younger audiences the studio sought to place him among its more youthful contract players, including Sandra Dee, Fabian (who appeared in both *Hobbs* and *Brigitte*), and John Saxon.

She had just heard from the family. Alexander had suffered a stroke. He had been taken to the Cleveland Clinic, then sent home. He was not expected to live.

Jimmy immediately left the set, drove home, picked up Gloria, and went to the airport. They arrived in Indiana the morning of December 28. Jimmy rushed directly to his father's bedside and stayed there until it was over.

After the funeral, he and Gloria returned to Hollywood, where he finished work on *Mr. Hobbs*. An inconsolable Jimmy Stewart did not step in front of a big-screen movie camera again for nearly a year and a half.

25

"This aging problem is not so bad for men as it is for the girls. I know that I have changed. I've lost a lot of hair and I'm getting some new lines in my face. I keep in pretty good shape though—play a lot of golf. What is amazing is how some of my friends keep looking so young. My old friend Hank Fonda still looks like a young man—and he's two years older than I am!"

—JIMMY STEWART

Grief was not the only reason Jimmy did not immediately return to making movies. At least part of it had to do with the ongoing crisis at Fox studios, where, just before Alexander's death, Jimmy had signed on to star in Koster's next domestic comedy, *Take Her, She's Mine*, based on the hit Broadway comedy by Henry and Phoebe Ephron, the team that had also written *The Jackpot*. To acquire the rights to the script. Fox had paid Broadway producer Harold Prince $150,000.

However, before it could go into production, virtually all ongoing Fox projects were shut down and new ones put on hold after the financial debacle that took place as a result of the making of *Cleopatra*. (The romance between Elizabeth Taylor and Richard Burton had brought international headlines and numerous delays that nearly bankrupted the studio.) It took nothing less than the return of Darryl F. Zanuck, who had gone into independent production to make the highly successful *The Longest Day*, to get things back on track.[1] For the better part of 1962, *Take Her, She's Mine* was put on hiatus. No one knew how long the film would be delayed, or if it would ever get made at all. Mean-

---

1. Like *How the West Was Won*, *The Longest Day* had several directors, each taking on a different aspect of the film, including Ken Annikan (British exteriors), Andrew Marton (American exteriors), Bernhard Wicki (German scenes), and Zanuck himself. *Cleopatra* was directed by Joseph L. Mankiewicz, and Rouben Mamoulian, who was fired and subsequently uncredited. He was replaced by Zanuck.

while, Jimmy, under contract, had to be ready to begin production on a moment's notice.

He kept busy on television, doing another *Jack Benny*; an episode of the popular Fred MacMurray TV show *My Three Sons* (in which he played Brigadier General James Stewart), and a previously signed episode of the *Alcoa Hour* drama series called "Flashing Spikes," directed by John Ford.

He also made a number of public appearances, including the Hollywood premiere at the Fox Wilshire Theater of *Mr. Hobbs Takes a Vacation*, notable for the turnout/tribute of several of Jimmy's former co-stars, including Joanne Dru (*Thunder Bay*), Ruth Hussey (*The Philadelphia Story*), Lee Remick (*Anatomy of a Murder*), and Rosalind Russell (*No Time for Comedy*), along with his current co-star in *Mr. Hobbs*, Maureen O'Hara. The ostensible occasion for the reunion was to celebrate Jimmy's first starring role at Fox back in 1937, in *Seventh Heaven*, but really, it was to give a show of support for him in his hour of personal darkness.

Despite the great showing, because of the death of his father his heart wasn't in it. He had already quietly begun to make plans to get out of his contract at Fox, retire, and move the family out of Beverly Hills to Santa Ynez, where he'd purchased half of an 1,100-acre ranch, for which he paid nearly half a million dollars, a significant addition to his growing portfolio of real estate investments in Beverly Hills, the Valley, and partnerships in dozens of profitable oil wells. The other half of the ranch had been bought by a Florida-based oilman who'd entered into an agreement with Jimmy to turn it into a cattle- and thoroughbred-horse-breeding farm, with the understanding that his interests be limited to business, while Jimmy and his family could live on the rest. One of the reasons Jimmy chose this site was that it was near the Santa Ynez County airport, where he had easy access to his private plane.

After closing on the ranch, Jimmy took the entire family on another trip to Africa—only the second time all the children had been permitted to come along—and this time, despite the official Stewart family policy of not killing wild game, young Michael, then seventeen, bagged a lion. Although not happy about it, Jimmy quietly congratulated his stepson and let it go at that. The only "weapons" Jimmy carried were Nikon cameras, preferring that brand because the lenses were made bayonet-style, and quickly interchangeable. Peter Stackpole, a former *Life* photographer and a frequent traveler with the Stewarts, had introduced photography to the family, telling Jimmy, "If you want a record of your trip, take as many pictures as possible; the law of averages is bound to work in your favor." As Jimmy later recalled, "We used to take movies in the jungle but our 8 mm camera was unfortunately eaten by a hyena one night. Now we just take stills."

Not long after their return to the States, Jimmy was off again, this time only with Gloria, for a ten-day holiday to Acapulco. He then sent Gloria back to California while he flew directly to Dallas to record the narration for several air force training films.

His first day back in L.A. from Dallas, a tour bus pulled up in front of the North Roxbury Drive house, by now a regular stop on the regular "See the Stars Homes" trips through Beverly Hills. Jimmy waved to the tourists and shouted "hi" to the drivers. He knew all of them by name. At that point the bus door opened and a little girl came out and ran over to him. He picked her up, smiled, gave her a little kiss, and put her back down. Her parents came rushing over to apologize. He laughed and invited them all in for some ice cream and soda. Later, when someone asked the family how they had felt during their visit, they smiled and said, "Right at home!"

— • —

That November, *How the West Was Won* was finally released, the long delay due mostly to technical problems and to everyone's surprise, no one's more than Jimmy's, the film was a smash hit at the box office. Counting both release formats, CinemaScope and regular widescreen, in its initial domestic release it managed to gross a total of $17 million, more than the long-delayed release of *Cleopatra;* Zanuck's other road show, *The Longest Day;* and David Lean's epic *Lawrence of Arabia,* to become the number one box-office film of the year.

The amazing success of what was a quite ordinary movie, its bigscreen technology notwithstanding, proved, among other things, that the name James Stewart still had some box-office pull, in this instance enough to thrust him back into the top rank of Hollywood movie stars. He decided to postpone indefinitely both his retirement and the move to the ranch. *How the West Was Won* proved the catalyst to get the moribund *Take Her, She's Mine* back into production, the first post-*Cleopatra* Fox project to get the green light, with a new, $3.5 million budget personally approved by Zanuck. When asked about the delay, Jimmy, who, up until the success of *West* had been hoping the film would never get made, put the most positive spin he could on the situation: "It was a profitable wait for the picture. I wish these waits could happen more often for the sake of the script. They've had time to polish and tighten it so we're starting with a script we'll actually be shooting, instead of one that has to be rewritten as we go along . . . it was sad that the studio had to shut down, but I think Darryl Zanuck was wise to do what he did."

In *Take Her, She's Mine*, Jimmy was cast in the role of Frank Michaelson (originally played on Broadway by Art Carney), paternal wisdom-spouting husband of Anne Michaelson (Audrey Meadows in the film) and father of twenty-one-year old Mollie Michaelson (Sandra Dee).[2] With less-than-laugh-riot dialogue—such as Dee's pouting, "Telling me your troubles would be like complaining to Noah about a drizzle"—Jimmy made the film without complaint, more or less walking through it until the last day of shooting.

— • —

In May 1963, news arrived that his father's widow, his second wife (Jimmy never referred to her as his stepmother), had decided to leave Indiana, Pennsylvania, and move back to her native Canada. He knew this meant the time had come to sell his father's beloved hardware store that had remained closed since Alexander's death. "After it was all over and I was alone, I went to the hardware store and let myself in, with a key I hadn't touched for thirty years. The interior smelled of metal, leather, oil and fertilizer, the odors of my childhood. I sat at his scarred oak desk and idly pulled open the middle drawer. It held a clutter of pencils and paper clips and bolts and paint samples. Something glinted dully among them. I picked up the funeral-train penny with the flattened Indian face and the burst grain. I had lost mine, so now I took his. Then I left the store, locking the door behind me. There have been many offers to buy the business, but I could not endure the thought of

---

2. The play, which opened on December 21, 1961, also starred Phyllis Thaxter as Carney's wife, and Elizabeth Ashley as his daughter.

another man's standing in the middle of Dad's life. I have sold off all the merchandise and today the store is vacant, just as a part of me will always be."

Aside from the penny, the only thing Jimmy took back with him to Beverly Hills was his Oscar for *The Philadelphia Story.* His single comment to the press about this episode was, "It's sad closing this chapter on a little town which has such deep memories for me."

— • —

Gloria could plainly see that Jimmy was depressed, and to try to cheer him up, suggested they do something they hadn't done in nearly ten years—go out to dinner at a public Hollywood nightspot. It was the kind of activity Jimmy had sworn off when he had begun seeing her, and he'd kept to his word, one of the reasons since his marriage that his name had rarely showed up in any of the gossip columns. This time, Gloria insisted, and they went for what he believed was going to be a quiet dinner at one of his favorite restaurants, Chasen's, the green-and-white bungalow-style establishment on Beverly Boulevard near Doheny Drive he still often frequented for lunch—either the chili and cheese toast—and maybe an afternoon Flame of Love cocktail if he happened to run into old friend Ronald Reagan, or half a salad followed by a house special called Sole Hitchcock ("So special it wasn't on the menu. It was a secret recipe given to Dave Chasen by Alfred Hitchcock," recalled Bill Frye). For dessert, Jimmy never varied in his selection—a single scoop of vanilla ice cream. No matter what mood Jimmy was in, he always behaved the same to the staff. Upon making his entrance, he would hand the hatcheck girl a twenty-dollar bill. After a while, there was no need for him to say anything. She would simply break it into three fives and five ones. When she'd hand it back to Jimmy, he'd give her two ones (before leaving the restaurant, he would hand Claude, the headwaiter, one of the five-dollar bills).

This night Gloria and Jimmy weren't in their banquette very long before radio and TV broadcaster Arthur Godfrey—a disciple of the New York City Winchell school of power-schmooze and report-it-the-next-day-on-the-air, who was in town and making the Hollywood rounds—stopped by for a chat. Before he left, Hedda Hopper spied the threesome and invited herself to join the party for a drink. All four were then forced to move to a larger banquette when Jackie Gleason and his drinking pal, Frank Fontaine, a regular on Gleason's TV show, decided to expand the jamboree. Comic actor Tom Poston came over as well, and pretty soon the night turned into a roaring drink fest. A wobbly Jimmy (who never held his liquor all that well), lost in the swirl of his own soused imagination, was later helped from the car to his front door by Gloria's firm arms.

— • —

Jimmy agreed to go on a promotional tour for *Take Her, She's Mine*. Although he didn't particularly like the movie, he had nothing much else going on. His ennui had as much to do with the movie itself as with the way the movie business was now being run, as it had changed so completely from his (and its) studio-system heyday. Personal promotion, for instance, during the height of the studio era, had been a relatively rare thing, confined usually to premieres, magazine interviews, and the occasional radio appearance or two. Now, having settled back into the business, he felt obligated to help develop an audience for his films. "It gets difficult to be optimistic in Hollywood," he said to one reporter, and therefore, found it necessary to "find the audience out there" for them, which he fully intended to do.

One story he didn't tell any reporters was that during the long delay he had decided to make up some reserve time with the air force. On a routine flight he was piloting, one of the engines of the aircraft conked out, and, with great difficulty, he'd managed to bring the hobbled craft to a safe landing. "All I could think of was not my personal safety," he wrote in his diary, "but what Congresswoman Margaret Chase Smith would say if I crashed such an expensive plane."

— • —

Take Her, She's Mine opened at New York's Criterion Theatre on November 13, 1963, to fairly awful reviews. Despite the thumbs-down from the critics and the Kennedy assassination nine days later, which produced one of the lowest box-office weeks in the history of movies, the film managed to do fairly well, outgrossing several "bigger" openings that year, eventually earning a fair profit for both the studio and the profit-sharing Jimmy.

By then he had already filmed a cameo screen appearance for John

Ford as Wyatt Earp in a bizarre scene in an even more bizarre film, *Cheyenne Autumn,* Ford's mea culpa for "having killed a lot of Indians in my time" and his newfound need to "make amends." The resultant film was a bloated mess, and a box-office failure. Ford would make only three more features before his death, none with Jimmy.[3]

Later that year, Stewart once again lamented in public about the death of the Hollywood studio system and how it reflected the culture's passing scene. As the *New York Times* described him during the interview, he was "rather stolid, conservative . . . so reticent that strangers often find it all but impossible to elicit responses to questions. At 56, Stewart's hair is gray and his face deeply lined. His speech is slow and deliberate. Stewart rarely mixes with fellow performers on a set but under suitably relaxed conditions and with the proper lubricants, he can be an entertaining raconteur. Stewart acknowledges that he misses Hollywood's old studio system, where top stars were carefully nurtured and assigned prime vehicles. Faced with the anarchy of present day Hollywood, Stewart complains that he has a difficult time finding movies that he wants to make. 'The Hollywood product today places too much emphasis on shock and not enough on old-fashioned sentiment,' he states. 'I still like to do movies that make the ladies cry.'"

The article went on to mention that, unlike his best friend, Fonda, Jimmy had not returned periodically to Broadway. And it slipped in almost as an afterthought that he was an ardent supporter of that fall's Republican presidential candidate, Sen. Barry Goldwater. In fact, Stewart's enthusiasm for Goldwater, the extremist right-wing candidate the party had put up against the Democrat post-assassination candidate, the (then) hugely popular and broadly liberal Lyndon Johnson, bordered on the obsessive. The Goldwater presidential campaign seemed to reignite Jimmy's passions, giving him the kind of energy that making films no longer did. He campaigned whenever he found the least bit of free time, between working on his newest film, *Shenandoah,* an imitation John Ford Civil War–lite family saga. Directed by Andrew V. McLaglen (actor Victor McLaglen's son), the film was filled with rifles,

---

3. *Young Cassidy* (1965), *Seven Women* (1966), *Vietnam, Vietnam* (1971); Ford died in 1973.

whiskers, chewed-on cigar butts, and a James Stewart that *Newsweek* described as not only "far from young, but [playing a role] of paterfamilias more tired than his eyes."

Earlier that year, Jimmy had completed work on *Dear Brigitte,* yet another dull domestic comedy, this one with Ed Wynn, a comic who brought anything but youth to the picture, and a scene in which Jimmy played the accordion, which just about stopped whatever discernible heartbeat the film had had until then. Understandably, it brought an end to the Koster/Johnson/Stewart Fox unit, by far the least memorable of the series. Brigitte Bardot's appearance in the film didn't do anything for its box office. Nor did the preposterousness of the fact that Jimmy, fifty-six but looking on the far side of sixty—his increased drinking, or use of "proper lubricants," as the *New York Times* had politely referred to it, didn't help his looks any—was supposed to be the father of an eight-year-old tyke. Jimmy's wife in the film was played by forty-one-year-old Glynis Johns. Moreover, Bardot had refused to allow her image or even full name to be used to promote the film, having reluctantly signed on strictly for the money (the reason the film's name was changed from *Erasmus with Freckles* to *Dear Brigitte*, the only way the producers had of suggesting her presence). She appeared in only one brief sequence, at the end of the film, for which the entire cast had to travel to Paris, as she refused to fly to Hollywood for the shoot.

The film holds no stylistic significance, no strong place in the canon of the James Stewart filmography; it does not accurately reflect the mood of the country during the time it was made (it appears more like a film from the mid-fifties than the early sixties). And yet, it somehow found an audience among aging loyalists of Jimmy's who would, apparently, go to see him in anything and among the younger people who wanted to catch a glimpse of the elusive Brigitte Bardot.

Released in 1965, *Shenandoah* did even better, placing sixth among the top-grossing films of that year, Stewart's biggest moneymaker since *Rear Window,* more than a decade earlier.

— • —

Although Lyndon Johnson had won the presidency in the fall of 1964 by one of the largest landslides in electoral history, Jimmy's campaigning for Goldwater had invigorated his political spirits. It also once again widened the personal distance between him and Henry Fonda, who, according to Jimmy's daughter, Kelly, was, through the years, "my father's only real close friend." What had further complicated matters between them was that Fonda's daughter, Jane, and son, Peter, had publicly come out against the growing conflict in Vietnam, which did not sit well at all with Jimmy. As far as he was concerned, the war was 100 percent justified, and anyone who thought otherwise was un-American. He told one reporter, in an uncharacteristic burst of public anger, in response to a question about draft-dodgers that seemed to be aimed directly at his Fonda godchildren, "I hate them! I absolutely hate them! Whether right or wrong, their country was at war and their country asked them to serve and they refused and ran away. Cowards, that's what they were."

As in virtually every home across America, TV had brought Vietnam into the living rooms of the Stewarts, where it became the nightly subject over dinner, and in this instance split the family into two factions as wide as the Mekong Delta. Each of Jimmy's two stepsons had his own opinion, one far different from the other's. Michael, the younger of the two, who, like all four of Jimmy's children, had expressed little or no interest in a show-business career, had set his sights on a major in political science. Soon his hair had grown long and he was openly student-protesting against the war, taking part in demonstrations that outraged his father.

Michael's stepsister, Kelly, although not really political, was sympathetic with Michael's commitment to his cause. "Michael and I were products of the times," Kelly recalled later. "The youth movement was taking hold, the war didn't seem to make much sense, and Michael and I didn't feel as if we had to pretend it did. My sister and I were still in high school, and we couldn't understand why anyone would want to go over to Vietnam voluntarily, to fight."

Generational and political walls went up between Michael and Jimmy, with stony dinner-hour silences, broken by ever-increasing outbursts from one or the other. The situation then completely unraveled when one day Michael came home from school and announced that he had declared himself a conscientious objector, which Jimmy took as tantamount to draft-dodging.

Ronald, on the other hand, could not have been more a model Maitland-Stewart if he had been born into the line. While away attending Colorado State, he decided that, in two years, immediately following his graduation, he would join the marines. During family dinners, the arguments that followed between the father and Michael intensified, and Michael and Ronald and Kelly and their father often ended the evening having shouted themselves hoarse, filled with angry emotions. Gloria, for the most part, tried to stay out of these politically heated battles.

What made Michael even angrier was his father's unwavering support of Ronald Reagan. The once-liberal head of the Screen Actors Guild had since moved considerably to the right. He had become an outspoken critic of the burgeoning student-based Free Speech Movement at the University of California at Berkeley, and was about to use that as a campaign platform for his 1966 run for the governorship of California, against incumbent Pat Brown, whom Reagan pointed the finger of blame at for all of Berkeley's troubles. It was this two-term residency at the State House that would lead, after a failed attempt in 1976, to Reagan's election in 1980 as president of the United States.

In the years before he became governor, Reagan loved to host fund-raising dinner parties with his wife, Nancy, at Chasen's, where Jimmy and Gloria were their most frequent guests, and it was at one of those occasions in the winter of 1966 that Reagan asked for and got Jimmy's support for a fall gubernatorial run. Jimmy enthusiastically agreed to do whatever he could for the cause.

Together, Reagan and Stewart made numerous public and private fund-raising appearances that helped finance the upcoming campaign. Jimmy enjoyed the endless receptions and always helped draw a big crowd, but consistently turned down offers from Reagan's campaign to accept any official post, and later on, after Reagan became president, to run for governor himself. He just wanted to help out his pal, he told any and all comers, and refused any type of payback, ceremonial or substantial, for his efforts.

Instead, after Reagan's election, he wanted to go back to making more movies and signed on to do another one for Andrew V. McGlaglen, *The Rare Breed*, opposite his *Hobbs* co-star Maureen O'Hara. Production went smoothly, almost mechanically, and once the film was in the can, Jimmy went into production on *Flight of the Phoenix* for director Robert Aldrich, a plane-crash-in-the-desert drama that Aldrich adapted from a novel he had optioned by British author Elleston Trevor. As it happened,

Gloria had read it at about the same time, and, independent of Aldrich, had suggested to Jimmy that he would be perfect in the role of the aging, grizzled pilot/hero of the story, Frank Townes. When Aldrich made his offer, Jimmy jumped at it.

The film had an outstanding supporting cast that included Richard Attenborough, Hardy Kruger, Peter Finch, Ernest Borgnine, Dan Duryea, and George Kennedy. The rough edge of Aldrich's heavy touch actually helped make the film an even more biting saga. Shot on location in Yuma, Arizona, it echoed, however faintly, the desert atmospherics of David Lean's *Lawrence of Arabia* (1962) and would go on to inspire such large-scale all-star miracle rescue fare as Ronald Neame's *The Poseidon Adventure* (1972).

During the unusually long and difficult production, according to his daughter Kelly, Jimmy went to extraordinary lengths to make sure he spent sufficient time with the family. "We had never all actually gone on a full safari together, with everyone there at the same time for the whole time. Mother had decided to take the kids and join some friends in Africa. When Father heard about this, he really wanted to join us, to be with the whole family together on a vacation no matter how brief, so he checked his schedule and found that he had just enough of a break during filming to board a plane, fly to Africa, spend one day with us, then return and head immediately to the set to resume filming."

On July 27, over the objections of director Aldrich and Fox head Richard Zanuck, Stewart simply walked off the set, leaving word that he would be back in a week, and that they should shoot around him until then. Late in the evening of August 2, just as he had promised, an exhausted Jimmy Stewart returned to his Holiday Inn suite in Yuma, and the next morning showed up on-set to resume working on the picture. There were no further interruptions until the film was finished, and also no further mention by anyone of the "furlough" taken by its star.

Flight of the Phoenix held its "world premiere" in December 1965 in order to qualify for the Oscars (thereby opening ahead of *The Rare Breed*), and began its regular domestic theatrical run on January 20, 1966, to indifferent-to-negative reviews and so-so box office, due at least in part to its total lack of younger stars or women to make the all-male plot more compelling (the only female character in the film is glimpsed in a brief mirage sequence, starring a young and unknown

Barrie Chase, a dancer mostly remembered for her TV work on Fred Astaire's specials). The film wound up placing a respectable forty-fifth among the highest-grossing movies of the year—not great, not awful; like the film itself, run of the mill.

— • —

As 1966 kicked in, Jimmy and Gloria took a long vacation during which they delivered their twin daughters to schools in Switzerland for their junior high school years abroad. Ronnie, meanwhile, had elected to go to Orme, a military prep school north of Prescott, Arizona, in anticipation of becoming an officer with the marines, while Michael chose Mercersberg, the same school his dad had attended as a youngster.

Shortly after the Stewarts' return to Los Angeles, Jimmy put in his annual Reserve stint with the air force; otherwise he and Gloria kept mostly to themselves, except to attend the occasional black-tie affair, such as the star-studded twenty-fifth anniversary celebration for Rosalind Russell and Freddie Brisson thrown by Frank Sinatra at the Sands Hotel in Las Vegas. The couple had first met via Cary Grant when Brisson had stayed at Grant's beach house in the late forties, after Grant's live-in partner, Randolph Scott, had moved out. The Brisson marriage was, besides Jimmy and Gloria's, one of the few Hollywood domestic success stories; to share in the festivities, a virtual Who's Who of Hollywood upper echelon of glitterati turned out. Even Grant, who lately had become increasingly uncomfortable being photographed in public with his new, much younger bride, the actress Dyan Cannon, nevertheless showed up in full-smile regalia, along with the Dean Martins, the Kirk Douglasses, the Mike Romanoffs, the Vincente Minnellis, Roddy McDowall, radio and film producer William Frye, book publisher and TV game show personality Bennett Cerf and his wife, Claudette Colbert, Pat Kennedy Lawford, the Alan Jay Lerners, the Leland Haywards (he had remarried), and the Josh Logans.[4]

---

4. Hayward was married four times. After Lola Gibbs, whom he divorced in 1922, and Margaret Sullavan, whom he divorced in 1947, he married Slim Hawks in 1949. They were divorced in 1960. His fourth and final wife was Pamela Harriman, whom he married in 1971 and stayed with for the rest of his life.

— • —

Early in 1967, Jimmy began work on a new picture at Warner Bros., *Firecreek,* for director Vincent McEveety, whose previous experience was limited to directing one TV movie for Disney, *Adventures of Hector, The Stowaway Pig,* one-hour episodes of television's neoclassic Western TV drama *Gunsmoke,* the neonoir series *The Fugitive,* and the popish spy satire *The Man from U.N.C.L.E.* Jimmy had originally assumed McLaglen would helm, but McLaglen had taken on an assignment instead to direct Kirk Douglas, Richard Widmark, and Robert Mitchum in *The Way West. Firecreek* was originally conceived as a feature-length film for TV, using most of the crew and talent from *Gunsmoke,* until its escalating budget dictated it had to go into theaters or be shelved.

Despite McEveety's uncertain film credits and the production's origination as a TV film, Jimmy was enthusiastic about it, mainly because Henry Fonda had agreed to co-star, and Jimmy was eager to bury their political differences. Eighteen years and complicated politics had kept them from doing screen time together since King Vidor's *On Our Merry Way.*[5] In the interim, everything in their lives had flowed along opposite shores, up to and including their opinions on the Vietnam War.

In the film, Jimmy and Fonda were cast as dire enemies, with Fonda in the role of an intellectual but deadly gunslinger, his familiar redemptive darkness swathed in a dark nobility. Jimmy, on the other hand, plays the town's part-time family-man sheriff, who is called upon to defend the townfolk from a band of outlaws (the land in question, the Missouri range, was more or less the same setting for the same plot—landowners vs. cattlemen—that framed George Stevens's *Shane* a decade earlier and that would again two decades later in Michael Cimino's *Heaven's Gate*). *Firecreek* also borrows liberally from *High Noon,* with a gunfight at the end between the surviving good guy, Stewart, and the surviving bad guy, Fonda, in which Fonda is about to kill Stewart until his granddaughter, played by the lovely Inger Stevens, shoots Fonda in the back, Grace Kelly style in *High Noon.*

---

5. Although they were both in the movie, Stewart and Fonda had no scenes together in *How the West Was Won.*

Filmed in Arizona in December, many of those who were on-set remember Jimmys' and Fonda's close relationship, how they would go off
together talking low so that only the other could hear, laughing at things
only they knew were funny, and then going their separate ways, Fonda to
play cards with the other "villains" of the film, Jack Elam and James Best,
while Jimmy would keep mostly to himself, working on his character,
thinking him through, and practicing hand gestures and faces that
would match his dialogue.

The film, Jimmy's seventy-first, opened on February 21, 1967, in
New York City; critics immediately saw the similarities between it and
High Noon, something that did not work in *Firecreek's* favor. Having
been tossed off by Warner, prior to its release, as part of a deal with its
new distributor, Seven Arts, the film never had much of a chance and
quickly disappeared (and because of the financial difficulties Seven
Arts eventually ran into, their catalog, including *Firecreek,* has had very
little subsequent TV play and remains largely unseen).[6]

Firecreek was followed by a long layoff of Jimmy from films. The hard
truth was that fewer producers and directors were willing to go with an
actor young people knew only as an old man, whose skin was weathered,
who wore toupees as obvious as top hats, whose eyes constantly watered
and whose hearing was permanently impaired (due, it was said, to the
plunge he had taken into the icy waters to save Clarence in *It's a Wonderful
Life.* That dive began the start of a long, slow descent into near-deafness in
one ear, not at all helped by his extensive flying for the air force).

Moreover, the screen was being taken over by the next wave of
independent-minded actors, producers, and directors all young enough
to be his children. Or grandchildren. While he was laboring as an aging
sheriff, actors such as Warren Beatty were creating a new kind of shoot-
out film (Arthur Penn's *Bonnie and Clyde,* 1967) younger audiences
would flock to. That same year, Dustin Hoffman in Mike Nichols's *The
Graduate* (also 1967) helped radically shift the notion of what a Hollywood leading man could be, from Jimmy Stewart/Henry Fonda/Gary
Cooper/Cary Grant—tall, handsome, and all-American (in spirit if not
birth)—to big-nosed, short, ethnic, immigrant-rooted neurotic "anti-

---

6. During production on the film, Jimmy received word that his childhood friend magician William Neff had died in his sleep early in February. He dedicated his work on
Firecreek to Neff's memory.

heroes," all of which set the stage, as it were, for 1969's epochal *Easy Rider,* directed by co-star Dennis Hopper, and produced by Henry Fonda's son, Peter. The film turned perennial "B" actor Jack Nicholson, the king of the celluloid neurotics, into an instant mainstream sensation, and established Peter, playing Captain America, a dope-smoking, free-loving hippie with a heart (and a Harley), as a big-screen Hollywood movie star.

As for Fonda Sr., he, too, felt the consequences from *Firecreek's* failure, blaming himself for believing he could get away playing a murderer against someone as beloved by his fans as Jimmy Stewart. "Jim and I played in a thing called *Firecreek,"* he later recalled in his memoirs, "You know, someone had the bright idea of making me the villain. I played a bad guy who tried to kill Jim Stewart. Now, any man who tries to kill Jim Stewart *has* to be marked as a man who's plain rotten. You can't get much worse than that."

— • —

In June of 1967, upon his completion of studies at Orme, Ronnie McLean Stewart was formally inducted into the United States Marine Corps as a second lieutenant, his bars personally pinned to his uniform at the colorful ceremonies by his father, Brigadier General James Stewart. It was an exceedingly proud moment for Jimmy. As he stood in the gleaming sunlight, he shook Ronnie's hand, pulled him in close, wished him well, and promised that he would come visit him first chance he got, no matter where in the world he wound up being stationed.

That no-matter-where turned out to be Vietnam.

Jimmy had begun to make annual visits to the troubled Asian country in his official capacity of brigadier general. In 1966, the year before he was scheduled to retire from the Air Force Reserve, he had volunteered to lead a B-52 bombing raid out of Guam over North Vietnam, after which he visited every American air base in South Vietnam and Thailand. Having promised Gloria he would see no further action, he went on an inspection tour for the Office of Information for the Pentagon, a "handshake" operation as they were known, during which he met with as many individual soldiers as possible.

Upon his return, he was given an unexpected honor. With mandatory retirement upon him, the Senate, where so much controversy had once swirled about his promotion to brigadier general, now chose to honor him, first with a spoken tribute by former Hollywood song-and-dance man Sen. George Murphy (R-California) for his "matchless record he has compiled of service to our nation and to the motion picture industry. . . . His face and his voice have become known to people in every country of the world and he has, through his profession, become one of the best international ambassadors of goodwill we could present abroad." In his speech, Murphy made note of the fact that Jimmy was only the second Air Force Reserve officer in history to be rewarded the Distinguished Flying Cross. Then, on June 25, 1968, Jimmy Stewart was written into history on the pages of the Congressional Record, which headlined his retirement and honored him with an editorial, excerpts of which included the following:

RETIREMENT OF BRIGADIER GENERAL JAMES STEWART FROM U.S. AIR FORCE RESERVE

On May 31, 1968, James Stewart formally retired as a brigadier general in the U.S. Air Force Reserve . . . As one who has long considered Jimmy Stewart his friend, I am proud of the matchless record he has compiled of service to our Nation and to the motion picture industry. I congratulate our good friend and there being no objection, the [following] Citation [is ordered to be printed in the] Record as follows:

Brigadier General James M. Stewart distinguished himself by exceptionally meritorious service to the United States in his mobilization assignment as Deputy Director, Office of Information, Office of the Secretary of the Air Force from 17 June 1959 to 31 May 1968. During this period General Stewart selflessly devoted his time, knowledge and broad experience in a concerted effort to publicize the Air Force contribution to our nation's security. As a result of his personal efforts he has brought about a greater awareness, throughout the nation, of the significant contributions Air Force personnel have made toward our country's defense. His sincerity, dedication and ability to communicate to people young and old, were significantly responsible for the general public's appreciation of the Air Force role in safeguarding freedom throughout the world. . . .

Jimmy was humbled to tears when he received this honor, but for the rest of his life made little mention of it, once again insisting that his military record not be used to promote any of his past or future movies.

As if to underscore the fact that he had not retired from his other career, show business, he booked a personal appearance on Dean Martin's surprisingly successful NBC variety TV show, taped in the summer of '67 and shown as the first episode of the '67–68 season. He did impersonations of James Cagney and Bette Davis that sounded nothing like the celebrities and everything like Jimmy Stewart.

Martin greatly enjoyed having Jimmy on his show, and Jimmy loved doing it so much that they decided to make a film together, Andrew McLaglen's *Bandolero!* It was Jimmy's third and Martin's first with McLaglen. In it, Martin, nine years younger than Jimmy in real life, played his younger brother in the movie. The fact that Raquel Welch was in the film had a lot to do with Martin and Jimmy having more fun off-set than on it, as the three went out drinking almost every night. However, despite a screenplay by James Lee Barrett, who had written the far superior *Shenandoah*, *Bandolero!* creaked where it should have snapped, and in June 1968 the film opened to near-instant obscurity.

Not long after *Bandolero!* wrapped, Jimmy and Gloria decided to spend Christmas in Kenya. Upon their return to Los Angeles, Jimmy, both rested and restless, started looking for new projects to keep him busy. One of the things they both loved to do was go to see the Dodgers, Gloria's favorite team. Jimmy rooted for the Yankees, but it made no difference; they liked going to Dodger Stadium at Chavez Ravine and drinking beer while sitting in the special seats kept for Hollywood royalty. They often ran into Cary Grant there, another intense baseball fan who spent many afternoons watching games in the warm sun with his wife, Dyan Cannon, and their baby daughter, Jennie.

About this time, Jimmy also agreed to join the American Red Cross as a fund-raiser, signing on to narrate a TV documentary, after which he was notified that he was to be honored by the British Film Institute, an award that meant a great deal to him because of the time he had spent in London during the war.

As 1968 turned into 1969, with no new feature film looming on the horizon, Jimmy signed on with the USO for a winter tour of Vietnam. This time he took Gloria along to accompany him for another round of handshakes with the troops. He later claimed to have shaken more than twelve thousand soldiers' hands during the trip. At one point, he broke away from the other entertainers, and Gloria, to visit the war zone and, although he had promised his wife he wouldn't, he unofficially accompanied a bombing crew on a mission along the Cambodian border.

The real reason he had taken Gloria along at all was that the air force had assured him that a visit with Ronald would be arranged, despite the fact that he was currently stationed closer to the DMZ—the demilitarized zone that officially separated North Vietnam from South Vietnam—than the military normally allowed any entertainers to get. Ronald, a member of the 73rd Reconnaissance Battalion of the 3rd Marine Division, was stationed at Dong Ha, 10 miles south of the DMZ, 406 miles north of Saigon. When his parents arrived, a surprised and delighted Ronald greeted them and barely had enough time to pose for a photo with his mom, before, all too soon, she and Jimmy were whisked back to safety.

Upon their arrival back in the States, a beaming Jimmy gave a press conference in which he lauded the outstanding valor and commitment of the servicemen and -women he had recently met. After settling back onto Roxbury, they began making final preparations for the upcoming marriage of their other son, Michael. Tension still rippled through the relationship between this son and his father, but Jimmy had promised Gloria to try to effect some kind of truce.

In mid-June, Kelly and Judy were both preparing for their graduation prom at Westlake High; Michael was already in Arkansas, where the bride's family was from; and Gloria and Jimmy were alone in the house on North Roxbury Drive when the knock came at the front door. They were both in the living room and glanced quickly at each other. No one ever knocked on their door without prior notice. Jimmy said nothing, went, and opened it. There before him stood a contingency of dress marines, and he knew. Gloria came up beside him and listened quietly as the spokesman for the organization recited the official notice. He began with the awful words "We regret to inform you . . ."

Ronald had been killed the day before by hostile machine-gun fire during an encounter with the enemy in Quang Tri province, along the DMZ. He and five other marines had been lured into an ambush by the North Vietnamese, even as half a dozen U.S. helicopters engaged the enemy in an attempt to save the men. They managed to get out all but Ronald.

He was twenty-four years old.

26

"People ask if we're bitter about having [the war] hit so close to home. Neither my wife nor I have any bitterness. We've gotten hundreds and hundreds of letters about it, but there was no bitterness in any of them. I don't think [Ronald] died in vain. I believe in the cause that he died for. The war has been a trial, and a tremendously difficult thing for the nation. But if there is a tragedy about it, it is the national tragedy that there has been so much sacrifice without a unified nation behind the cause. These are patriotic kids, patriotic Americans. All you have to do is go to Vietnam to see that the kids are still patriotic today. Everybody says that the war wasn't even declared. Well, I don't think wars *will* be declared anymore. It's like the old duel thing, where a man hits another in the face with a glove and says, 'Have your second ready in the bushes.' It's just a different world today. . . .

"There's our son, he wanted to be a marine. He was a good marine. I think of him all the time. It was a terrible loss, but I don't see it as a tragedy. He went to college for us. He wasn't a very good student. He said he didn't want to be drafted, he wanted to be a marine. He became a good marine. He conducted himself honorably on the field of battle. You can't consider that tragedy. . . .

"But losing a boy like that, you never get over it." —JIMMY STEWART

T he death of his stepson had brought the war home, but Jimmy was determined not to allow himself or Gloria to surrender to grief. Instead, they continued to prepare for Michael's wedding and insisted it take place as scheduled, three weeks hence, and they also planned on attending the girls' high school graduations as proud parents to cheer them, even as Jimmy quietly and methodically made arrangements to have Ronald's body returned to the States and prepared for burial.

Nor did the tragedy of Ronald's untimely passing immediately change Jimmy's politics. If it did anything at all, it pushed him even further to the right. To the public, he insisted that his son died a patriot, and for a good and just cause, and that he gave his life for his country and for freedom.

As his daughter Kelly remembered in a sad and poignant way, the loss of Ronald would serve to bring an end to the growing distance between Michael and Jimmy. This was, after all, at the core a close-knit, loving family, brought together by tragedy, in the kind of tight-lipped, stoic fashion that was the foundation of Jimmy's Presbyterian upbringing.

It was a shared grief that each member suffered from in his or her own way. "For me," Kelly said, "unlike Father, who was firmly set in his political ways, I was still developing my value systems, and the initial impact of Ronald's death was to turn me fully into the nihilist I was already leaning toward becoming. What's the point of believing in anything, I kept telling myself. Mom, too, had a change of her thinking, though not as severely as what I was going through. She became less political, and stopped believing in 'beliefs.' It took longer for Dad, but I think he did, too."

One thing Jimmy kept insisting, to friends and family alike, and to himself really, was that Ronald had not died in vain. However, if there were any cracks in the emotional armor that went up at the Stewart household, it was in the disappointment Jimmy felt from anyone who tried and failed to ease his way through this difficult time. The Beverly Hills Presbyterian Church, for instance, completely messed up the funeral ceremony. They were unable to unlock the massive organ, thus causing the services to take place without musical accompaniment. While never a regular churchgoer (Gloria was the one who directed that part of their Sundays, and also the one who stopped going to church for good after the funeral), his grief and anger lingered on this one incident for months, until he began attending services alone at the First Presbyterian Church of Hollywood instead.

Not long after, the marines sent a representative to the Stewart home who said he was there at the urging of the Nixon administration, which wanted to publicize Ronald's death, with all of Jimmy's conservative (pro-war) friends rallying to the cause, the entire horse-and-martyr show captured on film and distributed free throughout the media. In one of his very few displays of open anger, without saying a word Jimmy took the marine firmly by his elbow and threw him out of the house.

Next came the producers, the movie and TV big shots, all of whom wanted to make a feature motion picture about the life (really the death) of Ronald. Jimmy turned them all down, and threatened to sue anyone who tried to do it without the family's consent.

Tears, never something that flowed easily in the Stewart household, came nightly to Gloria who, it was reported by friends, cried herself to sleep for months after the death of her son. Jimmy as well could hardly keep his composure, breaking out in tears at the most unexpected (and sometimes expected) times and places, particularly in whatever dressing room he might be in when preparing to shoot a scene or make an appearance. Anything with the slightest references to sons, war, violence, or loss could set him off. He took to isolating himself, and kept out of the eye of the public more than usual. He spent numberless hours watching television, often with tears running silently down his cheeks. He moped around the house and began acting out the anger that lay atop his grief by bickering with Gloria. When he did go out, it was mostly to play a foursome of golf with Fred MacMurray, Bob Hope, and President Nixon. And his drinking increased dramatically.

It was, finally, Henry Fonda, who, when he got word of the depth and severity of Jimmy's depression, urged him to resume working on the film they had started before Ronald's death, *The Cheyenne Social Club*, which had temporarily shut down production when word of the tragedy arrived.

The film, an unrepentantly antique Western, was meant to provide a showcase for the friendship as well as the comic talents of its two stars. A couple of old cowboy coots think they're inheriting a ranch but actually gain possession of a whorehouse, Hollywood style, of course, where the women are all young and beautiful, wear expensive frilly white corsets and tons of lingerie, are intelligent, helpful, and having the time of their lives—and never seem to actually have sex with anyone. The madam was played by squeaky-clean Shirley Jones.

The film had been originally given the go-ahead by Jimmy himself, intending it to be directed by McLaglen. When he proved unavailable, Gene Kelly signed on as both producer and director. The aging Kelly had lately begun to appear in nondancing roles and to direct several movies, many of which he had starred in. He was eager to disappear from the screen altogether as a way of extending his timeless cinematic presence. A tongue-and-cheek look at a bygone era by a couple of Hollywood gray-hairs seemed to him to be the perfect vehicle. Production had just begun when word of Ronald's death hit the set, and production had temporarily shut down, with no guarantee when or if it would resume.

"The picture was rolling along fine," Fonda recalled, "when Jim and his wife, Gloria, suffered the worst kind of loss when their elder son was killed in action with the marines in Vietnam. Here we were, making this comedy, when the Defense Department notified them. Jim tried hard not to spread his grief through the company. He and I avoided discussing the war before the tragedy. Now, I did everything I could to take his mind off it. We chawed about old times at the Madison Square Hotel in New York, and our early bachelor days living together in Brentwood."

When production did finally resume, Fonda noticed that "Stewart would slip away each day with an apple or a piece of watermelon or a carrot in his hand. And I learned that he'd walk two or three blocks to the corral where the horses were kept. And he'd give a goodie to [Stewart's regular film horse] Pie. That's when I began to realize what Pie meant to him. His boy was gone, and I couldn't do anything about that, but now seeing the expression on Jim's face when he reached for something to take to his horse—I had an idea. On Sundays, when we weren't working, I'd have the wrangler bring Pie out and stand him in front of the barn. And then I made sketches of the horse, the barn, a carriage, and the gate. I planned it to be a surprise for Jim. I finished the watercolor after I got home. I had it framed and gave it to Jim. He was surprised all right. He just dissolved when he saw the painting . . . old Pie died about ten days later."

Jimmy's recollection of the making of the film focused on the laconic preparation, indicating how little either he or Fonda was actually interested in the content of the project. "I'd say to Fonda, 'Do yuh, do yuh want to go over this scene?' He'd say, 'No, no . . . uh, if you want?'

"I'd say, 'No, no . . .'

" 'Don't you know your lines?'

" 'Yes! I know my lines!'

" 'Well, uh, what, uh, uh, what are we rehearsing for?' "

— • —

The Cheyenne Social Club finished production late in the fall of 1969, and Jimmy decided to take Gloria and the two girls to Sun Valley, Idaho, for the Christmas holidays. The family, Jimmy realized, was slowly dissipating: Ronald was gone, Michael was married, the girls were off to college. He wanted one last time together with them. The only diversion he allowed himself on the trip was a rereading of *Harvey*, the play he had done on Broadway twenty-two years earlier and had made into a movie. Jimmy was considering once again playing the role of Elwood P. Dowd. Slipping backward in general held appeal to him, just as working and hanging out with Fonda on the set of *The Cheyenne Social Club* had allowed the both of them to cinematically time-travel to a simpler, happier time in their lives. A healthy dose of theatrical un-reality obtained by cozying up to the private world of a giant rabbit no-body else could see convinced Jimmy to seriously consider reviving the play for another Broadway run.

However, if he had been looking for redemption in the comfort of the happier past, he hadn't counted on what still lay before him, noth-ing less than full-scale resurrection, coming, of all places, from the mythic village of Bedford Falls, and not at all in the guise of Elwood P. Dowd, but old (young) George Bailey.

— • —

By the late sixties, the studio system, as Jimmy knew it, was on a one-way journey to oblivion. From its inception in the earliest years of the twentieth century, the movie business had been based on the no-tion of mass production, mass consumption, and mass disposability. Like automobiles, the thinking among the moguls was that films had limited values and that the American family had to be trained to buy one car every two years, two films once a week), and that when a film (or car) had run its course, it was ready for the junkyard. Old cars? There was no money in that for the likes of Ford. Old movies? Holly-wood couldn't care less about them. This is why the studios allowed the negatives of so many of the early silent films (and a considerable num-ber of sound ones as well) to literally disintegrate in their cans. Before satellite TV, before cable, before home video, before college courses in film, before television itself, very few films had any kind of shelf life.

The occasional "classic," such as *Gone With the Wind,* might be the-atrically revived every five or ten years, but that was the notable excep-tion. For the most part, films that had had their first run were considered by the industry to be as worthless and disposable as yester-day's newspaper.

When commercial television came into the homes it redefined the idea of entertainment for the American family. Although old films were a substantial part of the first generation of electronic offerings, by the mid-fifties, the great majority of network television was original pro-gramming that featured, for the most part, names that had never quite made it to the top in Hollywood and were on the downslide of their ca-reers—Lucille Ball, Sid Caesar, Milton Berle, Jackie Gleason—and whose childish brand of humor would hold a great appeal to a new, younger market.

Then, in the late sixties, a wondrous thing happened. After several TV networks began showing recent films as prime-time programming events—the NBC Film of the Week—it slowly dawned on the net-works that there might, indeed, be life in recycled movies after all. The unions quickly made deals with the studios to cover royalties for the ac-tors, directors, and other talent who had made the original films. At this point, smaller, independent stations, such as Channel 5 in New York City, searched for older films that had gone into the public domain, films that for one reason or another did not require royalty payments. In other words, free programming.

One such film Channel 5 discovered in the dust bin of discards was Frank Capra's *It's a Wonderful Life,* the film Capra had lost ownership of when Liberty Pictures had gone under. Most of Liberty's assets had gone to Paramount Pictures to repay distribution guarantees. Para-mount, however, had no interest in the negatives of the films it inher-ited and stored them away, not caring if or when the nitrate content turned the pictures, including *It's a Wonderful Life,* into dust.[1]

When Channel 5 went looking for films in the public domain that had a Christmas theme to compete with the big-name "specials" the networks were running, someone came across *It's a Wonderful Life.* A few days before Christmas 1969, the local station screened the badly

---

1. *It's a Wonderful Life* was later restored to near perfection by the American Film In-stitute.

scratched and faded film late on a Saturday night. To the station's amazement, a buzz quickly developed about this oddly dark "Christmas" comedy from "way back" in the forties, and Channel 5 began making plans for the following season to start to run the film as early as Thanksgiving, and keep it in frequent rotation through New Year's Eve.

The TV success of *It's a Wonderful Life* in New York City quickly spread to other independent stations all over the country, and by the time Frank Capra's memoirs were published, in 1970, both he and his book were in great demand. *The Name Above the Title* jumped onto the best-seller lists, Capra became a frequent guest on TV talk shows, and he developed a lucrative lecture-circuit career, primarily aimed at college campuses just beginning to introduce film studies into their curricula.[2] Donna Reed, who had made her career as an ingénue/leading lady in the late forties and early fifties, and who had become a TV mother in the late fifties with a sitcom that ran for eight seasons with her as a soothing, middle-aged mom, found a new audience for her talents, and went on to do a number of one-hour television dramas, thereby extending her career well into the seventies.

However, no one's career, or life, was changed more by the film's resurrection than Jimmy Stewart's. To the fabled baby boomers born either the year of or after the film was made, Jimmy became the everyman hero who takes on the establishment, who is for the "little people" and therefore an instant cultural hero. There he was again, courting Donna Reed, fighting old man Potter, raising his kids, taking the plunge off the bridge, the fight in the bar, Clarence, Zuzu's petals, all of it. College students in particular loved the film and watched it during the Christmas season religiously. Even general viewing audiences began to ritualize it, allowing *It's a Wonderful Life* to join a select handful of aging theatrical films that found an annual Christmas season television audience, including the 1951 Brian Desmond Hurst version of *A Christmas Carol* starring Alastair Sim, Judy Garland's magical turn as Dorothy in Victor Fleming's 1939 *The Wizard of Oz*, and Leo McCarey's 1944 *Going My Way* with Bing Crosby as Father O'Malley.

---

2. *The Name Above the Title* was originally sold by the William Morris Agency from a proposal Capra had written in 1968 to Macmillan, just before the film's TV renaissance, for the unprincely sum of $3,000.

By the time Jimmy had decided to slip back into the staged unreality of *Harvey*, the audience waiting to see him had grown to film-cult proportion. After a brief but successful tryout in Ann Arbor, co-starring Broadway legend Helen Hayes and supporting character actor Jesse White, the play opened on February 24, 1970, at the ANTA Theater on West Fifty-second Street, and caused a near riot. Thousands of fans who had not been able to get tickets turned out to try to catch a glimpse of their hero as he entered the stage door.

No one was more surprised by all of the excitement surrounding his return to Broadway than Jimmy, who had taken on the limited eight-week run as a way of being able to bow out gracefully if the show didn't sell any tickets.

He needn't have worried. Critics fell over themselves raving about his performance, and there wasn't an empty seat the entire eight weeks.

Still, prior to opening, he could not shake a bad case of the nerves returning to the live stage, even in a role he had played so many times before. Broadway audiences could be tough and cruel, and he was feeling particularly vulnerable those days. "I'm nervous," he told Judy Klemesrud of the *New York Times,* "When you haven't been onstage in twenty years, it's a pretty hard thing to get back into. Especially the voice projection. But my wife, Gloria, and I kind of welcomed the change. We found ourselves sitting around Beverly Hills having conversations with our two dogs. Hollywood is a little quiet and depressing right now. It's another one of our disaster times." He didn't have to elaborate, and Klemesrud kindly didn't press the issue. The cloud of grief that hung heavily over him was obvious.

The day after it opened *New York Times*'s chief drama critic, Clive Barnes, gave *Harvey,* and Jimmy's performance in it, the newspaper of record's official anointment of greatness when he declared: "Stewart's garrulous, genial presence is a delight. You feel that apart from Harvey himself, there is no one that you would rather encounter in your favorite neighborhood bar."

The *New York Daily News* called the production "marvelous," Jimmy's performance "a master class in acting."

The *New York Post* said Jimmy was "better than the late Frank Fay" in the role of Elwood.

Life magazine jocularly described Jimmy as "the perfect hippie hero, and with his hallucinatory rabbit he is taking the happiest trip on Broadway. Maybe, to draw a younger audience, the show should be called 'Hare.' "

Walter Kerr, in the *New York Times* Sunday Arts and Leisure section, wrote that "Mr. Stewart makes the play's last act astonishingly moving—was Frank Fay funnier? Who can honestly say now? He was nowhere near so touching."

And one local TV critic, John Bartholomew Tucker, compared the opportunity of seeing Jimmy in *Harvey* as akin to seeing Laurence Olivier in *Oedipus Rex* or "Yankee great Joe DiMaggio play center field."

Jimmy and Gloria had taken up residence on the thirty-fifth floor of the Waldorf Towers for the duration, where a color photograph of Ronald and his mother, taken by Jimmy when they briefly visited him in Dong Ha six months before the boy was killed, occupied center position on the suite's mantel.

They threw small post-theater cocktail parties almost every night, preferring a homey atmosphere, even if it was the luxe Waldorf, to going out on the town. In proper fashion of those who bow to show business royalty, everyone was willing to come up to their suite for drinks, talk, hors d'oeuvres, and good conversation. Everyone who came by when they first entered the suite always asked the same cute question: Where was Harvey?

At least part of the show's popularity could be traced to the revival of *It's a Wonderful Life,* once it became clear as many young people were coming to see the show as old ones, children who wanted their parents to take them to see Zuzu's father. Typical of the tykes who were taken by Mom and Dad backstage was one young man Stewart remembered this way: "A kid came with his dad, who said, 'Son, this is Elwood P. Dowd.' The kid said, 'I liked two things you said and I forget what they were,' but I said to myself, 'Thank the Lord for small favors. He could have said he didn't like anything!'"

— • —

Toward the end of the show's run, the Phoenix approached Jimmy about the possibility of extending the run at the ANTA a few more weeks, and he immediately agreed. He simply didn't want to stop playing Elwood. Another seven weeks was agreed upon, and again, the run sold out every seat. In a Broadway season that offered such new fare as *Sleuth*, which would go on to win the Tony for best drama; *Borstal Boy, Home, Child's Play, Conduct Unbecoming, Bob and Ray—The Two and Only*, and revivals of *Candide, Hay Fever, Othello*, and *Songs from Milk Wood, Harvey* remained among the year's top-grossing plays.

As May approached, the Phoenix once again sat down with Jimmy, this time to discuss the possibility of his staying with the show through the summer. After all, they told him, that was the time when most of the kids would be out of school and they could guarantee full houses. Besides, they were prepared to offer him a hefty raise to continue doing what he obviously loved so much.

To their surprise, but not Gloria's, Jimmy turned them down. He was feeling the grind of thirteen weeks, eight-shows-a-week on his aging body. He had had enough. His last performance, on May 2, 1970, was an emotional one. Gloria was in the front row, and dozens of his friends were in attendance as well. Everyone knew that this was most likely the last time Jimmy Stewart's presence would ever grace the Broadway stage, where so long ago he had begun his professional acting career. When the curtain fell, he came out alone for the final bow to a ten-minute standing ovation, as tears streamed down the surface of his pancaked face.

Jimmy and Gloria did not return directly to California. There was still the layer of grief that hung over their house the way smog did over L.A.—relentless, dense, and unhealthy. Instead, he booked a trip for them to one of their favorite retreats, the Aberdare mountains of Kenya, where Gloria could practice her photography. Both of them had, in fact, become fairly good at taking *National Geographic*–style photos. Gloria was by now so enamored of wildlife she had become a member of the board of directors of the Los Angeles Zoo (their daughter Kelly had found a focus for her "nihilism" by spending the summer on the south shore of Lake Rudolf in Northern Kenya, on a dig with Richard Leaky, the son of the famous anthropologist). Somewhere along the way, Jimmy, inspired by the grand vista of Africa's hills and mountains, began writing the singsong little verses that later on would become a talk-show staple whenever he appeared on them, particularly the Johnny Carson show, where Carson would love to hear Jimmy recite his non-sense poetry as if it were bubble-gum wrapper versions of the wit and wisdom of William Shakespeare.

— • —

They eventually arrived back at the North Roxbury house in June, just in time for Jimmy to turn down an offer to repeat his live portrayal of Elwood P. Dowd in Los Angeles. Helen Hayes had already agreed to be in it, but Jimmy still said no. What he really wanted to do was to make another movie, and signed on for what would be his fourth and final collaboration with Andrew McLaglen, *Fools' Parade,* an action adventure, shot on location in Moundsville, West Virginia.[3]

In it Jimmy plays Mattie Appleyard, a long-termer released from the penitentiary after serving his forty years for murder. He has a glass eye, a physical correlative to his lack of moral vision. Waiting for him is Anne Baxter, the madam of a local riverboat bordello, and assorted bad guys looking to corrupt what appears to be the nicest lifer who ever lived. He manages to kill a few more bad guys, goes to trial, is released, and sets off into the sunset on his merry one-eyed way.

The film was received indifferently, did little at the box office, and convinced Jimmy once and for all that his best filmmaking days were behind him. He was right; he would never again appear in a major motion picture with his name above the title. At the completion of the shoot, he accepted an offer to star in a half-hour TV series on NBC, slated for the 1971–72 fall season. His ratings on TV had always been high, from his earliest days on the tube with Reagan on *G.E. Theater,* to his many guest shots with Gloria on *Jack Benny* and his singing/accordion appearances on the enormously popular Dean Martin variety show.

The networks, sensing a real score, made Jimmy an offer he couldn't refuse, which turned him into what was then the highest-paid actor on TV.

Hal Kanter, a producer who had worked with Jimmy on *Dear Brigitte,* had known him since the war and had worked with virtually the cream of the movies-to-TV star set, including Dean Martin, Bing Crosby, and Elvis Presley. He had recently been at the forefront of integrating network family fare with such controversial shows as *Julia,* staring Diahann Carroll. After *Julia* proved a hit, NBC asked Kanter to develop a show for Jimmy Stewart, and he jumped at the chance. Jimmy

---

3. Retitled overseas as *Dynamite Man from Glory Jail.*

wanted to do a sitcom that stared Gloria as his wife, a cross between Jack Benny's show and *Ozzie and Harriet*. Kanter agreed, Gloria screen-tested, and she was all set to start rolling when the network turned her down, saying she wasn't a good enough actress to pull it off. Kanter then turned the casting of the part of Jimmy's wife into a major promotion for the upcoming series. "There hasn't been such a search since David O. Selznick hunted for Scarlett O'Hara's maid in 'Gone With The Wind,'" he announced to the press. "We've talked to every woman in this business over the age of 15 [itals added]. I've seen at least 50 actresses. Jimmy has read with 20 of them. We've screen-tested five and there are four more yet to be tested. Many of the actresses are well-known names. What surprised me is that some of them freeze up when they read with Jimmy. Especially the Broadway actresses. They are bowled over by his professionalism and I guess you could call it star power."

Jimmy smiled for the press but privately was infuriated that some hot shot at the network had decided that Gloria was not good enough to play Gloria on some silly TV show. The role eventually went to Julie Adams (Jimmy's co-star in *Bend of the River*). Adams, forty-four, was eighteen years Jimmy's junior, and it stretched the credibility of their relationship even further when they were supposed to have a grown son.[4]

The Jimmy Stewart Show (so named because, as Kanter put it, "the deep think boys at NBC gave a great deal of thought and research to the title and discovered the word 'show' is known to everyone") debuted September 19, and did not do well in the ratings. Jimmy looked old, tired, uncomfortable, and miscast. What's more, he had quickly discovered that he hated the grind of making what was, in effect, a short film every week. Early on, while still trying to make up his mind whether or not to go into television, he had talked it over with good friend Fred MacMurray, who told him it was the easiest thing he had ever done. And it was, for MacMurray. He had been doing it successfully for twelve years and had had it written into his contract that all his scenes for the complete season of his sitcom, *My Three Sons*, be shot together, with the rest of the cast doing the

---

4. As a consolation of sorts, Gloria actually appeared in the first episode as part of a flashback in which Jimmy Stewart's character, Jim Howard, played his grandfather, and Gloria played Grandmother Howard.

daily/weekly/monthly fill-ins. That allowed MacMurray to play golf for most of the year, while the show continued with his name and image effectively cut in when needed. Jimmy rejected that approach, preferring to shoot his show with the rest of the cast, something he had come to regret.

Not that it really mattered. The era of *Ozzie and Harriet* and the *Jack Benny Program* was coming to an end. On the horizon was a new crop of sitcoms; *The Mary Tyler Moore Show, Bob Newhart,* and *All in the Family* that would change forever the face of TV comedy, effectively warehousing the Lucys, the Gleasons, the Nelsons, the Bennys, the MacMurrays, and the Stewarts.

The Jimmy Stewart Show was canceled after one season and its star couldn't have been happier.

— • —

In 1972 at the age of sixty-four, Jimmy, along with Gene Autry, was inducted into the Hall of Fame of Great Motion Picture Performers at the National Cowboy Hall of Fame. The company was considerable: John Wayne's *The Cowboys,* directed by Mark Rydell, was voted the top Western film of the year, an episode of TV's *Gunsmoke* took the honors in that category, and John Ford received a special award for his contribution to Western heritage.

While Jimmy appreciated the honor, it made him a little uneasy. To him museums were like graveyards, he told one friend, and he wasn't quite ready to go there yet.

But death was hovering. A day after his induction, word reached him that his youngest sister, Virginia, had, after a brief illness, died in Hastings-on-Hudson. That news drove him back to *Harvey,* whose unreality had become his favorite escape from grief. He agreed to do it once more, this time as a TV film—once more calling upon Helen Hayes and Jesse White from the successful Broadway run, and adding John McGiver as the doctor and Madeline Kahn as the nurse (Kahn's appearance propelled her to stardom). But the one true constant for Jimmy, the one character that only he could cast because only he could see him, was Harvey the six-foot rabbit, who had, through the years, become part confessor, part shield, part comforter and all escape.

Harvey did well in the ratings, and Jimmy was soon offered another

TV series, this one more closely suited to his age, skills, and temperament. What also made it more feasible was the word in Hollywood that
Cary Grant, the elusive free agent was considering doing a TV series as
well, and that he was negotiating in the $35,000-per-show range. That
not only legitimized *any* screen actor going to the tube, but set a bar for
money that few would turn down.[5]

In November 1972, Jimmy put his signature on a contract with his
old studio, MGM, this time moving over to the TV division to star in
Hawkins on Murder, a made-for-TV movie. The character had already
become something of a TV staple thanks to Jimmy's original portrayal of
Paul Biegler in Otto Preminger's *Anatomy of a Murder,* a so-called backwoods attorney who outsmarts the big-city boys, and makes the audience love him for it. In true television style, he was now about to play a
derivation of his own original movie character.

The same week he inked the contract, Jimmy became a grandfather
for the first time. Michael and his wife, Barbara, were living in London
while Michael attended Oxford Law, and Barbara gave birth to a baby
boy they named Benjamin.[6]

Hawkins on Murder aired in March 1973 to surprisingly good reviews. Fred Silverman, the head of programming at CBS, a slightly
roundish, big man with a loping walk and slicked black hair, believed
that older audiences were the essential prime viewers of television, and
ordered seven ninety-minute episodes of *Hawkins* to rotate with the TV
version of *Shaft,* starring Richard Roundtree in the role he had originated in the movies. This time around, Jimmy had it written into his
contract that he would not work past six o'clock on any given day, no
matter how much the production needed him.

The end of the first season brought a Golden Globe Award for
Jimmy as Best Actor in a TV series. The network was ecstatic, and Silverman was planning an even more ambitious scope for the show the
second year. Jimmy took a meeting with him, listened to all he had to
say, including the considerable bump in salary, then politely turned him
down. There would be no second season, he told Silverman. Too much

---

5. Grant's series never materialized, as the actor ultimately decided he did not want
to compete with his younger movie image. Besides, he owned the negatives to most
of his movies, and did not want to compete financially with himself, either.

6. In 1973, Michael received his MA in jurisprudence.

hard work, he said, too little that was special about the medium, especially the lack of great directors. Instead, in April 1974, Jimmy made a
brief appearance in MGM's feature *That's Entertainment,* directed by
Jack Haley Jr., which highlighted the musical moments that had made
the studio a legend. Jimmy, appearing before a movie camera for the
first time in three years, introduced his version of "Easy to Love" from
Born to Dance as a bit of amusing trivia squeezed in between the great
sequences of Gene Kelly, Frank Sinatra, Fred Astaire, Debbie Reynolds,
Judy Garland, Eleanor Powell, Cyd Charisse, and many others.

Two months later, wanting to spend time with his new grandson, he
and Gloria traveled to London to appear yet again in *Harvey,* directed
this time by distinguished British actor Anthony Quayle. Equity rules
prevented Helen Hayes from repeating her role there, which went to the
London stage star Mona Washbourne. The run opened April 5, 1975,
the final performance underscored by six curtain calls for Jimmy, demanded by the tuxedoed, celebrity-studded audience.

For the run, Jimmy and Gloria moved into a small house on the out-
skirts of London, with room enough for their daughter Judy, who stayed
with them and never missed a single performance of the show.

As it happened, also appearing on the London stage was Henry
Fonda, reprising his successful one-man Broadway portrayal of Clarence Darrow. The cover of the September 1 issue of *People* magazine
featured them both on the front page, sitting on a park bench in
Grosvenor Square, Jimmy with his accordion on his shoulders, Fonda
with his long legs stretched out, together on the other side of their lives.

The two old friends did, indeed, go to the park often during the day;
they'd sit and speak little, Jimmy occasionally pulling apart the bellows
and softly playing a tune that came out sounding as thin as a whistle,
while Fonda sat wordless, slowly moving his feet back and forth in
rhythm. They hardly spoke a word to each other; they didn't have to.
There was nothing left between them that needed to be said.

27

"Jimmy loved to work. In 1975 he was asked to do a run of *Harvey* on the stage in London. It's about a nebbishy man who has an invisible six-foot rabbit for a friend. My producer friend Jim Wharton and I went over to see it, and Jimmy gave a magnificent performance. I'll never forget his curtain call. He came out, and took a bow, and the English audience gave him a standing ovation. Then he did something magical. He turned to the wings and said, 'Come on, Harvey, everyone wants to see you.' By his gestures, he brought Harvey to the middle of the stage and put his arm around him. Everybody in that theater would have sworn that he could actually see Harvey standing there with Jimmy. Then Jimmy stepped back and gave Harvey a solo bow, and the audience went wild."

—WILLIAM FRYE

*J*immy waited until the London run of the show closed before announcing his "semiretirement" from film. "I don't think I'll be making many more movies," he told a *People* magazine reporter upon his return to the United States. "I just don't fit in anymore." Having read a script he was offered, he said "Frankly, I don't even understand who the hell is doing what to whom—or why . . ."

With that, he settled back into the comfort and sanctity of North Roxbury Drive, aware that he had entered the final stretch and was moving headlong toward the finish line. The relatively quick succession of deaths—his mother, his father, his son, and his sister, had parted the clouds of life between him and the entrance to the gates of heaven. For the first time, he seemed resigned to take that last long walk into his own legend.

When the news that Leland Hayward had passed away that March, in 1971, at the age of sixty-eight, Jimmy dropped into an even deeper depression. Five months later, on August 31, during production of one of the occasional "special" episodes of *Hawkins,* word reached Jimmy on-set that John Ford had died. Not long after, Dave Chasen, the always gracious host of Jimmy's and Ronald Reagan's favorite restaurant, the ultimate Hollywoodian who had given Jimmy such a memorable bachelor party, met his maker. Then Bill Grady, the man who had been so crucial to Jimmy's early, formative film years at MGM, passed on. And then in December 1974, Jack Benny, Jimmy's good friend and neighbor, host of the TV show in which Jimmy appeared almost every Christmas with Gloria to replay what was essentially the same episode of them eating in a restaurant trying to avoid the company of the overbearing Benny and *his* wife.

At every one of their funerals, Jimmy was called upon to share his memories of the deceased, an obligation that became emotionally more difficult each time. It was why he had stressed to reporters, whenever asked, that he was only *semi*retired, believing that as long as he kept working, kept one hand in the game doing an occasional episode of *Hawkins,* he could prolong these last years as much as possible.

It did not mean, however, that he would do anything. As always, Jimmy maintained strict limits as to what he would allow himself to be in. When work did come his way, if he didn't think it was the right type of material, he'd turn it down, no matter how much he wanted to be back in front of a movie camera.

Such was the case when director Peter Bogdanovich and author Larry McMurtry, both of whom had hit it big with *The Last Picture Show* in 1971.[1] They wanted to return to the cinematic turf of melancholic Texas with something called *Streets of Laredo,* a late-nineteenth-century tale built around a group of aging rangers who travel the herd to Montana. Stewart read the script and rejected it, saying that it sounded like three old fogies, referring to the dream cast Bogdanovich had wanted—Jimmy, Fonda, and John Wayne.[2]

Jimmy still wanted to work with Wayne one more time, though, as a way to honor John Ford, and, after reading and rejecting dozens of

---

1. Bogdanovich directed the film and co-wrote it with McMurtry, based on his novel.

2. The screenplay eventually resurfaced as a highly regarded TV miniseries, *Lonesome Dove,* starring Robert Duvall in the Jimmy Stewart role, and Tommy Lee Jones in the one Bogdanovich had envisioned for Wayne.

scripts, found one both he and the Duke could agree on, *The Shootist*, to be directed by Don Siegel (1976). It was to be Wayne's last film, in which the character's death on-screen anticipated the actor's death off it. Wayne was in the late stages of terminal cancer and, in true (Hollywood) cowboy style, insisted on going out with his boots on. Jimmy played Wayne's doctor, who has the unenviable task of telling his character he's dying of cancer. At the end of the picture, when a climactic shoot-out has taken Wayne's life before the disease can finish him off, Stewart stands over the actor's bullet-riddled body and remembers the character. Less than three years later, in 1979, Jimmy would stand over the Duke's casket to remember the actor.

— • —

In the winter of 1976, the scales of life and death continued to balance. That February, Jimmy became a grandfather for the second time when his stepson Michael and his wife, Barbara, had another baby boy. The happy event occurred just after the completion of production on *The Shootist,* and when Jimmy had just begun to actively campaign for Ronald Reagan, then waging a furious campaign for the Republican nomination for president against the incumbent, the appointed but unelected Gerald Ford. Reagan, sensing he could beat Ford, even after he had pardoned Richard Nixon, a move that proved highly unpopular with the electorate, took Jimmy along to as many rallies as he could manage—seven key states in the Midwest, numerous one-stop airports, and enclosed lime green shopping malls with artificial flowers and fast-food courts, places where, Reagan knew, "his" people would turn out in large number to see not just him, but Jimmy as well.

In the speech Jimmy gave and never wavered from, he reassured audiences that despite all that had happened to him in his personal life, an oblique reference, perhaps, to the death of his son in Vietnam, "I'm more conservative now, if anything. I've always been a Republican conservative and promilitary, ever since I supported Eisenhower and Nixon."

Jimmy's campaigning persona was decidedly low-key, somebody resembling an older Jefferson Smith, as he'd tell the people that it was in their best interests to nominate and then elect Ronald Reagan.

Shortly after Ford won the nomination (but not the presidency, which went to Jimmy Carter, thereby setting up Reagan's 1980 victorious march to the White House), Jimmy and Gloria made plans to travel once more to Kenya, where Kelly had lived almost continually since the moment of her high school graduation and where she was now engaged to University of Cambridge professor Alexander Harcourt. Upon their return, Jimmy and Gloria spent time with Michael, Barbara, and the grandchildren, now living in Phoenix.

Whenever they were home in Los Angeles, Gloria ran their social lives, concentrating on various charitable activities. At one Annual Beastly Ball, sponsored by the Greater Los Angeles Zoo Association, Jimmy paid $4,600 to become the "adoptive father" of an orangutan. Mostly, however, she carefully limited their outings to places and events where Jimmy would feel most comfortable among their closest friends, among them the Reagans who, like the Stewarts, still loved to go to Chasen's for dinners, and perhaps do a little dancing afterward. Even here, among friends, Jimmy tended to stay by himself, withdrawn, pre-occupied, alone in the crowd. If he talked to anyone, he preferred it to be Reagan, sharing a drink while discussing politics in a corner some-where while Gloria played the role of life of the party for the both of them.

Later that year, good friend and producer William Frye got Jimmy to agree to star in *Airport '77,* a sequel to the smash *Airport* series of disaster films, part of the then-popular cycle that had followed in the wake of the amazing success of Ronald Neame's 1972 *The Poseidon Adventure,* with big stars doing cameos in larger-than-life nightmares. "Gloria, Jimmy and I were staying with friends at a ranch in Mexico, and I was working on the script of the film," Frye later recalled. "I asked him if he'd like to read it, and he said sure. The next day he said, 'Who's going to play Mr. Stevens?' referring to a small part in the picture. 'You, I hope,' I said, and to my delight he agreed."

Phillip Stevens is an aging billionaire (said to be based on J. Paul Getty), who is not on board the ill-fated crash but part of the obligatory cast of characters anxiously awaiting to find out who will survive and who won't.

The film premiered at the Anchorage Fine Arts Museum in Alaska and was well received by critics. It eventually grossed approximately $15 million in its initial domestic release and went on to be seventeenth on the list of top grossers for 1978. It wasn't a flop, but neither was it the kind of smash that would change anyone's life, especially Jimmy's.

Frye then asked Gloria and Jimmy if they would do some overseas promotion for the film, and they agreed. The world tour included Alaska, Australia, Bangkok, and Japan. "We got into Tokyo very late at night," recalled Frye. "When we were getting off the plane, an official told us we could get out the back way, and Jimmy said, 'Why? What's wrong?' The official said there were maybe eight or ten thousand people at the airport 'waiting for you.' 'Waaalll, in that case,' Jimmy said, 'I've gotta go out there. If they came all the way to see me, I'm not going out any back way!' It took us forever to get out of that airport!"

One of the stops was Hong Kong, where in their free time they toured the countryside. One afternoon a guide suggested that even though they didn't have the proper permits, they should all drive out to a high point where they could stand on a peak and look over to the Communist mainland. At the foot of the rise, the driver stopped the car and said he could go no farther. At that point, Jimmy got out and went alone up to the high point, where he stood gazing unsmiling into the great expanse, even as the official Hong Kong guards at the base of the hill pushed each other out of the way to get a glimpse of the legendary American movie star. *Mr. Glenn Miller! Mr. Shenandoah!* they shouted up at him. He turned, waved, and then went back down to his waiting ride.

— • —

In January 1978, Jimmy did something that struck many as odd and slightly defeatist, but that didn't bother him at all; he signed on to appear as spokesman in a series of sixty-second spots for the Firestone Tire and Rubber Company, to be aired during NFL games, the World Series of Golf, and the baseball playoffs, for a fee of more than $1 million. To Jimmy, being in front of the camera was what it was all about. Besides, he was friends with Leonard and Harvey Firestone, the sons of the corporation's founder, since they were all classmates at Princeton. When the brothers got word of Jimmy's desire to work, they came up with the commercial campaign. For his part, Jimmy was all too happy to lend his name and prestige to a company that had lately come under fire over safety issues involving its Firestone 500 tire.

After he finished shooting the spots, he took a brief vacation with Gloria to Denver. When a reporter there asked him what he was up to, he said he had come to celebrate the thirty-fifth birthday of an old friend. Who might that be the reporter asked? "Harvey," Jimmy replied.

In the fall, Jimmy appeared in Michael Winner's 1978 remake of Raymond Chandler's often filmed novel *The Big Sleep,* starring Robert Mitchum as the fabled Philip Marlowe. Mitchum, during production, rather ingloriously commented to the press that while the picture was all about corpses, one of his living co-stars, meaning Jimmy, looked deader than any of them. They did not remain friends.

Also that fall, Jimmy appeared in Don Chaffey's G-rated *The Magic of Lassie,* co-starring Mickey Rooney, and *The Green Horizon,* a Japanese-produced venture set in Kenya that went straight to cable TV and eventually video. The reason he agreed to be in it: Gloria wanted to go on safari and they both wanted the opportunity to visit Kelly, who was living in Rwanda.

— • —

One event that did matter a great deal to him was the 1979 American Film Institute Tribute to Henry Fonda, who had been chosen to join a prestigious handful of Hollywood greats, including John Ford, James Cagney, Orson Welles, William Wyler, Bette Davis, and Alfred Hitchcock. Jimmy couldn't resist using the opportunity to tease his old friend about his acting and his politics. "You know," Jimmy said, referring to the night he won the Best Actor Oscar over Fonda for *The Philadelphia Story:* "I voted for you against myself for your performance in *The Grapes of Wrath* in 1941 . . . of course, I also voted for Alfred Landon, Wendell Wilkie and Thomas Dewey."

In May 1979, his daughter Judy married Steven Merrill, a venture capitalist based in San Francisco ten years her senior. The marriage took place at North Roxbury, two weeks shy of Jimmy and Gloria's thirtieth wedding anniversary. The celebratory tone of the wedding was somewhat muted when word reached Jimmy that his one-time roommate in New York City and Los Angeles, Johnny Swope, had passed away.

Upon completion of *The Green Horizon,* Jimmy, now in his early seventies, reluctantly removed the *semi* from the retired of his future agenda. He also hung up his flying wings, when the latest round of qualifying tests revealed that his hearing had gotten so bad and his reflexes so slow, he should no longer pilot any aircraft.

After that life became, for Jimmy, a series of live memorials. Like George Bailey in *It's a Wonderful Life,* he gained the unique position of witnessing the value of his own life while still alive—at most of the events that chose to celebrate him, he was treated as if he were already dead. He made numerous "Grand Marshal" appearances at parades where he served as something of a living float, sat patiently through commercialized "lifetime tributes" on TV, numerous rubber-chicken Variety Club nights of honor; he accepted walls-full of lifetime achievement awards, including one from the Beverly Hills branch of the Friars Club attended by such Friars luminaries as Cary Grant, June Allyson, Frank Capra, William Wyler, George Cukor, Lucille Ball, Jack Lemmon, Gregory Peck, Mervyn LeRoy, and Henry Fonda, and which was presented by former president Gerald Ford.

When he wasn't out somewhere being honored, he spent long weekends at Roxbury dusting off old trophies and statuettes, or swimming in his unheated pool (not wanting to look extravagant during the energy crisis, he insisted on keeping the water at its natural temperature), answering some of the five hundred fan letters a month he still received, or if one of his movies was on TV—they played in Los Angeles and New York in the seventies on local over-the-air independent stations on the average of two to three times per week—watching without any apparent enjoyment, but rather with a critical eye, talking out loud about how "that was good," or "she should have said it that way," or "I wish I hadn't done it like that," or "that dialogue doesn't work."

All the while the ticking of the big clock grew ever louder. It was the only thing he could clearly hear without his cochlear aid.

His turn to be placed in the pantheon by the American Film Institute came on February 28, 1980.[3] Fonda, in turn, served as the emcee, and at one point told the audience "The point I want to lay on you, is that Jimmy Stewart never went out and looked for a job. The parts just kept happening for Jim and they kept getting bigger and bigger." Fonda's speech was followed by film clips from several of the classic features Jimmy had made. After, Richard Widmark said a few words about their experience making *Two Rode Together.* George Kennedy did the same about *Bandolero!* Ruth Hussey, Karl Malden, Ernest Borgnine, all spoke

---

3. The evening was videotaped and shown on CBS on March 16, 1980.

of acting with Jimmy; Mervyn LeRoy and Henry Hathaway recalled directing him; and Douglas Morrow represented the writers.

Then Frank Capra, hunched with age, his speech wet with saliva and roughened by a slight stutter that sounded as much the product of confusion as any speech defect, came to the microphone and, before a hushed audience, managed to say the following: "There is a higher level than great performances in acting. A level where there is no acting at all. The actor disappears and there's only a real live person on the screen. A person audiences care about immediately. There are only a few actors, very few, capable of achieving this highest level of the actor's art. And that tall stringbean sitting right over there, he's one of them."

Those words brought Jimmy to tears, as he stood with the rest of the crowd to a standing ovation for Capra while the aged director slowly left the stage. Jack Lemmon came on next and lightened the moment with his well-known (within the industry) impersonation of Jimmy, uncannily accurate and altogether hilarious. To ringing laughter, Lemmon concluded by getting close to the mike, looking in Jimmy's direction and saying, "You're a great actor, sir."

Grace Kelly was the next to approach the mike. Looking heavier than her ice-goddess years but still elegant and beautiful, she said a few soft words into the microphone, and then handed the podium over to, of all people, Dustin Hoffman.

It fell to Hoffman to give the last word, one that filled with unintended irony from the actor whose naturalistic screen skills caused many critics to hail him as the "next Jimmy Stewart." His words so accurately sum up the turning of Hollywood's generational tide, gratitude, awe, and respect that they bear repeating in total: "The truth of the matter is, Mr. Stewart," Hoffman began, speaking in the measured tones of an actor with a Bronx accent who has spent thousands trying in vein to lose it, "I wanted to be here tonight to see a lot of your work and to hear people talk about you, people I've never met, and hear stories I've never heard. My father grew up with you. My father worked on the lot when you were making Mr. Capra's *Mr. Smith Goes to Washington* and he's your age." Hoffman then paused before adding, "My mother is my age and that's one of the problems." The joke broke the tension and the black-tied audience loosened up and laughed out loud. "I saw *It's a Wonderful Life* two days ago for the first time. I think I'm maybe the only one here to have seen it recently. It's a great, great film and a great piece of work and you could have shown it tonight and it would have been a tribute in itself. I congratulate you for a really first-class piece of work, sir. I'm up here representing my generation of actors. . . . When I saw you on-screen in that performance, you made me laugh, you made me cry, and you made me wish for a country which perhaps we haven't seen for a while. I was told that *It's a Wonderful Life* was not a success, that you came back from the Second World War and made this film and were told by critics and people in this town that your career was at a low ebb and that you were down and out. I was also told you'd made the comment that you weren't sure whether you were an unemployed actor or an unemployed flier. Well, let me just say in closing that you made my parents very happy and you made me very happy, and if this world has any kind of Capra luck, you are going to make my children's children very happy."

At that point, the audience stood once more, this time to cheer Hoffman's heartfelt words. When the ovation began to fade, director George Stevens came to the podium to introduce the evening's honored recipient by reading the inscription on the award: "For one whose career has, in a fundamental way, advanced the film-making art and whose work has stood the test of time."

The crowd then hushed once more as Stevens gestured toward Stewart. Jimmy smiled in his familiar closed-lips fashion as he stretched to his full height, and the applause began like a storm from another county that blew into the center of town by the time he made it to the stage.

In typically soft-spoken manner, with his white hair bumping up against his orange-red toupee, and bifocals on his nose, he looked above the lenses to peer into the crowd. "Thank you all for sharing such a wonderful evening . . . which is about to go down hill fast . . . as I fumble around for the right words to express my appreciation. I know it's late and I promised myself to talk fast so as not to keep you up any later than is necessary. The problem is . . . I don't know how to talk fast."

The audience laughed with hearty, knowing, adoring appreciation. "I guess you could say that, until tonight, the American Film Institute has honored brilliance . . . daring . . . abundance of talent and attainment of the highest ideals of the motion picture community and that . . . er . . . brings us down to where we are now. When the American Film Institute . . . in all its *wisdom* . . . adds a new name and a new category to the Life Achievement Award—Jimmy Stewart, a remarkably fortunate fella," he told the twelve hundred movie stars and executives in attendance. And with that, as the houselights came up, as the crowd stood and cheered one last time, he turned and disappeared into the wings, a lifetime's memories of achievement and honor left behind in the empty spotlight.

— • —

Six months later, in the early evening of August 1980, seventy-two-year-old Jimmy Stewart was rushed to Saint John's hospital in Santa Monica, California, suffering severe chest pains. After initial reports of a heart attack, one saying he had died, the official word was released by a hospital spokesperson the next day that Jimmy had, in fact, not suffered a heart attack, but the effects of "an irregular pulse." He was released after two days.

Not much later, Jimmy found a new television outlet to replace both his former regularly recurring slots on the *Dean Martin Show,* which had been canceled, and the *Jack Benny Program,* which had ended a few years before with its star's death. *The Tonight Show Starring Johnny Carson* became a regular stop for him after his initial visit, in October 1979, to share with Carson and NBC the show's seventeenth birthday. Carson, who was not a relaxed or particularly spontaneous host, took an instant liking to Jimmy, identifying with his small-town ways, his Midwestern values, and his total lack of pretense.

Audiences responded as well. Like Carson, they loved the easy chat about safaris and old Hollywood and, most of all, the corny "poems" Jimmy liked to share with the audience, nonsense verses, mostly about animals, with a slightly risqué feel to them that kept audiences and Carson roaring with approval. Jimmy, always with pitch-perfect timing, exaggerated his drawl and his signature hand gestures, as he both poked fun and managed to pay tribute to himself without the slightest trace of ego, narcissism, cynicism, or bitterness.

— • —

January 1981 began with a stint as the grand marshal of the annual Tournament of Roses Parade in Pasadena, but the big deal of the year was the inauguration of Ronald Reagan as the fortieth president of the United States, held at the Capital Centre in Landover, Maryland.

The Stewarts were among the most honored private guests of the new president, for a week of three days and three nights of nonstop parties. Jimmy was asked to perform in the big show, hosted by Johnny Carson, on a bill that included Bob Hope, Ethel Merman, Mel Tillis, Debby Boone, Charley Pride, and Charlton Heston, the cream of Hollywood's conservative crop.

For his bit, Jimmy, in tuxedo decked out with his pilot wings and service medals, used the occasion to publicly salute his good friend: "It is an honor for me to salute you as the new commander-in-chief. It is an honor for me to be able to call you, from now on, Mr. President." Reagan was visibly moved by Jimmy's words, tears running from his eyes when he stood to return the salute.

It was a night that restored glamour in Washington, D.C., and set the black-tie tone for the duration of the Reagan presidency. Rather than bringing politics to Hollywood, Reagan had brought Hollywood to the capital, and it would be there that the country's prime cultural focus would remain for the next eight years. Nancy Reagan conducted a well-organized rondo of parties, galas, events, and evenings that dazzled the press and kept the country's populace glued to its television sets, beginning with the inauguration and continuing nearly uninterrupted for the two terms of the Reagan presidency.

The very next month, on February 6, 1981, Jimmy and Gloria were headed back to Washington as guests of the Reagans to help celebrate the president's seventieth birthday in a private party at the White House. It was the first of what were to be many nights the Stewarts would spend in the eighties sleeping in the grand old mansion.

At least partially due to his exposure at such close proximity to the White House, and also to his frequent appearances on the *Tonight Show,* Jimmy's schedule began to fill up, with still more honors and awards being given to him from all around the world. His life seemed newly reinvigorated, and he seemed to be enjoying his fame as never before. That spring, due to the popularity of his verses on the Carson show, in a deal brokered by the legendary agent Irving "Swifty" Lazar, he was offered a half-million dollars by Warner Books to write the story of his dog Beau, the subject of several of his goofy poems. He politely declined.

That May, Jimmy and Gloria were invited to take an audience with Pope John Paul II.

And then death returned with a vengeance.

The world had watched with a combination of joy and sadness as Henry Fonda had won the Best Actor award the previous March for his performance in *On Golden Pond,* the first and long-overdue Oscar for one of Hollywood's best ever (and most liberal) actors.[4] It was, to be sure, a sentimental award, given more for the sum of his work than the performance he gave in an otherwise ordinary movie, in which he played the cranky father to his real-life daughter, Jane, and distant, imperious husband to the great Katharine Hepburn. Everyone could plainly see that he was in poor health when he was shown at home by remote camera immediately after his name was read. However, the news that came on August 11, that Fonda had died, still managed to stun the nation. Jimmy had taken to visiting the bedridden actor regularly, sitting by his bedside and shouting to his best friend, who also suffered from severe hearing loss.

At the wake held in the Fonda home overflowing with friends, families, and show business luminaries, Jimmy sat alone, motionless, in

---

4. Not generally known is the fact that for virtually the only time in their careers, Fonda and Stewart were both up for the same part, that of the father in the film version of *On Golden Pond.* The "doubling" of Fonda as the real-life father to daughter Jane, in the film, proved irresistible and he got it. Fonda had shied away from "elderly" parts, until Edward Albee approached him in the early sixties to play George in his new play, *Who's Afraid of Virginia Woolf?* When Fonda acquiesced to his agent's decision, turning Albee down in favor of making *Spencer's Mountain,* directed by Delmer Daves, based on the autobiographical novel by Earl Hamner Jr. (which flopped on-screen but which would go on to be a smash-hit TV series in the seventies renamed *The Waltons*), Fonda fired his agent. Then, when he saw the stage production of *On Golden Pond,* he determined that he wanted to play the father.

Stewart had actually been offered the part in *On Golden Pond* and turned it down. "He didn't like the relationship the old man had with his daughter in the film," according to Bill Frye. "Jimmy loved both his daughters and couldn't imagine a father treating one the way the character did in the film, and therefore refused to play him." Stewart turned down other well-known roles as well. According to Frye, "He turned down *To Kill a Mockingbird* (Robert Mulligan, 1962) because he felt the racial thing was too controversial—too liberal really, but he would never say it in that way. He also turned down the lead in *Network* [Sidney Lumet, 1976] because of the language. He would never allow himself to use profanity on the screen." Ironically, all three of these roles brought the men who played them—Fonda, Gregory Peck (*Mockingbird*), and Peter Finch (*Network*) Academy Awards for Best Actor. "When Henry won, all I ever heard Jimmy say was how happy he was for him. He didn't have a jealous bone in his body." (William Frye's comments are from an interview with the author, Dec. 10, 2005).

Henry's study, in his comfortable old leather chair, staring ahead into the past while around him the air buzzed with compensatory energy and activities. He looked not unlike Scottie Ferguson, in *Vertigo,* after his nightmare turns him catatonic, except that this was no movie; this was real, the grief not dramatized and psychotically obsessive like in the film, but depressingly sane.

"Then, suddenly," remembered Shirlee, Fonda's wife, "he lowered his head very slowly over his lap and brought it back up at the same time that he raised his arms out as far as they would go and said, 'It was by far the biggest kite we ever flew'. . . . After about five minutes of talking about nothing except these kites, he fell back into the same silence and same position he'd been in before he started talking."

— • —

Ten days later, Jimmy was back in the coronary unit. The pain in his heart, the doctors told his wife, was something no medicine could cure.

PART EIGHT

—.—

The Final Rise; the Final Fade

Mr. and Mrs. James Stewart in the sunset of their lives.

28

"Rear Window has already started its new run with strong results at the box office, indicating that viewers are still spellbound by the Stewart-Hitchcock chemistry. *Vertigo,* perhaps Hitchcock's greatest work, *Rope,* one of his most rarely shown, will follow soon, along with the color-ful 1956 version of *The Man Who Knew Too Much* . . . It's a provocative notion, contrasting the glamorous Grant of *To Catch a Thief* say, with the troubled Stewart of *Vertigo.'"*   —DAVID STERRITT

*I*n September 1982, Grace Kelly, only fifty-two years of age, died in an automobile accident in Monaco. Coming as it did one month after the death of Henry Fonda, it deepened Jimmy's state of grief and mourning. Of all his leading ladies, Kelly had been his favorite, the only one who had become a life-long friend of the family.

At Gloria's urging, Jimmy went back to work. She hoped that the new project he was offered might take his mind off these two latest, incalculable losses. The film was for television, something called *Right of Way,* co-starring an aged Bette Davis, to be directed by TV producer George Schaefer. Despite the stellar star quality of its two leads, the film, shockingly, was turned down by all three broadcast networks (one executive at CBS described the story about terminal illness, and its geriatric stars, as having zero box-office power in the world of ever-younger over-the-air demographics). It was finally sold to then-fledgling HBO, whose average viewing numbers in those days rarely peaked above 500,000 subscribers, making *Right of* Way the first made-for-cable film in TV history.[1] Worse, for Jimmy (and Gloria), the script was all about

---

1. The salaries were reflective of the perceived stature of the film. HBO agreed to pay Stewart and Davis $250,000 each for their work in the film.

aging and death and afforded its two stars ample time to cry on each other's shoulders while thinking about their dear friend and co-star Fonda's recent passing. At one point, after nailing a particularly touching scene, Jimmy looked upward and said, simply, "Thank you, Hank."

— • —

It was the last live action feature film in any form that Jimmy Stewart would appear in. It aired in the fall of November 1983, and, was unfortunately (or fortunately, as the case may be) for the most part unnoticed and quickly forgotten by even his most loyal of fans. Jimmy, convinced more than ever his acting career was finally over, resigned himself to more rubber-chicken dinners, some in America, some abroad, some for the military, and some for charity.

If there was anything that occupied his time in a more pleasant way, it was the frequent visits he and Gloria made to the White House as guests of the Reagans—along with their frequent traveling and socializing companions Ruth and Tom Jones, an aircraft executive from Northrop, California; Betsy Bloomingdale; and Betty and Bill Wilson, the latter appointed by Reagan to be the U.S. ambassador to the Vatican, part of the president's famously informal "kitchen cabinet."

What particularly amused Jimmy, when he thought about it, was how throughout all the years they had been acting together in Hollywood, Reagan was always the supporting player and he, Jimmy, the star. Now, here, in Washington, it was all Ronnie Reagan; he had become the most powerful man in the world, and Jimmy, who had played a small but important part in getting him there, was what amounted to an extra—all of which was fine with him. If this was to be his final fade-out, the production values couldn't have been better. Anyway, he told himself, he had always prided himself on being a team player, and what better team could he have chosen to play on than this one?

On May 20, although he wasn't feeling in top shape—Jimmy believed he had aggravated a "bump" on his face by shaving with a new razor—he and Gloria traveled back to Indiana, Pennsylvania, to celebrate his seventy-fifth birthday. There he was greeted by three thousand cheering fans outside the county courthouse. Waving to the crowd, he told them that coming home was like meeting and getting reacquainted with an old friend. For the next three days, the entire town, including several of his World War Two unit who had traveled to Indiana for the occasion, devoted itself to its favorite son. The highlight of the celebration came when a nine-foot statue of the actor was unveiled across the street from the original location of his father's hardware store. It seemed to Jimmy a fitting end, a concrete wreath upon his own Hollywood life story.

And then, once again, his career took an unexpected and extraordinary turn, in what may be seen as nothing less than a miracle of cinematic resurrection.

— • —

It began, oddly enough, with the death of yet another close friend, Alfred Hitchcock, on April 29, 1980 (two years before Henry Fonda's and Grace Kelly's passings). As part of the director's fifties contract with Paramount deal, Hitchcock was given eventual ownership on five of the films. When his eight-year exclusive lease with the studio expired (each eight-year period commencing with that particular film's initial domestic release), most rights reverted to Hitchcock. Three of the five—*Rear Window, The Man Who Knew Too Much,* and *Vertigo*—starred Jimmy Stewart.

After Hitchcock's death, none of the five remained available for distribution. This was still the era of movie-screen–dominated exhibition—before the wide acceptance of cable, the existence of home video playback equipment, Blockbuster-type rental outlets, pay-per-view, or DVDs for rent via the mail. If one wanted to view certain classic films, such as Chaplin's *The Great Dictator* or Hitchcock's *Vertigo,* it necessitated either knowing someone with a clandestine print, or the willingness and financial wherewithal to hop a plane to Paris to catch a screening at that city's famed Cinémathèque.

Vertigo was briefly rereleased in 1973, by Hitchcock himself, but went largely unnoticed and was quickly pulled, after which none of the five features were seen again in any form of American theatrical release during his lifetime. In the late seventies, as film schools began to proliferate, requests for classic films became more frequent, and Hitchcock, for reasons unclear today, personally allowed the other four to be loaned out in numbered and encoded 16-mm prints (to prevent copying) to nontheatrical institutions, but absolutely refused to give anyone access to *Vertigo.*

Two years after his death, his wife, Alma, who was the sole executor of his estate, passed away and left everything to their only daughter, Patricia Hitchcock O'Connell, a sometime actress who played small but memorable roles in *Strangers on a Train* (the senator's pushy daughter) and *Psycho* (Janet Leigh's nosy co-worker). In 1983, O'Connell announced that a newly struck print of *Rear Window* would be shown, by request, at the Toronto Film Festival and at the most important and prestigious of all the annual American movie events, the New York Film Festival—and that she had arranged for Gloria and Jimmy Stewart to attend both.

Jimmy was delighted by the invitation and immediately accepted on condition that he was sufficiently recovered from the month's worth of radiation he was scheduled to undergo to treat that facial bump, which turned out to be a malignant skin tumor. It was the first serious health problem for Jimmy since his series of heart scares, and one that put a bit of a fright into him, especially when, while in attendance at the Toronto Film Festival, he had to leave before the actual screening due to facial pain. Despite his absence, the first public viewing in North America of *Rear Window* since the death of Hitchcock turned that festival on its head, and the buzz surrounding the upcoming New York showing was louder than any fall release that year was getting. The screening sold out weeks in advance.

— • —

October 2, the night of the festival, its positively euphoric director, Richard Roud, led a press conference attended by Universal Classics vice president Jim Katz, the company's entire East Coast publicity contingency, and Jimmy Stewart, whose presence had been iffy right up until the last minute. Roud completely charmed the crowd with a story about the Stewart/Kelly project intended as a sequel to *Rear Window*. "It was titled *Designing Woman* and it was going to be for MGM. We had the costumes all ready, the final touches were being put on the script and the sets were built. One Monday morning Grace Kelly came to Mr. Mayer and said, 'Mr. Mayer, I'm going to get married.' "

Jimmy then expressed regret at having quit the picture as well, leaving out that his decision had been made for personal, rather than professional, reasons; he simply wanted to be with and act alongside Kelly again. He then praised the eventual release that starred Lauren Bacall and Gregory Peck as a very successful and wonderful picture. Later on, joking with some other members of the press, he said that Hitchcock would have made more money with *Rope* if he had charged people five bucks a head to see how the picture was done.

That evening, Jimmy sat with the rest of the audience and, for the first time in nearly twenty years, watched *Rear Window*. When the film ended and the lights went up, the audience, already heavily applauding, broke into a thunderous ovation when Jimmy stood and waved to the crowd.

The next morning, in his hotel suite, he reflected on what it was like to see the film after so much time had passed. "The wonderful thing about it is that so much of it is visual. You really have to keep your eye open in the film, because it's a complicated thing. And the audience was really with it. I thought that was just amazing. It just bears out the feeling that so many of us had about Hitch and his way of doing things." And then, with carefully chosen words, he turned his attention to Kelly. "The wonderful thing about Grace was that she was just completely at ease with her lines. The emphasis was always in the right place, and this came from her. I remembered that very vividly, and it was really brought back last night. Absolutely fascinating woman. This was only her fifth picture." Still later on, Jimmy went about as far as he would ever go in describing his feelings for Kelly when he told a reporter that "I remember her so vividly . . . she had a warmth and a tenderness about her and you could see that it wasn't forced, that it wasn't her way of acting. It was the woman herself. This . . . this warmth and tenderness combined with the tremendous acting skill she had . . . she was something very, very special."

— • —

And then came *Vertigo*. Its long-awaited general U.S. release began in December 1983 and proved a smash at the box office, taking in $2.3 million in its limited release, a huge number for its day, *especially* for a twenty-five-year-old cult film. Writing in the *New York Times,* film critic Janet Maslin said, "An astonishing burst of applause greeted the penultimate moments of Alfred Hitchcock's 1958 *Vertigo* at the performance I attended—astonishing because only seconds later, the film's real ending left the audience in gasping disbelief. If *Rear Window* seemed a pleasant surprise when it re-emerged last fall, *Vertigo* now seems shocking."

Andrew Sarris had this to say: "There is something very darkly, very deviously funny in the spectacle of Stewart's meticulous effort to remake the shop girl into the femme fatale. On the one level it is a directorial parable on Hitchcock's own efforts with Novak, on another a critique of the eternal search for the ideal woman. The cream of the jest, however, is in the casting of supposedly all-American James Stewart in the role of the pathological Pygmalion . . . for the moment, let us say simply that *Vertigo* looks and sounds magnificent after more than a quarter of a century. Of how many contemporary films will we be able to say the same in 25 years hence?"

— • —

By the time all five Hitchcock films were rereleased, they had grossed more than $50 million, and, perhaps even more important, had restored both Hitchcock and Jimmy Stewart to the forefront of the country's cinematic imagination. Once again, as had happened with broadcast TV's discovery of *It's a Wonderful Life,* Jimmy was remembered and revered not as an aging time traveler through the memories of moviegoers, nor merely a contemporary, but a crucial, true modernist in a series of expressionist movies that showed off the best of both him and the medium within which he worked. Particularly among young people studying film in colleges, "Jimmy Stewart" attained an iconic preeminence, his career the reflection of both one man's extraordinary career as well as the history of American pictures.

Unfortunately, he was too old and frail to do much of anything about all the new celebrity other than to bask in the belated glory of his best work. Even if he had wanted to take advantage of the many offers that had started to come his way, he just wasn't physically strong enough. He was caught in both the curse and the blessing of film, in its Dorian Gray ability to hold up a mirror of perfection for all time. Those who give themselves over to it can never compete with their own long-gone youth, beauty, and talent. Their images provide moments at once caught and lost for all time, displayed by the unreachable past that will live forever as history, present, and future.

For Jimmy, revisiting his own past allowed him to take his mind off the darker events of his life that had taken place, the loss of his son, Hitchcock, Henry Fonda, and Grace Kelly at the top of that nightmare list. It allowed him to have his phone calls returned by the new studio heads born after his greatest moments of glory. It allowed him to pretend he was twenty, thirty, even forty years younger than he was, just by turning down the lights and turning on the projector. It allowed him an added layer of attention and respect during the remaining glitterati of the eighties Reagan era of American culture and politics.

And finally, it allowed him a way to ease into his own final fade with a dignity he might otherwise not have enjoyed. Unlike the fate of John "Scottie" Ferguson, Jimmy Stewart did not wander. Instead, he spent his last years in quiet reconciliation, prepared to face the last sunset of his life with peace and dignity.

29

"It's over. It's over. No, it's over."   —JIMMY STEWART

Scripts kept coming in, mostly for grandfathers of the grumpy type, either for TV or low-budget films, both categories Jimmy unequivocally rejected, refusing to play— as he often referred to the parts offered, loud enough for the studio boys to hear, even if they were listening—"grouchy old men."

Instead, he continued to frequent the White House until 1989, when the Reagans left the capital for retirement and life on their California ranch. Once the president left D.C., there was no longer any reason for Jimmy and Gloria to continue their sojourns east, except for the occasional award ceremony, of which there seemed to be no end.

Jimmy, in fact, planned to never visit D.C. again, and likely would not have had an issue not arisen that made his elderly blood boil as if he had been placed in a cauldron. Shortly after his eightieth birthday, he picked himself up and went to Washington, à la Mr. Smith, to testify against the growing practice of "colorizing" old black-and-white films to make them more palatable to television stations and video distributors looking to cash in by bastardizing the works of some of the greatest filmmakers in the world. To the producers and bottom liners of the studios, the only color that mattered was green, and they intended to harvest as much of it as they could, regardless of what it did to the original works. Colorize *It's a Wonderful Life*? That would be like replacing its shadows with sunshine, removing its furniture for the sake of showing off its wallpaper, and reducing its image of evil to the intensity of a cartoon.

None of which made the slightest difference to Ted Turner, whose need for color programming to feed his nascent cable movie stations seemed justification enough. He owned the MGM and 20th Century catalogs, many of the films of which were in glorious black and white. From 1965 through 1985, for instance, the black-and-white version of

George Seaton's *Miracle on 34th Street* (1947) earned about $50,000 from TV play-offs during the Christmas season, while the colorized version introduced in 1985 made a million dollars. Those kinds of numbers were hard to argue with. But argue with them Jimmy did, taking on not only the studios but also one of their biggest blowhards, Jack Valenti, LBJ's former White House aide, the studios' company man in Washington, and when filmmakers protested that their work was being destroyed, Valenti's callously cavalier response was that it was "a property issue. There's only one Lincoln Memorial and there are *copies* of films. Nobody says that when a film is colorized all the black-and-white versions are destroyed."

What was particularly galling to Jimmy, Frank Capra, and many of the younger, purist-schooled filmmakers such as Martin Scorsese, was that no one seemed interested preserving the films *as they were.* Hitchcock had proved that the old movies could earn new money, not because of their color, but because of their content.

"The colorization idea is a vicious lousy unkind thing to do to a motion picture," Jimmy told members of the press, and he was backed by such Hollywood heavyweights as Burt Lancaster and Katharine Hepburn.

Congressional hearings were held on the subject, and when Capra declined to testify, due to illness (heart problems), he asked Jimmy to go in his stead. His testimony was an impassioned plea for preservation, and included the following remarks: "I've said it before and I'm glad to say it again; the computer coloring of black-and-white films is wrong. It's morally and artistically wrong and these profiteers should leave our film history alone.[1]

"For fifty years or so, I've made my living as a screen actor in 80 films—one-half of them in black-and-white. I pray that they'll stay that way. Of course I remember the excitement that Technicolor film created back in the 1930's. It gave the studios a beautiful new option for their screen artistry. But for many creative reasons, we continued to make black-and-white films well into the 1960s. Some directors, like

---

1. These comments are taken from an article signed by Jimmy Stewart for *The Screen Actor,* a trade magazine, in which he duplicated much of his testimony before Congress. For continuity, much of the back-and-forth Q and A has been eliminated.

Woody Allen, still choose black-and-white today for the same reason; it tells a story in a unique and highly dramatic way. Black-and-white reduces character, settings and events to the very essence of darkness, light and shadow. . . .

"The first film I made after the war was Frank Capra's *It's a Wonderful Life.* Some people call it a perennial or a classic and that's all right by me. But those classics are the first targets of the colorizers, and the colorized version was shown on TV last year. I watched half of it and had to turn it off. I couldn't get through it. The artificial color was detrimental to the story, to the whole atmosphere and the artistry of the film. I felt sorry for the director, the cinematographer, the costume designer, the make-up man and all the actors. . . .

"A certain actor friend of mine named Ronald Reagan is fond of saying, 'If it ain't broke, don't fix it.' I agree with that kind of home-spun wisdom and that's exactly what I'd like to say to anyone who wants to paint up my face like an Easter egg. Our black-and-white films *ain't* broke, and they *don't* need fixin.' "

Unfortunately for Valenti, he had to follow Stewart's testimony. After being sworn in, Democratic representative Sidney Yates of Chicago, the chairman of the Appropriations Interior subcommittee, simply stared at Valenti in silence for several seconds, then began to speak. "Well, Jack, we've heard from Mr. Smith. Who are you going to be? Claude Rains or Edward Arnold?"

The halls of Congress exploded with laughter and applause, while a red-faced and furious Valenti sat and stared directly at Yates.

That was it. Show over, fade to black and white. Although several issues still remained to be settled, including questions of ownership that eventually became trademark and copyright hot buttons, a moral victory had been won. And, for one last time, it was Jimmy Stewart who played the people's hero, this time helping to keep alive, in all its pristine beauty, the cultural and artistic record of the century in movies he had played such a major role in. In an industry seemingly bent on self-destruction, his notion of preservation was ultimately a powerful, if vanishing, voice of an American way of life. What his pal Ronald Reagan had done for the nation's politics, Jimmy Stewart, it may fairly be said, did for the nation's culture. So it was that this time life wound up imitating art, instead of the other way around (which is what movies are usually all about), that glorious day the remarkable Mr. Stewart once more went to Washington.

For the rest of what had been yet another extraordinary decade for Jimmy, the public got little of him, beyond hearing his voice on an endearing Campbell's soup commercial (that significantly jacked up the gross sales of the venerable school lunch staple) and seeing him occasionally on the *Tonight Show*. The memoir he had once intended to write never happened. Instead, a book of his purposely corny Grandpa America poems was eventually published by Crown, to considerable success—it reached number three on the *New York Times* Fiction Best Seller list, and number four on the *L.A. Times* list. As Robert Osborne, writing for the *Hollywood Reporter*, stated, quite aptly, with a smile coming through his words: "Go Figure!" Jimmy went on a brief signing tour and capacity crowds turned out everywhere, to which he kept stating, under his breath as he got ready to write his signature in customers' copies, "I don't believe it . . . I just don't believe it . . ."

In 1991, he gave his voice to Fievel, the mouse in *An American Tail: Fievel Goes West*, directed by Phil Nibbelink and Simon Wells, with Jimmy's vocals personally directed by Steven Spielberg, who also produced the film (with Robert Watts). It was his final film, and, in truth, his heart wasn't really in it. He and Gloria completed their twenty-third African safari and took their pleasure still going to Chasen's for dinner with the Reagans, visiting their children, all in their thirties now and scattered to the four winds, and their four grandchildren (two by Michael, two by Judy, all boys).

They also still liked to entertain at both the house on North Roxbury and at the ranch, for a select, regular group of friends that included producer William Frye. After dinner, Jimmy always reached for his accordion, or simply sat at the piano, at which point, according to Frye, Gloria would playfully roll her eyes for the others and say "Oh no, not again." Jimmy would then launch into one of his favorite ditties, "Ragtime Cowboy Joe," or "Dear Ruth (I'm Telling You The Truth)," or both.

Only for very special occasions would they venture into the ceremonial spotlight. One such instance occurred in 1991. Gloria was a graduate of the American Academy of Dramatic Arts (AADA) and was invited to a ceremonial dinner that was being held on the West Coast, where the school had a branch, for what actor John Karlen calls "the hierarchy." Karlen said, "The dinner was held at L'Hermitage, a very upscale restaurant and hotel in Beverly Hills. I'm also an alumni, and I happened to be sitting a few tables away from Gloria and Jimmy, who looked dead drunk to me. I went up to him, hugged him, and gave him a kiss on the mouth, and he stuck this tongue right back and deep into mine. 'Jimmy,' Gloria said, playfully but with authority, 'That's enough!' Then she chuckled."

"It was funny but also sad to me," Karlen recalls. "He looked so old and frail, with watery eyes and no color in his cheeks. It reminded me of how, in the end, even the lions are brought down, only not by other lions, but hyenas. That's the law of nature, and the fate of man. Even movie stars!"

Death kept hustling its way through the gates, and that same year, 1991, Frank Capra passed away. He was ninety-four, and represented the last link, both off-screen and on-, to the glory days of the studio era that had given the world Jimmy Stewart, and Jimmy Stewart the world.

In April 1993, he went back into the hospital for heart surgery, a risky affair for an eighty-five-year-old man. A pacemaker was installed and he recovered enough to be released, but was in no condition to attend his birthday party that May, hosted by former president Ronald Reagan.

Nor was he able to attend any of the celebrations that took place when *Vertigo* was rereleased yet again, this time in 1993, fully and meticulously restored to its original 70-mm form, with its images considerably brightened, an entirely digitalized soundtrack that brought the beautiful Bernard Herrmann score, conducted by Muir Mathieson, to the forefront; and the warm, rich colors of the first Technicolor, Vista-Vision version, unseen in its proper ratio and spectrum balance since 1958. Once more, the film was hailed as Hitchcock's masterpiece, and Jimmy's acting a feat of contemporary wonder.[2]

Then, in October 1993, Gloria was diagnosed with terminal lung cancer. Preferring to die in the only home she had ever lived in with

---

2. The Hitchcock family has indicated they plan to rerelease the film to theaters every ten years. The last was a full digital video and audio restoration issued on DVD in 2005.

Jimmy, and hoping to do so with dignity, after the first of the new year, she refused any further treatments; she passed away on February 16, 1994, in his arms.

That was really the end for Jimmy. He told friends and family that he no longer wished to live, that his bad heart was shattered emotionally, and that they shouldn't grieve for him. "I'm devastated," he said. "I don't know how I'm going to live without her. The only consolation is knowing that we will soon be reunited. Our love will continue in heaven."

He spent his last months mostly in bed, drinking and watching television. On January 31, 1997, he tripped over a plant in his bedroom and had to be rushed to St. John's Hospital in Santa Monica for stitches to close a bloody gash in his forehead. There it was discovered that his skin cancer had returned, and this time it appeared to be untreatable. He was sent home, and six months later, on July 2, at the age of eighty-nine, the exact same age that Alexander had lived to, an embolism lodged in his lungs. The clot caused a heart attack that killed him instantly.

Tributes

"He was the last of that rare breed of male stars whose careers certified the star system as it operated virtually from the beginning of the sound era. Actors like Stewart, Spencer Tracy, Gary Cooper, Clark Gable, Cary Grant, John Wayne and Henry Fonda were larger than life, and because of the fusion of the performers' public and private personalities created something bigger than the sum of the two parts, something mythical. . . . The Stewart way of speaking—laconic, with a hesitant, nasal drawl—is instantly recognizable by virtually every American. His early screen image, like his personal life, epitomized a Middle American ideal in a confusing, sophisticated world."   **—FROM JAMES STEWART'S *NEW YORK TIMES* OBITUARY**

*W*ord of Jimmy Stewart's death spread quickly, first in Hollywood and then throughout the world. By the time of his funeral, it was clear that America had lost one of its most unique cultural heroes, an irreplaceable member of the cast of characters produced by the golden years of Hollywood's studio system, and America's most complete movie actor. Although he did not have the looks of a Cary Grant, he was able to play Americana better than the British-born matinee idol. Grant could do many wonderful things, but he couldn't ride a horse, wear a six-gun, or effectively play the little guy taking on the establishment. Against Grant's romantic exotic, Stewart's was the image of the American idealist.

He may not have been as tough as John Wayne, that other reigning movie star of twentieth-century patriotic Americana, but Wayne, with the exception of in John Ford's *The Quiet Man* (1952), could not play a believable romantic leading man. He was, rather, Hollywood's ultimate action hero. While Stewart could play hard-edged cowboys as well as Wayne (if not better), Wayne remains inconceivable opposite, say, Kim Novak in *Vertigo*.

Jimmy may not have been as intellectual as Henry Fonda, the conscience of the American liberal, but neither was he as doctrinaire. It was his innocence that redeemed him, that allowed his worship of Abraham Lincoln (as Jefferson Smith in *Mr. Smith Goes to Washington*) to ultimately outshine Fonda's dark portrayal of the sixteenth president of the United States (in John Ford's *Young Mr. Lincoln,* 1939).

Jimmy may not have been as funny as Bob Hope, but he was never irredeemably cowardly, as Hope was in his buddy-buddy "Road" pictures made with sidekick Bing Crosby (who did manage to overcome some of that Abbott-Costello adolescence in later movies). Whereas Hope never managed to win the girl via the self-redemptive notion of anything so unfunny as heroism or self-sacrifice, Jimmy made a virtue out of these qualities in John Ford's *The Man Who Shot Liberty Valance.* While it remains Hope-less to envision His Bobness in one of Ford's or Hitchcock's, Cukor's or even Capra's excursions, it is entirely plausible to see Stewart doing light comedy, as he did in Capra's *You Can't Take It with You,* Cukor's *The Philadelphia Story,* and even the humorous, if relentlessly shadowy, moments of Hitchcock's *Rear Window.*

The multiple facets, the complexities, the charm and the torment that combined into the film persona of "James Stewart" live forever in the endless revisitations of his movies, made by new, young viewers, pilgrims to the cultural museum of our collective American lives. Future movie-goers, in whatever form the art takes, will learn more about what America was like for most of the twentieth century from the films Jimmy Stewart and others made than from any textbook of the times.

— • —

More than three thousand people turned out for his funeral. He was laid to rest beside Gloria, at Forest Lawn Cemetery in Glendale, California, as a twenty-one-gun salute was provided by the military in honor of his war service. The following are a sampling of some of the thousands of public tributes that came in the immediate wake of his death:

"It was a wonderful life."—Leonard Klady, *Variety* reporter

"He was my favorite friend and he was a patriot."—Lew Wasserman

"He was the quintessential American face. He loved the work and respected the people who made him a star. He was a role model and inspiration."—Charlton Heston

"He was a shy, modest man who belonged to cinema nobility." —Jack Valenti

"He taught me that it was possible to remain who you are and not be tainted by your environment. He was not an actor . . . he was the real thing."—Kim Novak

"There is nobody like him today."—June Allyson

"Robert Mitchum died last week of emphysema, while James Stewart succumbed to heart failure (As if). The more probable cause is that someone asked God what America was like, and in order to save time He decided to call a couple of expert witnesses."—Anthony Lane, film critic for *The New Yorker*

"He was the most special actor I've ever worked with." —Betty Hutton

"He was a great actor, a gentleman and a patriot." —President Bill Clinton

"Jimmy Stewart's modesty meant he never understood that greatness that others saw in him. We shared so many of life's precious moments with him and his late wife, Gloria. We'll miss him terribly but know they're happy to be together. Our prayers are with his children during this very difficult time."—Ronald and Nancy Reagan

"He was uniquely talented and a good friend."—Frank Sinatra

"He was a gracious and generous man."—Tom Capra, son of Frank Capra

"America has lost its role model and I've lost a great friend." —Bob Hope

"He was one of the nicest, most unassuming persons I have known in my life. His career speaks for itself."—Johnny Carson

"Farewell, Mr. Smith."—Sony Pictures, in a full-page ad in the *Hollywood Reporter*

But none of these expressed the sense of both eternal joy and profound grief better than the two that follow. The first was from Jimmy's daughter Kelly Stewart Harcourt, who said, immediately after the funeral, "My parents' love and friendships with the familiar faces filling the church had sustained them . . . in the familiar closing line of *It's a Wonderful Life*, no man is a failure who has friends. So here's to our father, the richest man in town!"

And the second was from Karolyn Grimes, who played little Zuzu in that grand Capra film, whose petals represented the essence of life itself to young George Bailey. In her sixties when she heard of Jimmy's passing, she said, simply, "I think there will be bells ringing tonight."

Sources

RESEARCH INSTITUTIONS

The following research facilities were used by the author:

The Margaret Herrick Library of the Academy of Motion Picture Arts and Sciences, Beverly Hills, California.
The New York Public Library, New York City.
The New York Public Library for the Performing Arts, New York City.

BIBLIOGRAPHY

Allyson, June, with Frances Spatz Leighton, *June Allyson,* New York: Putnam's, 1982.
Auiler, Dan, *Vertigo: The Making of a Hitchcock Classic,* New York: St. Martin's Press, 1998.
Basinger, Jeanine, *The It's a Wonderful Life Book,* Norwalk, Conn.: The Easton Press, 2004.
Bazin, André, and Hugh Gray, translator, *What Is Cinema,* Berkeley: University of California Press, 1992.
Bogdanovich, Peter, *Peter Bogdanovitch's Movie of the Week,* New York: Ballantine, 1999.
Bogdanovich, Peter, *Pieces of Time,* New York: Arbor House/Esquire, 1973.
Bogdanovich, Peter, *Who the Hell's in It?* New York: Knopf, 2004.
Brough, James, *The Fabulous Fondas,* New York: David McKay Company, 1973.
Campbell, Joseph, *The Hero with a Thousand Faces,* Princeton, N.J.: Princeton University Press, 1972 (reprint edition, originally published in hardback in 1949).
Capra, Frank, *The Name Above the Title: An Autobiography,* New York: Macmillan, 1971.
Chandler, Charlotte, *It's Only a Movie: Alfred Hitchcock, A Personal Biography,* New York: Simon & Schuster, 2005.
Cooke, Alistair, *Alistair Cooke's America,* New York: Alfred A. Knopf, 1973.
Dewey, Donald, *James Stewart: A Biography,* Atlanta: Turner Publishing, 1996.
Dietrich, Marlene, *Marlene Dietrich: My Life,* New York: MacMillan, 1991.
Durgnat, Raymond, *The Strange Case of Alfred Hitchcock,* Cambridge: MIT Press, 1978.
Eyles, Allen, *James Stewart,* Briarcliff Manor, N.Y.: Stein and Day, 1984.
Fishgall, Gary, *Pieces of Time: The Life of James Stewart,* New York: Scribner, 1997.

Fonda, Jane, *My Life So Far,* New York: Random House, 2005.

Freedland, Michael, *Jane Fonda: A Biography,* New York: St. Martin's Press, 1988.

Gabler, Neal, *An Empire of Their Own,* New York: Anchor, 1989.

Gardner, Gerald, *The Censorship Papers: Movie Censorship Letters from the Hays Of-fice, 1934 to 1968,* New York: Dodd, Mead, 1987.

Gilbert, Julie, *Opposite Attraction: The Lives of Erich Maria Remarque and Paulette Goddard,* New York: Pantheon, 1995.

Grady, Billy, *The Irish Peacock: The Confessions of a Legendary Talent Agent,* New York: Arlington House, 1972.

Gussow, Mel, *Don't Say Yes Until I Finish Talking,* New York: Doubleday, 1971.

Harris, Warren G., *Clark Gable: A Biography,* New York: Harmony Books, 2002.

Hayward, Brooke, *Haywire,* New York: Alfred A. Knopf, 1977.

Heston, Charlton, *In the Arena,* New York: Simon & Schuster, 1995.

Higham, Charles, *Kate: The Life of Katharine Hepburn,* New York: W.W. Norton and Company, 1975.

Laurents, Arthur, *Original Story,* New York: Knopf, 2000.

LeRoy, Mervyn, *Mervyn LeRoy: Take One,* New York: Hawthorn Books, 1974.

Logan, Josh, *Josh: My Up and Down In and Out Life,* New York: Delacorte Press, 1976.

Martin, Deana, with Wendy Holden, *Memories Are Made of This,* New York: Harmony Books, 2004.

McBride, Joseph, *Frank Capra: The Catastrophe of Success,* New York: Simon & Schuster, 1992.

McClure, Arthur, Ken D. Johnes, and Alfred E. Twomey, *The Films of James Stewart,* Cranbury, N.J.: A.S. Barnes and Company, 1970.

McDougal, Dennis, *The Last Mogul: Lew Wasserman, MCA, and the Hidden History of Hollywood,* New York: Crown, 1998.

McGilligan, Patrick, *Alfred Hitchcock: A Life in Darkness and Light,* New York: Regan Books, 2003.

Meyers, Jeffrey, *Gary Cooper: American Hero,* New York: Cooper Square Press, 1998.

Morris, Edmund, *Dutch: A Memoir of Ronald Reagan,* New York: Random House, 1999.

Newquist, Roy, *Conversations with Joan Crawford,* New York: Berkley Publishing Group, 1981.

Pickard, Roy, *Jimmy Stewart: A Life in Film,* New York: St. Martin's Press, 1993 (originally published by Robert Hale, Ltd., England, 1992).

Quirk, Lawrence J., *James Stewart: Behind the Scenes of a Wonderful Life,* New York: Applause Books, 1997.

Quirk, Lawrence J., *Margaret Sullavan: Child of Fate,* New York: St. Martin's Press, 1986.

Robbins, Jhan, *Everybody's Man: A Biography of Jimmy Stewart,* New York: Putnam's, 1985.

Sarris, Andrew, *The American Cinema,* New York: Dutton Paperback, 1968.

Sarris, Andrew, *Confessions of a Cultist,* New York: Simon & Schuster, 1971.

Sarris, Andrew, *You Ain't Heard Nothin' Yet,* New York: Oxford University Press, 1998.

Sarris, Andrew, *The John Ford Murder Mystery,* London: British Film Institute, 1976.

Schickel, Richard, *The Men Who Made the Movies,* New York: Atheneum, 1975.

Shipman, David, *The Great Movie Stars: The Golden Years,* New York: Bonanza Books, 1970.

Smith, Starr, *Jimmy Stewart Bomber Pilot,* St. Paul, Minn.: Zenith Press, 2005.

Spada, James, *Grace: The Secret Lives of a Princess,* New York: Doubleday, 1987.

Spoto, Donald, *The Dark Side of Genius: The Life of Alfred Hitchcock,* New York: Ballantine Books, 1983.

Teichmann, Howard (as told to), *Fonda: My Life,* New York: New American Library, 1981.

Thomas, Bob, *King Cohn,* New York: Bantam Books, 1967.

Thomas, Tony, *A Wonderful Life: The Films and Career of James Stewart,* Secaucus, N.J.: Citadel Press, 1997.

Thomson, David, *The New Biographical Dictionary of Film: Expanded and Updated,* New York: Knopf, 2004.

Truffaut, François, *Hitchcock/Truffaut,* New York: Touchstone Books, 1985.

Wagner, Walter, *Beverly Hills: Inside the Golden Ghetto,* New York: Grosset and Dunlap, 1976.

Weinberg, Herman G., *The Lubitsch Touch: A Critical Study,* New York: Dutton, 1968.

Wiley, Mason and Damien Bona, *Inside Oscar: The Unofficial History of the Academy Awards,* New York: Ballantine, 1986.

Winters, Shelley, *Shelley II,* New York: Simon & Schuster, 1989.

Wood, Ean, *Dietrich: A Biography,* Cornwall, United Kingdom: MPG Books, 2002.

Notes

FRONTMATTER

page viii: **Thomas Mitchell** Lawrence Quirk, from an interview with Mitchell, referring to the actor's experience working with Stewart in *Mr. Smith Goes to Washington.*

page viii: **"That's the great thing"** Peter Bogdanovich, *Pieces of Time,* New York: Arbor House/Esquire, 1973, 140. (Bogdanovich writes Stewart's words with an implied accent—"and Gawd helps ya," which the author has eliminated for the sake of clarity.)

INTRODUCTION

page 3: **"All the great stars"** Allen Eyles, *James Stewart,* Briarcliff Manor, N.Y.: Stein and Day, 1984, 17.

page 4: **"His type is"** From a studio biography by house publicist Howard Strickling, written in 1938 for Metro-Goldwyn-Mayer studios, Culver City, California. There is no identifiable source for the "fan" who wrote the letter.

page 5: **Stewart's Oscar for Best Actor** Shortly after receiving the Oscar, the always gracious Stewart declared that his friend Fonda should have won. He was not alone in that sentiment. Many both in the Academy and the general public believed the award rightly belonged to Fonda but was likely denied him for two reasons. The first was that the politically conservative Academy would not want to reward Fonda's portrayal of a character as "radical" as Tom Joad. The second reason, many believed, was that Stewart should have won the previous year for his much stronger performance in Capra's *Mr. Smith Goes to Washington,* and felt his award was something of a payback for that oversight. The 1939 Best Actor Oscar went instead to Robert Donat for his performance as the title character in Sam Wood's *Goodbye, Mr. Chips,* over Jimmy Stewart; Clark Gable, in Victor Fleming's *Gone With the Wind;* Laurence Olivier, in William Wyler's *Wuthering Heights;* and Mickey Rooney, in Busby Berkeley's *Babes in Arms.*

CHAPTER I

page 13: **"The Garden of Eden"** Strickling, MGM bio.

page 14: **Jimsy** Bogdanovich, *Pieces of Time.*

page 17: **"I worshipped my parents"** quoted by Lawrence Quirk, a respected veteran show business journalist and biographer, in *James Stewart: Behind the*

Scenes of a Wonderful Life, New York: Applause Books, 1997. It must be noted, however, that Quirk gives little or no direct information on his sources, particularly quotes, and that his biography, more of a memory piece than a chronological fact sheet, offers no separate section of source notes.

page 17: **"I wouldn't say he was a loner"** Ibid., 6.

page 17: **"Doing things with my father"** Floyd Miller, "This Was My Father," *McCall's,* May 1964.

page 20: **"You are the"** Miller in *McCall's.*

page 20: **Now, present in spirit** This is an idea that informs the very structure of the Presbyterian Church, rooted in the Christian-Judeo belief in an invisible but all-pervasive God, and numerous Greek mythological figures, most often in the story of the virgin motherhood, wherein physical sex is bypassed as a method of impregnation in Mary, the physical absence but spiritual presence of the divine. More information on this subject may be found in the illuminating works of scholar Joseph Campbell's classic *The Hero with a Thousand Faces.*

page 21: **"There were . . . things"** Quirk, *James Stewart,* 10.

page 21: **"Jim claimed that he never"** Quoted by Quirk, *James Stewart,* 11.

page 21: **Stewart's height and weight** The Stewart side of the family was traditionally tall; Alexander was 6 foot 4 inches. Neither side had a history of underweight. Jimmy attributed a childhood bout with scarlet fever accompanied by a serious kidney infection as the reason for his lifelong slenderness.

page 24: **"hard work"** *People,* June 6, 1983.

CHAPTER 2

page 25: **"There wasn't a role"** From a June 26, 1964, 20th Century Fox studio press release interview to promote *Erasmus with Freckles,* released as *Dear Brigitte.* The original title was the name of the novel from which the film was adapted, by John Haase, and the film's shooting title, until it was changed, to capitalize on Brigitte Bardot's otherwise unbilled appearance. The actress, at the height of her American popularity, refused to be listed in the credits for her cameo appearance in the film.

page 26: **No steady girlfriends** Stewart mentions this fact many times in numerous interviews, including in Quirk, *James Stewart* (13), which quotes Bill Swope: "He said he was inhibited around them. He had the classic variation, even in those tender years, of the Madonna-Whore complex. *Good* girls were to be respected, *bad* girls avoided. . . . His mother's well meant injunctions had sunk in *too* well—more than she had intended, perhaps."

page 29: **"I don't think"** Alistair Cooke, *Alistair Cooke's America,* New York: Alfred A. Knopf, 1973, 332.

page 30: **"We had a real"** *New York Sun,* May 2, 1933.

page 31: **"excellent . . . swaggering . . . confident manner"** *Mercersburg News,* February 25, 1928.

page 32: **"We got there"** *Princeton Weekly Bulletin,* March 5, 1990.

page 33: **"Princeton and Jim Stewart"** Strickling, MGM bio, in this particular instance, although the sentiment and the lines appear identical in numerous later MGM studio "bios."

page 35: **"Look out"** and **"Kiss her"** Ibid., 11.

page 36: **"It wasn't Jim"** Ibid., 12.

page 37: **"Good Gawd"** Josh Logan, *Josh: My Up and Down In and Out Life,* New York: Delacorte Press, 1976, 36.

page 37: "**He walked away . . .**" Logan, *Josh*, 36.

page 40: "**gangling**" Logan, *Josh*, 41.

page 40: "**excellence easily equals**" *Time*, exact date unknown.

page 41: "**in order not to waste**" Quirk, *James Stewart*, 42.

page 42: "**an ingratiating personality**" and "**of no particular interest**" As a talent representative who reported directly to Louis B. Mayer and Irving Thalberg, it was Grady's job to travel the country scouting for new talent wherever he could find it, including at the many college performances he attended. Grady had begun his career as an agent in New York, where from 1917 to 1929 he handled the careers of W. C. Fields and Al Jolson; he played a key role in bringing them both to Hollywood after successful stage careers. Grady helped discover numerous future stars, including, besides Stewart, Eleanor Parker, Joan Blondell, Rock Hudson, and Van Johnson.

page 42: "**Returning to Princeton**" Logan, *Josh*, 32.

page 44: "**I went home**" Louise Sweeney, *The Christian Science Monitor*, February 19, 1980. Portions of the quote ("Mother, bless her heart . . . Dad shaking his head . . . No Stewart ever," etc.) are from an unattributed quote of Stewart, in Jhan Robbins, *Everybody's Man*, New York: Putnam's, 1985, 29. (Robbins is one of the many Stewart bios that offer no source notes.)

CHAPTER 3

page 45: "**If I hadn't become**" Bogdanovich, *Pieces of Time*, 130.

page 46: "**The [founders of] the University Players**" Donald Dewey, *James Stewart*, Atlanta: Turner Publishing, 1996, 102 (unattributed).

page 48: "**It was through**" Logan, *Josh*, 33.

page 48: "**Living with Sullavan**" Teichmann, *Fonda: My Life*, New York: New American Library, 1981, 64.

page 48: "**She was too**" Ibid.

page 48: "**She delighted**" Logan, *Josh*, 33.

page 50: "**You're my new**" Teichmann, *Fonda*, 68.

page 50: "**The rest of the time**" Gladwin Hill, *New York Times*, July 13, 1947.

page 51: "**He'd watch**" Jhan Robbins, *Everybody's Man*, New York: Putnam's, 1985, 30 (unattributed).

page 51: "**howlingly funny**" Logan, *Josh*, 35.

page 53: "**Perhaps**" Ibid., 36.

page 53: "**The reviews were**" Ibid.

page 54: "**I'll never forget**" Stewart, from local newspaper clippings in the collections of the Historical and Genealogical Society of Indiana County, Pennsylvania, and the Jimmy Stewart Museum, and also from portions of interviews originally conducted and referenced by Gary Fishgall in his book *Pieces of Time: The Life and Times of James Stewart*, New York: Scribner, 1997.

page 55: "**Oh yeah,**" Logan, *Josh*, 40.

page 56: "**icy**" and "**cold, shut-you-down**" Jane Fonda, *My Life So Far*, New York: Random House, 2005.

CHAPTER 4

page 58: "**It was a very**" Jimmy Stewart, interviewed by Paul Lindenschmid and John Strauss, *Ink* magazine, Winter 1977.

page 58: "**I was having a rough**" Jimmy Stewart, personal notes and diaries, June 1964, Historical and Genealogical Society of Indiana County, Pennsylvania.

page 59: **"I'm afraid Jim"** Teichmann, *Fonda,* 78.

page 61: **"We finished the . . ."** Ibid.

page 61: **"I played the accordion"** Stewart, from local newspaper clippings in the collections of the Historical and Genealogical Society of Indiana County, Pennsylvania, and the Jimmy Stewart Museum.

page 62: **"Appearing in 'Yellow Jack' "** Stewart, from local newspaper clippings in the collections of the Historical and Genealogical Society of Indiana County, Pennsylvania, and the Jimmy Stewart Museum.

page 62: **"Your soldiers"** Strickling, MGM bio.

CHAPTER 5

page 69: **[Stewart] has** *Collier's* magazine, 1936, exact date unknown.

page 70: **"Well, [on my way to California] I went home"** Teichmann, *Fonda,* 99.

page 73: **"Gosh, I never"** The Spencer Tracy anecdote is from a 1968 press release written by Jack Holland to promote the release of *Bandolero!*

page 75: **" 'I saw it"** Logan memory of the event is from Logan, *Josh,* 89–90.

page 77: **"that great new"** in Lawrence Quirk, *James Stewart,* 59.

page 78: **"She was protective"** Ibid., 61.

page 78: **"young all-American"** Quoted in Fishgall, *Pieces of Time,* 82.

page 78: **"They were both"** Brooke Hayward, *Haywire,* New York: Alfred A. Knopf, 1977, 87–88.

page 80: **"I'll never marry"** Jimmy Stewart, interviewed by Edith Driscoll for a syndicated fan magazine piece, 1935.

page 81: **"We were both"** Bogdanovich, *Pieces of Time.*

CHAPTER 6

page 84: **"I loved being in pictures"** Bogdanovich, *Pieces of Time,* New York: Arbor House/Esquire, 1973, 132.

page 87: **"James Stewart's and"** *New York Times,* February 18, 1938.

page 87: **"There is no fault"** *Movie Mirror,* May 1938.

page 87: **"[H]e has been denied"** Eyles, *James Stewart,* 44.

page 87: **"I was a contract player"** Ibid., 41.

page 88: **"The whores"** Quirk, *James Stewart,* 78.

page 89: **"I had to"** Ibid., 49.

CHAPTER 7

page 93: **"When Frank Capra"** Joseph McBride, *Frank Capra: The Catastrophe of Success,* New York: Simon & Schuster, 1992, 384. His quote of Capra is from information including McBride's interview with Capra, and from Glatzer's interview with him in Glatzer and Raeburn, eds., *Frank Capra: The Man and His Films,* Ann Arbor: University of Michigan Press, 1975.

page 94: **"I really felt"** Lawrence Quirk, *Margaret Sullavan, Child of Fate,* New York: St. Martin's Press, 1986, 89–90.

page 95: ***New York Herald Tribune* review,** July 18, 1938.

page 95: ***New Republic* review,** July 11, 1918.

page 97: **"In a moment of"** Logan, *Josh,* 135.

page 98: **"Jimmy gave Norma"** Donald, Dewey, *James Stewart: A Biography,* Atlanta: Turner Publishing, 1996, 180.

page 98: **Stars in Your Eyes** In his memoirs, Logan sheds more light on the connection between the Shearer/Stewart romance and the eventual play. Originally intended as a musical biography of the early life of Orson Welles, who, in the script, matures into a left-wing Hollywood radical, a popular, romantic theme often used in Hollywood and theater at the time. However, as Logan explains, he and the others connected to the show discard all the "unfunny Communist stuff, and do a show about the crazy way Hollywood people mix *sex* [rather than politics] and movies. I had an idea that just might be wild enough for a start. What if the young director was someone like Stewart, all wide-eyed and virginal, and Ethel Merman [as Shearer], the studio big star and owner because her [dead] husband had left it to her, was hot for him . . . the show was rewritten as *Stars in Your Eyes*." (Logan, 141.)

page 101: **Clark Gable in *It Happened One Night*** It has often been reported that Gable was loaned out by Mayer as punishment. According to Joseph McBride, "Mayer wanted to teach [Gable] a lesson for making what the MGM chief considered extravagant money demands" despite the failure of Robert Z. Leonard's *Dancing Lady* (McBride, *Capra*, 304). However, according to Warren G. Harris, Gable's biographer, "Between his illnesses and his suspended salary, Gable had been punished enough. It was simply a business deal that benefited both studios. MGM had no project of its own ready for Gable, and it also earned $5,600 per week by charging Columbia $2,500 instead of the $2,000 [Gable] received at home."

page 102: **"I had seen"** Frank Capra, 242.

CHAPTER 8

page 105: **"He's the easiest"** Capra, *The Name Above the Title,* 220.

page 106: **"He grabbed you"** Joseph McBride, *Frank Capra: The Catastrophe of Success,* New York: Simon & Schuster, 1992, 384–85.

page 106: **"I just had"** Ibid., 385.

page 106: **"the accumulation"** Ibid., 384.

page 109: **Member of the Academy and member of the Directors Guild** Nothing demonstrates Capra's duality more than this. Capra was elected president of the Academy in 1935, a year when it nearly disbanded over internal disputes involving the formation of the Directors Guild. Capra, already a millionaire, had less to gain than most directors, and was reluctant to support the guild. It was only after the guild gained power and recognition that Capra joined it, seeming to adjust his loyalties to the pragmatic consideration of survival, both his own and the industry's. Widespread boycotts threatened to bring down the Academy, its PR Awards ceremonies, and the entire industry itself, when Capra came up with the inspired notion of giving a special Lifetime Achievement Oscar to pioneering director D. W. Griffith—one of the most important figures in the formation of the feature film that spawned Hollywood as an industry, but, with the advent of sound had, despite being one of the founders of United Artists, fallen hard and fast into alcoholic obscurity. Capra understood the gesture would be taken universally as an irresistibly reconciling one, which not even the most committed anti-Academy unionist would dare miss. When *Mr. Deeds* won Capra his second Oscar that same year, 1936, it was presented to him by master of ceremonies George Jessel, who, after listening to Capra say with all modesty, "I don't see how anyone could look over these [other] nominees [Gregory La Cava for *My Man Godfrey*, Robert Z. Leonard for *The Great Ziegfeld*, W. S. Van

Dyke for *San Francisco,* William Wyler for *Dodsworth*] for the director and pick one out," a disgusted Jessel replied, "Well, they all may be president of the Academy some day and then they can select whom they please."

CHAPTER 9

page 111: **"My father first"** Frank Capra Jr. interviewed by author.

page 115: **"At the New York premiere"** Robbins, *Everybody's Man,* 67.

page 115: **"It was a great"** Elsie West Duval, from a piece published in *Reminisce,* May–June 1998.

page 116: **"man or woman."** Source wishes not to be identified.

page 116: **"prayed like mad"** *Parade* magazine, January 28, 1990.

page 117: **"Save your clean"** Eddie Mannix, an MGM executive and friend of Stewart, quoting a letter to Jimmy from Bessie, Quirk, 105.

page 117: **Stewart and Fonda** Here is what Andrew Sarris wrote about these two performances: "It is hard to believe that Fonda was once the third-ranking Fox leading man, behind Tyrone Power and Don Ameche, but such he was and such he might have remained had he and John Ford not made film history together. Still, Fonda never achieved either the mythic magnitude of the personality movie stars like Cagney, Stewart, Grant, Wayne, Bogart, Cooper, and Gable. . . . Fonda's young Lincoln was a case in point as an intermediate performance in 1939 between James Stewart's forceful projection of his own personality in *Mr. Smith Goes to Washington* and Robert Donat's uncanny incarnation of old age in *Goodbye, Mr. Chips.* . . . Significantly, Stewart won the New York Film Critics Award that year, and Robert Donat the Oscar, but Fonda's performance fell by the wayside." Sarris, *You Ain't Heard Nothin' Yet,* New York: Oxford University Press, 1998, 187.

page 118: **"Everyone was out"** Interviewed by Roy Newquist, *Conversations with Joan Crawford,* New York: Berkley Publishing Group, 1981, 103.

page 119: **"general unflattering portrayal"** Gerald Gardner, *The Censorship Papers: Movie Censorship Letters from the Hays Office, 1934 to 1968,* New York: Dodd, Mead, 1987.

page 122: **"Director Frank Capra"** "The Role I Liked Best," *Saturday Evening Post,* October 26, 1946.

page 125: **"obligatory Capra scene"** Sarris, *You Ain't Heard,* 355.

page 126: **"It was the filibuster"** *Los Angeles Times,* October 15, 1967.

page 126: **"When Jimmy was"** McBride, *Frank Capra,* 416.

page 127: **"He played"** Quirk, *Stewart,* 113.

page 129: **"lean, gangling"** . . . **"the most complete"** Sarris, *You Ain't Heard Nothin' Yet.*

CHAPTER 10

page 130: **"She'd slept with him"** This and other quotes that appear in this chapter are from the published diaries of Erich Maria Remarque as quoted throughout in Julie Gilbert's *Opposite Attraction: The Lives of Erich Maria Remarque and Paulette Goddard,* New York: Pantheon, 1995.

page 137: **"I liked taking"** Ean Wood, *Dietrich: A Biography,* Cornwall, United Kingdom, MPG Books, 186.

page 143: **Sarris quotes re Stewart and Sullavan in *The Shop Around the Corner*** Sarris, *You Ain't Heard Nothin' Yet,* 306.

page 143: **Doubling** See André Bazin's essay in *What Is Cinema*, Berkeley: University of California Press, 1992.

page 146: **"When people stared"** Ginny, quoted in "My Brother Becomes a Star," *Coronet* magazine, February 1940.

page 147: ***The Mortal Storm* and German response** Despite the great pains MGM took to keep from identifying Germany as the country where the film is set (for economic reasons as much as for any other, fearing a boycott of their films throughout a lucrative, Nazi-dominated Europe), Borzage was targeted as anti-Fascist; i.e., pro-Jewish, and, later, as at least sympathetic to the Communists by HUAC, so the German government actually protested to the studio during the making of the film. Robert Stack, one of the young players in the film, recalled that while filming, a representative from the Swiss consulate showed up and announced that he had been told by the Germans to warn MGM, "Your picture will be remembered by Berlin after they win the war." (Donald Dewey, direct attribution or source not provided by author.)

CHAPTER 11

page 150: **"Stewart's most distinctive"** David Freeman, "The Last American," *Buzz* magazine, August 1997, 89.

page 154: **"When I first"** Dewey, *James Stewart*, 217 (unattributed).

page 156: **Stewart's humorous behavior during the filming of *The Philadelphia Story*,** Charles Higham, *Kate: The Life of Katharine Hepburn*, New York: W.W. Norton and Company, 1975, 103 (unattributed).

page 156: **"I had learned"** From local newspaper clippings in the collections of the Historical and Genealogical Society of Indiana County, Pennsylvania, and the Jimmy Stewart Museum.

page 163: **"The only lottery"** Starr Smith, *Jimmy Stewart Bomber Pilot*, St. Paul, Minn.: Zenith Press, 2005, 29.

page 164: **"You know my views"** Pickard, *Jimmy Stewart, A Life in Film*, New York: St. Martin's Press, 1993. The story about the anonymous phone call has been reproduced in numerous articles and books, never denied by either Fonda or Stewart. (unattributed)

page 166: **"Look what I won"** Stewart's and Burgess's responses are from Sidney Skolsky's "Tintypes: James Stewart," *Hollywood Citizen-News* and syndicated, August 31, 1963.

page 167: **"I wanted him"** Quirk, *James Stewart*, 131 (unattributed).

page 167: **"I never thought"** Dewey, *James Stewart*, 220 (unattributed).

page 168: **The phone conversation between Stewart and Alexander** Pickard, *Jimmy Stewart*, 53.

page 168: **"a military secret"** The official is unidentified in a story that appeared in the *Los Angeles Herald Express* on March 7, 1941.

CHAPTER 12

page 173: **"I'm sure tickled"** "Film Star Stewart Wears Olive Drab," *Los Angeles Examiner*, March 23, 1941.

page 176: **Jimmy's letter to Hayward re agent commission** This was reproduced in whole in Sidney Skolsky's column that appeared in the *Hollywood Citizen-News* on May 3, 1941, and in syndication across the country.

page 183: **Alex's letter** It and similar memories of James Stewart are part of "Recollections of J. M. Stewart," an unpublished manuscript that is held by the Historical and Genealogical Society of Indiana County, Pennsylvania.

page 183: **"shy and taciturn . . . unavailable for an interview"** *Los Angeles Times,* November 29, 1943.

page 184: **"I found that"** Lawrence Quirk, *James Stewart,* 146.

page 184: **"women reporters"** This and other information and quotes from the PR session are from an article that appeared in the *New York Herald Tribune* on December 19, 1943, headlined "Capt. James Stewart Exhibited to the Press by 8th Air Force."

page 186: **"I was really afraid"** Dewey, *James Stewart* (unattributed). Some background into the military experiences and Stewart's fear are from a two-part series that appeared in the *Saturday Evening Post,* beginning December 8, 1945, and concluding December 15, 1945, by Col. Beirne Lay Jr. It was one of the few pieces that ran detailing Stewart's combat, one that, significantly, contained no direct quotes from Stewart, who declined to participate in the writing of the article by a fellow officer.

page 186: **"Fear is"** As told to Richard M. Schneider, *Guideposts,* n.d. This and the related quotes that follow are from Schneider.

page 186: **"braved mud"** and **"If you think"** *Los Angeles Times,* January 10, 1945.

page 187: **"I watched the way"** Walter Matthau, speaking at the American Film Institute regarding the Life Achievement Award given to Jimmy Stewart, February 1980.

page 190: **"they shot [his men up]"** Fishgall, *Pieces of Time,* 171.

page 191: **"[Leland] was always"** Hayward, *Haywire,* 307.

page 191: **"The country's had enough"** *Hollywood Citizen-News,* September 4, 1945.

CHAPTER 13

page 192: **"*It's a Wonderful Life*"** Jeanine Basinger, *The It's a Wonderful Life Book,* Norwalk, Conn.: The Easton Press, 2004, Introduction.

page 192: **"After World War II"** Andrew Sarris, *Village Voice,* May 19, 1987.

page 192: **"In my files"** Hedda Hopper, *Chicago Tribune Magazine,* April 18, 1954.

page 193: **"Hey, Jimmy, where"** This question and the others asked at the train station and Stewart's responses are from the *Los Angeles Examiner,* October 3, 1945.

page 194: **The game of Pitch** Michael Freedland, *Jane Fonda: A Biography,* New York: St. Martin's Press, 1988, 10.

page 194: **Footnote about Jimmy living in Fonda's house** During this visit, Jimmy made time to visit with Clark Gable, whose wife, Carole Lombard, had been killed, along with her mother, a few days earlier (January 16) when her plane crashed into the mountains shortly after takeoff, following a war bond drive in Las Vegas. Gable, a newly commissioned air force officer, was determined to see action, despite the fact that he was forty-one years old. Quote from James Brough, *The Fabulous Fondas,* New York: David McKay Company, 1973, 90.

page 195: **"the whole town"** Hedda Hopper, syndicated column, October 1945.

page 195: **Stewart's dates and sleeping attire** Sidney Skolsky, "Tintypes," *Hollywood Citizen-News,* November 15, 1945.

page 200: **"Four years ago"** Capra, *The Name Above the Title: An Autobiography,* New York: Macmillan, 1971, 371.

page 201: **"uniting producer-directors"** Ibid., 372.

page 202: **"It was the story"** Ibid., 376.

page 203: **"For crissake"** Capra, *The Name Above the Title,* 377.

page 207: **"wildly melodramatic"** Sarris, *You Ain't Heard Nothin' Yet,* 355.

page 208: **"Jimmy didn't feel"** Bogdanovich, *Pieces of Time,* 135.

page 208: **"Both Capra and Stewart"** *Life* magazine, September 23, 1946.

page 208: **"the pain and sorrow"** Sarris, *You Ain't Heard,* 356. Here is more of what Mr. Sarris wrote about *It's a Wonderful Life:* "The last-minute happy ending never quite compensates for all the suffering that precedes it, and yet there is something unyieldingly idealistic in Stewart's persona that clears away any sour aftertaste from what in the final analysis is one of the most profoundly pessimistic tales of human existence ever to achieve a lasting popularity. Yet even in its darkest moments, *It's a Wonderful Life* achieves a mini-epiphany with a burly, surly patron sitting grimly at a bar near the despondent Bailey. When he hears the name 'Bailey' mentioned, he hauls off and socks the already tortured protagonist seemingly without provocation until we learn that the assailant's wife is the schoolteacher whom the distraught Bailey has unfairly scolded on the telephone for letting his little girl go home alone in the snow and cold. The 'heavy' in every sense of the word emerges as one of us as he movingly describes his wife's crying over the episode. In this one moment the humanism of *It's a Wonderful Life* cancels out all the cute, cloying embarrassments of the angel played by Henry Travers."

page 209: **"The film was"** Frank Capra Jr. interview with author.

page 209: **"it was when"** Sarris, *Village Voice,* May 19, 1987.

CHAPTER 14

page 217: **"Later, over coffee"** Barbara Heggie, *Woman's Home Companion,* April 1947.

page 218: **"something has to be done"** Hedda Hopper, syndicated column, *Chicago Tribune,* February 1948.

CHAPTER 15

page 219: **"Stewart claimed"** Alfred Hitchcock, as told to Favius Friedman. *Popular Photography,* November 1948.

page 222: **"raise eyebrows"** Charlotte Chandler, *It's Only a Movie: Alfred Hitchcock, a Personal Biography,* New York: Simon & Schuster, 2005, 170.

page 222: **"Both Cary Grant and"** Arthur Laurents, *Original Story,* New York: Knopf, 2000,

page 223: **"*Rope* wasn't my favorite"** Chandler, *It's Only a Movie,* 169.

page 223: **"The only thing"** Laurents, *Original Story,* 128.

page 223: **"Jimmy Stewart was not"** Chandler, *It's Only a Movie,* 170.

CHAPTER 16

page 232: **"One morning I"** Robbins, *Everybody's Man,* 103 (unattributed).

page 235: **"I could tell"** and **"The romance"** Ibid., 70 (unattributed).

page 237: **"I knew Jimmy"** June Allyson with Frances Spatz Leighton, *June Allyson,* New York: Putnam's, 1982, 95.

CHAPTER 17

page 240: **"If the prewar"** Martin Scorsese speaking at the American Film Institute presentation of the Lifetime Achievement Award to Jimmy Stewart, February 1980.

page 242: **"When I first"** Quoted by Aline Mosby, *Los Angeles Daily News,* August 8, 1949.

page 243: **"rather bewildered"** This and other details of the wedding are from the *Los Angeles Daily News,* August 10, 1949.

CHAPTER 18

page 247: **"*Winchester '73* was"** Stewart quoted in McBride, *Frank Capra.*

page 250: **"When the picture"** Dewey, *James Stewart* (unattributed).

page 250: **"was not only"** Richard T. Jameson, "Anthony Mann," *American Film: A Journal of Film and Television Arts,* January 1990.

page 251: **"Mann's reputation"** Elliott Stein, *Village Voice,* August 11, 2004.

page 251: **"The Westerners"** Terrence Rafferty, *New York Times,* August 8, 2004.

CHAPTER 19

page 256: **"I played"** Allyson, *June Allyson,* 77.

page 257: **"Where Gloria and I"** *Coronet,* July 1970.

page 257: **"I remember painfully"** Jimmy Stewart interview with Jack Holland, 1968 (Universal press release).

page 261: **"Fonda, his long-time"** Teichmann, *Fonda.*

CHAPTER 20

page 269: **"Hitchcock saw in Stewart"** Dan Auiler, *Vertigo: The Making of a Hitchcock Classic,* New York: St. Martin's Press, 1998, 19.

page 275: **"A lot of things"** James Spada, *Grace: The Secret Lives of a Princess,* New York: Doubleday, 1987.

page 275: **"I was absolutely"** *USA Today,* March 6, 1987.

page 275: **"We were all so"** Patrick McGilligan, *Alfred Hitchcock: A Life in Darkness and Light,* New York: Regan Books, 2003.

page 275: **"Every man who"** Ibid.

page 276: **"It gave me"** Quirk, *James Stewart,* 190.

page 277: **"When you think"** Roger Ebert, *Chicago Sun-Times,* March 16, 1968.

CHAPTER 21

page 279: **"I've never got much"** *Los Angeles Times,* October 15, 1967.

page 279: **"the biggest single"** *Newsweek,* May 9, 1955.

page 280: **"For a long time"** Paramount press release, circa July 1955.

page 281: **"When Richard [Powell] and I"** Allyson, *June Allyson,* 95.

page 283: **"In *The Man from Laramie*"** Stein, *Village Voice,* August 11, 2004.

page 283: **"That [film] distilled"** Eyles, *James Stewart,* 130, further unattributed.

page 285: **"My dad had"** Eleanor Harris, *Los Angeles Examiner,* January 1, 1956.

page 286: **"One Sunday"** *McCall's,* May 1964.

page 286: **Quotes regarding the Far East trip** Louella Parsons, *Los Angeles Examiner,* May 1, 1955.

page 293: **"Hitchcock and I met"** Donald Spoto, 389.

page 295: **"interrupts the harmony"** Ibid.

page 295: **"The first time"** Ibid.

page 295: **"[Hitchcock] was very"** Ibid., 391.

page 295: **"In the beginning"** Ibid., 392.

page 296: **"Hitch believed"** Neil P. Hurley, "The Many-Splendored Actor: An Interview with Jimmy Stewart," *The New Orleans Review,* Summer/Fall 1983.

CHAPTER 22

page 298: **"Leading my list"** Kim Novak, *TV Guide,* March 7, 1987.

page 298: **Excerpts of conversation at Hayward dinner pary** *Los Angeles Examiner* (American Weekly supplement), January 1, 1956.

page 299: **against a cement** Fishgall, *Pieces of Time,* 258.

page 299: **"I wanted to"** Ibid.

page 300: **"Like Lindbergh"** Ibid.

page 301: **embarrassment** Andrew Sarris, *Village Voice,* May 19, 1987.

CHAPTER 23

page 323: **"Ford, Hitchcock, Wilder"** *Los Angeles Times,* October 15, 1967.

page 325: **"The common wisdom"** Peter Bogdanovich, *Who the Hell's in It?,* New York: Knopf, 2004, 245–46.

page 325: **"First of all"** Kim Novak interviews with author.

page 327: **"to make sure"** Mervyn LeRoy, *Mervyn LeRoy: Take One,* New York: Hawthorne Books, 1974, 199.

page 328: **Stewart comments about the studio system** *Variety,* October 3, 1958.

page 333: **"As the flashbulbs"** Charlton Heston, *In the Arena,* New York: Simon & Schuster, 1995.

CHAPTER 24

page 337: **"Of the westerns"** "Films and Filming," April 1966.

page 337: **"I love him . . . "** Peter Bogdanovich, 174.

page 338: **"In accepting"** Andrew Sarris, *The John Ford Movie Mystery,* 180.

page 339: **"I remember the first"** Stewart interviewed by Hurley.

page 340: **"I went up"** Bogdanovich, *Pieces of Time,* 174.

page 340: **"a load of crap"** Dewey, *James Stewart,* 412 (unattributed).

page 344: **Bogdanovich on *Liberty Valance*** Peter Bogdanovich, *Peter Bogdanovich's Movie of the Week,* New York: Ballantine, 1999, 89.

CHAPTER 25

page 349: **"This aging problem"** Dick Kleiner, *Show Beat,* July 22, 1964.

page 351: **"If you want a record"** and **"We used to take movies"** Susan Squire, *Los Angeles Herald Examiner,* July 22, 1976.

page 351: **The story of the girl and the tour bus** *Los Angeles Times,* September 28, 1963.

page 352: **"It was a profitable"** Wolfson, in a 20th Century Fox press release, approximately April 1963.

page 352: **"After it was all over"** *McCall's,* May 1964.

page 353: **"It's sad closing"** *Los Angeles Herald-Examiner,* May 22, 1963

page 353: **Information regarding Chasen's, and the quote from Bill Frye** William Frye, interview with author.

page 354: **"It gets difficult"** and **"find the audience"** *The Film Daily,* November 19, 1963.

page 354: **"All I could think of"** Jimmy Stewart's personal notes, June 26, 1964.

page 355: **"having killed a lot of Indians"** and **"make amends"** John Ford to producer Bernard Smith as quoted in Fishgall, *Pieces of Time,* 294.

page 355: **"rather stolid"** Peter Bart, *New York Times,* October 11, 1964.

page 357: **"my father's only real close friend"** Kelly Stewart Harcourt, interview with author.

page 357: **"I hate them!"** Dewey, *James Stewart,* 444.

page 357: **"Michael and I"** Kelly Stewart Harcourt, interview with author.

page 359: **"We had never"** Kelly Stewart Harcourt, interview with author.

page 363: **"Jim and I played"** Teichmann, *Fonda,* 305.

CHAPTER 26

page 367: **"People ask if we're bitter"** Combined public comments of Stewart, Klemesrud, *New York Times,* February 22, 1970.

page 367: **"There's our son"** Aljean Harmetz, *New York Times,* February 22, 1970.

page 367: **"But losing"** *Coronet,* July 1970.

page 368: **"For me"** Kelly Stewart Harcourt, interview with author.

page 370: **"The picture was"** and **"Stewart would slip"** Howard Teichmann, *Fonda.*

page 370: **"I'd say to Fonda"** Angela Fox Dunn, *Boston Herald,* December 7, 1983.

page 375: **"A kid came"** Joyce Haber, *Los Angeles Times,* March 15, 1970.

page 378: **"There hasn't been"** Vernon Scott, *Los Angeles Herald-Examiner,* May 21, 1971.

page 378: **"the deep think boys"** Ibid.

CHAPTER 27

page 382: **"Jimmy loved to"** William Frye, *Vanity Fair,* April 2003.

page 382: **"I don't think"** McLaughlin, *People,* September 1, 1975.

page 384: **"I'm more conservative"** Arthur Bell, "Talking on the Turnpike with My Father's Favorite Star," *Village Voice,* August 14, 1978.

page 385: **"adoptive father"** of an orangutan Walter Wagner, *Beverly Hills: Inside the Golden Ghetto,* New York: Grosset and Dunlap, 1976, 127.

page 385: **"Gloria, Jimmy and I"** Frye, *Vanity Fair,* and interview with author.

page 386: **"We got into Tokyo"** Ibid.

page 387: **"Harvey"** *Los Angeles Times,* December 11, 1978.

page 387: **"You know"** Teichmann, *Fonda,* 352.

page 388: **"that was good"** From Bell, "Talking on the Turnpike," and from Kelly Stewart Harcourt ("that was good," "she should have said it that way," "I wish I hadn't done it that way," "that dialogue doesn't work," describing to the author her father watching himself on television.

page 394: **"Then, suddenly"** Dewey, *James Stewart,* 482.

CHAPTER 28

page 397: *"**Rear Window** has already"* David Sterritt, *The Christian Science Monitor,* October 20, 1983.

page 400: **"It was titled"** *Variety,* October 5, 1983.

page 401: **"The wonderful thing"** Janet Maslin, *New York Times,* October 9, 1983.

page 401: **"I remember her so vividly"** Dunn, BH December 5, 1983.

page 401: **Janet Maslin and Andrew Sarris** Their reviews of the rerelease of *Vertigo* are here taken from Aulier, *Vertigo,* 190–91.

CHAPTER 29

page 404: **"It's over"** Paul Hendrickson, *Life* magazine, July 1991.

page 405: **"a property issue"** Jane Birnbaum, *Los Angeles Herald-Examiner,* July 3, 1988.

page 408: **"the hierarchy"** John Karlen, Interview with the author.

page 409: **"I'm devastated"** *New York Daily News,* July 3, 1997.

Filmography

All films are feature length, except where noted by asterisk (*), and are listed in the order of their release (year noted), which sometimes differs from the order in which they were made. Production companies are listed separately if they are different from the major studio distributor.

1. **ART TROUBLE** (1934).* A Vitaphone Corporation short. Directed by Ralph Staub. Producer uncredited. Screenplay (story) by Jack Henley, Dolph Singer. Principal cast: Harry Gribbon, Shemp Howard, Beatrice Blinn, Leni Stengel, James Stewart (uncredited).

2. **THE MURDER MAN** (1935). MGM. Directed by Tim Whelan. Produced by Harry Rapf. Screenplay by Tim Whelan, John C. Higgins (from a story by Tim Whelan and Guy Bolton). Principal cast: Spencer Tracy, Virginia Bruce, Lionel Atwill, Harvey Stephens, Robert Barrat, James Stewart, Fuzzy Knight, Ralph Bushman.

3. **ROSE-MARIE** (1936). MGM. Directed by W. S. Van Dyke II. Produced by Hunt Stromberg. Screenplay by Frances Goodrich, Albert Hackett, Alice D. G. Miller, from an operetta with books and lyrics by Otto A. Harbach and Oscar Hammerstein II. Principal cast: Jeanette MacDonald, Nelson Eddy, Reginald Owen, Allan Jones, James Stewart, Alan Mowbray, Gilda Gray, George Regas, Robert Greig, Una O'Connor, Lucien Littlefield, David Niven, Herman Bing.

4. **NEXT TIME WE LOVE** (1936). Universal. Directed by Edward H. Griffith. Produced by Paul Kohner. Screenplay by Melville Baker (Doris Anderson and Preston Sturges both worked, uncredited, on the script, from the Ursula Parrott story "Say Goodbye Again"). Principal cast: Margaret Sullavan, James Stewart, Ray Milland, Grant Mitchell, Anna Demetrio, Robert McWade, Ronnie Cosby, Florence Roberts, Christian Rub (uncredited), Charles Fall, Nat Carr, Gottlieb Huber.

5. **WIFE VS. SECRETARY** (1936). MGM. Directed by Clarence Brown. Produced by Hunt Stromberg. Screenplay by Norman Krasna, Alice Duer Miller, John Lee Mahin (from the short story by Faith Baldwin). Principal cast: Clark Gable, Jean Harlow, Myrna Loy, May Robson, George Barbier, James Stewart, Hobart Cavanaugh, Tom Dugan, Gilbert Emery.

6. **IMPORTANT NEWS** (1936).* An MGM Miniature (10 minutes). Directed by Edwin Lawrence. Produced by Metro-Goldwyn-Mayer. Principal cast: Charles "Chic" Sale, James Stewart.

7. **SMALL TOWN GIRL** (1936). MGM. Directed by William A. Wellman. Produced by Hunt Stromberg. Screenplay by John Lee Mahin, Edith Fitzgerald,

Frances Goodrich, and Albert Hackett (from the novel by Ben Ames Williams). Principal cast: Janet Gaynor, Robert Taylor, Binnie Barnes, Lewis Stone, Andy Devine, Elizabeth Patterson, Frank Craven, James Stewart, Douglas Fowley, Isabel Jewell, Charley Grapewin, Nella Walker, Robert Greig, Edgar Kennedy, Willie Fung.

8. **SPEED** (1936). MGM. Directed by Edwin L. Marin. Produced by Lucien Hubbard. Screenplay by Michael Fessier (from an original story by Milton Krims and Larry Bachman). Principal cast: James Stewart, Una Merkel, Ted Healy, Wendy Barrie, Weldon Heyburn, Ralph Morgan, Patricia Wilder.

9. **THE GORGEOUS HUSSY** (1936). MGM. Directed by Clarence Brown. Produced by Joseph L. Mankiewicz. Screenplay by Ainsworth Morgan, Stephen Morehouse Avery (from the novel by Samuel Hopkins Adams). Principal cast: Joan Crawford, Robert Taylor, Lionel Barrymore, Franchot Tone, Melvyn Douglas, James Stewart, Alison Skipworth, Louis Calhern, Beulah Bondi, Melville Cooper, Edith Atwater, Sidney Toler, Gene Lockhart, Phoebe Foster, Clara Blandick, Frank Conroy, Nydia Westman, Willard Robertson, Charles Trowbridge, Greta Meyer, Fred "Snowflake" Toones.

10. **BORN TO DANCE** (1936). MGM. Directed by Roy Del Ruth. Produced by Jack Cummings. Screenplay by Jack McGowan and Sid Silvers (from their screen story written with B. G. DeSylva). Principal cast: Eleanor Powell, James Stewart, Virginia Bruce, Una Merkel, Sid Silvers, Frances Langford, Raymond Walburn, Alan Dinehart, Buddy Ebsen, William Mandel, Joe Mandel, Juanita Quigley, Georges and Jalna, Reginald Gardiner, J. Marshall Smith, L. Dwight Snyder, Jay Johnson, Del Porter.

11. **AFTER THE THIN MAN** (1936). MGM. Directed by W. S. Van Dyke II. Produced by Hunt Stromberg. Screenplay by Frances Goodrich, Albert Hackett (from unpublished story material by Dashiell Hammett). Principal cast: William Powell, Myrna Loy, James Stewart, Elissa Landi, Joseph Calleia, Jessie Ralph, Alan Marshal, Teddy Hart, Sam Levene, Dorothy McNulty (as Penny Singleton is credited), William Law, George Zucco, Paul Fix.

12. **SEVENTH HEAVEN** (1937). 20th Century Fox. Directed by Henry King. Produced by Darryl F. Zanuck, associate produced by Raymond Griffith. Screenplay by Melville Baker (from the play by Austin Strong). Principal cast: Simone Simon, James Stewart, Jean Hersholt, Gregory Ratoff, Gale Sondergaard, J. Edward Bromberg, John Qualen, Victor Kilian, Thomas Beck, Sig Rumann, Mady Christians, Rollo Lloyd, Rafaela Ottiano, Georges Renavent, Edward Keane, John Hamilton, Paul Porcasi, Will Stanton, Irving Bacon, Leonid Snegoff, Adrienne D'Ambricourt.

13. **THE LAST GANGSTER** (1937). MGM. Directed by Edward Ludwig. Produced by J. J. Cohn. Screenplay by John Lee Mahin (from a story by William A. Wellman and Robert Carson). Principal cast: Edward G. Robinson, James Stewart, Rose Stradner, Lionel Stander, Douglas Scott, John Carradine, Sidney Blackmer, Grant Mitchell, Edward S. Brody, Alan Baxter, Frank Conroy, Louise Beavers.

14. **NAVY BLUE AND GOLD** (1937). MGM. Directed by Sam Wood. Produced by Sam Zimbalist. Screenplay by George Bruce (from his novel). Principal cast: Robert Young, James Stewart, Florence Rice, Billie Burke, Lionel Barrymore, Tom Brown, Samuel S. Hinds, Paul Kelly, Barnett Parker, Frank Albertson, Minor Watson, Robert Middlemass, Phillip Terry, Charles Waldron, Pat Flaherty, Stanley Morner (as Dennis Morgan is billed), Matt McHugh, Ted Pearson.

15. **OF HUMAN HEARTS** (1938). MGM (Loew's Inc.). Directed by Clarence Brown. Produced by John W. Considine Jr. Screenplay by Bradbury Foote (from the story "Benefits Forgot" by Honore Morrow). Principal cast: Walter Huston, James Stewart, Gene Reynolds, Beulah Bondi, Guy Kibbee, Charles Coburn, John Carra-

dine, Ann Rutherford, Leatrice Joy Gilbert, Charley Grapewin, Leona Roberts, Gene Lockhart, Clem Bevans, Arthur Aylesworth, Sterling Holloway, Charles Peck, Robert McWade, Minor Watson.

16. **VIVACIOUS LADY** (1938). RKO. Directed by George Stevens. Produced by Pandro S. Berman. Screenplay by P. J. Wolfson, Ernest Pagano, Anne Morrison Chapin (uncredited) (from a novelette by I. A. R. Wylie). Principal cast: Ginger Rogers, James Stewart, James Ellison, Beulah Bondi, Charles Coburn, Frances Mercer, Phyllis Kennedy, Franklin Pangborn, Grady Sutton, Jack Carson, Alec Craig, Willie Best.

17. **THE SHOPWORN ANGEL** (1938). MGM (Loew's Inc.). Directed by H. C. Potter. Produced by Joseph L. Mankiewicz. Screenplay by Waldo Salt, Howard Estabrook (uncredited) (from the story "Private Pettigrew's Girl" by Dana Burnet). Principal cast: Margaret Sullavan, James Stewart, Walter Pidgeon, Hattie McDaniel, Nat Pendleton, Alan Curtis, Sam Levene, Eleanor Lynn, Charles D. Brown.

18. **YOU CAN'T TAKE IT WITH YOU** (1938). Columbia. Directed by Frank Capra. Produced by Frank Capra. Screenplay by Robert Riskin (from the stage play by George S. Kaufman and Moss Hart). Principal cast: Jean Arthur, Lionel Barrymore, James Stewart, Edward Arnold, Mischa Auer, Ann Miller, Spring Byington, Samuel S. Hinds, Donald Meek, H. B. Warner, Halliwell Hobbes, Dub Taylor, Mary Forbes, Lillian Yarbo, Eddie "Rochester" Anderson, Clarence Wilson, Josef Swickard, Ann Doran, Christian Rub, Bodil Rosing, Charles Lane, Harry Davenport.

19. **MADE FOR EACH OTHER** (1939). United Artists. Directed by John Cromwell. Produced by David O. Selznick Production Company. Screenplay by Jo Swerling (jokes contributed by Frank Ryan) (from a story idea by Rose Franken). Principal cast: Carole Lombard, James Stewart, Charles Coburn, Lucile Watson, Harry Davenport, Ruth Weston, Eddie Quillan, Alma Kruger, Esther Dale, Renee Orsell, Louise Beavers, Ward Bond, Olin Howland, Fern Emmett, Jackie Taylor, Mickey Rentschler, Ivan Simpson.

20. **THE ICE FOLLIES OF 1939** (1939). MGM (Loew's Inc.). Directed by Reinhold Schünzel. Produced by Harry Rapf. Screenplay by Leonard Praskins, Florence Ryerson, Edgar Allan Woolf (from a screen story by Leonard Praskins). Principal cast: Joan Crawford, James Stewart, Lew Ayres, Lewis Stone, Bess Ehrhardt, Lionel Stander, Charles D. Brown, Roy Shipstad, Eddie Shipstad, Oscar Johnson.

21. **IT'S A WONDERFUL WORLD** (1939). MGM (Loew's Inc.). Directed by W. S. Van Dyke II. Produced by Frank Davis. Screenplay by Ben Hecht (from a screen story by Ben Hecht and Herman J. Mankiewicz). Principal cast: Claudette Colbert, James Stewart, Guy Kibbee, Nat Pendleton, Frances Drake, Edgar Kennedy, Ernest Truex, Richard Carle, Cecilia Callejo, Sidney Blackmer, Andy Clyde, Cecil Cunningham, Leonard Kibrick, Hans Conried, Grady Sutton.

22. **MR. SMITH GOES TO WASHINGTON** (1939). Columbia. Directed by Frank Capra. Produced by Frank Capra. Screenplay by Sidney Buchman (from the story "The Gentleman from Montana" by Lewis R. Foster). Principal cast: James Stewart, Jean Arthur, Claude Rains, Edward Arnold, Guy Kibbee, Thomas Mitchell, Eugene Pallette, Beulah Bondi, H. B. Warner, Harry Carey, Astrid Allwyn, William Demarest.

23. **DESTRY RIDES AGAIN** (1939). Universal. Directed by George Marshall. Produced by Joe Pasternak. Screenplay by Felix Jackson, Gertrude Purcell, Henry Myers (from a screen story by Felix Jackson, from the novel by Max Brand). Principal cast: James Stewart, Marlene Dietrich, Mischa Auer, Charles Winninger, Brian Donlevy, Allen Jenkins, Warren Hymer, Jack Carson.

24. **THE SHOP AROUND THE CORNER** (1940). MGM. Directed by Ernst Lubitsch. Produced by Ernst Lubitsch. Screenplay by Samson Raphaelson, Ben

Hecht (uncredited), (from the play *Parfumerie* by Miklós László). Principal cast: James Stewart, Margaret Sullavan, Frank Morgan, Joseph Schildkraut, Sara Haden, Felix Bressart, William Tracy, Inez Courtney, Sarah Edwards, Gertrude Simpson.

25. **THE MORTAL STORM** (1940). MGM. Directed by Frank Borzage. Produced by Sidney Franklin (Frank Borzage, Victor Saville, both uncredited). Screenplay by Claudine West, Andersen Ellis, George Froeschel (from the novel by Phyllis Bottome). Principal cast: James Stewart, Margaret Sullavan, Robert Young, Frank Morgan, Irene Rich, Maria Ouspenskaya, William T. Orr, Robert Stack, Bonita Granville, Gene Reynolds, Russell Hicks, William Edmunds, Ward Bond, Dan Dailey, Esther Dale, Sue Moore, Granville Bates.

26. **NO TIME FOR COMEDY** (1940). Warner Bros. Directed by William Keighley. Produced by Hal B. Wallis. Screenplay by Julius J. and Philip G. Epstein (from the play by S. N. Behrman). Principal cast: James Stewart, Rosalind Russell, Charles Ruggles, Genevieve Tobin, Louise Beavers, Allyn Joslyn, Clarence Kolb, Robert Greig, Frank Faylen, Robert Emmett O'Connor.

27. **THE PHILADELPHIA STORY** (1940). MGM. Directed by George Cukor. Produced by Joseph L. Mankiewicz. Screenplay by Donald Ogden Stewart, Waldo Salt (uncredited) (from the play by Philip Barry). Principal cast: Cary Grant, Katharine Hepburn, James Stewart, Ruth Hussey, John Howard, Roland Young, Virginia Weidler, John Halliday, Mary Nash, Henry Daniell, Lionel Pape, Rex Evans, Russ Clark, Hilda Plowright, Lita Chevret, Lee Phelps.

28. **COME LIVE WITH ME** (1941). MGM. Directed by Clarence Brown. Produced by Clarence Brown. Screenplay by Patterson McNutt (from an original story by Virginia Van Upp). Principal cast: James Stewart, Hedy Lamarr, Ian Hunter, Verree Teasdale, Donald Meek, Barton MacLane, Edward Ashley, Ann Codee, King Baggot, Adeline de Walt Reynolds, Si Jenks, Dewey Robinson.

29. **POT O' GOLD** (1941). Released in Great Britain as *The Golden Hour*. United Artists. Directed by George Marshall (dance director Larry Ceballos). Produced by James Roosevelt (Globe Pictures). Screenplay by Walter DeLeon (from a screen story by Monte Brice, Andrew Bennison, and Harry Tugend, based on a story idea by Haydn Roth Evans and Robert Brilmayer). Principal cast: James Stewart, Paulette Goddard, Horace Heidt and His Musical Knights, Charles Winninger, Mary Gordon, Frank Melton, Jed Prouty, Dick Hogan, James Burke, Charlie Arnt, Donna Wood, Henry Roquemore, Larry Cotton, William Gould, Aldrich Bowker.

30. **ZIEGFELD GIRL** (1941). MGM. Directed by Robert Z. Leonard. Produced by Pandro S. Berman (musical numbers directed by Busby Berkeley). Screenplay by Marguerite Roberts, Sonya Levien (from a story by William Anthony McGuire). Principal cast: James Stewart, Judy Garland, Hedy Lamarr, Lana Turner, Tony Martin, Jackie Cooper, Ian Hunter, Charles Winninger, Edward Everett Horton, Philip Dorn, Paul Kelly, Eve Arden, Dan Dailey Jr., Al Shean, Fay Holden, Felix Bressart, Rose Hobart, Bernard Nedell, Ed McNamara, Mae Busch, Renie Riano.

31. **IT'S A WONDERFUL LIFE** (1946). Liberty Films (distributed by RKO). Directed by Frank Capra. Produced by Frank Capra. Screenplay by Frances Goodrich, Albert Hackett, Frank Capra (uncredited), Michael Wilson, Clifford Odets, Jo Swerling (from the short story "The Greatest Gift" by Philip Van Doren Stern). Principal cast: James Stewart, Donna Reed, Lionel Barrymore, Thomas Mitchell, Henry Travers, Beulah Bondi, Frank Faylen, Ward Bond, Gloria Grahame, H. B. Warner, Frank Albertson, Samuel S. Hinds, Todd Karns, Mary Treen, Virginia Patton, Charles Williams, Sarah Edwards, Bill Edmunds, Lillian Randolph, Argentina Brunetti, Karolyn Grimes.

32. **MAGIC TOWN** (1947). Robert Riskin Productions (distributed by RKO). Directed by William A. Wellman. Produced by Robert Riskin. Screenplay by Robert Riskin (from a screen story by Robert Riskin and Joseph Krumgold). Principal cast: James Stewart, Jane Wyman, Kent Smith, Ned Sparks, Wallace Ford, Regis Toomey, Ann Doran, Donald Meek, E. J. Ballantine, Ann Shoemaker, Mickey Kuhn, Howard Freeman, Harry Holman, Mickey Roth, Mary Currier, George Irving, Selmer Jackson, Robert Dudley, Julia Dean.

33. **CALL NORTHSIDE 777** (1948). 20th Century Fox. Directed by Henry Hathaway. Produced by Otto Lang. Screenplay by Jerome Cady, Jay Dratler (from newspaper articles by James P. McGuire adapted by Leonard Hoffman and Quentin Reynolds). Principal cast: James Stewart, Richard Conte, Lee J. Cobb, Helen Walker, Betty Garde, Kasia Orzazewski, Joanne De Bergh, Howard Smith, Paul Harvey, John McIntire, Moroni Olsen, George Tyne, Richard Bishop, Otto Waldis, Michael Chapin, E. G. Marshall, John Bleifer.

34. **ON OUR MERRY WAY** (1948). Aka *A Miracle Can Happen*. Miracle Productions. Directed by King Vidor, Leslie Fenton (uncredited), John Huston, and George Stevens (the segment in which James Stewart appears). Produced by Burgess Meredith. Screenplay by Laurence Stallings, Lou Breslow, John O'Hara (the segment in which James Stewart appears) (from a story by Arch Oboler). Principal cast (in the segment in which James Stewart appears): James Stewart, Burgess Meredith, Henry Fonda, Eduardo Ciannelli, Dorothy Ford, Carl "Alfalfa" Switzer, Harry James.

35. **ROPE** (1948). Warner Bros. Directed by Alfred Hitchcock. Produced by Alfred Hitchcock and Sidney Bernstein (Transatlantic Pictures). Screenplay by Arthur Laurents, Ben Hecht (uncredited, adapted by Hume Cronyn from the play by Patrick Hamilton). Principal cast: James Stewart, John Dall, Farley Granger, Joan Chandler, Sir Cedric Hardwicke, Constance Collier, Edith Evanson, Douglas Dick, Dick Hogan.

36. **YOU GOTTA STAY HAPPY** (1948). Universal. Directed by H. C. Potter. Produced by Karl Tunberg. Screenplay by Karl Tunberg (from a serialized magazine story by Robert Carson). Principal cast: Joan Fontaine, James Stewart, Eddie Albert, Roland Young, Willard Parker, Percy Kilbride, Porter Hall, Marcy McGuire, Arthur Walsh, Paul Cavanagh, William Bakewell, Halliwell Hobbes, Stanley Prager, Mary Forbes, Edith Evanson, Peter Roman, Houseley Stevenson.

37. **THE STRATTON STORY** (1949). MGM. Directed by Sam Wood. Produced by Jack Cummings. Screenplay by Douglas Morrow, Guy Trosper (uncredited), George Wells (from a screen story by Douglas Morrow). Principal cast: James Stewart, June Allyson, Frank Morgan, Agnes Moorehead, Bill Williams, Bruce Cowling, Gene Bearden, Bill Dickey, Jimmy Dykes, Cliff Clark, Mary Lawrence, Dean White, Robert Gist.

38. **MALAYA** (1949). Released in Britain as *East of the Rising Sun*. MGM. Directed by Richard Thorpe. Produced by Edwin H. Knopf. Screenplay by Frank Fenton (from an original story by Manchester Boddy). Principal cast: Spencer Tracy, James Stewart, Valentina Cortese, Sydney Greenstreet, John Hodiak, Lionel Barrymore, Gilbert Roland, Roland Winters, Richard Loo, Lester Matthews, Ian MacDonald, Charles Meredith, James Todd, Paul Kruger, Anna Q. Nilsson.

39. **WINCHESTER '73** (1950). Universal-International. Directed by Anthony Mann. Produced by Aaron Rosenberg. Screenplay by Robert L. Richards, Borden Chase (from a story by Stuart N. Lake). Principal cast: James Stewart, Shelley Winters, Dan Duryea, Stephen McNally, Millard Mitchell, Charles Drake, John McIntire, Will Geer, Jay C. Flippen, Rock Hudson, John Alexander, Steve Brodie, James Millican, Abner Biberman, Tony Curtis (as Anthony Curtis), James Best, Gregg Martell.

40. **BROKEN ARROW** (1950). 20th Century Fox. Directed by Delmer Daves. Produced by Julian Blaustein. Screenplay by Albert Maltz, fronted by Michael Blankfort (from the novel *Blood Brother* by Elliott Arnold). Principal cast: James Stewart, Jeff Chandler, Debra Paget, Basil Ruysdael, Will Geer, Joyce MacKenzie, Arthur Hunnicutt, Raymond Bramley, Jay Silverheels, Argentina Brunetti, Jack Lee, Robert Adler, Harry Carter, Robert Griffin, Billy Wilkerson, Mickey Kuhn.

41. **THE JACKPOT** (1950). 20th Century Fox. Directed by Walter Lang. Produced by Samuel G. Engel. Screenplay by Phoebe and Henry Ephron (from a magazine article by John McNulty). Principal cast: James Stewart, Barbara Hale, James Gleason, Fred Clark, Alan Mowbray, Patricia Medina, Natalie Wood, Tommy Rettig, Robert Gist, Lyle Talbot, Charles Tannen, Bigelow Sayre, Dick Cogan, Jewel Rose, Eddie Firestone, Estelle Etterre.

42. **HARVEY** (1950). Universal-International. Directed by Henry Koster. Produced by John Beck. Screenplay by Mary Chase, Oscar Brodney, and Myles Connolly (from the original Broadway play by Mary Chase). Principal cast: James Stewart, Josephine Hull, Peggy Dow, Charles Drake, Cecil Kellaway, Victoria Horne, Jesse White, William Lynn, Wallace Ford, Nana Bryant, Grace Mills, Clem Bevans, Ida Moore, Dick Wessel.

43. **NO HIGHWAY IN THE SKY** (1951). 20th Century Fox. Directed by Henry Koster. Produced by Louis D. Lighton. Screenplay by R. C. Sherriff, Oscar Millard, Alec Coppel (from the novel *No Highway* by Nevil Shute). Principal cast: James Stewart, Marlene Dietrich, Glynis Johns, Jack Hawkins, Janette Scott, Elizabeth Allan, Ronald Squire, Jill Clifford, Niall MacGinnis, Kenneth More, Wilfred Hyde-White, Maurice Denham, David Hutcheson, Hugh Wakefield.

44. **THE GREATEST SHOW ON EARTH** (1952). Paramount. Directed by Cecil B. DeMille. Produced by Cecil B. DeMille. Screenplay by Fredric M. Frank, Barré Lyndon, Theodore St. John, and Frank Cavett. Principal cast: Betty Hutton, Cornel Wilde, Charlton Heston, Dorothy Lamour, Gloria Grahame, James Stewart, Henry Wilcoxon, Emmett Kelly, Lyle Bettger, Lawrence Tierney, John Kellogg, John Ridgely, Frank Wilcox, Bob Carson.

45. **BEND OF THE RIVER** (1952). Released in Great Britain as *Where the River Bends* (to avoid confusion with *The End of the River*). Universal-International. Directed by Anthony Mann. Produced by Aaron Rosenberg. Screenplay by Borden Chase (from the novel *Bend of the River* by Bill Gulick). Principal cast: James Stewart, Arthur Kennedy, Julie Adams, Rock Hudson, Lori Nelson, Jay C. Flippen, Harry Morgan, Chubby Johnson, Howard Petrie, Royal Dano, Stepin Fetchit, Jack Lambert, Frank Ferguson, Frances Bavier, Cliff Lyons, Jennings Miles, Frank Chase, Lillian Randolph.

46. **CARBINE WILLIAMS** (1952). MGM. Directed by Richard Thorpe. Produced by Armand Deutsch. Screenplay by Art Cohn (from a nonfiction magazine article by David Marshall Williams). Principal cast: James Stewart, Jean Hagen, Wendell Corey, Carl Benton Reid, Paul Stewart, Otto Hulett, Rhys Williams, Herbert Heyes, James Arness, Porter Hall, Fay Roope, Ralph Dumke, Leif Erickson, Henry Corden, Howard Petrie, Frank Richards, Stuart Randall, Dan Riss, Bobby Hyatt, Willis Bouchey.

47. **THE NAKED SPUR** (1953). MGM. Directed by Anthony Mann. Produced by William H. Wright. Screenplay by Sam Rolfe, Harold Jack Bloom. Principal cast: James Stewart, Janet Leigh, Robert Ryan, Ralph Meeker, Millard Mitchell.

48. **THUNDER BAY** (1953). Universal-International. Directed by Anthony Mann. Produced by Aaron Rosenberg. Screenplay by Gil Doud, John Michael Hayes (from a screen story by John Michael Hayes based on an idea by George W. George and

George F. Slavin). Principal cast: James Stewart, Joanne Dru, Gilbert Roland, Dan Duryea, Marcia Henderson, Robert Monet, Jay C. Flippen, Antonio Moreno, Harry Morgan, Fortunio Bonanova, Mario Siletti, Antonio Filauri.

49. **THE GLENN MILLER STORY** (1953). Universal-International. Directed by Anthony Mann. Produced by Aaron Rosenberg. Screenplay by Valentine Davies, Oscar Brodney. Principal cast: James Stewart, June Allyson, Charles Drake, Harry Morgan (as Henry Morgan), George Tobias, Barton MacLane, Sig Ruman, Irving Bacon, James Bell, Kathleen Lockhart, Katharine Warren, Dayton Lummis, Marion Ross, Phil Garris, Deborah Sydes, Frances Langford, Louis Armstrong, Gene Krupa, Ben Pollack, the Modernaires, and the Archie Savage Dancers.

50. **REAR WINDOW** (1954). Paramount. Directed by Alfred Hitchcock. Produced by Alfred Hitchcock. Screenplay by John Michael Hayes (from the short story by Cornell Woolrich). Principal cast: James Stewart, Grace Kelly, Wendell Corey, Thelma Ritter, Raymond Burr, Judith Evelyn, Ross Bagdasarian, Georgine Darcy, Sara Berner, Frank Cady, Jesslyn Fax, Rand Harper, Irene Winston, Havis Davenport.

51. **THE FAR COUNTRY** (1955). Universal-International. Directed by Anthony Mann. Produced by Aaron Rosenberg. Written by Borden Chase. Principal cast: James Stewart, Ruth Roman, Corinne Calvet, Walter Brennan, John McIntire, Jay C. Flippen, Harry Morgan, Steve Brodie, Connie Gilchrist, Robert Wilke, Chubby Johnson, Royal Dano, Jack Elam, Kathleen Freeman, Guy Wilkerson, Allan Ray, Eddy Waller, Eugene Borden, John Doucette, Robert Foulk, Paul Bryar.

52. **STRATEGIC AIR COMMAND** (1955). Directed by Anthony Mann. Produced by Samuel J. Briskin. Screenplay by Valentine Davies, Beirne Lay Jr. (from a screen story by Beirne Lay Jr.). Principal cast: James Stewart, June Allyson, Frank Lovejoy, Barry Sullivan, Alex Nicol, Bruce Bennett, Jay C. Flippen, James Millican, James Bell, Richard Shannon, Rosemary DeCamp, John McKee, Don Haggerty.

53. **THE MAN FROM LARAMIE** (1955). Columbia. Directed by Anthony Mann. Produced by William Goetz. Screenplay by Philip Yordan, Frank Burt (from the magazine serialization of the novel by Thomas T. Flynn). Principal cast: James Stewart, Arthur Kennedy, Donald Crisp, Cathy O'Donnell, Alex Nicol, Aline MacMahon, Wallace Ford, Jack Elam, John War Eagle, James Millican, Gregg Barton, Boyd Stockman, Frank DeKova.

54. **THE MAN WHO KNEW TOO MUCH** (1956). Paramount. Directed by Alfred Hitchcock. Produced by Alfred Hitchcock. Screenplay by John Michael Hayes, Angus McPhail (from a story by Charles Bennett and D. B. Wyndham-Lewis— original version made by Hitchcock in 1934, with Leslie Banks in the Stewart role). Principal cast: James Stewart, Doris Day, Brenda De Banzie, Bernard Miles, Ralph Truman, Daniel Gelin, Mogens Wieth, Alan Mowbray, Hillary Brooke, Christopher Olsen, Reggie Nalder, Noel Willman, Richard Wattis, Alix Talton, Yves Brainville, Carolyn Jones.

55. **THE SPIRIT OF ST. LOUIS** (1957). Warner Bros. Directed by Billy Wilder. Produced by Leland Hayward. Screenplay by Billy Wilder, Wendell Mayes (adaptation with Charles Lederer from the original book by Charles A. Lindbergh). Principal cast: James Stewart, Murray Hamilton, Patricia Smith, Bartlett Robinson, Robert Cornthwaite, Sheila Bond, Marc Connelly, Arthur Space, Harlan Warde, Dabbs Greer, Paul Birch, David Orrick, Robert Burton, James Robertson, Maurice Manson, James O'Rear, David McMahon, Griff Barnett.

56. **NIGHT PASSAGE** (1957). Universal. Directed by James Neilson. Produced by Aaron Rosenberg. Screenplay by Borden Chase (from the story by Norman A. Fox). Principal cast: James Stewart, Audie Murphy, Dan Duryea, Dianne Foster,

Elaine Stewart, Brandon de Wilde, Jay C. Flippen, Herbert Anderson, Robert J. Wilke, Hugh Beaumont, Jack Elam, Tommy Cook, Paul Fix, Olive Carey, James Flavin, Donald Curtis, Ellen Corby.

57. **VERTIGO** (1958). Paramount. Directed by Alfred Hitchcock. Produced by Alfred Hitchcock. Screenplay by Alec Coppel, Samuel Taylor (from the novel *D'entre les morts* by Pierre Boileau and Thomas Narcejac). Principal cast: James Stewart, Kim Novak, Barbara Bel Geddes, Tom Helmore, Henry Jones, Raymond Bailey, Ellen Corby, Konstantin Shayne, Lee Patrick, Paul Bryar, Margaret Brayton, William Remick, Julian Petruzzi, Sara Taft, Fred Graham.

58. **BELL BOOK AND CANDLE** (1958). Columbia. Directed by Richard Quine. Produced by Julian Blaustein. Screenplay by Daniel Taradash (from the play by John Van Druten). Principal cast: James Stewart, Kim Novak, Jack Lemmon, Ernie Kovacs, Hermione Gingold, Elsa Lanchester, Janice Rule, Philippe Clay, Bek Nelson, Howard McNear.

59. **ANATOMY OF A MURDER** (1959). Columbia. Directed by Otto Preminger. Produced by Otto Preminger (Carlyle Productions). Screenplay by Wendell Mayes (from the novel by Robert Traver, pen name for Justice John D. Voelker). Principal cast: James Stewart, Lee Remick, Ben Gazzara, Arthur O'Connell, Eve Arden, Kathryn Grant, Judge Joseph N. Welch, Brooks West, George C. Scott, Murray Hamilton, Orson Bean, Alexander Campbell, Joseph Kearns, Russ Brown, Howard McNear, Ned Wever, Jimmy Conlin, Ken Lynch.

60. **THE FBI STORY** (1959). Warner Bros. Directed by Mervyn LeRoy. Produced by Mervyn LeRoy. Screenplay by Richard L. Breen, John Twist (from the book by Don Whitehead). Principal cast: James Stewart, Vera Miles, Murray Hamilton, Larry Pennell, Nick Adams, Diane Jergens, Jean Willes, Joyce Taylor, Victor Millan, Parley Baer, Fay Roope, Ed Prentiss, Robert Gist, Buzz Martin, Kenneth Mayer, Paul Genge, Ann Doran, Forrest Taylor, Scott Peters, William Phipps.

61. **THE MOUNTAIN ROAD** (1960). Columbia. Directed by Daniel Mann. Produced by William Goetz. Screenplay by Alfred Hayes (from the novel by Theodore H. White). Principal cast: James Stewart, Lisa Lu, Glenn Corbett, Harry Morgan, Frank Silvera, James Best, Rudy Bond, Mike Kellin, Frank Maxwell, Eddie Firestone, Leo Chen, Alan Baxter, Bill Quinn, Peter Chong, P. C. Lee.

62. **TWO RODE TOGETHER** (1961). Columbia. Directed by John Ford. Produced by Stan Shpetner (John Ford Productions). Screenplay by Frank Nugent (from the magazine serialization and novel *Comanche Captives* by Will Cook). Principal cast: James Stewart, Richard Widmark, Shirley Jones, Linda Cristal, Andy Devine, John McIntire, Paul Birch, Willis Bouchey, Henry Brandon, Harry Carey Jr., Olive Carey, Ken Curtis, Chet Douglas, Annelle Hayes, David Kent, Anna Lee, Jeanette Nolan, John Qualen, Ford Rainey, Woody Strode.

63. **THE MAN WHO SHOT LIBERTY VALANCE** (1962). Paramount. Directed by John Ford. Produced by Willis Goldbeck (John Ford Productions). Screenplay by Willis Goldbeck, James Warner Bellah (from the story by Dorothy M. Johnson). Principal cast: James Stewart, John Wayne, Vera Miles, Lee Marvin, Edmond O'Brien, Andy Devine, Ken Murray, Jeanette Nolan, John Qualen, Willis Bouchey, Carleton Young, Woody Strode, Denver Pyle, Strother Martin, Lee Van Cleef, Robert F. Simon, O. Z. Whitehead, Paul Birch, Joseph Hoover.

64. **MR. HOBBS TAKES A VACATION** (1962). 20th Century Fox. Directed by Henry Koster. Produced by Jerry Wald. Screenplay by Nunnally Johnson (from the novel *Mr. Hobbs' Vacation* by Edward Streeter). Principal cast: James Stewart, Maureen O'Hara, Fabian, John Saxon, Marie Wilson, Reginald Gardiner, Lauri Peters,

Valerie Varda, Lili Gentle, John McGiver, Natalie Trundy, Josh Peine, Minerva Urecal, Michael Burns, Richard Collier, Peter Oliphant, Thomas Lowell, Stephen Mines, Dennis Whitcomb, Michael Sean.

65. **HOW THE WEST WAS WON** (1962). MGM (in Cinerama). Directed by John Ford, Henry Hathaway (Stewart's segment), George Marshall (uncredited), Richard Thorpe. Produced by Bernard Smith. Screenplay by James R. Webb, John Gay (uncredited). Principal cast: Spencer Tracy, Carroll Baker, Lee J. Cobb, Henry Fonda, Carolyn Jones, Karl Malden, Gregory Peck, George Peppard, Robert Preston, Debbie Reynolds, James Stewart, Eli Wallach, John Wayne, Richard Widmark, Brigid Bazlen, Walter Brennan, David Brian, Andy Devine, Raymond Massey, Agnes Moorehead, Harry Morgan, Thelma Ritter.

66. **TAKE HER, SHE'S MINE** (1963). 20th Century Fox. Directed by Henry Koster. Produced by Henry Koster. Screenplay by Nunnally Johnson (from the original Broadway play by Phoebe and Henry Ephron). Principal cast: James Stewart, Sandra Dee, Audrey Meadows, Robert Morley, Philippe Forquet, John McGiver, Bob Denver, Monica Moran, Jenny Maxwell, Cynthia Pepper, Maurice Marsac, Irene Tsu, Charla Doherty, Marcel Hillaire, Charles Robinson, Janine Grandel.

67. **CHEYENNE AUTUMN** (1964). Warner Bros. Directed by John Ford. Produced by Bernard Smith (Ford-Smith Productions). Screenplay by James R. Webb (from the novel by Mari Sandoz). Principal cast: James Stewart, Edward G. Robinson, Richard Widmark, Carroll Baker, Karl Malden, Sal Mineo, Dolores Del Rio, Ricardo Montalban, Gilbert Roland, Arthur Kennedy, Patrick Wayne, Elizabeth Allen, John Carradine, Victor Jory, Judson Pratt, Mike Mazurki, Ken Curtis, George O'Brien, Shug Fisher.

68. **DEAR BRIGITTE** (1965). 20th Century Fox. Directed by Henry Koster. Produced by Henry Koster (Fred Kohlmar Productions). Screenplay by Hal Kanter, Nunnally Johnson (uncredited) (from the novel *Erasmus with Freckles* by John Haase). Principal cast: James Stewart, Fabian, Glynis Johns, Cindy Carol, Billy Mumy, John Williams, Jack Kruschen, Ed Wynn, Charles Robinson, Howard Freeman, Jane Wald, Alice Pearce, Jesse White, Gene O'Donnell, Brigitte Bardot.

69. **SHENANDOAH** (1965). Universal. Directed by Andrew V. McLaglen. Produced by Robert Arthur. Screenplay by James Lee Barrett. Principal cast: James Stewart, Doug McClure, Glenn Corbett, Patrick Wayne, Rosemary Forsyth, Phillip Alford, Katharine Ross, Charles Robinson, Paul Fix, Denver Pyle, George Kennedy, Tim McIntire, James McMullan, James Best, Warren Oates, Strother Martin, Dabbs Greer, Harry Carey Jr., Kevin Hagen, Tom Simcox, Berkeley Harris.

70. **THE FLIGHT OF THE PHOENIX** (1965). 20th Century Fox. Directed by Robert Aldrich. Produced by Robert Aldrich. Screenplay by Lukas Heller (from the novel by Elleston Trevor). Principal cast: James Stewart, Richard Attenborough, Peter Finch, Hardy Kruger, Ernest Borgnine, Ian Bannen, Ronald Fraser, Christian Marquand, Dan Duryea, George Kennedy, Gabriele Tinti, Alex Montoya, Peter Bravos, William Aldrich, Barrie Chase.

71. **THE RARE BREED** (1966). Universal. Directed by Andrew V. McLaglen. Produced by William Alland. Screenplay by Ric Hardman. Principal cast: James Stewart, Maureen O'Hara, Brian Keith, Juliet Mills, Don Galloway, David Brian, Jack Elam, Ben Johnson, Harry Carey Jr., Perry Lopez, Larry Domasin, Alan Caillou, Bob Gravage, R. L. "Tex" Armstrong, Ted Mapes, Larry Blake, Charles Lampkin.

72. **FIRECREEK** (1968). Warner Bros.–Seven Arts. Directed by Vincent McEveety. Produced by Philip Leacock. Screenplay by Calvin Clements. Principal cast: James Stewart, Henry Fonda, Inger Stevens, Gary Lockwood, Dean Jagger, Ed

Begley, Jay C. Flippen, Jack Elam, James Best, Barbara Luna, Jacqueline Scott, Brooke Bundy, J. Robert Porter, Morgan Woodward, John Qualen, Louise Latham, Athena Lorde, Harry "Slim" Duncan, Kevin Tate, Christopher Shea.

73. **BANDOLERO!** (1968). 20th Century Fox. Directed by Andrew V. McLaglen. Produced by Robert L. Jacks. Screenplay by James Lee Barrett (from a screen story by Stanley L. Hough). Principal cast: James Stewart, Dean Martin, Raquel Welch, George Kennedy, Andrew Prine, Will Geer, Clint Ritchie, Denver Pyle, Tom Heaton, Angel Munoz, Sean McClory, Harry Carey Jr., Donald Barry, Guy Raymond, Perry Lopez, Jock Mahoney, Big John Hamilton, Dub Taylor.

74. **THE CHEYENNE SOCIAL CLUB** (1970). National General. Directed by Gene Kelly. Produced by Gene Kelly. Screenplay by James Lee Barrett (who also executive produced). Principal cast: James Stewart, Henry Fonda, Shirley Jones, Sue Ann Langdon, Elaine Devry, Robert Middleton, Arch Johnson, Dabbs Greer, Jackie Russell, Jackie Joseph, Sharon DeBord, Richard Collier, Charles Tyner, Jean Willes, Robert Wilke, Carl Reindel, J. Pat O'Malley, Jason Wingreen, John Dehner.

75. **FOOLS' PARADE** (1971). Released in Great Britain as *Dynamite Man from Glory Jail.* Columbia. Directed by Andrew V. McLaglen. Produced by Andrew V. McLaglen. Screenplay by James Lee Barrett (from the novel by Davis Grubb). Principal cast: James Stewart, George Kennedy, Anne Baxter, Strother Martin, Kurt Russell, William Windom, Mike Kellin, Katherine Cannon, Morgan Paull, Robert Donner, David Huddleston, Dort Clark, James Lee Barrett, Kitty Jefferson Doepken, Dwight McConnell.

76. **THE SHOOTIST** (1976). Paramount. Director: Don Siegel. Produced by M. J. Frankovich, William Self (Dino De Laurentiis Productions). Screenplay by Miles Hood Swarthout, Scott Hale (from the novel by Glendon Swarthout). Principal cast: John Wayne, Lauren Bacall, Ron Howard, James Stewart, Richard Boone, Hugh O'Brian, Bill McKinney, Harry Morgan, John Carradine, Sheree North, Richard Lenz, Scatman Crothers, Gregg Palmer, Alfred Dennis, Dick Winslow, Melody Thomas, Kathleen O'Malley.

77. **AIRPORT '77** (1977). Universal. Directed by Jerry Jameson. Produced by William Frye (Jennings Lang Productions). Screenplay by Michael Scheff, David Spector (from a screen story by H. A. L. Craig and Charles Kuenstle, inspired by the film *Airport* [1970] based on the novel by Arthur Hailey). Principal cast: Jack Lemmon, Lee Grant, Brenda Vaccaro, Joseph Cotten, Olivia de Havilland, Darren McGavin, Christopher Lee, George Kennedy, James Stewart, Robert Foxworth, Robert Hooks, Monte Markham, Kathleen Quinlan, Gil Gerard, James Booth, Monica Lewis, Maidie Norman, Pamela Bellwood.

78. **THE BIG SLEEP** (1978). ITC. Directed by Michael Winner. Produced by Elliott Kastner. Screenplay by Michael Winner (from the novel by Raymond Chandler). Principal cast: Robert Mitchum, Sarah Miles, Richard Boone, Candy Clark, Joan Collins, Edward Fox, John Mills, James Stewart, Oliver Reed, Harry Andrews, Colin Blakely, Richard Todd, Diana Quick, James Donald, John Justin, Simon Turner, Martin Potter, David Savile.

79. **THE MAGIC OF LASSIE** (1978). International Picture Show. Directed by Don Chaffey. Produced by Bonita Granville Wrather, William Beaudine Jr. (Lassie Productions). Screenplay by Jean Holloway, Richard M. Sherman, Robert B. Sherman (from a story by Richard M. Sherman and Robert B. Sherman). Principal cast: James Stewart, Mickey Rooney, Pernell Roberts, Stephanie Zimbalist, Michael Sharrett, Alice Faye, Gene Evans, Mike Mazurki, Robert Lussier, Lane Davies, William Flatley, James V. Reynolds.

80. **AN AMERICAN TAIL: FIEVEL GOES WEST** (1991). Universal. Directed by

Phil Nibbelink and Simon Wells. Produced by Steven Spielberg and Robert Watts. Screenplay by Flint Dille (from a story by Charles Swenson). Principal cast (cartoon voices; audio only): Dom DeLuise, James Stewart, John Cleese, Amy Irving, Phillip Glasser, Cathy Cavadini, Nehemiah Persoff.

ADDITIONAL FILM APPEARANCES

1. **FELLOW AMERICANS** (1942). Direced by Garson Kanin for the Office of Emergency Management. Documentary dramatizing the Japanese attack on Pearl Harbor, 10 minutes.

2. **WINNING YOUR WINGS** (1942). Produced by the Office of War Information. Short film about the Army Air Corps.

3. **AMERICAN CREED** (1946). Released in Great Britain as *American Brotherhood Week*. Directed by Robert Stevenson. Produced by David O. Selznick.

4. **THUNDERBOLT** (1947). Directed by John Sturges and William Wyler. Introduction by James Stewart. Short documentary about fighter plane support of ground troops.

5. **10,000 KIDS AND A COP** (1948). Directed by Charles Barton. Documentary. Introductory narration.

6. **HOW MUCH DO YOU OWE?** (1949). Columbia. Short documentary for the Disabled American Veterans.

7. **AND THEN THERE WERE FOUR** (1958). Socony-Vacuum Oil Company. Directed by Frank Strayer. Short documentary about road safety.

8. **AMBASSADORS WITH WINGS** (1958). Ex-Cello Corp. Short documentary.

9. **X-15.** (1961). United Artists. Directed by Richard Donner. Narrated by James Stewart. Full-length documentary.

10. **DIRECTED BY JOHN FORD** (1971). The American Film Institute. Directed by Peter Bogdanovich. Interview with James Stewart included.

11. **PAT NIXON: A TRIBUTE TO THE FIRST LADY** (1972). David Wolper short film for the Republican Party, narrated by James Stewart.

12. **THAT'S ENTERTAINMENT!** (1974). MGM. Directed by Jack Haley Jr. Produced by Jack Haley Jr. Screenplay by Jack Haley Jr. Documentary musical compilation that includes a clip of James Stewart from *Born to Dance*.

13. **SENTIMENTAL JOURNEY** (1976). Directed by Ferde Grofé. Produced by Ferde Grofé. Commemoration of the fortieth anniversary of the DC-3.

14. **MR. KRUEGER'S CHRISTMAS** (1980). Sponsored by the Mormons. Directed by Kieth Merrill. Short documentary featuring James Stewart and the Mormon Tabernacle Choir.

TELEVISION APPEARANCES

This list does not include the numerous apperances on *The Jack Benny Show, The Dean Martin Show, My Three Sons,* and the *Tonight Show Starring Johnny Carson,* all of which he played himself. The following are dramatic roles in which Stewart played a character, either once or in a series, or was interviewed for documentary purposes, only for television.

1. **"THE WINDMILL," *GENERAL ELECTRIC THEATER*** (1955). 22-minute episode. First airdate: April 24, 1955.

2. **"THE TOWN WITH A PAST," *GENERAL ELECTRIC THEATER*** (1957). 22-minute episode. First airdate: February 10, 1957.

3. **"THE TRAIL TO CHRISTMAS,"** *GENERAL ELECTRIC THEATER* (1957). 22-minute episode. First airdate: December 15, 1957.

4. **"CINDY'S FELLA,"** *LINCOLN-MERCURY STARTIME* (1959). Director: Gower Champion. Screenplay by Jameson Brewer (from a radio script by Frank Burt). First airdate: December 15, 1959.

5. **"FLASHING SPIKES,"** *ALCOA PREMIERE* (1962). Directed by John Ford. Produced by Frank Baur and Avista. First airdate: October 4, 1962.

6. *THE JIMMY STEWART SHOW* (1971). Directed by Hal Kanter. Produced by Hal Kanter (for Warner Bros. Television). Screenplay by Hal Kanter. 22-minute episode. First airdate: September 19, 1971.

7. **"HARVEY"** (1972). *THE HALLMARK HALL OF FAME*. Directed by Fielder Cook. Produced by David Susskind. Adapted for TV by Jacqueline Babbin, Audrey Gellen Maas (from the play by Mary Chase). 66 minutes. First airdate: March 22, 1972.

8. *HAWKINS ON MURDER* (1973). Subsequently retitled *Death and the Maiden*. Directed by Jud Taylor. Produced by David Karp (Arena/Leda). 66 minutes. First airdate: March 13, 1973.

9. *HAWKINS* – **"MURDER IN MOVIELAND"** (1973). Also known as "Murder in Hollywood." Director: Jud Taylor. Screenplay by David Karp. 66 minutes. First airdate: October 2, 1973.

10. *HAWKINS* – **"DIE, DIE, DARLING"** (1973). Directed by Paul Wendkos. Screenplay by Gene L. Coon. 66 minutes. First airdate: October 23, 1973.

11. *HAWKINS* – **"A LIFE FOR A LIFE"** (1973). Directed by Jud Taylor. Screenplay by David Karp. 66 minutes. First airdate: November 13, 1973.

12. *HAWKINS* – **"BLOOD FEUD"** (1973). Directed by Paul Wendkos. Screenplay by David Karp. 66 minutes. First airdate: December 4, 1973.

13. *HAWKINS* – **"MURDER IN THE SLAVE TRADE"** (1974). Directed by Paul Wendkos. Screenplay by Robert Hamner. 66 minutes. First airdate: January 22, 1974.

14. *HAWKINS* – **"MURDER ON THE THIRTEENTH FLOOR"** (1974). Directed by Jud Taylor. Screenplay by David Karp. 66 minutes. First airdate: February 5, 1974.

15. *HAWKINS* – **"CANDIDATE FOR MURDER"** (1974). Directed by Robert Scheerer. Screenplay by Robert Hamner. 66 minutes. First airdate: March 5, 1974.

16. *THE AMERICAN WEST OF JOHN FORD* (1971). Directed by Denis Sanders. Interview with James Stewart. Shown on CBS television.

17. *THE GREEN HORIZON* (1981). Japanese title: *Afurika Monogatari*. Directed by Susumu Hani. Produced by Terry Ogisu, Yoichi Matsue. Executive in charge of English production: Ken Kawarai. Released overseas in theaters, seen in the United States on Showtime (premium cable), first in November 1981. Released on video-cassette in Great Britain by Skyline Video, through CBS/Fox Video.

18. *RIGHT OF WAY* (1983). Home Box Office. Directed by George Schaefer. Screenplay by Richard Lees (adapted from his original play). 106 minutes. First showing: August 23, 1983, at the Montreal Film Festival. First HBO cablecast: November 1983. Principal cast: James Stewart, Bette Davis, Melinda Dillon, Priscilla Morrill, John Harkins, Louis Schaefer, Jacque Lynn Colton, Charles Walker.

19. *NORTH AND SOUTH, BOOK II* (1986). ABC/Warner. Miniseries. Broadcast fall 1986. Stewart cameo as southern lawyer.

Final Thoughts and Acknowledgments

*T*here are several people I would like to acknowledge for their cooperation, assistance, and invaluable insights.

I wish to thank Kelly Stewart Harcourt, one of Jimmy's twin daughters, whom I initially connected with via literary agent Alan Nevins. For the record, Ms. Harcourt says she has never really liked anything written about her father, but nevertheless agreed to talk to me with the understanding that it did not mean she was authorizing this biography. She sat for several lengthy interviews (by phone and mail) and provided numerous valuable insights as well as dozens of previously unseen photos that otherwise would have been impossible for me to acquire. She proved intelligent, articulate, charming, and fascinating, and an invaluable source for this biography.

I wish to thank Frank Capra Jr., whom I was able to contact via my friend and colleague Zack Norman. Mr. Capra proved a valuable source of information, was direct and open, extremely helpful, and informative. Several years ago, Mr. Norman also introduced me to Peter Bogdanovich, who was also informative, and has also since become a friend. Thank you for everything, Zack.

I wish to thank Kim Novak for agreeing to give me an extremely rare interview. To make this one happen, my agent for many years, Mel Berger of the William Morris Agency, went to Norm Brokaw, the chairman of the board who also happens to be Ms. Novak's longtime agent. After several months, she agreed to talk. Ms. Novak and I spoke at length many times, both by phone and in person. Her insights provided valuable source material, especially regarding the making of *Vertigo* and *Bell Book and Can-*

dle.

I wish to thank William Frye, who I first met and interviewed for my biography of Cary Grant. Then as now, he provided great anecdotal material on both Grant and Jimmy Stewart. He is a wonderful fellow, an extremely knowledgable film veteran, extraordinarily generous, and now a very good friend.

I wish to thank the late June Allyson, who I interviewed via fax (in the form of questions and answers). Although in frail health, she was friendly, cooperative, and informative.

I wish to thank John Karlen.

I wish to thank Andrew Sarris for his many years of inspiration, his insights, and for his introduction of the auteurist theory into the consciousness of modern American film theory and criticism. I had the privilege of studying with Mr. Sarris while I earned my MFA at Columbia University, and for several years after while I studied film history there at the doctoral level. I left Columbia without writing my PhD dissertation when my good friend Phil Ochs committed suicide in 1976. I chose instead to write my version of his life, *Death of a Rebel,* and, except for an occasional teaching or lecturing assignment, never again returned to the academic world.

During my years of formal study and thereafter in my writing career, I have not been able to find much relevant historical writing on James Stewart or his place in the history of American film. Most of what passed for American film criticism in the thirties, forties, and fifties—the three most important decades in Mr. Stewart's career—were either studio generated PR releases, gossip column writing, or the kind of conventional day-after reviews that newspaper film critics such as Dwight MacDonald specialized in. This is not to slight James Agee or Otis Ferguson, or even André Bazin, but, in truth, none of them wrote very much, if at all, about James Stewart, at least not directly. Some of this may be due to the fact that for nearly six years in the forties, when Stewart was in the military, he made no commercial films, and therefore slipped through the critical cracks (Bazin's writings flourished a few years prior to Stewart's major film work). Another significant factor is the large number of movies that Stewart made that, prior to the extraordinary, groundbreaking publication in 1968 of Andrew Sarris's *The American Cinema,* were considered "genre" films, too easily categorized and dismissed by reviewers as American studio product, their directors functionaries rather than visionaries, products low on art and high on action (comedy or the two-fisted kind). More "adult" films, with themes of romance, mystery, and historical world drama were, for the most part, thought of by "serious" American critics as made better by the Europeans. The snobbery that passed for insight in mainstream American movie criticism and by extension against "all those stars in heaven" was the product of an elitist generation of film writers who looked down on their assignments, and therefore their subjects, as some sort of relegation of their own careers. Film reviewing came in a distant last in the hierarchy of art worth writing about (after theater number one, *of course,* books, art exhibits, baseball, the Detroit Auto Show, etc.). It wasn't until Sarris restructured the importance of American studio movies that the careers of such great filmmakers as John Ford, Alfred Hitchcock, Howard Hawks, Charlie Chaplin, Orson Welles, Josef Von Sternberg, Frank Capra, and so many others were reevaluated and resurrected. The accompanying stars who illuminated these directors' visions were also thusly reexamined—on the pages of others' critical writings and in the imaginations of audiences all over the world. Among the most resilient of these actors is, in my opinion, James Stewart. Because of the auteurist revisionism of American film rankings (auteurism being a critical tool, not a career goal—no filmmaker becomes an "auteur"), Hitchcock is restored to his proper role as the superior filmmaker, more "important" than, say, Cecil B. DeMille, and therefore, it follows, James Stewart is more cinematically significant than Charlton Heston.

I wish to thank everyone at Harmony Books, beginning with Shaye Areheart, who first brought me to the house; my editor, Julia Pastore, Trisha Howell, Linnea Knollmueller, Barbara Sturman, Andrea Peabbles, Robin Slutzky, and Mel Berger at William Morris. Mr Berger's assistant, Eric Lupfer, was extremely helpful in tracking down contacts for many of the others included in this book.

I leave you now, but will meet with you again a little further on up the road.

Index

C

D

𝒩

T

About the Author

MARC ELIOT is the *New York Times* bestselling author of more than a dozen books on popular culture, among them the highly acclaimed biography *Cary Grant*, the award-winning *Walt Disney: Hollywood's Dark Prince*, *Down 42nd Street*, *Take It from Me* (with Erin Brockovich), *Down Thunder Road: The Making of Bruce Springsteen*, *To the Limit: The Untold Story of the Eagles*, and *Death of a Rebel*. He has written on the media and popular culture for numerous publications, including *Penthouse*, *L.A. Weekly*, and *California Magazine*. He divides his time among New York City; Woodstock, New York; and Los Angeles, California. Visit him at www.marceliot.net.